Head of the Line

A Holocaust Survivor's Memoir

Donated to the Blynn Holocaust Collection
in honor of my parents,
Nina + Michael Jackson,
two Survivors, two very brave Souls.

— Renata Jackson

Printed in the U. S. A. By:
Moriah Offset Corp.
115 Empire Blvd. Brooklyn, N.Y. 11225, Tel: (718) 693-3800

Dedication

To my mother, my brothers, their wives and children, and our extended family – all of whom perished during the Holocaust at the hands of the Nazi executioners. G-d alone knows where they fell and where they gasped their last breaths.

To my father, whose life was shortened due to the indescribable pain and sorrow he suffered because of the *Shoah*. These pages are my memorial to them, my recitation of the *Kaddish* for our family's martyrs.

Contents

Editors' Note

Our father's personal and historical record of the Holocaust is linguistically unique: first, it's translated from a patchwork of six languages (Yiddish, Hebrew, Polish, German, Hungarian and Russian); second, the resulting English version has survived numerous editorial passes. At each phase in producing this volume, we labored to maintain his original tone and intent – balancing that with our shared goal of improving its readability in English.

To aid the reader's appreciation of this *Shoah* testimony, while remaining true to the original manuscript, we adopted certain conventions that we hope improve its clarity.

1. We made every attempt to minimize foreign language references in the text. Our rule was to ask, "If Dad's first language had been English, how would he have said this?" Then we'd translate or keep the term, accordingly, to simplify the prose.

2. However, we preserved foreign words that, in our view, were vital to portraying the Holocaust. We could not in good conscience produce a text that eliminated *Shoah*-specific terms such as *häftling* or *kapo*. Thus, anyone browsing these pages will see a still-abundant supply of non-English references.

3. Consequently, we were careful to define the remaining foreign words in text on first-mention and to create a glossary of these terms so the reader need not be an expert in seven languages to get through the book.

4. Details we judged tangential to the main text appear in footnotes. Rather than force the reader to flip to the back of the book each time, it was our strong preference to present these notes on the same page. It's left to the reader to decide whether to read or ignore this supplemental material.

5. We purposely maintained some of Dad's linguistic nuances, most notably his habit of referring to "Jewish *boys*" (emphasis added) in the labor or concentration camps. Although the term refers to males from their teens into their 40s, it captures the sense of oneness he feels with his fellow *Shoah* victims.

6. To convey the correct pronunciation of certain words, we introduced an underlined C̲H̲ to stand for the sound expressed in the Scottish term Lo̲c̲h̲ Ness — non-existent in English but very common in Hebrew.

7. We relied on the wonderful book *The Joys of Yiddish,* by Leo Rosten, as a rich source of spelling and usage conventions.

8. Many Hebrew and Yiddish terms — including holidays such as Rosh Hashanah, Yom Kippur, Torah, Yeshiva and months of the Jewish calendar — are defined in Webster's New World Dictionary (Third College Edition, Simon and Schuster). We followed its spelling conventions as appropriate.

Jack Jackson and Renata Jackson, December 2000

Acknowledgement

A person worries about the loss of his money, and not about the loss of his days. His money does not help him, and his days do not return.

from *The Book of Life*

Adam doeg al ibud damav, v'aino doeg al ibud yamav. Damav ainam ozrim, yamav ainam chosrim.

(Hebrew) *Sefer ha-Chaim*

I have always wanted to chronicle my experiences during the *Shoah* years. In the early 1940s, when I was hiding in Debrecen, Hungary, I did start a journal, but of course those pages were lost during the war. When my wife Nina and I came to this country, our first order of business was to support ourselves and, later, our children, Jack and Renata. But over these many years, I still harbored the desire to record my memoirs. It lay heavily on my mind. Thoughts kept convulsing through my head: about my bitter past, as well as the present and future. Yet time went by, and I simply could not take pen in hand, despite the frequent urging by my son and daughter to put down on paper the details of what happened to Nina and me, their grandparents, aunts, uncles and cousins. I kept procrastinating, actively postponing the task, day after day and week after week. It was as though some kind of curse prevented me from starting. There was a *shalvat nefesh*, Hebrew for contentment of the soul, that was missing.

At last I realized, however, that time was flying by very quickly, that money isn't everything and that in every life comes a time of reckoning. The spiritual and material lives must balance. You cannot write valid checks when the checkbook balance is zero. The same principal applies to life; you must know from whence you came and where you are going: *da'a mi ayin batah u-l'an atah holech.*

I finally began to chronicle my story in January of 1986. Writing Yiddish in longhand on the pages of a bound notebook, I recorded a series of memories about my birthplace, my family and my early schooling. I worked through that August and produced only a fraction of the manuscript, and then neglected the project entirely until January 1990 – a hiatus of almost three and a half years. From January to March of 1990, I added only a few more paragraphs. Ultimately, despite my self-generated interruptions and the passage of time, I found the strength to finish documenting my story. I was able, as they say in Yiddish, *a rup redden fun hartzen,* "to talk it out from the heart."

Eventually I filled over 625 pages with my handwritten Yiddish reminiscences. Then, working with a stack of dictionaries (Yiddish, Hebrew, English), I translated the manuscript into English. I kept many Yiddish and Hebrew words and phrases, to perpetuate the mother tongue spoken in my birthplace, the Carpathian region. (I will for all my days regret that I didn't teach my children Yiddish when they were young. They are missing out on the rich heritage of an almost 1,000-year-old culture that was created and written in the Yiddish language. During the *Shoah*, when Jewish martyrs, our parents and brothers and sisters, gasped their last breath, the majority of them expressed their final thoughts in Yiddish.)

I dictated my translated history, sentence by sentence, into a tape recorder. Renata then saw to it that all 22 tape cassettes were transcribed: I must thank both her and typist Steven Schwab for tackling this difficult task. From there, my son Jack – in spite of the fact he was extremely busy with the pressing needs of raising his own family – oversaw and coordinated the entire project. He reorganized the original manuscript chronologically, rewrote extensive passages, raised editorial questions about details I had overlooked and arranged the material into chapters. We then enlisted the editorial help of oral historian Jeannie Miller to address stylistic issues, and author Mordechai Staiman, who made invaluable suggestions affecting the manuscript's tone and readability. I thank both of them for their work on interim drafts. I'm likewise appreciative to artist Ed McCormack who rendered the cover art and was gracious about various changes I requested. Jack and Renata then worked with me to smooth language in the final version, polish the transliterations, finish the glossary and fill in as many missing facts as we could. I want to express with great joy and pride my appreciation to my two children. Without their help it wouldn't be possible for me to publish this book in English.

Last but not least, I must acknowledge deep gratitude to my wife Nina, who understood and coped with the depression that hung over me while writing about death, loss and genocide. She helped me despite the great emotional burden that dealing with the *Shoah* places on her. She applied her artistic skills to first conceptualize the book's cover art, and I relied heavily on her language expertise to translate idiomatic words and expressions from Polish and German into English.

Although my writing consists mainly of personal experiences, I nevertheless believe my memories of the *Shoah* have a general, especially Jewish, significance. Elie Wiesel, Primo Levi and K. Zetnik (the pseudonym of Yechiel Dinur, *né* Feiner) have eternalized the *Shoah* in their writings. These authors are considered *m'konanim* of the Holocaust – a Hebrew word interpreted as "mourners." I have never liked that translation, however, because of its association in ancient Jewish history with professional mourners hired to wail at a person's funeral. I prefer "witnesses and recorders of tragic history" (like our great prophet Jeremiah, the *m'konen* of the destruction of the First Temple). Even though human language falls short of accurately expressing the enormity of the cruelty that produced the *Shoah's* ocean of blood, tears and agony, anyone who bore witness to it has an obligation to record whatever he or she saw and experienced.

I had no literary ambitions in recounting my own bitter memories of the *Shoah*. My intent has always been to leave this text for my children and grandchildren – stories I had great difficulty relating because I bear the *Shoah's* indelible stain. I know that even by their best intentions, my children could not and cannot comprehend what we Holocaust survivors went through. We ourselves sometimes cannot understand how and why we survived. Through these writings, though, I hope to communicate with and instruct my children and grandchildren. I have recorded my experiences *l'zecher olam*, for everlasting memory, and to serve as a warning for the coming generations. If future generations of Jews will have a justification for their existence, it is only if they will not forget the Holocaust.

Allentown, Pennsylvania, December 2000

Preface

Day of Mourning

"THIS IS ALL I HAVE TO SHOW FOR MY LIFE'S LABORS?" my Uncle Zecharia asked, pointing to a small satchel of his belongings as our family was rounded up like cattle and driven from our homes in 1941.

On that day we observed Tisha b'Av, a day of fasting and meditation in solemn commemoration of the destruction of the Second Holy Temple in 70 CE (Common Era). In 1941, Tisha b'Av (the 9th day of the Hebrew month of Av) fell on the Sabbath. In keeping with Jewish tradition that forbids fasting on Sabbath, the fast is delayed one day, to the 10th, and thus was called Tisha b'Av *nidcheh* (postponed).

When they snatched us from our homes, allowing us to take only a small suitcase or backpack of our possessions, little did we know that we were at the beginning of the third destruction, the *chorban shlishi*, more terrible than all previous tragedies in our nearly 4,000 year history.

There were times, in our ancient past, when Jews stood up and fought for themselves. There were those in Jerusalem who revolted against our Roman oppressors in 66 CE, and held them at bay for four years despite great odds. Later, in 135 CE, Bar Kochva and his defiant fellow Jews rebelled against the tyrannical Emperor Hadrian. Many of our Jewish brothers and sisters perished then, but they nevertheless stood on their own two feet and fought their enemy to the bitter end.

But something went wrong in the 20th century. Even after the Kishiniev pogrom of 1903, Chaim Nachman Bialek, the Hebrew poet of anger, wrote with some frustration about the lack of resistance by his fellow Jews: "They had no 'flavor' in their lives and neither did they in their deaths." Some 40 years later, during the *Shoah*, despite clear warning signs of our impending destruction, we also went like sheep to the slaughterhouse. Our shame from this can never diminish the outcome of our paralytic response. We died as cowards. A heavy narcotic-like sleep befell us, and when we awoke it was already too late. The fires of the Holocaust engulfed us on all sides.

Unlike millions of others who perished, I lived to tell my story and bear witness to the murder of many Jewish souls. For more than 50 years, my *Shoah* experiences have tormented me. Somehow, I found at least some solace by sharing my complicated mixture of anger, guilt and pain with surviving fellow death-camp inmates, and by making sure that my children knew what happened to their fallen family.

As with all such survivors, I came through the Holocaust because of a series of often inexplicable circumstances, all of which were beyond my control. For instance, my 6-foot-2-½-inch height positioned me at the head of the line in forced marches across Europe. For a time, I benefited from this – at least minimally. In other cases, sheer luck found me a few steps away from where the Angel of Death struck. Four pin-holes in a document spared my life, as did heeding a stranger's advice to walk south rather than north. Sometimes I recognized these factors as they occurred; more often, I did not.

I don't know what other Jews thought as they daily faced the Nazi tyrant. But I personally have blamed myself for not anticipating the coming disaster and not leaving the accursed land of Europe in time. In this memoir, I feebly explain my actions not to flee and leave my family behind.

The prominent Zionist leader Ze'ev Jabotinsky tirelessly warned the Jews of Poland and the rest of Europe, "You are sitting on top of a volcano. Jews, evacuate!" Yet we turned a deaf ear, especially to Hitler, who never hid his intentions. As early as 1935-'36, he enacted the Nuremberg Laws that stripped the German Jews of their citizenship. But Jabotinsky had the foresight to see what was coming. At that time Palestine was under British rule, and there was a quota system that allowed very few Jews to enter legally, but Jabotinsky strongly advocated our defying the British quota.

The problem was that most European Jews were under the influential opinions and leadership of the Orthodox rabbis, the most powerful of whom were opposed to Zionism: there were those who believed that Jews should not return to their homeland until the arrival of the Messiah. Because of this, the Jewish leadership itself was in conflict.

Even within the Zionist movement, there were differences of opinion. When Jabotinsky published his evacuation warning in *The Warsaw Daily Moment*, he was denounced by Yitzchak Greenbaum, then head of the Jewish members of the Polish Parliament and a Zionist who believed that the cure for anti-Semitism was found not by running away but rather by staying and fighting for Jewish rights.

Adding to the already deeply problematic situation created by this controversy at the leadership level was the attitude of incredulity on the part of the general Jewish population, which never believed that a systematic annihilation could ever be planned, let alone carried out.

At such crucial times, Jews needed a united governorship to help steer us to effective action. In its absence, we became hypnotized – like a python's victim – swallowed up by the snake known as Nazi Germany.

These thoughts still lie heavily on my heart and mind, and on my spirit. They manifest themselves in my dreams. Very often my dreams and self-criticisms focus on the question, "Why?" Why were we so passive?

Why didn't we Jews of Europe resist? I can't forgive myself for not doing enough to fight back.

I'm greatly concerned that our descendants will see only our failure to resist the Germans' crimes against us. In English, historical records of the Holocaust utilize the word "extermination," as though one is simply eliminating cockroaches or other pests. But of course, "extermination" was an outright euphemism for the calculated murder of million of human beings, and the post-Holocaust generations must come to realize that fact fully.

My shame and pain regarding the Holocaust are partially diminished, however, by the heroic struggles of the entire Jewish community in Palestine (the *yishuv*) who fought for independence, along with all the remnants of European Jewry in Displaced Persons camps who refused to go back to their birthplaces and instead boarded dilapidated ships, risking their lives against the mighty British fleet, in order to help establish the State of Israel.

We Jews are described by the gentile prophet Balaam (Numbers XXIII:9) as "a people who shall dwell alone, who shall not be reckoned among the nations."[1] Biblical commentators explain that the word "alone" in this passage means not only a nation living apart from the gentile population, but also a people distinguished by their religious and moral laws. Furthermore, an alternative interpretation of "reckoned" is "conspire." Thus the latter phrase may also be interpreted as "the people of Israel do not conspire against the gentile nations."

These two points are utterly important. First, we Jews are a unique and invaluable people among the nations of the world. Second, throughout the ages, we have not been the aggressors but rather consistently the victims of persecution.

I feel that unity is the way towards overcoming all our enemies. This we can accomplish only by eradicating the brotherly hate *(sinat achim)* among us. To accomplish this goal of unity, we must teach our offspring *ahavat Yisroel,* love of the Children of Israel. So now, in this vein, I present this memoir – so we never forget our past, and use it to draw important lessons for our future.

---

[1] In Hebrew: *"Am l'vadad yishkon, u-ba-goyyim lo yitchashav."*

Chapter 1

Torun

"YOU WILL HAVE A LOT OF *MAZEL* [LUCK]," my mother told me when I was old enough to understand. She explained that I was born in a birth-sack, meaning I was delivered still surrounded (and protected) by the placenta. "Children born this way are blessed with good luck," she said. I have often wondered whether this fact played a role in the many times I escaped certain death during the *Shoah* years.

When I arrived in this world, my father, Avraham Zalman Jakubowics, was 50 years old, and my mother, Rivkah (Drimmer) Jakubowics, was 49. I can imagine what a big surprise I must have been to them, coming as I did in their later years. My birth took place during Passover, the Festival of Freedom, falling on the second day of *chol ha-mo'ed*, the holiday's interim period, in the Hebrew year 5679. On the modern Julian calendar this is April 18, 1919. My mental image of my parents has always been as elderly people, because my earliest memories occurred when they were already in their mid- to late-50s.

My birthplace of Torun was situated at the northern end of the Carpathians, the mountainous border then shared by Czechoslovakia and Poland, but now part of the Ukraine. Carpathia was incorporated as an autonomous region of the Czechoslovakian Republic after World War I. Its official languages were Small Russian (Ukrainian) and Czech, and the alphabet was Russian Cyrillic. With a population of a little more than one million, the area was home to roughly 100,000 Jews, or 10-11 percent of the residents. Overall, the region was quite poor. Natural resources consisted solely of lumber – huge forests of mainly pine and spruce – and a few salt mines. There was no coal, though we really didn't need any, as lumber was a plentiful fuel source. The area also was excellent for raising cattle and sheep, so dairy products were in abundance. In fact, Carpathian cheeses were famous and very good.[1]

---

[1] Singer Theodore Bikel performs a number of songs, including *"Mammeh Liggeh," "Romania, Romania"* and *"Brinzeh,"* which glorify cheeses produced in this region.

What Carpathia lacked in natural resources, G-d more than compensated for in natural beauty. The region was an Eden for scenery painters and poets. A green, pine forest fragrance permeated the spring and summer breezes, filling the air with a delightful perfume. Majestic backs of the Carpathian Mountains stretched as far as the eye could see, and rivers meandered through the foothills. Waterfalls filled the serene, quiet forest with a bubbling, rushing roar. This combination of beautiful panoramas, striking fragrances, and soothing sounds was quite literally intoxicating. One had the feeling of witnessing the product of Biblical Creation.

Near Torun, atop the Plashiveh Mountain, is a remarkable natural wonder: a lake called the Eye of the Sea. It measures one kilometer long, but is no more than five hundred meters wide and is about a third of a kilometer in depth. Tourists from all over the Czechoslovakian Republic would come just to see it. To get to the mountaintop, they had to climb three to four hours simply to view it because the lake is surrounded on all sides by pine forest. In the center of the lake is a tiny island, forming the "pupil" that helps give this body of water its name.

Across the valley below, houses were built along a highway running through the foothills. These were primarily Jewish homes. The Small Russians, or Ukrainians, lived by and large in the surrounding mountains and fields, where they farmed or raised their livestock. Torun's entire population totaled roughly 3,000. Many villages this size dotted the landscape. The nearest "official" city – Chust (pronounced CHOOST) was 80 kilometers (50 miles) away to the southwest.

In Torun alone there were three synagogues and two *mikvahs* (ritual baths). Here the Torah lived in great affluence. Jewish holidays reigned supreme. Every *Shabbos* (Sabbath) was like a new *matan Torah*, a new giving of the Torah. And while Jewish families toiled hard during the week – "From the sweat of your brow shall you eat bread"[2] – their Sabbaths were restful, rich in spiritual content and contentment. People truly felt as though they had acquired an additional soul[3] – a metaphor for the spiritual enrichment of *Shabbos*.

---

[2] *"B'zaiyut apechah tochal lechem."*
[3] In Hebrew, this is called the *neshama y'seira*.

Torun was home to 135 *tallesim* (prayer shawls), our shorthand way of maintaining the tradition of not directly counting the number of Jews. Instead, we counted *tallesim*, each one represented a married man and his family. (In our region, boys did not wear *tallesim* before marriage, as opposed to the custom in many places in the United States.) The 135 families, therefore, represented roughly 700-800 souls. On average, families had four or five children apiece, and it wasn't rare for them to have more. By my estimate, only 80 to 100 of my fellow Toruners survived to see the end of the war – and many of these only because they left as pioneers to Israel before and during the 1930s.

The streets of Torun were unpaved gravel, and there were no street lamps. In winter, when darkness fell early, children returning from <u>ch</u>eder (Jewish primary school) would have to make their way home by torch or flashlight. Only three Jewish families in the town owned an automobile or truck. Everyone else relied on horse and buggy (we had neither) or the twice-daily buses to <u>Ch</u>ust.

Since Torun's only real industry was lumber, there were two lumber mills in town. In addition, there were two grain mills, a few grocery stores and some bars. All these businesses were in Jewish hands; not a single gentile owned a store in town. Local gentiles knew that anything they required had to be obtained before a Jewish holiday or *Shabbos*, when everything would be closed.

Families in the lumber business were considered upper class. Other families engaged in farming or buying and selling livestock, and could be considered middle class. Another group owned horses and buggies and made their living transporting freight. We referred to them as *balegulas*, or literally "owners of wheels." They'd transport building materials – two-by-twos, two-by-fours and lumber for furniture – the 80 kilometers to <u>Ch</u>ust. On the return trip, they'd bring basic food items such as flour, sugar and all kinds of produce, along with kerosene and oil. Normally, the trip to <u>Ch</u>ust and back via horse and buggy would take three days. If a *balegula* wanted to make two trips a week, he'd start right away after *Shabbos* – as soon as a minimum of three stars were visible in the night sky (meaning that the Sabbath had officially ended). If some obstacle delayed his second trip back from <u>Ch</u>ust, he would show up a little late on Friday evening, *erev Shabbos*, when the Jews were already on their way to synagogue. When this would happen to one poor fellow, Bore<u>ch</u> the

Balegula, we used to say that Bore<u>ch</u> drove his wagon shaft right into the Friday night noodle soup.

Bore<u>ch</u> was a bachelor in his 40s. Earlier in his life he had been a yeshiva *bu<u>ch</u>ar*, a student of the Talmud.[4] When people would kibitz him – "Bore<u>ch</u>, why don't you get married? You don't have a queen for your *Shabbos*" – he'd answer: "Such a disease the rich Jews should get!" The source of his response was a rhetorical question in Hebrew: "I should get married and have daughters so they will be maids for the rich Jews? Let them serve themselves!" Unfortunately, it often did come down to that – girls from poor families frequently would become maids in the homes of the wealthy.

In fact, two very wealthy Jews once lived in Torun. However, these families – Pickel and Krauss – had moved away to <u>Ch</u>ust before my time. They owned many thousands of acres of forest. It was said in Torun that during the Austro-Hungarian Empire, in the time of Emperor Franz-Yosef, Pickel and Krauss were once candidates to become barons. Their religion, however, prevented them from being granted the title.

In 1925, my parents bought the house in which I grew up (literally; I grew *up* in that house). They purchased it from the Pickel family, and at one time it had been the most lavish house in all of Torun. What my father bought, however, was a skeleton. World War I battles fought in our area of the Carpathians had left the structure gutted, with only its outer stone walls standing. Houses in Torun were always built of lumber, which was never in short supply. This house, however, was the only one in the area built entirely of stone, like a castle, leading people to call our house the *mo'ar* (stone house). The only other stone structure in Torun was City Hall. Its status as a skeleton actually worked to my father's financial advantage: there was a national law that allowed a 15-year tax exemption on new houses; my father applied for this abatement and received it.

The restoration took quite a few months, but the house was transformed into a real beauty. There wasn't another like it for miles around. Only in Volova, which was the county seat, could one find

---

[4] If somebody knew the Talmud, we'd say that *Abya v'Ruva* are not alien to him (this is a reference to two men, often mentioned in the Talmud, who ran yeshivas in Babylonia in the 3rd and 4th centuries CE).

similarly imposing homes. It had massive doors and windows; all the rooms were painted, every one a different color. While other houses in the area were plain white, we had a silver room, a golden room, a green room, and so forth. Circling the wall of each room, up by the ceiling, was multicolored floral stenciling. All the ceilings were painted pure white. For almost two months, a pair of painters from the city of Munkatch (pronounced MOOHN-kotch) had labored to paint the house inside and out.

Not only was our house big and pretty, but it also was cheerful and spiritual. Often, famous rabbis would travel through the region, and invariably they stayed in our home. We had enough spare rooms to host them, and also enough space in the yard to accommodate all those who would come by horse and buggy from the surrounding villages to meet or listen to them. Each rabbi had many followers in the region so sometimes they would stay at our house for a week at a time. My mother loved to prepare meals for them, and especially to prepare the *Shabbos* tables. It was very spiritually uplifting when the rabbis stayed with us. The majority of people in the Carpathian region believed these were holy men who had the capacity to perform miracles.

Chapter 2

Family

OUR HOME WAS WARM AND JOYOUS My parents were products of the second half of the 1800s, so the current philosophy of "Did you hug your child today?" would have been alien to them. Saying good-bye to my parents when I left home for yeshiva may have been the only time in my life that we hugged and kissed. In spite of this, I never felt unloved or unwanted. Their love for my brothers and me manifested itself in many other ways.

My mother stood as tall as my father – about six feet – and was statuesque. In the style of the day, she wore a brown wig *(sheitel)* fashioned in the shape of a bun, long-sleeve blouses, and her skirts to mid-calf. Back then, not just observant religious women wore long sleeves – everyone did. We always had a maid, so my mother didn't have to clean, but she prepared all our meals. Her social life consisted of spending time with her three daughters-in-law, her grandchildren, her other in-laws, her own brothers and sisters (she was one of nine) and her friends. As for my father's appearance, even in his later years he had a full head of black hair. He wore a short red beard and, when he died, he still had all his teeth.

They married when he was 19 and she was 18. He started in the lumber business shortly after their marriage and worked very hard – first contracting (buying and selling lumber) in Slovakia, and then later buying 500 acres of the Leptitsia Forest. Very active in community life, my father for many years was the head of the congregation of the largest *shul* in Torun. He was also considered a very wise man, and people frequently came to him to arbitrate business disputes. Every *Shabbos* afternoon, for many years, about seven or eight yeshiva *buchars* would come to our house to study *Mishnah* and *Gemara* with him. Unfortunately, my most vivid memories of my father coincide with the Depression years, so I remember him as a worry-wart, obviously concerned about his business. Like many people, he lost a lot of money during this period. My mother, on the other hand, was an optimistic type who worked hard to raise his spirits and the morale of the family.

Once my mother confided that she had hoped to have a girl

when she was pregnant with me because our family consisted entirely of boys: Eliezer, born in 1897; Moshe, in 1899; and Zvi, in 1907. Of the three, Zvi was closest to me in age, but even he was twelve-and-a-half years my senior. That left me the baby of the family – the Yiddish term was *mezinkeh* – and my parents certainly spoiled me. I grew up enjoying many privileges that I knew my older brothers hadn't experienced when they were young. For instance, it was customary at that time for boys of yeshiva age to wear *pais* (side-locks), but to shave the rest of their heads to be able to lay *tefillin* (to don phylacteries, worn in daily morning prayer). But my parents were more Zionistic and modern, so I didn't have to wear *pais* and I got to keep my hair.

As I mentioned, there was *Shabbos* learning in my house every Saturday afternoon, and my father of course wanted me to participate. But these boys were in their early 20s and I was just in my teens, so I resisted. I had other things I would rather do with friends my own age and from the Zionist youth group I belonged to, the Betar Organization. We used to sneak out of Torun, to the outskirts of town, to play soccer. Playing soccer was not considered an especially Jewish thing to do, but on *Shabbos* it was an altogether forbidden activity: one should only be studying Torah. So when the Chief Rabbi of the area, Aaron Teitelbaum, found out, he journeyed from Volova, called a meeting of the Torun townspeople to publicly scold the parents and reprimand all the players. (People were contacted by announcements in *shul*.) My parents knew about this meeting, but didn't attended, and they didn't make me go, either.

I was named Michael, in honor of my mother's grandfather, Mechel (Michael) Drimmer. Lots of stories about him were told in our house. He was a very, very religious man. They used to say of him that he would conduct special midnight worship,[1] which not everybody would do. And I heard he had a very beautiful voice, that he was a cantor, but he sang just for the High Holidays, and this honor he performed free. He was born in Dolina (a city on the other side of the Carpathian mountains that was actually part of Austria-Hungary in his time), and the woman he took as his wife was named Malya.

Mechel Drimmer was a very devoted lover of Zion. He was the first Jew from our area in Torun to emigrate to Palestine (then under

---

[1] In Yiddish, this is referred to as *"Uprechten chatsosn."*

Turkish rule as part of the Ottoman Empire) in 1903 or 1904. My maternal great-grandfather truly had to love Zion very dearly to leave all his children and his belongings and go, in his sixties, to Jerusalem. Self-sacrifice and love of Zion were flaming in his soul, just as the flame of the burning bush in the Sinai burned yet was never consumed. My uncle Zvi Drimmer (my mother's brother who later changed his name to Armin Darvosh) once told me, in 1941 when I visited him, that he helped his grandfather Michael obtain the necessary papers and make the arrangements to leave for Palestine. At that time passage was over land through Romania and then by ship across the Black Sea to Turkey. It had to be a lengthy trip.

Great-grandfather Drimmer lived in Jerusalem until his death in 1916. He died a few years before I was born, and was buried on the Mount of Olives, the *Har Ha-Zetim*, in the Romanian section. My eldest brothers, Eliezer and Moshe, always bragged that our great-grandfather Mechel had sent them *tefillin* from the city of Jerusalem. With great pleasure, my parents often recalled how he sent us an *esrog* for *Succos*, and that it was the only *esrog* in Torun from the Holy Land. This was a very, very big honor. Also, they mentioned his *nusach*,[2] the way my great-grandfather used to sing the prayers during the High Holidays. When they sang "*Adon Olam*," they'd unfailingly recall that my great-grandfather brought that tune from Dolina, Poland, when he settled in Torun. According to legend, this melody dates back to our Patriarch Jacob, who sang it when he was courting his future wife, Rachel, the pretty daughter in the house of Lavan.

Eliezer and Moshe, *Hashem yimkom dammam*,[3] both married in 1925 when I was five-and-a-half or six years old. They each moved into their own houses with their families at that time; Zvi continued to live in our parents' house until 1938, the year he married. Eliezer was the oldest, and the most learned of us brothers. He was a student

---

[2] *Nusach* refers to the prayer rites traditionally followed by a particular group.
[3] Hebrew for "G-d should avenge their blood"; abbreviated HYD.

frequently tore up and threw out Jewish books during this time. Many of our treasures were lost in the fires of the *Shoah*.

Shari and Eliezer had two children, both boys: Berzi, named after Shari's father who died not too long after their wedding, and Willi. Though I was their uncle, they were really more like younger cousins to me than nephews. Berzi (who was born about 1928) had trouble speaking Yiddish in the beginning because his mother was very slow in learning it herself. Willi was about three years younger. Berzi was 16 and Willi was 13 when the German snake devoured them, together with their parents, HYD.

Moshe and his wife Montze also had two beautiful children. Montze miscarried twice, but then gave birth to Channaleh, their eldest, a dark-haired, blue-eyed girl, and a younger boy, also dark-haired, named Shloimi. Montze was my mother's cousin. (Montze's mother Etyeh and my maternal grandmother Hudyeh were sisters, making Moshe and Montze second cousins. Marriage between second cousins is allowable by Jewish tradition.) My parents were not happy with Moshe's choice, but to this day I don't understand why. It was after all from the same family. My parents tried to talk him out of it, but nothing helped. Their mutual romantic desire was very strong, and Moshe married his beloved Montze. And when Moshe and Montze returned from their honeymoon they brought me a special present: a toy railroad, with tracks and a locomotive that ran on batteries. I was the happiest boy in Torun! Nobody my age, certainly none of my friends, had such a toy. I also got a set of building blocks with which I could construct a house with windows and doors. All my friends were envious of such wonderful toys, especially the train that went round and round on its tracks.

Moshe had his own business, trading lumber and building materials. He used to travel to Chust quite a bit, and he always brought me presents when he returned from the city. I had a special affection for Moshe. In later years, when I reached my teens, my

in the famous yeshiva in Bonyhad (pronounced BON-yeh-hahd), Hungary. My uncle Armin had been a student there, too, along with the famous Hebrew poet Avigdor Fierstein (who later changed his name to Avigdor Hameiri). Under his penname, he authored the famous book *Ha-Shiga'on Ha-Gadol* (*The Great Madness*), which described World War I, as well as many other books, and the song "*Shalom Lach Yerushalayim*" ("Peace to You, Jerusalem"). Later on, this song was incorporated into the Friday night service prayers of some Reform congregations.

Eliezer joined our Uncle Armin in the scrap iron business in Sighet, Romania. They didn't stay in business very long, eventually selling it. But while in Sighet he met a girl, Shari, with whom he fell in love and later married. Shari was the granddaughter of a famous rabbi, Benyamin Zev Krauss, *zichrono l'vracha*,[4] head of a neologue temple in Debrecen. He authored a very respected commentary on the Torah, *Ma'aros Ha-Bozek* (*ma'aros* means "views" and *Bozek* is an acronym for his name, Benyamin Zev Krauss.)

Shari's mother tongue was Hungarian, and she spoke a bit of German. We used to have a lot of laughs when my mother and Shari would "converse." Both of them spoke in Italian – with their hands. Shari would call my mother "Mommo," which we found very funny. It didn't take very long for Shari to learn two new languages, though: a bit of Yiddish and also Ukrainian (or Ruthenian, Small Russian, as we called it). She learned Ruthenian faster than Yiddish because Eliezer had hired a Ruthenian housekeeper. Shari had to learn Ruthenian quickly, because it was the only language the maid spoke.

Eliezer's wedding took place in Sighet, Romania, and the family needed passports to travel outside the Czech Republic. The wedding had been set for a certain date, until Shari's father became very ill and the wedding was postponed for four or six weeks. It was very disappointing because the delay occurred at the last minute. My mother had baked quite a few cakes and other goodies for the wedding. In those days we didn't have freezers, so we all ate lots of cookies and cakes for a time.

Eventually the wedding took place, but I was left at home with my grandmother Hudyeh (Judith, in English), who stayed behind to baby-sit me. She was probably in her 70s then, and it was hard for her to travel. Our maid Calina also helped out; I spoke to her in

---

[4] Hebrew for "of blessed memory"; abbreviated ZL.

Ruthenian. She was in our house a long time, eight or 10 years.

Sighet was home to a very famous *badchen*, a type of wedding entertainer specializing in humorous and sentimental improvised rhymes. The *badchen* was paid handsomely for his performance. This particular entertainer – Hersch Leib Gottlieb, born in 1844 – was known throughout the Carpathian and Maramaros regions as a great talmudic scholar, a fine writer and poet, and a strong lover of Zion. Zionism was neither very common nor accepted among the greater Jewish population of this area in the early 1900s. But to a growing number of people, who called him "Hersch Leib Sigheter" (the Sighet resident), he indeed was very popular. Even Dr. Theodore Herzl, the founding father of Zionism, heard of him. Herzl presented him with a Yiddish printing press so he could spread his Zionist ideals. Almost single-handedly, Hersch Leib Sigheter started publishing a bi-weekly paper in Hebrew called *Zion*, in 1924. Four years later, he and a partner by the name of Eliyahu Blanc launched a monthly Hebrew magazine called *Ahavat Zion* (*Love of Zion*). He also published a Hebrew newspaper called *Ha-Shemesh* (*The Sun*) and a Yiddish paper, the *Yiddisheh Volks Zeitung* (*Jewish People's Newspaper*). Hersch Leib wrote under a few pseudonyms, but one that he used very often was "*Vemen Got hat Lieb*," or "Whom G-d Loves." He wrote poetry and also translated into Hebrew some of the works of Goethe and Schiller. In 1933, his grandchildren published a compilation of his poetry under the title *Lieder fun Mein Leben* (*Songs From My Life*).

Eliezer subscribed to one of Hersch Leib's magazines, saving every back issue. We'd all discuss the articles, and from these family discussions I could see how sympathetic our house was to the Zionist movement. In the glow of these feelings, everyone wanted very much to have Hersch Leib Sigheter as the entertainer for Eliezer's wedding. Hersch Leib was already in his 80s at that time, but my father enlisted my Uncle Armin, who lived in Sighet, to ask Hersch Lieb whether

he'd be the *badchen*. At first he declined. "These Hungarians," he told my uncle, "they won't understand me anyway, and that's why I don't want to do it." But when my uncle revealed that half the wedding party – the groom's side – was from the Carpathian and that the groom himself was a former Bonyhad Yeshiva student, he consented. It was a great honor to have Hersch Leib Sigheter as the *badchen*. They used to speak about it often in our house.

Returning from the wedding in Sighet, my parents brought me a gift: a small violin. I was very happy with this present, and I squeaked and creaked on it immediately. My interest waned quickly, though; I grew bored and dropped it. Ten years later, in 1935, I took it up again. This time it gave me a lot of joy and pleasure, but it only lasted until 1938. That year on the Hebrew calendar, 5698, is signified by the letters *taf-resh-tzadi-chet*, and spells the word *tirzach* (murder). It coincided with the Kristalnacht (November 1938), when the situation for European Jewry, already bad, turned even worse.

Eliezer received a dowry from Shari's father – a library that included many rare and valuable books. Some were bound in leather, and according to Czech law, there was a high import duty for leather goods. (These volumes were considered leather goods even though leather was simply the book's cover.) Eliezer couldn't afford to bring the entire library to Torun at one time; instead, he carried a few books in his suitcase each time he returned from visiting Shari's mother. Among the limited number of books he was able to transport was one very rare edition: a book of records from the Jewish congregation of Frankfurt-on-Mein. This record book dated from the beginning of the 17th century (over 300 years old in 1926-'27) to the 20th century, and was a treasure for historians on early Jewish life in Germany and throughout Europe. Many other titles in the library were notable, including books of the *Kabbalah* (Jewish mysticism), including the *Zohar*. One of the oldest was a compilation of Josephus's writings in Hebrew called *Yosephen*.

At the time I was too young to understand the significance of these books, or what became of them. When the Hungarians dragged us from our homes on Tisha b'Av *nidcheh*, Eliezer managed to escape. He joined his wife and children in Debrecen where they had been visiting her mother. Of course, he had to leave these books behind (not to mention all his other possessions). I'll never know for certain what the Hungarians did with these rare editions, but gent teenage friends and I always wanted to know the current styles in snap-brim caps and knickers and so forth. When Moshe traveled to the city, I'd ask him to bring me sweaters, shirts, or any type of clothing that was in style at the time.

In 1930, Moshe built a new house for his family, catty-corner from our home. Next to it (and directly across from our house) was the Hebrew public school: a wooden tablet on the school proclaimed, in blue and white Hebrew letters, "National Hebrew Day School."[5] Founded in 1919, this was the only Hebrew school in the Carpathian region at that time. There were already such schools in Munkatch, but in our area and until the mid-1920s, this school was unique.

Zvi (who was age 13 when I was born) grew up with me because he lived at home well into his 20s. Moshe (21 years my senior) and Eliezer (23 years older) had each married and moved out to raise their own families. When I became a Bar Mitzvah at age 13, our family once again had a *mezumin* (meaning three men of Bar Mitzvah age or older). It is customary, when three adult males dine together, for them to offer a special prayer after the meal. After Eliezer and Moshe moved out, and until my Bar Mitzvah, there were only Zvi and my father. After my Bar Mitzvah, one of the three of us would lead the blessing; my father used to rotate this job every meal, between himself, Zvi and me. Secretly, I was unhappy about this arrangement because I had to wait every time we had a meal together, and couldn't get away from the table until we *benched mezumin* (offered grace).

Zvi attended yeshiva away from home in Pistchan and in Nitra (both in Slovakia). In 1927, he was 20 years old and was drafted into the Czech army. After serving for a standard tour of 18 months, he returned home – and promptly fell into a relationship with a cousin, our Uncle Zecharia's daughter, Channa. It wasn't hard to understand why Channa fell in love with Zvi. He was the most handsome among us four brothers. He was tall, but not overly tall or gangly, really a young man with nice features.

Their engagement party was held in the future bride's home. It was a big affair and the family was supportive. But after a year, their love for each other trickled away; by the end of the year they broke up. Who knew why their great love leaked out. I was too young for Zvi to confide in me about such matters. But he did tell me he'd

---

[5] "*Bet Sepher Ivri Amami.*"

never again get engaged to a girl who is an only child. Some years later, he met a pretty girl by the name of Piri. She lived in a neighboring village called Kalin in the Carpathians. They met – let's attribute it to Divine Providence – and my brother was happy. Piri later became his wife. Ironically, Piri was also an only child. It seems as though romantic desire is a lot stronger than personal resolutions.

Zvi and Piri made a very happy pair. Sadly, their joy didn't last long. Only a few weeks after their marriage (in 1938), rumors swirled through the country that German troops were massing on the border. Czech president Edvard Benes (on the night of May 20-21) ordered five classes of military service personnel to man the country's border fortifications. As a reservist, Zvi was called up as soon as the mobilization took place.

in the famous yeshiva in Bonyhad (pronounced BON-yeh-hahd), Hungary. My uncle Armin had been a student there, too, along with the famous Hebrew poet Avigdor Fierstein (who later changed his name to Avigdor Hameiri). Under his penname, he authored the famous book *Ha-Shiga'on Ha-Gadol* (*The Great Madness*), which described World War I, as well as many other books, and the song "*Shalom Lach Yerushalayim*" ("Peace to You, Jerusalem"). Later on, this song was incorporated into the Friday night service prayers of some Reform congregations.

Eliezer joined our Uncle Armin in the scrap iron business in Sighet, Romania. They didn't stay in business very long, eventually selling it. But while in Sighet he met a girl, Shari, with whom he fell in love and later married. Shari was the granddaughter of a famous rabbi, Benyamin Zev Krauss, *zichrono l'vracha*,[4] head of a neologue temple in Debrecen. He authored a very respected commentary on the Torah, *Ma'aros Ha-Bozek* (*ma'aros* means "views" and *Bozek* is an acronym for his name, Benyamin Zev Krauss.)

Shari's mother tongue was Hungarian, and she spoke a bit of German. We used to have a lot of laughs when my mother and Shari would "converse." Both of them spoke in Italian – with their hands. Shari would call my mother "Mommo," which we found very funny. It didn't take very long for Shari to learn two new languages, though: a bit of Yiddish and also Ukrainian (or Ruthenian, Small Russian, as we called it). She learned Ruthenian faster than Yiddish because Eliezer had hired a Ruthenian housekeeper. Shari had to learn Ruthenian quickly, because it was the only language the maid spoke.

Eliezer's wedding took place in Sighet, Romania, and the family needed passports to travel outside the Czech Republic. The wedding had been set for a certain date, until Shari's father became very ill and the wedding was postponed for four or six weeks. It was very disappointing because the delay occurred at the last minute. My mother had baked quite a few cakes and other goodies for the wedding. In those days we didn't have freezers, so we all ate lots of cookies and cakes for a time.

Eventually the wedding took place, but I was left at home with my grandmother Hudyeh (Judith, in English), who stayed behind to baby-sit me. She was probably in her 70s then, and it was hard for her to travel. Our maid Calina also helped out; I spoke to her in

---

[4] Hebrew for "of blessed memory"; abbreviated ZL.

Ruthenian. She was in our house a long time, eight or 10 years.

Sighet was home to a very famous *badchen*, a type of wedding entertainer specializing in humorous and sentimental improvised rhymes. The *badchen* was paid handsomely for his performance. This particular entertainer – Hersch Leib Gottlieb, born in 1844 – was known throughout the Carpathian and Maramaros regions as a great talmudic scholar, a fine writer and poet, and a strong lover of Zion. Zionism was neither very common nor accepted among the greater Jewish population of this area in the early 1900s. But to a growing number of people, who called him "Hersch Leib Sigheter" (the Sighet resident), he indeed was very popular. Even Dr. Theodore Herzl, the founding father of Zionism, heard of him. Herzl presented him with a Yiddish printing press so he could spread his Zionist ideals. Almost single-handedly, Hersch Leib Sigheter started publishing a bi-weekly paper in Hebrew called *Zion*, in 1924. Four years later, he and a partner by the name of Eliyahu Blanc launched a monthly Hebrew magazine called *Ahavat Zion* (*Love of Zion*). He also published a Hebrew newspaper called *Ha-Shemesh* (*The Sun*) and a Yiddish paper, the *Yiddisheh Volks Zeitung* (*Jewish People's Newspaper*). Hersch Leib wrote under a few pseudonyms, but one that he used very often was "*Vemen Got hat Lieb*," or "Whom G-d Loves." He wrote poetry and also translated into Hebrew some of the works of Goethe and Schiller. In 1933, his grandchildren published a compilation of his poetry under the title *Lieder fun Mein Leben* (*Songs From My Life*).

Eliezer subscribed to one of Hersch Leib's magazines, saving every back issue. We'd all discuss the articles, and from these family discussions I could see how sympathetic our house was to the Zionist movement. In the glow of these feelings, everyone wanted very much to have Hersch Leib Sigheter as the entertainer for Eliezer's wedding. Hersch Leib was already in his 80s at that time, but my father enlisted my Uncle Armin, who lived in Sighet, to ask Hersch Lieb whether he'd be the *badchen*. At first he declined. "These Hungarians," he told my uncle, "they won't understand me anyway, and that's why I don't want to do it." But when my uncle revealed that half the wedding party – the groom's side – was from the Carpathian and that the groom himself was a former Bonyhad Yeshiva student, he consented. It was a great honor to have Hersch Leib Sigheter as the *badchen*. They used to speak about it often in our house.

Returning from the wedding in Sighet, my parents brought me a gift: a small violin. I was very happy with this present, and I squeaked and creaked on it immediately. My interest waned quickly, though; I grew bored and dropped it. Ten years later, in 1935, I took it up again. This time it gave me a lot of joy and pleasure, but it only lasted until 1938. That year on the Hebrew calendar, 5698, is signified by the letters *taf-resh-tzadi-chet*, and spells the word *tirzach* (murder). It coincided with the Kristalnacht (November 1938), when the situation for European Jewry, already bad, turned even worse.

Eliezer received a dowry from Shari's father – a library that included many rare and valuable books. Some were bound in leather, and according to Czech law, there was a high import duty for leather goods. (These volumes were considered leather goods even though leather was simply the book's cover.) Eliezer couldn't afford to bring the entire library to Torun at one time; instead, he carried a few books in his suitcase each time he returned from visiting Shari's mother. Among the limited number of books he was able to transport was one very rare edition: a book of records from the Jewish congregation of Frankfurt-on-Mein. This record book dated from the beginning of the 17th century (over 300 years old in 1926-'27) to the 20th century, and was a treasure for historians on early Jewish life in Germany and throughout Europe. Many other titles in the library were notable, including books of the *Kabbalah* (Jewish mysticism), including the *Zohar*. One of the oldest was a compilation of Josephus's writings in Hebrew called *Yosephen*.

At the time I was too young to understand the significance of these books, or what became of them. When the Hungarians dragged us from our homes on Tisha b'Av *nidcheh,* Eliezer managed to escape. He joined his wife and children in Debrecen where they had been visiting her mother. Of course, he had to leave these books behind (not to mention all his other possessions). I'll never know for certain what the Hungarians did with these rare editions, but gentiles frequently tore up and threw out Jewish books during this time. Many of our treasures were lost in the fires of the *Shoah*.

Shari and Eliezer had two children, both boys: Berzi, named after Shari's father who died not too long after their wedding, and Willi. Though I was their uncle, they were really more like younger cousins to me than nephews. Berzi (who was born about 1928) had trouble speaking Yiddish in the beginning because his mother was very slow in learning it herself. Willi was about three years younger. Berzi was 16 and Willi was 13 when the German snake devoured them, together with their parents, HYD.

Moshe and his wife Montze also had two beautiful children. Montze miscarried twice, but then gave birth to Channaleh, their eldest, a dark-haired, blue-eyed girl, and a younger boy, also dark-haired, named Shloimi. Montze was my mother's cousin. (Montze's mother Etyeh and my maternal grandmother Hudyeh were sisters, making Moshe and Montze second cousins. Marriage between second cousins is allowable by Jewish tradition.) My parents were not happy with Moshe's choice, but to this day I don't understand why. It was after all from the same family. My parents tried to talk him out of it, but nothing helped. Their mutual romantic desire was very strong, and Moshe married his beloved Montze. And when Moshe and Montze returned from their honeymoon they brought me a special present: a toy railroad, with tracks and a locomotive that ran on batteries. I was the happiest boy in Torun! Nobody my age, certainly none of my friends, had such a toy. I also got a set of building blocks with which I could construct a house with windows and doors. All my friends were envious of such wonderful toys, especially the train that went round and round on its tracks.

Moshe had his own business, trading lumber and building materials. He used to travel to Chust quite a bit, and he always brought me presents when he returned from the city. I had a special affection for Moshe. In later years, when I reached my teens, my teenage friends and I always wanted to know the current styles in snap-brim caps and knickers and so forth. When Moshe traveled to the city, I'd ask him to bring me sweaters, shirts, or any type of clothing that was in style at the time.

In 1930, Moshe built a new house for his family, catty-corner from our home. Next to it (and directly across from our house) was the Hebrew public school: a wooden tablet on the school proclaimed, in blue and white Hebrew letters, "National Hebrew Day School."[5] Founded in 1919, this was the only Hebrew school in the Carpathian region at that time. There were already such schools in Munkatch, but in our area and until the mid-1920s, this school was unique.

Zvi (who was age 13 when I was born) grew up with me because he lived at home well into his 20s. Moshe (21 years my senior) and Eliezer (23 years older) had each married and moved out to raise their own families. When I became a Bar Mitzvah at age 13, our family once again had a *mezumin* (meaning three men of Bar Mitzvah age or older). It is customary, when three adult males dine together, for them to offer a special prayer after the meal. After Eliezer and Moshe moved out, and until my Bar Mitzvah, there were only Zvi and my father. After my Bar Mitzvah, one of the three of us would lead the blessing; my father used to rotate this job every meal, between himself, Zvi and me. Secretly, I was unhappy about this arrangement because I had to wait every time we had a meal together, and couldn't get away from the table until we *benched mezumin* (offered grace).

Zvi attended yeshiva away from home in Pistchan and in Nitra (both in Slovakia). In 1927, he was 20 years old and was drafted into the Czech army. After serving for a standard tour of 18 months, he returned home – and promptly fell into a relationship with a cousin, our Uncle Zecharia's daughter, <u>Ch</u>anna. It wasn't hard to understand why <u>Ch</u>anna fell in love with Zvi. He was the most handsome among us four brothers. He was tall, but not overly tall or gangly, really a young man with nice features.

Their engagement party was held in the future bride's home. It was a big affair and the family was supportive. But after a year, their love for each other trickled away; by the end of the year they broke up. Who knew why their great love leaked out. I was too young for Zvi to confide in me about such matters. But he did tell me he'd

---

[5] *"Bet Sepher Ivri Amami."*

never again get engaged to a girl who is an only child. Some years later, he met a pretty girl by the name of Piri. She lived in a neighboring village called Kalin in the Carpathians. They met – let's attribute it to Divine Providence – and my brother was happy. Piri later became his wife. Ironically, Piri was also an only child. It seems as though romantic desire is a lot stronger than personal resolutions.

Zvi and Piri made a very happy pair. Sadly, their joy didn't last long. Only a few weeks after their marriage (in 1938), rumors swirled through the country that German troops were massing on the border. Czech president Edvard Benes (on the night of May 20-21) ordered five classes of military service personnel to man the country's border fortifications. As a reservist, Zvi was called up as soon as the mobilization took place.

Chapter 3

Growing UP

I RECEIVED A PAIR OF PIGEONS as pets when I was nine or 10. I don't remember exactly how or from whom I got them, but the pigeons gave me a great deal of joy for three or four years, until I left for yeshiva. In a brief time, from about 1928 to 1932, my one pair of pigeons multiplied until I had a flock of over 100 housed in the attic of a wooden and stucco structure behind our *mo'ar*. Flying about our property, they made a horrible mess of the back porch that ran the entire length of the house. It was covered with pigeon droppings and had to be cleaned all the time. The structure's walls, too, were ruined. There were even occasions when the pigeons almost flew into the kitchen of the main house.

By this time, Calina had left us and was replaced by a Russian woman, Anna, who did most of the cleaning. Cleaning up after the pigeons had to be done every few days, and sometimes I would help. (Unbelievably, for a while, we had rented the downstairs living quarters of this building to a Czech teacher. I have no idea how he lived there with my pigeons always overhead.)

My mother constantly asked me to get rid of the pigeons, or at least to reduce the population. I resisted simply by crying or pleading; as a child, I couldn't understand what she was complaining about. Despite her feelings, she showed great equanimity in letting me keep them. Privately, my parents must have appreciated how much pleasure I had in raising the pigeons, because they used to buy corn, wheat, or other grains wholesale so I was able to feed the entire flock. It's only now, as an adult, that I can appreciate how much patience they demonstrated in tolerating those pigeons, because they were terrible pests. (That my parents continued to tolerate the birds shows much patience on their part; that I persisted in keeping them also shows a great deal of stubbornness on mine.)

One day, a hawk chased one of my pigeons across the nearby Rika River. I took off in pursuit, to try to protect this poor bird, but couldn't cross the river where they had flown, and had to run to a nearby bridge. The pigeon managed to evade the hawk by flying into the attic of a house. To its terrible luck, there was a stray cat in the attic. By the time I got there, the pigeon had met its end from the cat. How upset I was!

For ages, pigeons have been celebrated by poets and song

writers. King Solomon mentions them in his Song of Songs (*Shir Ha-Shirim*). Pigeons are monogamous, unlike other birds; their devotion to their mate is phenomenal, and is something worth emulating. Just as a naturalist observes animals in the wild and records their habits, I began to note the pigeons' tendencies from my countless hours of watching them. Pigeons lay two eggs each month. The male helps incubate them, remaining in the nest during the day, and turning them over to the female at night and for part of the morning. When they hatch, the eggs always yield one male and one female.

If a cat or a hawk killed one member of a nesting pair, the surviving partner would remain with the nest – incubating the eggs or feeding the hatchlings – for a very long time. Whenever this happened, I used to act as a *shadchen*, a matchmaker. If I had a "widowed" female from one pair and a male from another, I would put them together in a cage. For the first few days they'd fight constantly; then the fighting would subside and, finally, they reluctantly would consent to mate. But the pigeons that hatched from this pairing were always two males or two females – never again a male-female couple. Naturally, that gave me more work as a *shadchen*. My skill in observing the pigeons grew to the point where I could tell their age by inspecting the color of their plumage.

It was no coincidence that during the years I devoted my every free hour to the pigeons, I also suffered from swollen tonsils and sore throats. My mother blamed these problems on my spending so much time in a drafty attic with the birds. I didn't believe her, though, and my love for the pigeons remained very strong. If a pigeon was killed, I used to cry and cry. Today I know that pigeons indeed do spread disease. Looking back, I can appreciate how much love my parents had for me to endure all the consequences of my "hobby."

One such illness occurred when I was 10, during Passover. I was very sick with infected tonsils. My mother offered me some *kremslach*, potato pancakes, which were my all-time favorite. Normally, I would have devoured them, but couldn't even touch them now because of the pain I experienced in swallowing. Sympathetically, my mother said, *"Es, Mecheleh, es Mecheleh di kremslach"* – "Eat, little Michael, eat the potato pancakes." And then she added, "Today is your birthday." It was the second day of *chol ha-mo'ed Pesach.* This was the only time in my life that either of my parents directly mentioned my birthday.

Once, when I was older, I found a note my father had inscribed on the inside cover of his *Chumash.*[1] In Hebrew, he wrote: "My son Michael, his light should shine, was born …,"[2] along with the year and the Torah chapter being read in the synagogue that week. I noticed similar inscriptions for each of my three brothers' birthdays, also in Hebrew. (It seems that anything that has to do with the soul is written in Hebrew, the Holy Language.)

Other than instances like these, birthday celebrations were alien to the Carpathian Jewish communities. I think, partly, the reason had to do with the Jewish philosophy about life. Birthday celebrations have little meaning in a world view that asserts:

> In spite of yourself you are born, and in spite of yourself you are alive, and in spite of yourself you will die, and in spite of yourself you are destined to give account of yourself before G-d.[3]
> *Chapters of the Fathers*, Chapter IV, Verse 29

If anything, birthdays were seen as a Christian custom. Christians celebrate the birth of Jesus, and Christmas always represented a time of great danger to Jews. It wasn't safe for us to go outdoors during this holiday, for fear of pogroms or other atrocities. For that reason, I think European Jewry purposely avoided emulating this Christian practice. Jews have always meticulously, even under tremendous pressure, guarded their distinctions from other people with great care. Despite it all, I used to love this time of the year for two reasons. First, since it wasn't safe to go out at Christmas time, we Jewish children did not have to go to *cheder* those evenings. Second, a number of young people, some of Zvi's friends, used to come to our house to play cards, and I loved to watch them.

In April 1932, I became a Bar Mitzvah. It wasn't our custom to throw a blowout party as it is today. It must have been a Monday or

---

[1] Hebrew for the Pentateuch, or Five Books of Moses.
[2] *"B'ni Michael nairo ya-ir nolad …."*
[3] *Pirkei Avot. Al korchecha attah nolad, v'al korchecha attah chai, v'al korchecha attah mait, v'al korchecha atta atid litain din v'cheshbon lifnai Ha-Kadosh-Baruch-Hu.*

Thursday morning – the only weekdays that we read from the Torah during morning prayers – and after Passover, since we do not lay *tefillin* on a holiday or during *chol ha-mo'ed*. I was called up to the Torah for the first time in my life, and my father said the appropriate blessing: "Thank you, G-d, that I have been absolved from the sins of my son,"[4] meaning that from now on the son is an adult and responsible for his own actions. And that's all. A bottle of whiskey and some *kichel* were given to the congregants, and that was the extent of the celebration. (It's interesting to note that in his book *The Joys of Yiddish*, author Leo Rosten defines *kichel* as the "unpretentious little biscuit" that has been "present at Jewish celebrations for hundreds of years." The current style, he comments, "of elaborate Bar Mitzvahs and weddings has upstaged the *kichel*.")

After my Bar Mitzvah, I went away to school at Yeshivas Yitzchak Bais Yoseph, an academy founded by the famous Spinka Rebbe (Yoseph Meir Weiss, 1838-1909) and continued by his son Isaac in the Czech city of Sevlush, about 120-130 kilometers from Torun. (Rebbe Isaac Weiss was murdered in 1944, HYD.) By this time, my pigeons had been multiplying for several years, and I could hardly leave them behind unattended. Pigeons are kosher to eat, like chicken. In fact, at the time of the Holy Temple, pigeons were allowed to be brought as a sacrifice, though it was mainly poor people who did so. Supposedly, roasted pigeon meat is very delicious, but I would have none of that! Naturally I wouldn't allow my mother to take the pigeons to be slaughtered and prepared as a meal. Instead, I sold all of them to a Czech border guard who said he was going to take care of them. Shortly thereafter, he was transferred over 100 kilometers away to another post. Amazingly, some of the pigeons escaped and actually flew back to my house.

The period from 1932-'33 was the first time in my life that I was away from home. In Sevlush (the Hungarian name for the town was

---

[4] "*Baruch sheh pateranu m'onsho shel zeh*"

Sölish), I stayed at the home of my Aunt Faiga, my father's younger sister, and her husband, Yitzchak Popper. The yeshiva was conveniently not too far from their house, but I was very lonesome and longed for my own home, in spite of the fact that I had some playmates: I lived in a small structure behind their main house, sharing a room with their son, my cousin, Zvi. My cousins Rivka and her older sister Esther shared a second bedroom in the same building. The four of us spent much too much time in the main living area of this house, hovering over a table and playing a table-top soccer game. We'd use oversized coat buttons, shooting them like tiddly-winks through a goal, and arguing forcefully over each play.

A zealous student I was not. To my benefit, two yeshiva "upper classmen" were also from Torun, and they kept encouraging me and helping me with my studies. Yeshiva hours began early: we had to rise by seven o'clock for morning prayers. Then, after breakfast, the *rosh yeshiva* (headmaster) lectured us on *Mishnah* and *Gemara*. In the afternoon, we'd study the day's passages, leading up to weekly exams before *Shabbos* on Friday.

I wish I could have had more academic diligence. But I didn't put my heart into my yeshiva studies, because in those days I longed to be a student in the Hebrew *gymnasium* in the city of Munkatch. My parents would have had to pay tuition for *gymnasium* (a secondary school education resulting in something beyond an American high school diploma), not to mention food and housing, while yeshiva was free, and I could stay with my relatives. Those were tough years financially in our house. The Great Depression of 1929 had reached our region by then, and my father's lumber business lost a lot of money. It was a very, very hard time, and our family didn't have the means to send me anywhere else.

I did finish the year, completing two semesters in Sevlush before coming home in September 1933. I had grown extremely tall while I was away. I returned, looking very thin and pale, towering over everyone at 186 centimeters (over 6-foot-2) in height. When my mother saw how tall I had grown she said, "I'm so happy now that you are a boy. What would I have done with a *langer moit* [very tall maiden] like you?"

My parents took me to the family doctor, Dr. Marton, in Volova, 20 kilometers from Torun. He suspected I might develop tuberculosis, which was very prevalent in those days, and advised my parents not to send me back to the city right away. So I remained in Torun's country air for a while. To continue my schooling, my father hired a private tutor who taught me *Gemara* and *Mishnah* for two hours every day. For another hour each day my cousin Zvi taught me *Chumash* and Rashi.[5] Cousin Zvi was also the one who taught me the *ta'amim* (the notation that prescribes the musical chanting of passages from the Torah) before my Bar Mitzvah.

Israel Gross, my private tutor, was the son of Rabbi Yitzchak Gross. He was a young man in his 20s, very knowledgeable in Talmud study. For some reason, the first tractate he selected for me was the *Mishnah* of *Niddah,* which deals with a whole range of sexual issues, such as the menstrual cycle, the time of abstinence, and so on. I suspect he wanted to impress me that he was no dumb *buchar*, that he knew something about the birds and the bees.

---

[5] "Rashi" is the acronym for "*Rabbainu Shlomo Yitzchaki*," author of the 11th century commentary on the Bible and the Talmud.

Chapter 4

Political Cauldron

THE ZIONIST MOVEMENT swept up the youth of Torun in the years 1933 to 1939 and this period was one of great intellectual development for me. A whole range of political parties were organized, representing all shades of the Zionist political spectrum: on the right were the Revisionists (I was a member of this group[1]); left of center was the *Mapai* organization[2]; and the *Shomer Ha-Tza'ir* (The Young Guardians) was on the extreme left. All of these groups wanted to establish a Jewish homeland, but differed significantly in how they conceived of it: as an orthodox Jewish State (the preference of the Revisionists) or a non-religious socialist system (*Shomer Ha-Tza'ir*).

The original founders of the Zionist movement in Torun were called <u>Ch</u>ovavai Zion (Lovers of Zion); generally, they were older and credited with the singular achievement of having built the structure for the Hebrew public school and the modern Yiddish and Hebrew library that the building housed.

The library consisted of works of Jewish, Yiddish and Hebrew classical writers like Shalom Alei<u>ch</u>em, Mendele Moi<u>ch</u>er Sphorim, Shalom Ash, Y. L. Peretz, <u>Ch</u>aim Na<u>ch</u>man Bialik, A<u>ch</u>ad Ha-Am, and so forth. The library also had Yiddish books that were translated from classical writers like Tolstoy, Gorky, Pushkin, Shakespeare, Byron, Thomas Mann, de Maupassant and others. We also received a host of Yiddish dailies: the Warsaw *Hyndt* (*Today*), a socialist newspaper; *The Moment* (a right-leaning paper, also published out of Warsaw), and the YIVO *Bletter* (*Pages*), which was published in Vilna.[3] To enlarge the library's holdings, Zionist youth of all stripes put on plays twice a year, the proceeds going to purchase new books.

For the most part, Torun's youth were also very idealistic <u>ch</u>ovavai Zion. The Zionist movement strengthened and expanded in 1933-'34. Many of our young people – sometimes entire nuclear families – left their homes and relatives to be pioneers in what was then still called

[1] The Hebrew acronym for the Revisionist group is *Hatzohar – Ha-Zionim Revizionim*.
[2] The Hebrew acronym *Mapai* stands for *Mifleget Po'alai Eretz Yisroel*, or Workers Party for the Land of Israel.
[3] YIVO is the acronym for *Yiddischer Wiesenschaftlecher Institut*, or the Institute for Jewish Research.

Palestine. In hindsight, I see that destiny took a hand in saving the lives of each of those who left Torun at that time.

In 1933, a tragic chapter in the history of Zionism occurred, igniting a polarization of the Jewish people and weakening the Zionist movement for years to come. On a Tel Aviv beach one Friday evening, an Arab shot and killed Dr. Chaim Arlazarov. Dr. Arlazarov was a brilliant man, head of the *Misrad Ha-Chutz* of the *Va'ad L'Umi* — essentially, the secretary of state for the coming Jewish State. But the British mandate government in Palestine cleverly and deceitfully seized this opportunity to accuse the right-wing Revisionist organization of being behind Dr. Arlazarov's murder, to cause Jews to fight among themselves.

The ploy succeeded, fostering an enormous division within the Jewish population. Tremendous hatred flared, not only in Palestine, but in the Diaspora as well. This was always the British policy: divide and conquer — so the local population would be easier to govern. They arrested and tried three members of the Revisionist organization: Abba Achimeir (who was a newspaper journalist), Avraham Stafsky and Zvi Rosenblatt. The trial lasted a bit more than a year. Achimeir and Rosenblatt were exonerated, but Stafsky was sentenced to death. His sentence was appealed and ultimately overturned, but month after month during the judicial process created real anger and hatred — a war among brothers. Even siblings and friends didn't speak to each other if they supported opposing Zionist camps.

Hate engulfed the Jewish population and left ugly scars. Even before Stafsky's sentence was handed down, Ze'ev Jabotinsky warned in an article published in *Moment* that hanging Stafsky would accomplish nothing. ("There will be no peace on the other side of the gallows," he wrote.) The whole Zionist movement was terribly divided. On the one hand, Rabbi Yitzchak *Ha-Cohen* Cook, the Chief Rabbi of Palestine, was ready to swear that Stafsky was not the murderer. At the other extreme, the *Mapai* group saw an opportunity to use the circumstances to blunt the growth of its opposition. This conflict remains a black mark on the *Mapai* organization in the history of the Israel's rebirth. Even people like David Ben-Gurion, whose contribution to the State of Israel was monumental, couldn't erase this sad and dirty chapter in modern Jewish history.

All this made a significant impression on me, a 14-year-old *buchar*, and left me deeply pained for a long time. One *chaver* (close friend) of mine from Torun, a boy who went to *cheder* with me, believed the Revisionist organization committed this terrible crime. Even non-Zionist Jews were divided. Some contended that Jews were capable of spilling blood, while others believed that this was a libel by Jews against Jews.

Many years later, when the State of Israel was already in existence, a governmental official came clean on the Arlazarov affair. Bechor Shitrit had been the highest ranking Jewish officer serving in the British police force; he had access to top-secret British material revealing the real story. Shitrit's conscience, it seems, bothered him, and he disclosed publicly that his own party, the *Mapai*, had collaborated with the British – that the British had intentionally used the situation to drive a wedge between Jewish groups, and that the purpose had been to make it easier for the British to manage Palestine.

The lies concocted about Dr. Arlazarov's death were like a virulent strain of bacteria, infecting Palestine and the Diaspora and making the Jewish body very sick. The Zionist movement suffered for many years that followed. I believe, for instance, that this series of events was one of the reasons that the Revisionist organization, under Ze'ev Jabotinsky's leadership, withdrew from the World Zionist Organization and established a group of its own, called the New Zionist Organization, under his leadership.

The same year that Dr. Arlazarov was murdered, 1933, Hitler, *yemach shemo*,[4] came to power in Germany. Hitler didn't hide his beastly intentions. Over radio and in the printed press, he declared his war against the Jews. Even as he openly shrieked his threats, we Jews didn't believe him. Perhaps due in part to the Arlazarov affair, Jewish leaders throughout the world were *fartumult*, very confused. Only in 1935 and 1936, when refugees started to flee Germany and some came to Czechoslovakia, did we begin to recognize the mortal threat behind Hitler's ranting.

Two such refugee families came to Torun. One, from Frankfurt-on-Mein, stayed in our house for a while. Listening to their experiences, I really started to worry about what would happen to us and Jewish people the world over. Jabotinsky was in Poland then, and had already issued his famous call to evacuate Europe:

---

[4] Hebrew for "may his name be erased" – abbreviated YS.

For three years, I have been imploring you, Jews of
Poland, the crown of Polish Jewry, appealing to you,
warning you unceasingly that the catastrophe is near.
My hair has turned white and I have grown old over
these years, for my heart is bleeding that you do not
see the volcano that will soon begin to spew out its
fires of destruction. ... Listen to my words at this, the
eleventh hour. For G-d's sake: let everyone save
himself; so long as there is time to do so, for time is
running short.[5]

Sadly, we Jews didn't hear his SOS. But Jabotinsky was not
alone. In those years, all Zionist organizations were actively preparing
Jewish youths to settle in Palestine. Groups of young pioneers,
hachsharot, were organized to learn the skills they'd need once they
arrived there. Most of these young people were students who lacked
any trade at all. In Sevlush, there was a *hachsharah* to teach people
how to lay bricks and build. Another focused on agriculture. One
hachsharah, organized by the Revisionists in the Italian port city of
Civitavecchia, was set up to teach young Jews how to handle ships
and be mariners.

I was 16 then, and it was this sea-faring *hachsharah* that I very
much wanted to join, in preparation for living in Palestine. Maybe
I'm from the tribe of Zevulun, because our patriarch Jacob blessed
his son Zevulun by saying that he and his children would be sailors
and mariners.[6]

My parents, ZL, didn't want to hear anything about this. They
were already in their early 60s. "You want to go to Palestine?" my
mother would ask. I loved fresh milk and drank so much every day
that she reasoned I couldn't go "unless we send you with Linche,"
the dairy cow that had been with our family since World War I. My
mother said she would never sell that cow; she couldn't conceive of
letting the cow go any more than she would me.

---

[5] From a speech in Warsaw on August 10, 1938, one year before the Nazis invaded
Poland.
[6] In Genesis XLIX:13 — "(The trible of) Zevulun shall dwell at the shore of the
sea" (*Zevulun al chof yamim yishkon'*).

Zvi also wanted to go into a *hachsharah* (I don't recall what type of trade he was interested in learning) and my parents wouldn't let him go either. Like all my contemporaries, I faced a choice: either to act according to my feelings (pursue the dream of emigrating to Palestine), and thereby perhaps survive the impending Holocaust; or to uphold the fifth of the Ten Commandments ("Honor your father and mother"[7]). In the horrifying days and nights I experienced from 1941 through 1945, I often thought about this paradox. Why, I agonized, hadn't I taken my destiny in my own hands? The pain and shame I endured during the *Shoah* years were even greater because I accused myself of not having acted. I concluded that I deserved all these humiliations because my Zionist convictions mustn't have been strong enough: I felt I was a coward for not having gone to the *hachsharah* in Civitavecchia anyway.

I was not the only member of my generation who faced this dilemma. And I know there were others who chose a path different from mine.

---

[7] *"Kibud Av v'Em."*

Chapter 5

Six-Month Window

A YEAR AFTER THE GREAT WAR ENDED in 1918, the world was full of hope, and people believed there would finally be an era of peace. Unfortunately, it lasted fewer than 20 years. As early as 1933, a cancer started growing in Europe: Hitler and his Nazis. The plague that emerged was unlike any the world had seen before. Especially for us Jews, it became the catastrophe (*chorban*) that surpassed in atrocities and cruelty all the previous calamities in Jewish history.

Even as we tried to convince ourselves that we would be okay, we saw the storm approaching. We could have gotten out. From the time of the Munich dictate in October 1938 (appeasing Hitler by granting Germany the Sudentland region of Czechoslovakia) until his troops moved into Prague on March 15, 1939, we could have escaped. My closest boyhood friend, Zvi Fixler, got out. I *wanted* to leave then, too, to go to Palestine. During that six-month window, we could have fled and might have been spared the *Shoah*. But home ties were too strong. The threads that knitted our family together held us in place. And by the time we recognized what had transpired – when we saw the reality of our predicament – it was too late.

When Czechoslovakia was being torn apart in 1938, Torun was already in political upheaval, charged with great danger for the Jews. Our region, the Carpathian, was populated by the Ruthenians (Small Russians). But ethnic Ukrainians (living in Poland and, of course, Soviet-held Ukraine) considered Small Russians to be Ukrainians, as well. In great secrecy, Ukrainian nationalists organized an underground movement to erect an independent Ukrainian state. They hoped that once an independent Ukraine was established in Carpathia, it would be a springboard for their own later expansion into the Polish-held Ukraine and ultimately the greater Soviet-held Ukraine. Jewish families had lived among the local Ruthenians in relative peace for hundreds of years. We didn't see among them any great desire for independence. In general, they seemed happy to belong to the Czechoslovakian state, because they enjoyed autonomy.

During my childhood, there was for the most part an atmosphere of mutual tolerance between Jews and non-Jews throughout the region. In public school, for instance, children would sing three national anthems: the Czech anthem, *Kde Domov Muj* ("Where My Home Is"); the Slovak hymn, *Nad Tátro* ("On the Tatro

Mountains"); and the Ruthenian anthem, *Podkarpatsky i Rusini* ("Under the Ruthenian Carpathian Mountains." Also, the Czech government had always been very friendly toward the Jews, especially in the Carpathian region, because they knew we were loyal citizens. We lived under a Czech Republic that was a benevolent government. For example, the first president, Thomas G. Masaryk (1850-1937; held office from 1918-'35) was a true friend of the Jews. (In the year 1899, while he was a professor of philosophy at Prague Czech University, he defended Leopold Hilsner in a blood libel. Masaryk believed that it was not possible to be a good Christian and an anti-Semite at the same time. He also came to the defense of Mendel Beilis in 1913 during his blood libel case. To this day, his courageous work is commemorated in Israel: the kibbutz K'far Masaryk was established in his honor; later, a forest was planted in his memory.)

Nationalistic unrest among Ukrainians in neighboring Poland, secretly incited and encouraged by Hitler in the mid-1930s, was exported to our region. When Hitler started to threaten Czechoslovakia about the Sudetenland, he quietly urged the Ruthenians in Carpathia to split from Czechoslovakia and form an independent nation. Once separate, the argument went, they could join the Ukrainian region of Poland (where Hitler was also fomenting unrest by promising to help create an independent Ukraine). Months before the real invasion of Czechoslovakia took place, Polish Ukrainians stole across the frontier into Torun and vicinity to organize paramilitary units. These armed bands, called "*sitches*" (pronounced SEETCH-ehz), actively incited the locals against the Jewish population. "You will soon be independent," they told the Ruthenians, "and will have all the property we confiscate from the Jews."

Although throughout my childhood we experienced a period of calm among the various local nationalities, we Jews had a long, bloody history with the Ukrainians that went all the way back to the year 1648-'49. During that period, Bogdan Chmielnicki led a revolt and perpetrated pogroms that wiped out hundreds of Jewish villages in the Ukraine. In the twentieth century (1917-'18), the Ukrainian leader Simon Petlyurah also decimated Jewish communities, such as Zhitomir, Proskurov and others. As in previous Ukrainian independence movements, the first thing the Ukrainians promised was to kill the Jews and plunder their fortunes. (In May 1926, a Jew by the name of Shalom Schwartzbard took revenge against Petlyurah. By then, Russia had taken over the area and quelled the uprising; many Ukrainian leaders fled to Czechoslovakia and, in Petlyurah's case, to France. Schwartzbard, whose family had perished in pogroms that Petlyurah incited, shot and killed him one day on a Paris street. His trial took place from 1926 to 1927. It took a while, but the French court finally acquitted Schwartzbard in October 1927 because he was able to prove that these gangsters murdered members of his family.)

The Carpathian Jews survived those events. But Hitler's desire to dominate Eastern Europe was tearing apart the Czechoslovakian Republic from within. In April and May of 1938, Hitler made a series of moves designed to agitate factions within the country. At the same time, he pressured Britain and France for Sudentland concessions, all as a prelude to his greater goal of taking the entire country by force. In late September, diplomats once again gathered in Munich and – in an attempt to defuse the situation – Chamberlain submitted to Hitler's demands by ordering Czechoslovakia to immediately evacuate the Sudetenland area. We were stunned to find out then that the mighty British and French empires, which we thought would stand by us, were merely paper tigers.

In a desperate effort to forestall the Anglo-French appeasement to Hitler, Czech President Benes ordered a general mobilization of troops on September 23, 1938. The infamous Munich Pact dictated that the Czech Republic evacuate the Sudetanland completely by October 10 of that year. As a result of this, President Benes resigned his presidency on October 5, and was succeeded by Emil Hacha.

During that last week of September, our entire country was in a state of great confusion and chaos. We were unable to get in touch with Zvi, who was in Kalin at that time, where he and Piri had been living at her parents' house. Zvi was still in the reserves (the *Strash obranu statu*, or *SOS*, meaning "Defender of the State" in Czech) and with the national crisis, the Czech military was looking for him in Torun. We knew that with the mobilization, Zvi's military assignment would bring him back home. Torun was situated just inside the border between Czechoslovakia and Poland, and the *SOS* was charged with defending this frontier. Even though Poland was a Slavic-speaking country like Czechoslovakia, relations between the two peoples were generally hostile.

On October 1, 1938, Rosh Hashanah, I was attending a separate *minyan*[1] conducted in the Hebrew school across the street from my house. I happened to be gazing out the window when I saw a motorcycle roaring up the street. It was Zvi, returning from Kalin on the only transport he could find. Right away I ran out to greet him. His biggest worry seemed to be that he was late for his posting. We considered this a lucky assignment, much safer than having to guard the German border. Immediately he reported to the command post. Whatever excuse he gave for his tardiness, the commandant gratefully took him in, because they trusted the Jewish soldiers much better than the Ruthenians.

The Sudetanland was surrendered to Germany by October 10. But from then until mid-March, we were still safe as Czech citizens, free to come and go as we pleased. The Czech police and administration maintained control over the greater part of the Carpathian region, and we still hoped that we'd escape the worst: that the *Ashmedai* (in Jewish lore, the king of the demons) would be satisfied with the terms of the Munich Agreement, and not push for more. In spite of the fear and anxiety that Hitler was getting closer, only two or three people left Torun to make *aliyah*. We were hoping for G-d's intervention, even though our sages warned us never to rely on miracles.[2]

No miracles prevented Hitler, YS, from moving into Bohemia-Moravia in mid-March, 1939. At the same time as Hitler's troops invaded Prague, a motorcycle messenger from Chust arrived in Torun. He stopped at the Ruthenian school, where the local *sitches'* headquarters were located; the messenger brought a written order to launch an uprising against the Czech administration. Half an hour later we saw a whole gang of *sitches* pile out of the school, armed with machine guns. They marched to the local Czech headquarters, just a half-kilometer away, and were able to take the Czech garrison by surprise. They overpowered the reservists and declared independence from the Czech government. Zvi was still in the *SOS* unit then, but fortunately he was off-duty that day, at home when the attack occurred. The *sitches* were vicious anti-Semites; who knows what they might have done to Zvi if they caught him. (Later, we found a list the *sitches* had prepared for Torun, naming which Jews they intended to hang and which ones to shoot.)

With these events, our six-month window for escape abruptly slammed shut. The Ruthenians declared their independence from the

---

[1] The number of Jewish men, traditionally 10, required by Jewish law to be present to conduct a communal religious service.

[2] "*Ain somchim al ha-nais.*"

Czech Republic, and to our horror we found ourselves no longer Czech but Ukrainian citizens. All of us were scared stiff, but the immediate danger from the Ukrainians lasted only 24-36 hours. Almost immediately, Hungarian troops moved into the Carpathian region, on March 15 or 16. The result was that a very short-lived Ukrainian independence movement collapsed. Hungary annexed the territory, based on claims dating back to the Austro-Hungarian Empire. We Jews all knew what the Ukrainians were capable of, so with Hungary's move into our area we felt that the threat of immediate danger was past: between the Ukrainians and Hungarians, we thought the Hungarians were the lesser of the two evils. Of course, the Hungarians were no *tzaddikim* (righteous people) either, but in 1939 their occupation of our region — ironically, with Hitler's blessing — saved Carpathian Jewry from potential Ukrainian atrocities.

Sadly, this was only a temporary reprieve. "And there arose a new Pharaoh over Egypt who didn't know Joseph" (Exodus I:8).[3] The Hungarians also started to bare their teeth. Some time at the end of 1939, a whole series of evil decrees were issued against the Carpathian Jews. The first decree forbade Jews from engaging in the lumber trade. This weighed heavily on the whole Jewish population because the majority of us sustained ourselves from that industry.

The situation deteriorated from day to day. Increasingly we became concerned about the conditions around us. We coped with every change, but each new evil decree slowly strangled our remaining freedoms. First they took away our livelihood; soon after, they banned our freedom of assembly. We used to gather quite often as members of the Zionist movement, which was well organized in Torun. One day, my brother Eliezer and cousin Zvi Heimowitz, both leaders of the *Chovavai Zion* organization, were called to Volova. Somehow, Hungarian officials discovered that they had had a meeting, even though nothing about it had been published. Summoning Eliezer and Zvi, the Hungarian authorities accused them of this "crime." I don't know how they beat the accusation, but the matter was dropped and the two of them were let go with just a scare.

We immediately stopped having such meetings, however, and

---

[3] "*V'yokom melech chadash al Mitzrai'im asher lo yadah et Yoseph.*"

also began eliminating our library of books that were published in the Soviet Union. In the early 1930s, a Yiddish version of the Communist newspaper *Pravda* (Truth), called *Emes*, was published in Moscow that printed selected works of Yiddish writers – Shalom Aleichem, Mendele Mocher Sphorim, Shalom Asch and others. The library had ordered this newspaper, as well as books by these authors. The Soviet publisher was giving away crates of these works, absolutely free – the catch being that whoever ordered them also was inundated with communist propaganda. We didn't want it to look obvious to the publisher that we were interested only in the "non-Red" volumes, so we ordered a few propaganda texts, too, just to get the books we really wanted. But now we started to clean out the communist "*chometz*,"[4] since "Red" texts would have attracted the ire of anti-Soviet Hungarians).

During this time, Hungary sent in lots of troops and started to requisition homes, mostly Jewish ones, for quartering soldiers. They also commandeered the building that housed our Hebrew school and library. A while later, they requisitioned our synagogue. In our own home they expropriated two rooms, but allowed us to continue living in the rest of the house. We never forgot that Torun was on the Polish border. Although Poland and Hungary had friendly relations, the Hungarians started building fortifications on the mountains all around. Hungary was already allied with Germany, and we saw these preparations as a harbinger of conflict yet to come.

In the summer of 1939, the Hungarians organized a paramilitary youth group called "Levente." All boys aged 15 to 20, Jewish as well as Ruthenian, had to attend training exercises twice a week for two hours at a time. I was one among that group. The Hungarian instructor was a terrible anti-Semite, and he constantly bullied, jeered at and beat us Jewish boys. The punishment for not attending the session was severe, so we had no alternative but to go and suffer his humiliation and lashes. The verbal humiliation was harder to bear than the occasional physical abuse, because we were singled out; we had never before in the former Czechoslovak Republic felt such anti-Semitism. How blind and numb we were that we hadn't seen this black future awaiting us. Maybe, in the summer of 1939, maybe we still could have gotten out. Yet we remained.

It got worse. New decrees were issued that called for all Jewish males, ages 20 to 50, to register in military labor camps the

---

[4] Metaphorically speaking, any forbidden possessions; literally, any leavened food products prohibited during Passover.

Hungarians called *munkotabors*. Each camp comprised a company of 150-200 men (a *munkoszazod*). It was said then that this was only for three months' time. Rumors flew through the Jewish community – false optimism – that the Hungarians only wanted to please the Germans and had no intention of harming the Jews too badly.

How deluded we were that we didn't see where all this would lead. Maybe it's human nature, especially among Jews, to hope for miracles and mercy.[5] As the Hebrew saying goes, "Don't give up hope, even if a sharp sword is held against your neck."[6] But our optimism and that hope cost us very dearly.

My dear parents hoped very much that *y'shias Hashem* (G-d's help) would come soon; they wanted to protect me from the Hungarian labor units. I had already turned 20 in April 1939, so my father paid off a man in charge of birth records in City Hall. For the bribe, he altered the documents by changing my birthday to November 18, 1920, to make me one-and-a-half years younger. For now, I was saved. I did not have to go into a *munkotabor* in 1939. Despite all this *tsuris* (trouble), we continued to hope Hitler would surely meet a bloody demise and bring an end to our travails.

---

[5] For *nissim* and *rachamim*.

[6] "*Al timnah mi-rachmim, aphilu cherev chadah munachat al tzavarechah.*"

Chapter 6

The Approaching Storm

TIME STRETCHED ON LIKE THAT, with all of us depressed yet somehow full of hope that the approaching storm would pass us by. Not even the most pessimistic among us could have imagined what a bleak future awaited us. Before Rosh Hashanah, our community was able to arrange with the military commander – naturally in return for a nice "present" – to have the troops vacate the synagogue before the High Holidays. The building was cleaned out nicely and we awaited the new year in hope of better days to come. Rosh Hashanah 1939 fell on September 1. We were all in the synagogue, and suddenly, somehow, the news that Warsaw was being bombarded spread throughout the congregation. Hitler had begun his move into Poland.

A great shiver went through everybody. Many of us subscribed to the great Jewish dailies published out of Warsaw (*Hyndt, Moment*), and we were very familiar with Jewish life in Poland. In Torun, especially, and the Carpathian in general, we drew spiritual nourishment from Warsaw – it was often referred to as the "crown jewel" of European Jewry.[1] We had no details, but we all felt a great tragedy had befallen the Jewish people of Europe. Poland was home to Europe's largest Jewish community, over three million souls, and formed the greatest reservoir of Jewish spiritual thinking and creativity – perhaps the greatest Jewish spiritual center in the world.

Four days after Hitler began his attack on Poland – on September 5 – England and France declared war on Germany, and World War II began. But the modern army of the *Ashmedai* seemed invincible. Within three weeks, Poland had been overrun and the country was divided between Russia and Germany – the result of a secret agreement between Stalin and Hitler, YS.

Across the frontier from Torun was a small Polish town called Vishkoff. About a week or 10 days after Germany's first attack, thousands of Polish soldiers began streaming into Hungary, and many of them passed through Vishkoff to Torun. Hungarian troops manning the border allowed Polish soldiers to enter, but only on the condition that they surrender their weapons.[2] The main guard station

[1] It was also called an *ir v'aim b'Yisroel* – literally, a metropolis or mother city, but figuratively, a great Jewish city outside Israel.
[2] Border guards were called *finantzen*, not to be confused with "finances!"

was in the middle of town, a wooden building with a large front yard. Escaping Polish soldiers had to deposit their weapons there. Weapons were stacked in a huge pile in front of the building, like a small mountain. I saw some of the soldiers crying when they had to lay their weapons down.

Among the Polish soldiers were some Jews. One Jewish soldier, who visited our house, related the horrific destruction in Poland, mainly from German air force bombardment. He also spoke of the deep anti-Semitism in Poland and in the Polish army. Even now, when the Poles see what the German *Ashmedai* is doing to them, he said, their anti-Semitism does not abate. We offered the soldier civilian clothing and help to get him deeper into Hungary where he might blend in with the still-large Jewish communities in big cities like Budapest and Debrecen. He declined, saying, "I want to see the Poles' end already."[3] That's how bitter he was about Polish anti-Semitism in the Polish army.

Near the end of September, Russia annexed the Polish Ukraine, the carving-up of Poland being the final element in the secret pact between Hitler and Stalin. All of a sudden, we in Torun became neighbors of the Soviet Union. Under the Czech constitution the Communist Party had been legal, and a small number of committed Communists seized the opportunity to leave, since Russia now was only a two-hour walk over the mountain.

On one hand, we were very happy that at least a *part* of Poland's Jewry was saved, because, as cruel as Stalin was, he did not compare to Hitler in his treatment of the Jews. And the Polish Ukraine was home to large Jewish enclaves, in cities such as Lemberg, Stanislaw, Stri, Kolomei, Kamieniec Podolski, Dolina and others. On the other hand, we weren't naïve about Stalin. We knew what kind of beastly behavior the Communists were capable of, including the "show trials" Stalin staged in 1935-'36, the purges he carried out against some of his highest ranking officials (Zinoviev, Kamenev, Tukachevski and Radek, to name a few), and his crimes against ordinary citizens (charging them with conspiracy, forcing "confessions," and then executing them).

It took a few months, but now that they had the Soviet Union

---

[3] "*Ich vil shön sehn zayer sof.*"

on their border, the Hungarians deployed a larger military contingent in the region. Frantically, they started building bunkers and other fortifications along the mountains and in the villages. They strengthened border patrols and curtailed movement of the local population, especially for us Jews. On the other side of the frontier, Russia also beefed up its border patrols. For anybody inclined to cross the border, the opportunity for passage swiftly slipped away.

In short order, Torun overflowed with Hungarian soldiers and we felt like we were living in the middle of a war zone. Worse, the Hungarians suspected we Jews would be sympathetic to the Russians. And I might say they were correct: we *surely* didn't have any sympathy for Hitler and his allies. So the Hungarian authorities curtailed our movement. By this time, Jewish males between 20 and 50 were already taken to the Hungarian military labor camps, so all the Carpathian villages were emptied of young boys and men. For those of us who remained, life was suffocating and scary.

Despite the danger, we tried to monitor radio broadcasts from London. The Hungarians had prohibited Jews from owning radios or from listening to foreign broadcasts. Anyone caught was beaten up or arrested (or both) and sent to jail. In spite of that, we did have a radio hidden in the cellar of my Cousin Zvi Heimowitz's house, who lived about a half-kilometer from us. Whenever we dared, we tuned in to the BBC, which aired its broadcasts in all European languages during the war; we listened to the German language version. The reports were designed to lift the spirits of millions of people in occupied countries like Poland and Czechoslovakia, predicting that Germany eventually would be defeated. The question for us was: when? And the BBC didn't lead us to believe it would occur quickly. Just the opposite. In May 1940, when Winston Churchill became Prime Minister of Great Britain, we were full of hope that the end of the Chamberlain/appeasement era would hasten Hitler's fall. But we were very disappointed by Churchill's famous speech when he said, "I have nothing to offer but blood, toil, tears and sweat."[4] Certainly this was a realistic appraisal by a great leader, but unfortunately it also was a clear message that Hitler would not be defeated any time soon. Another clear message: we Jews justifiably came to the realization that we wouldn't be able to survive a long conflict. Still, against all odds, we hoped for a miracle.

One miracle did occur in our family that year. Sometime in 1940, Zvi and Piri were blessed with a baby boy. They named him Baruch,

---

[4] First statement as Prime Minister, House of Commons, May 13, 1940.

meaning "blessed." We all hoped that blessings had come upon them.

In the summer of 1940, another large contingent of Hungarian troops arrived in Torun, settling in almost every Jewish home in town. (Most of the Jewish residences were located along the highway, giving the soldiers a central location.) If a house had four or five rooms, they'd take two away. We were not spared. Our house, in fact, was "host" to the military contingent's commanding officer, a Hungarian *ezredesh* (the rank of colonel). He occupied one room and the other room was for his attaché. The Hebrew school, located directly across from our house, was transformed into military headquarters for all units in Torun.

We continued to listen secretly, of course, in Cousin Zvi's basement, to the BBC for good news from the battlefront, but the miracles we craved never arrived. Just the opposite. We heard reports detailing German victories in the face of massive British and French setbacks. Then, at the close of one such ominous broadcast, the BBC announced that Ze'ev Jabotinsky, ZL, had died in New York City. It was the 29th day of the Hebrew month of Tammuz. Tammuz is loaded with sad and tragic happenings in Jewish history. The Roman siege of Jerusalem, more than nineteen hundred years earlier started on the 17th day of Tammuz. In more recent history, Dr. Binyamin Ze'ev Herzl – the man who had sown the seeds for our coming independence – died when just in his forties, on the 20th day of Tammuz in 1904. Chaim Nachman Bialek, beloved Zionist and "poet of anger,"[5] died on the 21st of Tammuz, 1934. Now with Jabotinsky's death, another great Jewish leader passed from among his people. For a long time this loss lay heavily on my mind and I couldn't put it aside.

I grew very scared, fearing every unknown that tomorrow might bring. It must have shown on my face, because my mother tried hard to lift my mood. She must have been scared, too, but she'd always comfort and reassure me, telling me not to worry and predicting that everything will turn out all right. She emphasized our very strong faith in the eternity of the Jewish people.[6] To this day, I don't know

---

[5] "*Meshorer ha-za'am.*"
[6] In Hebrew, *bitachon b'netzach Yisroel.*

whether she truly had this strong faith herself, or if it was a façade to improve my morale. My father was always the anxious one, the worrying kind – especially in those days. He didn't speak much about our situation, at least not with us, but we saw deep concern on his face. I inherited this unfortunate trait from him. Generally, one cannot change one's character, and under those circumstances it would have been better for me to have my mother's nature.

Deep down, no Jew was convinced, yet we deluded ourselves that conditions were more or less tolerable. By now, for one thing, many of the Jewish males who had been drafted into military companies had been released and sent home. We also concocted theories about the Hungarian Prime Minister, Count Kaloi. In the Hungarian parliament, he delivered virulent anti-Jewish speeches. Wishful thinking led us to believe this was only to please Hitler – that Kaloi wasn't as bad as he sounded. After all, in Budapest and other Hungarian cities, Jews still owned businesses. True, anti-Jewish laws in the Carpathian region were harsher, but this was because Carpathian Jews had been Czechoslovakian citizens before; it didn't take much of a stretch for us to believe that's why Hungary was more severe with us. A majority of Hungarian Jews thought they'd get through this with only a little trouble. How sad it was, how they deceived themselves from reality!

As the winter of 1940-'41 approached, my brother Zvi was called to a *munkotabor*. He managed to bribe someone and get a nine-month postponement. We were always trying to buy time, still hoping for miracles. The Hebrew saying, "It's enough to worry about troubles when they arrive, not beforehand," was the general Jewish mindset at the time.[7]

By now our house had become quite crowded. Beside Zvi, Piri and the baby, we still quartered the two Hungarian officers. Piri's parents lived in a big house in Kalin, so Zvi decided the three of them should move there. Kalin, in contrast to Torun, seemed safer, as it was away from the border. Throughout the winter, Zvi remained with his in-laws. When he returned to Torun on business, after *Pesach* 1941, he left Piri and the baby with her parents. Eliezer's wife Shari also left Torun with their two children, Bertzi and Willi, in this case for Debrecen, to live with Shari's mother. Eliezer remained alone in his house, about a kilometer away from us. Moshe, Montze and their two children, Channaleh and Shloimi, had nowhere else to go, so they stayed in Torun in their house, diagonally across the street from

---

[7] "*Dai l'tzarah b'sha'atah.*"

us. With all the restrictions and the constant presence of the military, life in Torun was stifling. We had to depend on the kindness of individual military officers to let us breathe.

Spring turned to summer. It was a nice, warm day and the windows of our house were open. So were the windows of the Hebrew school across the street, and we could hear the Hungarian *ezredesh* addressing his officers. It was a pre-battle pep-talk. I didn't understand Hungarian then, but Eliezer had heard him, too, and translated the gist of it. "We are getting ready," he had said, "with our allies, the Germans and the Italians, shortly, to attack and destroy Communist Russia."

My reaction was immediate. "What a fool that colonel is," I told Eliezer. "I hope they do try to attack the mighty Soviet Union." Unfortunately, we didn't know the real situation in the Soviet Union, the same as we misjudged the true strength of Great Britain and France.

Not long after this, the colonel told my father in confidence that it would be prudent for him to leave Torun, as war could break out at any time. It would be best, he said, to be far from the border. We couldn't believe he was actually concerned about our safety or welfare. We thought perhaps he was telling us this to get us to move out, so he could have the whole house for himself. We simply weren't prepared to believe that this small country of Hungary – even allied with Germany – would dare attack the powerful Soviet Union. All the same, my father hired a man with a horse and buggy, loaded up our clothing, jewelry, and other valuable possessions, and dispatched Zvi to accompany him to my beloved Aunt Jutta (YOO-tah), who lived 70 kilometers deeper in the Carpathian, in Bereziv. The colonel granted us a special permit to make the trip because Jews weren't allowed to come and go easily.

When other Jews saw us carting away possessions from our house, they reacted immediately with fear that the war was coming to Torun and that the Hungarians would force them out of their homes. Although they discussed this potential situation, they ignored their panicky feelings and stayed. As I write these lines now, I cannot understand why *all* of us Toruners didn't try to leave the town at that time. We would have saved ourselves two years of grief and trouble. But I guess it's human nature to be tied to one's place of birth – to the land and to the possessions one has toiled to accrue over a lifetime.

June 22, 1941, began as a beautiful, sunny summer day. The only thing on my mind that morning was to get over to the synagogue (*shul*) to pray. When I arrived there, the news on everybody's lips was that Germany had attacked the Soviet Union. The Hungarian army, concentrated in Torun, was on the move, too, and had crossed the border into Poland. We were all elated by the news, convinced that this action marked the end of Germany. But our feelings of joy were quickly tempered by the realization that we were now in the middle of a battle zone.

A day or two passed, and we started to hear of the great German "*Blitzkrieg*" victories. Even the Hungarians were advancing. We couldn't believe our eyes, either, when we saw more and more Hungarian troops passing through Torun on their way deep into the former Poland. The so-called mighty Red Army was not putting up even token resistance. Hearing about those easy victories completely devastated us. Our morale sank even lower than before, our hope drained away. We were trapped in a terrible nightmare.

"From where will come my helper?"[8]

---

[8] "*Mi ayin yavoh ezri?*" (from Psalm 121:1).

Chapter 7

Deportation

OUR NEIGHBORS AND LIFELONG FELLOW RESIDENTSof Torun knew of the deportation decree before it was carried out. Eliezer had been a town councilman. One Friday, a week before we were dragged from our homes, he learned that there had been a town council meeting, but he hadn't been informed or invited. "I don't know," he said. "I wasn't called, and I don't like it. Something is going on." He couldn't know what orders were being given behind the scenes, but his suspicions ran high because of the way gentile townspeople were acting.

This was the beginning of the *Shoah* for Carpathian Jewry. "And it was in those days ...."[1] Our great commentator Rashi tells us that, in Jewish history, each time a story starts with the words "and it was,"[2] it signifies the beginning of a tragedy. And it was in those days, the ninth and tenth days of the Hebrew month of Av 1941, Tishah b'Av *nidcheh*, that began the violent deaths of my family. As it happens, Tisha b'Av fell on a Saturday that year (August 2).[3] According to tradition, our fast to lament the destruction of the Holy Temple in Jerusalem and the loss of Jewish independence nineteen hundred years earlier was not to be held on the Sabbath, but instead was postponed to Sunday. Tragically, our own postponed day of devotion and contemplation, Sunday, August 3, would mark the beginning of our plunge into four years of darkness.[4]

We needed all the spiritual uplift we could get. During this already difficult period, our rabbis tried to raise our spirits by finding contemporary messages in the weekly Torah readings. In Exodus XXX:12, for example, which was read in the synagogue back in

---

[1] "*Va'yehi b'yamim ha-hem.*"

[2] "*Va'yehi.*"

[3] The expulsion of Jews from Spain in 1492, the same year Columbus "discovered" America, was based on a decree issued March 31 of that year: Jews were given four months either to convert or leave. The last Jews left on Tisha b'Av, which that year coincidentally also fell on August 2. Columbus sailed a day later.

[4] Even now, almost 60 years later, it is very hard for me to retell the bitter and terrifying days and nights that started that month of Av. Not too long ago, I read excerpts of a book by Primo Levi, the Italian Jew. He describes with great talent the *gehenom* (hell) known as Auschwitz. He concludes, and I agree, that a person tortured once remains forever tortured.

March 1941, G-d promises that when Moses will tally the Children of Israel, there will not be a plague among them.[5] The rabbis considered this particular passage meaningful to our circumstances because the letters of the Hebrew word for taking the sum of something ("*thissa*") had the numerical value corresponding to the current Hebrew calendar year, 5701 (which correlates with the Julian calendar year of 1941).[6] This is just one of many instances of our rabbis in Torun referring to Torah portions as "proof" that nothing would happen to us. But I'm afraid that all this looking for and relying upon numerological connections misled us into thinking we would be alright.

Now, early in the evening of August 2, strains of the beautiful prayer that begins "G-d, Master of the Universe" ("*Ya Ribon Olam*") emanated from Torun's *shul.* It is a deeply emotional plea: "G-d, Master of the Universe, save the Jewish people from the lion's mouth, the people whom You selected from among the nations. Return us from exile." The congregation understood very well that this prayer was recited in mourning for the destruction of the Holy Temple. What we could not have known was that our own destruction would begin six or seven hours later, the same night and in the same *shul.*[7]

"Oh, G-d, my G-d, why did You forsake us?[8]

Opposite our *shul* was Zecharia Godinger's house. We used to gather there since it was always a joyful place for young people. Malkah, the eldest sister, was of my brother Zvi's generation, but she was her family's matriarch: her parents had died a few years earlier, and now, as a married woman, she took care of the house and her siblings. Her brothers were away in labor camps, but her unmarried sisters Bailah and Yenta still lived there. With the sound of "*Ya Ribon Olam*" still lingering in my ears, I left the depressing atmosphere of the *shul* and went over to their house.

---

[5] "*Ki thissa et rosh b'nai Yisroel lifkudaihem … v'lo yihyeh bahem negef bifkod otam.*"

[6] In Hebrew, each alphabet letter corresponds to a numerical value. The letters that spell "*thissa*" – *taf* (400) - *shin* (300) - *aleph* (1) add up to 701. *Taf-shin-aleph* was the short-hand notation for 5701 (the fifth millennium being understood).

[7] In that very *shul,* Carpathian Jews, our fathers and forefathers, celebrated Jewish holidays and rituals for more than a hundred years: Bar Mitzvahs, circumcisions (*brit milot*), the calling up to the Torah of a groom on the day before his wedding (*aufruf*), midnight prayers (*chetzosn*), and celebrations for completing the study of Talmudic tractates (*siyumim*), etc. How many tears fell on the Book of Psalms (the *tehillim*) and on open prayer books (*siddurim*); and how many blasts of the ram's horn (the *shofar*) were heard there!

[8] "*Eli, Eli, lamah azavtanu?*" (from Psalm 22:2).

A Jewish *munkoszazod* had been stationed at the Godinger's. Almost all these boys were from deep inside Hungary. They referred to themselves as "Jews from the Hungarian motherland" ("*onyo orszagi Zsidos*"; in Yiddish we called them the "*mammalandische Yidden*") and they believed that their Hungarian heritage would spare them the treatment of other European Jews. Most of them were very assimilated and couldn't speak or understand a word of Yiddish. Among the group was a talented musician who played the accordion and piano. On the Godinger's porch, this fateful night, he was churning out Hungarian tunes on his accordion. I knew that the next morning all the Jews of Torun would sit on low benches (as was the custom during the fast of Tisha b'Av) and recite the melancholy Lamentation from Jeremiah: "How does the city [Jerusalem] sit, solitary, that was full of people."[9] But here I was, listening to Hungarian folk melodies. It struck me as bizarre and made me very uncomfortable.

After 15 or 20 minutes I left and went home, wondering what kept these young Jews from feeling depressed or scared like me. I felt very alone, because most of my friends were already in the labor camps. (As it turned out, this was fortunate for them: they escaped deportation to the Polish Ukraine.)

Around eleven o'clock, Zvi and I retired to the room we shared. Tomorrow would be the fast in commemoration of the destruction of the First and Second Holy Temples, I reminded him, and it seemed to me that those Hungarian Jews at the Godinger house, playing and singing like that, don't know what day tomorrow is. Steamed with resentment, Zvi and I finally dropped off to sleep around midnight, on what was to be our last night ever together in our own home. For that matter, it would be the last time for the next four years that I even had a real bed I could call my own on which to sleep.

Around one-thirty in the morning, wild, ferocious screams in Hungarian and banging on our windows broke our sleep. "Open up! Open up!" Frightened, we opened the door, and three Hungarian soldiers pushed through the doorway, bayonets fixed to their rifles. They reeked of whisky. Later, we found out that they'd been given

---

[9] "*Aicha yashvah b'dad ha-ir rabbati am*," in Jeremiah, Lamentations I:1.

lots of whisky, to be more savage in carrying out their orders. Banging their rifle butts on the floor and on the tables, they screamed, "Faster, faster, get dressed, pack your clothing, you dirty Jews, you are not allowed to stay here anymore!"

From room to room they moved, rifling through drawers on my night table and dresser. My wristwatch lay on the night table. When one of the soldiers spotted it and put it in his pocket, I protested. Without hesitating, he hit me in the chest with his rifle, and accompanied it with a Hungarian curse: "You dirty Jew!" I stopped protesting.

In a low voice, my mother told me to get dressed in my newer clothing. I didn't understand the reason then, but later I did. This was no time for saving something nice for later. It took us less than an hour, though it seemed like an eternity with the Hungarians hovering around us. Then the soldiers herded us out, my father, my mother, me and my brother Zvi, into the *shul*, where only a few hours earlier we had been praying. Inside were other Jews who'd been routed from their homes. Hungarian soldiers were all over the place, inside and surrounding the building. In front, by the *shul*'s Western wall near the Holy Ark (the *Aron Ha-Kodesh* that housed our Torah scrolls), was a local official with a list of all the Jews of Torun. Next to him in civilian clothes were two Hungarians whom we had never seen before. We surmised they must be members of the Hungarian secret police. Soul by soul, they checked the "merchandise" off their list – people already delivered by the troops, and those of Torun's 700-800 Jews who were still to come.

Every few minutes, soldiers would deliver more families into our *shul*. No one knew what would happen to us, and we were terrified. We found out later that this evil deportation decree had been issued on Friday, the week before. In secret, local Ukrainians were told what the Hungarian forces were preparing to do. But our neighbors had kept silent: they did not warn us. We believed we lived in harmony with Torun's gentile population, where we resided together in the Carpathians for hundreds of years. Just the opposite: they seemed very happy that they would soon acquire all the Jewish possessions. [10]

---

[10] My cousin Zipporah (who is also from Torun but now lives in Israel) traveled back to Torun in the 1990s to achieve some closure on this part of her past. She visited my old house (one of the few structures still remaining from the time we lived there) and talked with some of these neighbors, one of whom still recalled Zipporah's parents, my aunt and uncle, even without prompting. The intervening 50 years, mostly under Soviet rule, had resulted in economic and environmental ruin. The lush mountainsides had been over-logged and completely denuded. *When*

(We also learned later that in Bereziv, a village where my favorite aunt lived, the mayor had resisted the Hungarians. "My Jewish neighbors lived here for hundreds of years," he protested, "and I will not stand for that." But he was successful only in delaying the decree for a while, not in eliminating it.)

Everybody was in a state of complete shock and panic. "Where are they taking us?" one asked the other, and nobody knew the answer. When they came to our row, officials told my father that he and my mother weren't on the list because they were over 75 years old. A soldier was ordered to escort them back home. (Apparently, my father's birth certificate listed him as 10 years older than he really was. The reason for this had something to do with World War I, and that was his good fortune now.)

"Thank G-d, Mom and Dad are out," Zvi said to me. He tried to relieve my anxiety by reminding me, "We're young, and we shall overcome all this." The local official who released my parents had a friendly (and profitable) relationship with my father. He was the person who, for a bribe, had removed my brother Zvi's name from the list ordering boys into the labor camp; this was also the same person who had taken a bribe to alter my birth certificate and register me as younger. Although my mother was in her 60s, he had the authority to dismiss her with my father. In total, 17 Jews – all of whom were supposedly older than 75 – were allowed to remain in Torun.

A while later we saw soldiers bringing in my brother Moshe and his wife Montze with their two children, Shloimi, 5, and Channaleh, 8. By now, the *shul* was overflowing with men and women, old ones, young ones and babies. Had I all my senses about me, I am certain I could have escaped from there – it was pure pandemonium. I'll never forget the terrible scene before my eyes: the plaintive cries from babies, screams of women, all those people crushed together.

As dawn approached, we saw buses stop near the *shul*. Hungarian soldiers rushed Jews out and loaded them onto these buses. "Where are they taking us?" we asked. Despite the women and small children among us, the soldiers, the drivers, everyone, all said

---

the Jews were here, we had jobs, they told her. *Today we have nothing.* What Zipporah learned may be taken as at least some measure of retribution.

we were being taken to a labor camp. They jammed us onto the buses, overloaded, shoulder to shoulder, and drove off in the direction of <u>Ch</u>ust. Zvi, Moshe, Montze, their children and I somehow managed to remain together on one bus. As for our brother Eliezer, we had not seen him in the *shul* and didn't know where he was. Months later, we learned that he had heard the soldiers coming for him and managed to escape.

The buses passed through villages like Bistra, Maidan, Soimi, Volova and others, all home to Jewish communities similar to Torun, with 700-1000 souls apiece. Through the windows, we could see Jews going to *shul* in the morning for Tisha b'Av services. They stared at the buses with frightened faces and scared eyes, buses jammed with babies and women, men old and young. Because Torun was a border village, we were the first to be wrested from our homes. These villages would be next: a deportation decree was in effect for them as well – and that, too, was a secret well-kept by the local population.

When we arrived in <u>Ch</u>ust, the buses drove to a huge lumberyard. The yard was enclosed by a high wooden fence and surrounded by soldiers. It was a warm, sunny day, and they unloaded us into the open area. Families struggled to remain together. Men, women, children, the elderly, the sick, and the helpless, all were deposited there, sitting on the ground with their small bundles of belongings (*pecklech*). Children cried. A constant wailing filled the air.[11]

There was no place in the yard for dealing with human necessities, neither for ladies nor men. After sitting there a few hours, people tried to relieve themselves in corners of the yard. Women would go in groups and hold up a coat or cloth to shield themselves. Children relieved themselves all over the place. Every hour or so, new buses arrived, delivering Jewish cargo from different villages.

I walked around the fence inside the yard, and found a loose board. I was convinced I could get out through the hole. Although I had no idea where I would go, I rushed back and told Zvi about it, urging him to join me. "Let's get out, let's get out of here, and we'll worry where to go later."

Zvi disagreed. "How could we leave Moshe alone with the two children? No, we have to stick together. Whatever happens, happens." As it turned out, we could help Moshe very little, but perhaps just having us there made him feel a little more secure.

---

[11] The poet Bialek wrote, "Vengeance for the blood of a baby, even the devil has not yet created" – "*Nikmat dam yel'ed katan od lo barah ha-satan.*"

Scorched from the sun and the heat, we nevertheless fasted the whole day, and suffered greatly from thirst. Toward evening, several young Jewish boys from this town of <u>Ch</u>ust managed to get close to the yard, and from outside the high fence they whispered in to us, to try to calm our fears. They told us we would be taken to Poland where there were lots of empty houses that people left after the Hungarians marched in there. This was only a rumor – who knew where we were going to be taken – but I guess these boys didn't know what else to tell us to calm our anxieties. [12]

Overnight we remained in that yard. Mothers and fathers tried to make the best of it, laying down jackets or other clothing on which their children could sleep. Infants and babies literally went to sleep on their mothers' breasts. Thank G-d it was a warm night and didn't rain. Late at night, most of the cries subsided, and we could only hear occasional sighs, the moans and groans of the adults. I could barely sleep; nor for that matter could many others. Stunned by my predicament, I gazed absentmindedly up at the clear summer sky. Who knew what to think, what to expect, what to do! Zvi kept trying to calm me, saying, "We will overcome, we will overcome." As far as we knew then, Zvi's wife, Piri, and their baby, Baru<u>ch</u>, were still in Kalin. We didn't know their fate, yet we hoped they'd be spared deportation and may be safe by being further from the border.

Like a flock of sheep, we huddled in the yard that night, still not believing we were in imminent danger. I'm certain now that had we known we were being earmarked for destruction, we would have resisted. I am forced to the same conclusion: our eternal Jewish belief in hope contributed to our own demise during the *Shoah*.

In the morning, soldiers and gendarmes entered the yard, and started chasing us toward the gate with sticks and rifle butts. Again I heard anguished screams from all over the place, cries that reached up to the sky. Families struggled to stay together and share the same destiny. Once outside, we saw that military transport trucks had pulled up for us. The trucks were open, uncovered. Gendarmes and

---

[12] A few days later, we found out that <u>Ch</u>ust, too, was half-emptied of its Jewish population. These deportations occurred under the pretext that the residents lacked citizenship papers. Those who by chance did have their papers, or who had connections in high places, were spared for at least for a little while, until early May, 1944.

soldiers pushed and beat people with their sticks and rifles, and loaded us onto the·trucks until it wasn't possible to force even one more person on board. I have no idea how many of us were jammed onto each truck, but we managed to stay together – Moshe, Montze, the two children, Zvi and I.

On the truck, we recognized other neighbors in the crowd: the mother of Zvi Fixler, my friend who had left for Palestine a few weeks before the Czech Republic was torn apart, and his siblings; the family of Zecharia Godinger; and the family of Yosel Davidovitch.

We used to call this man "Yosel the *Grober*" (Yiddish for plump or fat) because he was such a heavyset man. He was also a witty person: he talked slowly and quietly and had a joyful side, always telling jokes. But I'll never forget when, on that truck, he suddenly turned to his son, Moishe Leib, and in a very earnest, somber voice said, "I told you to put my *tallis* and *tefillin* bag in [with their belongings], and you forgot!" Continuing to criticize, he added, "How can a Jew travel without his *tallis* and *tefillin*? This, I'm afraid, is our last journey, our last road."

As I listened, a great fear overcame me, because I knew Yosel was a wise man and I figured he had evaluated the situation correctly. Two or three weeks later, I found out that this really was his and his son's last road traveled. Among thousands of others – including my Uncle Zecharia, my father's only brother, and his entire family; my cousins Yoseph and Channah and their baby; Zvi Fixler's mother and his brother and sister; and my cousin Zvi Heimowitz and his entire family – they were slaughtered in the city of Kamieniec Podolski (kahm-YEHN-nyets poh-DOHL-ski), a large city in what was then the Polish Ukraine.

Later we arrived in Yassin, a border town between the former Czechoslovakia and Poland. It was at this location that a railroad tunnel had been cut through the Carpathian Mountains. They unloaded us from the military trucks and ushered us onto freight train; these particular train cars happened to be covered. For some reason, the train didn't move. We stayed there for more than a day, that night and the next morning. It was a sticky August, and being packed so tightly together inside the closed rail car made it unbearably hot.

Somehow Zvi and I managed to get out of the car, and we found a wide wooden plank from a fence. We brought it back to the train, set it between two cars, and laid down on it. The Hungarian soldiers watching the train saw us but didn't say anything. For some reason they didn't stop us from getting out, and they didn't chase us back in, either. Maybe they pitied us because they were also uncomfortable: they knew that it was even hotter inside the crowded car, and noisy too from the ongoing yelling and crying of little children.

Zvi and I discussed escaping. But where would we go? And what about our brother Moshe and his family? How could we leave them? Over and over, we experienced the same haunting feelings and gnawing questions, and we couldn't come to a satisfactory solution. Think, think, think, yet we couldn't think, and were unable to decide. We accepted our Jewish destiny as the chosen people, with its sad fate of suffering: this is the Jewish sacrifice on G-d's altar. We have carried this destiny for generations and generations. "We have wandered in strange and alien lands in poverty and destitution and shame, and we still guarded our ornamental beauty and splendor for you, our G-d."[13]

Finally, the next day, the train started moving, and we were transported to the town of Kolomaya (in Yiddish we called it Kolomayeh). Arriving around noon, we stopped for a few hours at the train station there. But this time they did not let us out of the cars.

By coincidence, a Jewish *munkoszazod* had been assigned to work on the Kolomaya railroad station, laying rails and loading cargo. When they spotted our boxcars jammed with women and children, young and old, peering through the slats (some even had relatives on our car), they reacted visibly. Their faces revealed deadly fear and anxiety. Clearly, they did not know what was happening back at their homes. These boys had been shipped out of their towns right at the start of the upheaval, when the Hungarians marched in at the end of June 1941. Now they were seeing whole families deported.

Some tried to approach our boxcars with their water and food rations, but to no avail. As soon as our train pulled into the Kolomaya station, it was surrounded by the Ukrainian civil guard, the *sitches*, who prevented anyone from getting too close to us. These same local *sitches* had rounded up Kolomaya's Jews for heavy labor. The Ukrainians considered this a neighborly good deed they had

---

[13] "*Nadadnu b'naichar b'oni u b'chlimah, shamarnu tiferet rak-lach.*" I believe this is a line from a Hebrew song, but I can't recall its title, source, or author.

performed for their Jewish friends. They selected the most prominent members of the city's Jewish community — the richest, those in business, and those who had never before done manual labor — and then rejoiced in tormenting them with hard work.

Among these Jews was Kolomaya's rabbi, a frail, elderly man with a long white beard. With a shovel on his shoulder, he moved his lips, muttering to himself: "My G-d, my G-d, why did You forsake us?" He kept repeating it, walking alongside our boxcars.

For two days and two nights, we remained in Kolomaya. When finally we moved again, it was in the direction of the Dniester River, which is one of the longest rivers in Europe. At the next station we stopped again, this time for a whole day and a night. It seemed that they had no idea what to do with us. And all we could do was wait. Every minute was an ordeal. Up to this point in the journey, no food or water had been provided. Besides being hungry and thirsty, we were cramped into impossible quarters in the boxcar, with hardly any room to sit down on the floor, and the cries from the children and women never ceasing. We choked from the hot August weather and our own perspiration-soaked odor, it now having been more than five days since anyone had been able to bathe. Simply to be able to relieve ourselves required a great humanitarian gesture on the part of the *sitches*, who periodically allowed groups of us out of the car for a few moments.

It was *Shabbos* morning when all the deportees were unloaded from the boxcars. This time, Hungarian soldiers herded us to a nearby place where open Hungarian military trucks awaited. It was the same scene all over again: soldiers yelling "Quick! Quick! Quick!" and screaming the Hungarian curse "Dirty Jews!"[14] as they crowded us onto the trucks. Families tried to stay together; soldiers beat and shoved them with rifle butts, pushing them onto the trucks. When one truck filled up and a family member was left out, they pushed him onto another.

The cries and screams were unbearable. Most of our group once again managed to make it onto the same truck. But this time, Uncle Zecharia, his family and our cousin Zvi Heimowitz did not. When they tried to board our truck, soldiers beat and pushed them away onto another one. This was the last time we saw any of them. Their truck, and others, drove off in the direction of Kamieniec Podolski. After a week or 10 days, we found out later, they were rounded up by the local Ukrainian *sitches* and again robbed of their belongings,

---

[14] *"Bidesch Jidos!"*

especially jewelry, and within a day or so taken to a cemetery where they were slaughtered. Some of them were also thrown into the Dniester River to drown. A few of these individuals managed to survive; about one such individual, I shall write later.

Our truck took a bridge across the Dniester. In the early weeks of the war, amidst great German victories, the Russians had simply abandoned this area and left this bridge intact. Hungarian soldiers now stood guard at both ends of the bridge. The Hungarian Army, allied with the Germans, controlled this entire area. Around noon, we arrived in a small village, close to the city of Tlust. It was a hot afternoon, and the trucks halted near a large open field. They unloaded us into the middle of that field. A Hungarian lieutenant ordered us to sit down, and he made a very short speech.

"Jews! This is your Palestine. If anyone dares to cross to the other side of the Dniester River, he will be shot on the spot! I warn you! Don't you dare attempt to cross back and try to come into Hungary. This is your Palestine. Here is where you stay." That was the whole speech. Then he turned around and ordered the truck drivers back across the bridge into Hungary.

There we sat, approximately 800 souls, men, women, children. We were absolutely confounded. Turning to one another, we asked each other, "Where will our help come from?"

I don't know how long we sat in the middle of that field, paralyzed. Someone said, "Let's go to the highway." Another said, "Let's go back." A third suggested, "Let's look for a village." In the meantime, we sat in the same place, with our meager belongings that we had hastily thrown together one week earlier on Saturday night. We had some Hungarian money with us, but we didn't know whether anyone would accept it. We had been thrown to the wolves, left there like unclaimed baggage. We had become, in Yiddish terms, *hefker:* people without sanctuary; property outside the protection of the law.

And the wolves did come. They smelled the fresh meat that the Hungarians put out for them. Local Ukrainians came to see this amazing sight: Jews with lots of baggage. Straight off, they tried to barter bread for clothing. They were starved for clothing, because under the Russian occupation of the past two years, they couldn't get any. Before long, as more and more locals kept gathering, two young men arrived and identified themselves as sons of the mayor. We should go with them, they said, and they'd arrange places for all of us to stay the night. Tomorrow, they said, they would decide what to do with us.

Though suspicious of their seemingly humanitarian gesture, we had very little choice. Reluctantly, we agreed, and these two young men led all of us away. As we entered the village, more young Ukrainians came running to see this wild sight: tired, disheveled refugees, their pitiful belongings in tow. The sons divided us into groups, and ordered the groups into villagers' yards. Each yard had a large barn, and people were literally driven in. My brothers, Montze, the two children and I wound up in the mayor's yard, along with a widow and her two very pretty grown-up daughters.

Once inside the barn, we asked one of the mayor's sons whether any Jews lived in his village. "Just one family," he said, "not far from where we were – down the street near the town well." While we spoke, Montze was trying to sell one of her skirts to get some milk for the children.

It was still daylight, so Zvi and I decided to look for this Jewish family. Heading off in the direction that the mayor's son indicated, we quickly came upon a house with a *mezuzah* on the door post. We walked right into the front room, and found a man sitting by a table; on it was a white tablecloth and a candelabra. "peace be with you" ("*Shalom aleichem*") we greeted him. Then, all of a sudden it dawned on us: with the sight of the candelabra, we realized it was *Shabbos*, Saturday afternoon. In our daze, we'd completely lost our sense of time; but now we knew that it had been six days since we last saw our home.

The way this man rose from his chair, it looked to us as if we startled him awake. His face showed tremendous fear and anxiety, but he invited us to sit down. We explained who we are and what had happened to us. The poverty in that house was plainly evident. We could see only a few crumbs of food set out on the *Shabbos* table. It seemed there were flies everywhere, especially on the tablecloth. Why, we asked, were there so many flies? He replied, "This is all the result of the war." And he kept on repeating it, as though he were talking to himself, "The war, the war."

He mentioned his daughter; evidently she had abandoned him. But while he complained about her leaving, he also tried to justify it to us. She'd been a member of the Communist Party. Remaining here would have put her at grave risk, because the local population was very sympathetic to the Nazis. Ultimately, we left his house, feeling deep pity for this man. We realized that he couldn't help us, and we certainly couldn't help him.

We still were very hungry, and didn't know where to turn. There were no stores in sight — not that our money was any good. We found out later that our Hungarian currency (*pengas*) would be accepted only by Hungarian soldiers. They'd sell us cigarettes (at inflated prices, of course), and we could exchange these with the locals for bread, eggs, milk, butter, whatever. But right now we didn't see any Hungarian soldiers, and we were saving the limited amount of food we had with us for the children.

In wandering aimlessly, Zvi and I chanced upon some farm land. The field appeared abandoned, and was heaped with stalks of corn and wheat that had been cut down some time earlier. We grabbed ears of corn, rubbing them with our hands to strip off the kernels. We ate raw kernels of corn until our hunger pangs quieted.

Then we returned to the barn where Moshe was. Montze had exchanged another dress for bread, eggs and cheese, along with the milk she bartered for the children. We didn't want to make Moshe's life harder, so we refused to share their bread. We said that we had eaten at the home of that Jew down the street, and omitted telling them what the old man's house really looked like.

The barn floor was covered with straw, so we gathered some up and then spread it down in several areas, for make-shift beds. It had been almost a week since we had any real sleep, and when we finally did drop off, we slept deeply, as though we'd been drugged.

Chapter 8

Leaving 'Palestine'

WE REMAINED IN THE MAYOR'S BARN for nearly a week, not knowing what to do or where to go. Day after day, we sold more clothing and undergarments to buy food, enough to satisfy our hunger. Hungarian soldiers were nowhere to be found, so our *pengas* were still useless to us. This might have gone on for a while, but one day the mayor's sons came and ordered us to leave immediately. This was a ploy they had concocted to rob us of our possessions, but, of course, we didn't know it at the time.

During the few days we'd camped in this village, we learned there was a larger community, Istichkeh, with some Jewish families, back in the direction of the Dniester River. In the opposite direction was Tlust, a sizable city with an even larger Jewish population. We decided to take our chances in the direction of Istichkeh. As we started on to the main road, we met more and more families that had been staying with locals and were being ordered to leave. Family by family, they linked up with us. The whole group that was to have stayed here in our "Palestine" was on the move again.

Standing on the outskirts of the village, everyone had a different opinion about which way to go. Finally, one group broke away and started off toward Tlust, but our group continued toward Istichkeh. What a terrible sight we were: everyone with what was left of their belongings, mothers and fathers carrying their babies, and some small children walking under the weight of their own small *pecklech*. We trekked for no more than an hour. Suddenly we saw a military truck coming toward us. We split into single file lines on either side of the road, as a truck full of German soldiers, staring at us in amazement, rumbled past our group.

Thank G-d they didn't stop, because we were far more frightened of the Germans than of the Hungarians. Relieved, we veered off the highway into an adjacent field, to rest. It must have been around 11 a.m. or noon, and some men took out their *tallesim* and *tefillin* to pray. That sparked a heated argument. One group yelled at the other, "Put away the *tallis* and *tefillin*! Don't put them on! Do you want to draw the Germans' attention to us?" Who knew if more military trucks would come by.

Suddenly, an elderly Jew in our group jumped into the argument. I hadn't noticed him before, but when he spoke I recognized him. He was a cantor from a Carpathian village, deported with his daughter and her two children at the same time we had been. But being from outside Torun, they must have been in a different group of deportees originally, and were "unloaded" at another location along the Dniester. He told us his daughter and two grandchildren had been robbed, murdered, and thrown into the Dniester River by the *sitches* and drowned.

I don't know how the old man escaped their fate, but he did, and somehow he managed to latch on to our group. He looked like a madman, as though he had lost his sanity from grief. He began cursing like a "blasphemer and insulter of G-d".[1] "I am sorry that I laid two sets of *tefillin* all my life," he screamed at those people who had their *tallesim* on.[2] "Throw your *tallesim* and *tefillin* away! There is no G-d to pray to!"

I was terribly shocked to hear words like that from a Jew. It produced great fear in me; I fully realized how we were all in mortal danger. A few men put their *tallesim* away to avoid drawing attention to themselves from the passing trucks, but others stood their ground and continued to pray.[3]

The weather was sunny and nice, so we remained in the field for a few hours. When we returned to the road, our group split up again. We were still marching to Istichkeh, but a few decided to go back toward Tlust. In fact, nobody knew where to go: there was no overriding rationale for one direction or the other. By then, we were down to about 200 or 250 souls, grownups and children. We were still headed in the direction of the Dniester River, but we knew it would be impossible to cross the bridge. We'd seen how well it was guarded, and we hadn't forgotten the Hungarian officer's warning: we would be shot on the spot if we tried to cross the river.

And yet we still headed for the Dniester. After two or three miles the women and children complained of being tired, so we left the road to rest in a field. Truthfully, we were all exhausted, more

---

[1] "*Mechareif u'megadeif*" (from Psalm 44:17).

[2] Extremely religious Jewish men would lay two sets of *tefillin* every morning.

[3] In our wanderings, I witnessed two kinds of religious transformations. Some devoutly religious people lost their faith completely, like this cantor, in reaction to horrible circumstances. Others experienced an opposite reaction. Life-long non-believers, exposed to great danger, became fervent believers in G-d.

from anxiety than from the walking. The Hungarian officer's threat kept echoing in our minds, and this nightmarish thought paralyzed us with fear. To stay or go — either course of action held potential danger.

Toward evening, voices in our group started to lobby to stay in this field overnight. "Tomorrow morning, we'll try to reach the village of Istichkeh." The argument went back and forth, no one really knowing what to do, until finally it got too dark to travel, so the decision to stay overnight in the field was made by default. Everybody opened their packs and ate what little food remained, mainly bread and cheese. Mothers and fathers fed the babies and the small children whatever they had. Around nine or ten o'clock, our encampment grew quieter as everyone submerged into his or her own thoughts. The central question on everybody's mind continued to be "From where will our help come?" How would we get out of this situation?

Moshe, Montze, Channi, Shloimi, Zvi and I banded tightly together. By this time, even the youngest children in the camp sensed we were in a most unusual situation and that we were in danger. Filled with fear, they clung to their parents, falling asleep on their mothers' and fathers' chests. Suddenly, around midnight, the quiet was shattered by screams and loud cries. A hail of rocks pelted down on us from all sides. Stones split open people's heads. I got hit hard on my back. Our screams were indescribable. Parents lost sight of their children and frantically called for them. In the pandemonium, children shrieked for their parents. I heard Moshe screaming, "Where is Shloimi?" And during it all, the stones kept raining down on us.

We barely knew where to turn, but Zvi and I managed to run in the direction of the highway. Under cover of darkness, we circled back around to the encampment, and met up with Montze and Shloimi. We told them to stay put, and edged closer to the camp to find Moshe and Channi. We were fortunate to find them, and returned with them. But as we reassembled, we realized we left all our belongings behind. Zvi and I ran back to where we had bedded down and luckily found our *pecklech* right way. Quickly we grabbed them and hastened back to Moshe and Montze. In the meantime, our group was churning and crying. Running in different directions, they called out for each other in the dark.

As soon as we were all together again, we ran, packs in hand, down the highway. It was pretty dark night that night; we could barely see the road. When we reached a good distance from the encampment, we stopped to catch our breath and consider what to do next. All this time, Moshe had been carrying little Shloimi, and Montze was running while holding <u>Chann</u>i's hand. Here, in the dead of night, neither child had cried or uttered a peep.

Later on, we found out this attack had been organized by the locals. A number of Ukrainian teenagers secretly watched us and, when they saw us bed down for the night, they decided to start stoning us. They figured that, in the ensuing panic and confusion, we'd leave our meager belongings behind.

In the aftermath of the Ukrainian hooligans' attack, I and the remnants of my family were alone, separated from the larger group. We continued walking. Come dawn, we spied a barn in the distance and made our way toward it. The barn door was open, so we went inside and closed the barn door behind us. My back ached from where I been struck by the rock, but (along with the others) I sank into the straw piled on the floor and fell into a deep sleep. We were all exhausted from our fright.

When we awoke, it was past noon. Whatever became of everyone else in our group, we had no idea. We never saw those other people again. Of greater concern was our own immediate fate. Suddenly we heard the clatter of a horse and buggy come to a halt outside the barn. Then a man swung the barn door open and, seeing us lying down on the straw, he demanded: "What are you doing here? I am the owner of this barn."

We begged and pleaded with him, telling him about our being attacked the previous night, and offered to pay him to take us to a Jewish family in Istichkeh. He refused to accept our Hungarian money, but he noticed a woolen blanket we had. In exchange for that blanket and a pair of men's pants, he said, he'd take us there – after dark. In the meantime, he'd let us stay in the barn.

. Did we have a better option? No. We were totally drained of strength and nerve, so we agreed to his trade-off. We settled in to wait, dividing up our remaining bread so everyone would have a few bites. Then we lay back down on the straw to wait for a miracle that this man wouldn't betray us.

That miracle did happen. Toward evening, the man returned with his horse and buggy. We paid the agreed-upon price of blanket and trousers, boarded the buggy and started on our way. Istichkeh is not far, the man said, and he'd take the less-traveled side roads. In no more than an hour, we arrived at the edge of the village, stopping at a house built into the side of a small hill. Hopping off his buggy, the man went inside; it seemed he knew the widow who lived there with her daughter and son-in-law. These people were very merciful and took us into their home, giving us one room. Montze and the children slept in the bed, and we three brothers slept on the floor.

It was wonderful to hear Yiddish being spoken again. The widow's daughter and son-in-law had no children. The son-in-law's first name was Lyoveh (his wife called him "Lyovitchkah," a term of endearment for Leib or Ze'ev). They informed us that there were also other Jewish families in Istichkeh, and that every day Hungarian military trucks transported more and more Jews across the Dniester and dumped them in the vicinity of Kamieniec Podolski.

This family's home, we could see, was a house of poverty. We realized they could not help us with anything more than a roof over our heads. Of course we were very grateful for that, but we knew we'd have to continue bartering for food. At least the house had a stove and a kitchen, so we could cook. It had been more than two weeks since the children and the rest of us had eaten a hot, cooked meal. Here we were also able to wash ourselves – something else we hadn't been able to do since being deported. This alone was a great relief for us.

The widow knew a Ukrainian Catholic priest. I don't know the nature of their friendship, but he stopped by to see her almost every day. Montze made a point of speaking to the priest and told him that in Torun, many Ukrainian nationals, like the *sitches*, lived in harmony with the Jews. She therefore urged him to write an open letter, addressed to the local Ukrainian people, which might help clear our return to the Carpathian. This wasn't exactly the truth, but it's how she tried to curry favor with him to get the letter. The priest glanced at the ring Montze had on her finger. He hinted a few times that he liked that ring, but we decided this was too high a price to pay for a letter that we weren't certain would be of any help to us.

Eventually, he did write us a letter of recommendation with a priestly stamp affixed to it – for 100 Hungarian *pengas*. What we found was that people in Istichkeh did accept Hungarian money because a Hungarian battalion was stationed nearby along the Dniester. Of course, the soldiers took *pengas* in exchange for cigarettes and other items. (The 100 *pengas* was a lot of money, but it was worth it. Later in our wanderings, around the city of Stanislav, this letter saved us from being robbed and G-d knows what else.)

The widow's son-in-law Lyovitchkeh was a very nervous person, and he drank too much alcohol to calm his nerves. He reeked of very strong whiskey. He must have had the bottles hidden somewhere in the house because he never went out at all. His wife did go out into the village, and brought back tomatoes, potatoes and corn on the cob, and cooked them. Evidently, it was more dangerous for Jewish males to walk the streets than for Jewish females. Lyovitchkeh would pace back and forth, muttering to himself in Yiddish: "Stomach, stomach, what are you bothering me for! Do I have it and I'm not giving it to you?"[4]

For some time, we stayed in Istichkeh. Zvi and I went to the surrounding farms (sometimes even Moshe did) roughly every other day to barter for food with our clothing. Some farmers also took Hungarian money. We'd return with flour, milk, eggs, whatever the farmers would sell, and Montze would bake bread, cook potatoes, and so forth.

In the meantime, we heard frightening news. The situation around Kamieniec Podolski was very tense and harsh for Jewish Hungarian refugees. Jews were being slaughtered almost every day. This convinced us even more that we must do whatever we can, by whatever means possible, to return to Hungary.

From Hungarian soldiers stationed in the area, we learned that most Hungarian Jews were still in their country; only Carpathian Jews, like us, and Jews who were unable to prove their citizenship had been deported. We also met up with another Carpathian refugee who ran away from Tlust, where we had relatives. Did he know the welfare of our uncle Zechariah and his family, our aunt Sarah's children and their families, or my mother's brother Berel and his family? we asked. He seemed sure that Berel and his family were still in Tlust, though he was uncertain about the others.

Based on this information, Zvi and I decided to head toward Tlust in search of the rest of our family. The city was only 20-30 kilometers from Istichkeh, and we estimated it was a four- or five-hour walk. Talk about folly, talk about stupidity. How could we even entertain such a dangerous journey in such an alien and hostile place? But we decided to anyway. We'd leave Moshe, Montze, and the

---

[4] *"Mugen, mugen, nidda nit! Hob ich den in gib dir nit?"*

children in Istichkeh, and walk to Tlust to find out about our extended family. We would stay overnight and then return the following day.

The next morning was clear and sunny, and we started out quite early. After having been on the main road for only an hour, we saw a young local girl coming toward us. When we met, she stopped us and asked in Ukrainian where we were going. Our accents instantly told her we were not locals and, to our shock, she started talking to us in Yiddish. When we told her what we were doing, she broke down and began crying. She was dressed in gentile attire, but she was a Jew from Istichkeh, trying to find her mother and father. We shouldn't go to Tlust, she told us, because every day local Jews and Hungarian refugees were being killed there.

When the war broke out, this girl had run away with the retreating Soviet army and left her parents behind. Later, in a change of heart, she managed to cross the battle lines to seek her parents. She asked us about them, but of course we knew nothing about her family. We parted shortly thereafter: the girl headed south toward Istichkeh, and Zvi and I marched on in the opposite direction. Only now, after hearing what was happening in Tlust, we were more scared and more unsure about our plan. After only five or ten minutes heading north, we decided to return to Istichkeh. When we got back and told Moshe of this encounter, he admitted he was very worried that we had gone, and said we had the done the right thing to return. We must give up our effort to search for our extended family, he said, and concentrate on getting across the Dniester River.

Chapter 9

Isaac Tzumer

INTENT ON BUYING MORE FLOUR AND FOOD FROM A FARMER, Moshe, Zvi and I headed to a neighboring village some days later. On the way there, we encountered two Ukrainian *sitches* armed with rifles. They stopped us and started interrogating us: where were we going, what were we doing there, where were we from, and so forth. They finally ordered us to go with them, and, after walking a while, brought us to a house. The owner of this house was a man by the name of Isaac Tzumer, who owned and operated the only flour mill in that entire area. I shall never forget this man as long as I live. He turned out to be a *malach*, a true angel.

In a commanding voice, the *sitches* told Mr. Tzumer, "Isaac! We brought you these three Hungarian Jews. Take care of them until tomorrow. Tomorrow we'll come and then will take them away. And if they aren't here tomorrow, you will become a head shorter. Remember what we are telling you! You are responsible for them."

Mr. Tzumer was sent to us by G-d to save our lives. When the *sitches* left, this angel of a Jew told us, "First of all, sit down to the table and I'll prepare something for you to eat." Evidently he was a bachelor because we didn't see signs of anyone else in the house. Isaac Tzumer was the only Jew in this village. He knew all the farmers in the area; his was the only mill for grinding their corn, wheat or whatever. He told us that he didn't know how much longer he would be able to hold on to the mill, which was now run by one of his gentile employees who had been established as the legal owner. Under the current political situation, this type of surreptitious contractual agreement was often arranged between a Jewish business owner and a trusted gentile employee, so the Jew could continue to operate relatively free of intervention from the military authorities. In Yiddish, the gentile "owner" was referred to as a *Strohmann* (literally, a "straw man" or a "front"), who would provide the true, previous owners with a percentage of the profits.

While we conversed, he loaded the table with a large loaf of corn bread, cheese, cream and milk. He knew he was dealing with hungry people. We ate ravenously and, for the first time in a long time, satisfied our hunger.

When we finished eating, he said to us, "Listen, my brothers. You must disappear from here tonight. Get across the Dniester River to the city of Horodenka, because your lives are in danger."

Moshe told him that his wife and two children were in Istichkeh at the home of the widow. Isaac knew this woman, and where she lived. But, he told us, he also knew those two *sitches*. If we didn't disappear, he predicted, these two local thugs would take us to Kamieniec Podolski and surrender us to the Germans there. Evidently, Isaac knew what was happening to our people in that Ukrainian town.

"But what will happen to you tomorrow when the *sitches* come for us?" we asked him. "What will you do? You're putting your own life in jeopardy."

"A plurality counts for more than a single person," he replied. "I am only one, and you are six souls. I will cope somehow with those two *sitches*. Shortly, I'll go see a man who has a small boat, and I'll pay him off. He will ferry you across the Dniester tonight, at one o'clock in the morning, and deliver you to a place a half kilometer from a Jewish family who will let you stay the night. In time, they will bring you to the city of Horodenka. In Horodenka there are still lots of Jews and a Jewish Council (*Judenrat*) that has organized a public kitchen where they take care of Hungarian Jewish refugees.[1] Meanwhile, stay here until it gets dark. Then you'll go back to Istichkeh [to reunite with Montze and the children]. At 1 a.m., a man will come for you and take you to the place where the boat is anchored."

Isaac Tzumer left us in his house and told us to wait until he returned. While we waited, Moshe was especially nervous, thinking about his wife and children back in Istichkeh, and knowing that they were undoubtedly worried about us, too. Every minute seemed like an hour. Finally, Isaac Tzumer returned, and told us he arranged for a reliable man, a gentile who had transported Jews across the river previously. Then Isaac described in detail how we'd get to safety once we reach the opposite bank of the Dniester. From the landing we first must go to the right, he said, a couple hundred steps. There, we will come to a road. "Follow it to the left for about half a kilometer. On the right-hand side of the road you'll see three large buildings in a row. All three are painted white. In the last of the three, there will be a dimly lit lantern on a table, visible from the road. Knock on the door, and people will let you in."

---

[1] The public kitchen would provide a bowl of soup and piece of bread a day.

He told us that the first two structures are huge grain storage buildings, and that the Jew who lives in the third house is a grain dealer, someone Isaac said he'd known and trusted for years. Isaac also told us the man's name; to my regret, I no longer remember it. Finally, Isaac promised to come to Horodenka to visit us. While relating all this, he had been packing a bag full of bread, cheese, and tomatoes for us. When it began to get dark, we left his house and, retracing our steps, made our way back to Istichkeh. On arriving there, we found Montze sobbing hysterically. The children were terribly frightened to see their mother like that. Everyone was worried that we'd been gone so long – even the widow, her daughter, and son-in-law. After a while everybody calmed down, and we told them about the *sitches*, the *malach* Isaac Tzumer, and our plans to cross the Dniester – hopefully, on our way back to Hungary.

Moshe and Montze put the children to bed. While they slept, we packed what remained of our belongings. We kept on checking the time. We knew the man would come no later than 1 a.m. Not wishing to wake our hosts at that hour of the morning, we bade them good-bye earlier and thanked them for their hospitality. They wished us a successful journey (*hatzlachah ba-derech*), but in the end they were awake anyway when we departed. They saw how nervous we were, and stayed up to try quieting our fears. "We know Isaac Tzumer," they said, "and if he says he's sending a man, then that man is reliable. You can rest assured you won't have to worry about him."

Moshe and Montze were overwrought with anxiety. Their biggest concern was that the children would cry when we woke them up to leave. With all this going through our minds, time once again stretched into an eternity. Moshe took his prayer book out of his *tallis* bag and started to recite the psalms (*tehillim*). He asked what day it was. We had lost track of the date, but now we calculated that it must be the week before Rosh Hashanah, the fourth day of *Selichot*.[2] (That must have been either Wednesday or Thursday, September 17 or 18, 1941.) From the time we left Torun on Tisha b'Av *nidcheh* (Saturday and Sunday, August 2 and 3) until now had been close to six weeks.

---

[2] This refers to the days leading up to the Jewish New Year. Literally meaning "foregiveness," *Selichot* are penitential prayers and hymns recited daily (usually before dawn) during the week prior to Rosh Hashanah.

As Moshe prayed, I noticed tears running down his cheeks. Moshe was the most pious of us four brothers. Watching him, Zvi and I were greatly moved; we couldn't utter a word.

Around 12:30, the man arrived. Moshe woke up the children, and to our great amazement and luck, they didn't cry — indeed, they were very quiet. Some instinctual understanding of our precarious situation must have helped them cope, despite their young ages. One last time we said good-bye to our hosts and slipped quietly out of the house, following this escort. It was a very dark night, so we moved along in a tight group. Moshe carried little Shloimi. Channi started out walking on her own, but couldn't keep up, so I picked her up and carried her the rest of the way, maybe a kilometer. At this point, the Dniester had turned into a mighty river. Drawing closer, we could hear its roar. Finally, we came upon a boat moored by a rope. What we saw terrified us: a tiny boat, barely bigger than a large bathtub. Seven of us in this little boat? Had we seen this vessel before leaving, we would surely have refused to go. But now there was no turning back. We had no time to think. So we all squeezed in, Moshe holding Channi, Montze holding Shloimi. Neither child made a sound.

By then, our eyes had grown accustomed to the dark, and we could see a little better. The river water looked muddy and moved very fast. The current carried us quickly down river while the man, working hard at the rudder, struggled to cut across the flow. We were all breathless, our hearts pounding with fear. We dared not utter a word; even the children held their breath. The roar of the river was deafening. I may have forgotten many things, but this is a date I will remember forever, the fourth day of *Selichot*, 1941. The crossing took only 15 or 20 minutes, perhaps even less. For us, it seemed forever. Finally we reached the other side safely. The man showed us what direction to take, said goodbye, and pushed off the bank to begin his trip back.

We climbed a small hill and, after a short while reached the road we needed to take. We turned left, as instructed, and quickened our pace from a walk to a slow run. According to what we were told, it should have been only half a kilometer to the three buildings. G-d was on our side: we didn't see or meet a living soul. Again the minutes seemed to stretch. Finally we could make out three buildings alongside the road. I sprinted to the third house and cautiously approached the front door. It was dark, but I ran my hand alongside the door post. As my fingers came across the *mezuzah* there, a feeling of great relief came over me: I was sure we had arrived at the right place.[3]

Together we walked around to the window. It was covered by a curtain, but through it we could see a dim light on a table. We knocked on the window three times, as Mr. Tzumer advised, and a woman asked us in Yiddish, "Hungarische? Hungarische?" Yes, we said. She asked how many of us there were. We told her and she opened the door for us. When we came inside, we saw more people sleeping on the floor. She led us into another, smaller room. The only furniture there was a bed, and we were happy that at least Montze and the children would be able to curl up in it. The woman offered us warm tea, but the enormous excitement of crossing the Dniester had left us drained and spent. We thanked her and said no, we didn't want anything other than to sleep. We made ourselves comfortable on the floor and tried to drop off.

In the morning, after we managed to clean ourselves up a bit and wash the children, we finally saw where we were and just who had taken us in: the grain dealer, his wife, their daughter and son-in-law. These four people lived in a huge house. The son-in-law was a physician and held a permit from the German authority to travel to and from Horodenka, which was quite a distance away. The Jewish community in Horodenka had not yet been driven into a ghetto, and, as Isaac Tzumer informed us, they had a *Judenrat*. In fact, this physician secretly served as a liaison: he would inform the *Judenrat* how many refugees made it across the Dniester, and the Council would designate Jewish homes in Horodenka where they could be temporarily housed.

Horodenka also served as a Hungarian military command center in the Polish Ukraine. Hungarians were supposed to be in charge of this part of the battle line but it was actually the Germans at the helm. (Although it had been only three months since war broke out between Germany and Russia, the Germans were very fast to force Jews to wear white arm bands with a blue Star of David [*Mogen David*]

---

[3] When my son bought a house, I reminded him a few times not to forget to put *mezuzahs* by the doors. He was surprised at how often I kept reminding him. I never mentioned my motive, until now: it is related to this experience in crossing the Dniester. To this day whenever I come to a Jewish house and see a *mezuzah*, I am always reminded of that night and that the presence of a *mezuzah* meant safety.

on them, so they could mark us as *hefker*.) The presence of Hungarian soldiers, we found out later, meant that our Hungarian *pengas* could be used to buy all sorts of items. Soldiers would accept the *pengas* for their canned foods, chocolates, candy, cigarettes, anything they had. And if we had cigarettes, we could barter with the local farmers for butter, cheese, eggs, milk, even chickens. But cigarettes served as the gold standard because they were in short supply.

We remained in the grain dealer's house a day or two, no more. Then one by one, we were ferried to a Jewish home in Horodenka. Mainly it was the grain dealer's daughter (the physician's wife) who took us: a couple of times by horse and buggy, but usually on foot. She procured Star of David arm bands for us, but we did not put them on while we were traveling to Horodenka.

We all rejoined at the home of Reb Berel Geffner. His house was large, but poverty screamed from all corners. Reb Berel and his wife, an elderly couple, lived there alone, with barely enough food for themselves; certainly they could not help us out with any meals. We were, of course, very thankful for the roof over our heads. We still had some of the bread that Isaac Tzumer had given us; we also had Hungarian money.

Reb Berel did manage to offer us one thing: matches. In his possession were two large cartons full of them. This was all he had to show for the last two years of Communist occupation. How he came by so many matches, he never revealed. He simply said to us, "This is everything I have. That's all I can help you with." I guess in time of war, matches are nearly as valuable a currency as cigarettes.

Zvi and I donned the white armbands and headed into town, following the directions given to us by Reb Berel, to go to the *Judenrat* building. From the number of white armbands we spotted along the way, we could tell Horodenka had a large Jewish community. When we arrived, we found the *Judenrat* had a sizable office building, and the ground floor housed its public kitchen. A large contingent of volunteers, Jewish boys and girls, caring youths, helped Hungarian refugees and local needy Jews. We went directly to one office to register, and there they told us that the German military authority issued passes to Hungarian Jews, allowing them to travel back to Hungary. We were very suspicious about this, fearing some kind of trick. But at the same time the thought of being able to return home raised our spirits. They instructed us to return the next day; the passes would be ready by then.

As we emerged from the building, we saw Hungarian soldiers milling around the area. We approached one and struck up a conversation. In general, Hungarian soldiers spoke only their own mother tongue. Being in a Slavic-speaking country, they couldn't communicate with the locals; they might have been the most virulent anti-Semites, but when someone addressed them in their own language, they somehow mellowed. This was something I observed during the war. Our particular soldier was scheduled to be rotated back to Hungary the next day, so he had come into town to sell anything he could for Hungarian *pengas*: his military ration of bread, some fish and meat conserves and cigarettes. We bought it all and paid him well.

Zvi also begged him to take a letter back to Hungary and mail it from inside the country. Remarkably, he agreed. The military would supply their soldiers with postcards to write home to their families; thankfully, this soldier had a blank one, which he then handed to me. Cradling it in my palm right there on the street, I wrote a few words to our parents. Zvi kept up the conversation with the soldier while I scribbled (at the time, I knew only a few words of Hungarian). I wrote my parents that we were in Horodenka; that all of us, Zvi, Moshe, Montze and the children, were together; and that we were planning to travel on the road to Dolina. (Dolina was the closest town on the other side of the border to Torun.) I also mentioned that in Horodenka we met a friend of ours from Torun, a man by the name of Friedman. This soldier must have been a noble person, because he did mail the card and my parents did receive it. That postcard was the first sign of life they got from us after our deportation, and it let them know we were trying to return. As my parents told us later, my few words had helped ease their anxieties and lessen their agony.

We returned to the house of Reb Berel with a fresh loaf of bread and the canned conserves in hand, and related our adventures. It was a great relief for Moshe, Montze and all of us. We offered some of our food to the Geffners, but they adamantly refused to accept any. The next morning, Zvi and I went into the city again to buy more produce, and we returned to the *Judenrat* offices. To our great surprise, the passes were ready. Each pass bore the official stamp of the German command post with a swastika, and was signed by a first-lieutenant (an *oberleutnant*). I've no idea how the Jewish Council was able to obtain these. Maybe the first-lieutenant issued passes on his own responsibility. It was also possible the passes were fake — forged by the Council.

The day before Rosh Hashanah, our angel appeared again: Reb Isaac Tzumer visited us in the house of Reb Berel Geffner. We were delighted and relieved to see him, because we were worried the *sitches* who detained us would carry out their threat on his life. But Isaac told us that when the *sitches* returned, he simply bribed them with a watch, and they left. He dismissed the whole thing as unimportant. Now he arranged for Zvi and me to journey 2-3 kilometers with him to a nearby village, to a friend's farm. When we arrived, Isaac Tzumer said to the farmer, "Give these people 10 kilograms of flour, and if you have any baked bread, give them that, too. Whatever you give them, I'll give it back to you double." Tzumer knew everyone in the farmer's family, and asked the man about his children. In the meantime, the farmer's wife invited us to the table; she set out bread, cheese and butter, and we ate until we were full.

The farmer filled a bag with flour — in fact with more than 10 kilos — then another sack with bread, cheese, butter and eggs, as well as a bunch of apples and a head of cabbage. When we returned to the Geffner's house, together with our *malach*, no one could believe such a miracle. It was the day before Rosh Hashanah 5702 (September 1941). Montze now had flour and eggs, and she would be able to bake bread (*challah*) for the New Year. We told Mr. Tzumer that, G-d willing, after Rosh Hashanah, we'd set out in the direction of Dolina.

On hearing this, Mr. Tzumer produced a package — one he'd originally brought to the Geffner's house — opened it and revealed a half pound of tobacco. He handed it to us, saying that the area around Dolina in the Polish Carpathian is experiencing great hunger, a famine, and that we should keep the tobacco until we got there, and use it as currency. We couldn't thank him enough. This man, this Jew, was truly a self-sacrificing soul. He and his name will forever be engraved in my memory. This was a Jew without a beard, without *pais*. He walked without a head covering. For me, it was a revelation that one can be a very pious Jew without the traditional external trappings. He bade us farewell, and as we parted we all had tears in our eyes.[4]

The next day at sundown would begin Rosh Hashanah, so that morning Montze set out to make dough and bake *challah* for us. It

---

[4] When my wife and I came to the United States in 1949, I placed an ad in the daily Yiddish newspaper, *Der Tag*, searching for Isaac Tzumer. I described him and asked whether anyone knew about him, and whether he survived the war. Unfortunately, I never received a single response to the ad.

was such a gift to have freshly baked _challah_ for the holiday. We also had obtained some soap, so for Rosh Hashanah we had clean undergarments to wear. While Montze was baking and cleaning, Moshe stayed with the children, and Zvi and I went back to the _Judenrat_ to inquire about procuring a man with a horse and buggy to take us to Stanislav. We told them that we have Hungarian currency, which was acceptable in Horodenka. They promised to arrange it for us after _yontif_ (the holiday). While there, we also found out that a prominent rabbi of Munkatch was somewhere in Horodenka, at a house near us.

We related all this when we returned, and inquired of Reb Berel about Rosh Hashanah services. He explained that there was no one _minyan_ in Horodenka, that _minyans_ were formed in private houses. He himself was not planning to go anywhere, just to pray in his own home. He found two High Holy Day prayer books and gave us one. Ironically, despite the two large cartons of matches he had, there were no candles to light in Reb Berel's home that evening.

That is how we ushered in the Jewish New Year, 5702, in the fading light of sundown.[5] We were all depressed. Memories of past Rosh Hashanahs filled our thoughts, and we hoped that G-d would not forsake us.

---

[5] In Hebrew, the letters signifying the Jewish calendar year 5702 are _taf-shin-beth_. Because these letters can also be rearranged to spell the word '_Shabbat_' (meaning rest, and implying peace and tranquility), our rabbis (always looking, as I mentioned earlier, for cabalistic clues) still therefore believed that we Jews would be safe from harm.

Chapter 10

High Holy Days, 1941

THE NEXT MORNING STARTED OFF NICE AND SUNNY We recited some of the Rosh Hashanah prayers, Moshe more than Zvi or me. We ate a cooked meal that day: soup, potatoes and apples. From our windows we could see Jews (wearing white and blue arm bands), congregating at a house down the street. It appeared they had a *minyan* there, but we stayed in Reb Berel's house.

Around one or two o'clock in the afternoon we tried to doze off, Montze with the children in one bed, Mrs. Geffner in another, and the rest of us lying on the floor or on the two bunk beds in the room. Suddenly we heard a German military truck stop right in front of the house. An officer and four soldiers burst through the front door.

One yelled out sarcastically, "What is this? A hospital?"[1] Somebody answered, I don't remember who, "Today is a Jewish holiday." To which the German replied, "What? You have a holiday today?"[2] In a snide tone, he repeated, "Holiday?!"

Eyeing the furniture in the room, the officer and soldiers evidently didn't like what they saw. We overheard one saying to the other, "Poor Jews"[3] – not expressing sympathy, obviously, but contemptuously implying that here were not wealthy Jews from whom there was anything to steal. Just as quickly as they came, they left, empty-handed. We got away that day with just a little scare. As we peeked through the window, we saw the officer and soldiers force their way into the house across the street. Later we saw them carrying out furniture – sofas, tables, other things – and load it onto their truck. When the truck was filled, they left. The family in that house, Reb Berel said, had been well-to-do.

This was our first close encounter with the Germans, Rosh Hashanah, September 1941, when Jewish property was *hefker*, and so was Jewish life.

The second day of Rosh Hashanah, I visited the house down the street. Indeed there was a *minyan* there and, among those who were praying, I found a few Hungarian refugees. They told me the Munkatcher Rebbe was staying nearby, and a messenger had been

---

[1] "*Was ist das? Ein Krankenhaus?*"
[2] "*Was? Haben sie heute Feiertag?*"
[3] "*Arme Juden, arme Juden.*"

sent by the Jewish community in Munkatch to inform him that a Hungarian officer would be dispatched to bring him back to Hungary after *yontif*. (Horodenka had become a staging area for the Hungarian army; from there, troops would be sent deeper into the Ukraine with the advancing German army. As a result, Hungarian officers traveled back and forth to Hungary from Horodenka, and one could transport the Rebbe.) Of course this was all illegal, but it was the first hint I heard that suggested the Jews in Hungary were actually striving to help us. The Rebbe in turn promised to keep the Jewish committee in Horodenka posted about the situation around the former border area between Poland and Hungary.

Indeed, after Rosh Hashanah, an emissary came for the rabbi and escorted him safely to Yasina, the first border village on the other side of the Carpathian Mountains. It must have taken three days, but the rabbi managed to get a note back to the Jewish Council in Horodenka. The border was heavily guarded, he wrote, and the region was suffering a massive food shortage. He advised refugees not to attempt a border crossing for now. This message had a very discouraging effect on all of us Hungarian refugees. Nevertheless, we decided to go, but in the direction of Dolina, Vishkof and Torun. It had never been our intention to reach Yasina. Besides, we reasoned, we were armed with travel passes that the Jewish Council had obtained from the German command, as well as a "To whom it may concern" letter from the priest in Istichkeh, asking locals not to hinder our travel but, in fact, to aid us.

Right after Rosh Hashanah, we returned to the *Judenrat* to see about the horse and buggy driver they promised to procure for us. Unlike the travel passes, which had been prepared overnight, this request took longer to fill: it was almost a week before they were able to find us a driver. A day before Yom Kippur, we rose early in the morning, before first light. We all got into the buggy and started in the direction of Stanislav. We knew that Stanislav had a large Jewish population, and we expected to use it as a jumping-off point to get closer to Dolina. Dolina was only 40-50 kilometers from Torun, and was home to relatives from my mother's side, the Drimmer family.

The driver explained he'd avoid the main highway and stick to side roads instead. He also told us he would go only as far as a village outside Stanislav and no farther. We would have to cover the remaining distance on foot.

Around noon, the buggy man stopped in a small village to feed and rest his horse. Zvi and I meanwhile had gone over to a house to try buying food for *pengas*, when suddenly Moshe came running and yelling. While we were away, a whole gang of Ukrainian teenagers surrounded the wagon to rob us. Moshe's face literally was white from terror. We ran back and found Montze and the petrified children sitting atop the wagon. Montze had produced the letter from the priest in Istichkeh, and was showing it to the buggy man. It clearly had a profound effect on him, because he started to protest in a loud voice and told the gang not to try anything. Then he lashed his horse with a riding whip and we quickly continued on toward Stanilsav, getting away safely.

In the afternoon, we reached a small village that was actually beyond Stanislav; the driver, having been paid in advance, left us by the road. We started toward town, Zvi and I in the lead. We noticed a woman, whom we could identify as Jewish by her arm band, standing in a little garden in front of her house. We approached her to ask about Stanislav. She recognized us right away for what we were: Hungarian refugees. The woman advised us to stay away from Stanislav because the Germans were rounding up all the Hungarian Jews they found there – and then these people just disappear. The Germans also were taking local Jews into custody, allegedly for work. But they in turn also disappeared.

By this time, Moshe, Montze and their children had caught up with us, and the woman invited all of us inside. She gave the children some fresh milk and suggested that, since the next day was Yom Kippur, we should stay in her village along with several other Hungarian Jewish families. They were being housed at the local *shul* and they, too, wanted to reach Dolina after *yontif*. We asked, "What about the next village, away from Stanislav, closer to Dolina? Are there Jews living there?" Yes, she replied, but as far as she knew, there were lots of Germans there now, too.

We left this woman's house not knowing what to do. Should we heed her advice and remain there? Or should we proceed to the next village toward Dolina? The hardest challenge any person faces is when he doubts the correctness of his action. But we never discussed it; we never really consciously decided. We just headed toward Dolina. As we kept walking, it seemed as if a mysterious force propelled us. This mysterious force, whatever it was, saved our lives.

Zvi and I continued on in single file. We'd devised a signal – a raised arm and a wave of the hand, either to the right or the left, depending on which direction we should bolt – in order to warn Moshe and Montze if we sensed danger, giving them a chance to slip off the highway with the children without being seen, and to hide in grain fields on either side of the road. After a fair distance, we suddenly noticed a convoy of German military trucks barreling toward us. Signaling Moshe, we darted off the highway into the adjacent field. Although it was a sunny day, the trucks were draped with their rain covers and we could not see what was inside them.

Once the trucks passed by, we carefully emerged from the field and continued our single-file walk again. Eventually, we reached a village. On the right side of the highway was a house, its front and side yards surrounded by a low fence. By some miracle, I spotted an arm reaching out of the doorway, as it grabbed the door and pulled it shut. The arm had a white armband. I leaped over the fence and ran quickly to the door, assured this was a Jewish house. I knocked, but no one answered. I called out in Yiddish, "Let us in, let us in! Jews! We are also Jews!"[4] Slowly the door opened, and a deathly scared man abruptly yanked me in and slammed the door behind me.

Inside, the house was very gloomy. All the windows were covered, curtains drawn. I told him I was there with two of my brothers, my sister-in-law and two children. He allowed me to go back outside and retrieve them. I vaulted the fence again and signaled for Moshe and Montze to come quickly. Zvi and I ran toward them, snatched up the children and hurried back to the house (this time entering the yard via the gate!). Getting all six of us inside probably took only five minutes, but it felt uncomfortably long. The people hiding in the house told us that the Germans had been rounding up all the Jews of this village all day long, and that the Germans camouflaged their atrocities with different names. One was called an "*aktion*," which translates as "action" or "campaign" – as if they were simply conducting something as benign or noble as a Red Cross campaign. Or the German word "*überziedlung*," which means "to transfer"; this is the term the Nazis used when they rounded up people to be killed in the concentration camps. The euphemism they

---

[4] "*Lozt aran, lozt aran, Yidden. Mir zinnen och Yidden*"

employed for the gassing and killing was "*entlausungsanstalt*," meaning de-lousing establishment.

The people in this house were so terrified that it seemed as though one could reach out and touch the fear in the air. They told us that local *sitches* had pointed out the Jewish homes to their Nazi masters, and the Germans obliged by rounding up all the Jewish families in town, young and old. They then put them onto military trucks and took them to Stanislav. From there, the Jews just disappeared; nobody knew to where. But in this particular house, they told us, a member of the family was the only dentist in this village. He had been befriended by one of the *sitches*, who tipped him off to the impending "*aktion*." The village needed a dentist, after all, so their family was spared. Now we realized what was in those covered trucks that we had seen along the road.

Throughout this harrowing experience, the children displayed an extraordinary level of understanding and bravery, despite their tender ages. They seemed to sense our danger, but didn't cry or make demands. As much as possible, we tried to conceal our own fear and worry from them. But they must have sensed our true mood instinctively, especially now, with all of us huddled in this single room.

As evening fell, of course it grew darker, but our hosts didn't light candles: better not to advertise that anyone was home. We fed the children some of the canned rations we had bought from the Hungarian soldiers. We also had bread and some cold potatoes. This was the meal we had in preparation for our fast, on the eve of Yom Kippur, 1941.

As we sat in the dark, my thoughts wandered back to Torun and a previous Yom Kippur. I could see my mother lighting the Yom Kippur candles at home. In our shul were hundred of tall candles brought in by every family and lit by the men. I could see Jews wearing the special white cover garments (*kittels*) for the High Holy Days, and *tallesim*. Everybody experienced a solemn chill, as we watched the very pious men kneeling to receive ritual lashings. We waited expectantly for old Reb Yaikel to lead us in prayer and recite the solemn Kol Nidre,[5] and, later, for Rabbi Yitzchak Gross to delivery the homily. Rabbi Gross would urge everyone to ask forgiveness from each other. No prayers (*tefillot*) to G-d can atone for

---

[5] "All Vows"; this prayer asks G-d to exempt the individual only from oaths made to oneself, not vows made or obligations held toward others. Reb Yaikel was both a *shochet* (ritual slaughterer of kosher animals) as well as our *ba'al tefillah* (one who leads a congregation in prayer).

sins between a human being and his friend, he would tell us. Human beings must ask forgiveness of each other, in order for the wrongdoing to be erased.

A scene replayed vividly in my mind: I saw antagonists in Torun approach each other, beg forgiveness and shake hands. This optimistic image of reconciliation spun before my eyes, but now, in the darkness of this house, my heart was depressed and grieving.

Not too far away from the city of Stanislav, this small village was emptied of Jews, on the eve of Yom Kippur 1941 (5702).

Chapter 11

Guten Morgen

THE DENTIST'S FAMILY OFFERED US ONE BED that evening, and we promptly put Montze and the children to sleep in it. Moshe, Zvi and I spread out on the floor, submerged in our sad thoughts. Out of sheer exhaustion we finally fell asleep. I awoke late the next day, Yom Kippur. No one left the house. The curtains remained drawn all day long; the shutters were closed, too, barely letting any light inside. In the gloom, we spoke with the young dentist. We learned about his village and we told him our story. When we related our attempts to get to Dolina (on the promise of our German travel passes and the letter from the priest), he said he'd try to find a new horse and buggy man for us after *yontif.*

The next day the dentist finally dared to venture outside. From others he learned that, on Yom Kippur, the Germans had continued their *"aktion,"* rounding up all the Jews in a neighboring village. That was the village we'd just left – where the woman advised us to join the other Hungarian refugees in the local synagogue. We found out much later that my mother's younger brother, Berel, was in that synagogue with his family: 10 souls. Uncle Berel had been looking for us, just as we had been searching for them. Had we learned earlier that they were nearby, I'm certain we would have stayed together as a family. And we would have shared their fate (they were murdered in Stanislav, the day after Yom Kippur). But that mysterious power that led us to ignore the woman's advice kept us moving and spared our lives.

Only one member of Berel's family survived: his daughter, Zipporah, who was 14 or 15 years old at the time. Cousin Zipporah managed to escape, making her the only direct living link to her martyred parents; she eventually made her way to Palestine and started a family.[1]

We waited in this village another two or three days until the dentist succeeded in hiring a man with a horse and buggy. Paying the

---

[1] Zipporah later told me that when her family had been in Tlust, they continually sought our whereabouts. Zvi and I had wanted to go to Tlust earlier in 1941, but met up with that girl who urged us not to go there. In that instance, we took her advice. Our sages say people never recognize miracles when they occur *(ehn adam makeer b'niso),* only in hindsight. Meeting that girl by chance along the road contributed directly to my survival.

driver in advance (in *pengas*), we traveled by daylight and were transported to the outskirts of Dolina, without incident. The driver knew a Jewish family there, and so he deposited us in their yard. Immediately, the family took us into their home. We inquired if they knew a family in Dolina by the name of Drimmer. Yes, they replied. Excitedly, we related that our mother's family originated from there, and these people were our extended family.

For some three months now, the war had been underway, but in Dolina, the Germans had not yet set up a ghetto. Instead, they were just plain harassing the Jews, ordering them to form a *Judenrat* so they could more easily rob the Jews of all their valuables, like gold or jewelry: all the Germans had to do was threaten the *Judenrat* with death if the Council failed to make ransom payments. But that was only part of the Germans' idea behind setting up a *Judenrat*. They also used the Jewish Council to round people up to do all kinds of hard labor. Nevertheless, our host advised us to register with the *Judenrat*, since (as in Horodenka) the Council maintained a public kitchen and tried to help out Hungarian Jewish refugees where it could.

In the early evening, the head of this household sent his son to show us where the Drimmer family lived. Moshe, Montze and the children stayed behind, while Zvi and I walked to their house and introduced ourselves. Dolina was in Poland, of course, and Torun in Czechoslovakia, and since political relations between the two countries were never very friendly, we had little contact with the Polish Drimmers. But even though we were distant cousins who had never seen each other before, we were welcomed into their home and made to feel like we were among close family. This branch of the Drimmer clan had beautiful twin boys, about sixteen years old. (Despite their young age, they were both graying, which I thought was odd.) Immediately, the senior Drimmers fed us and informed us that they only had room enough to accommodate one of us, but that their brother-in-law, a family across the street, could take in the other.

It was my lot to stay with the people across the street. To my regret I cannot remember their names. This family had a daughter who worked as a secretary for the *Judenrat*. She was a good looking girl, just about a year or two older than I was, and she belonged to the same Revisionist youth group in Dolina as I did in Torun. To both of us, Ze'ev Jabotinsky had been a hero, so through our shared Zionist sympathies we immediately felt a fraternal closeness. When I told her of my plans to register with the *Judenrat*, she warned me immediately. Almost every day the Germans ordered the *Judenrat* to hand over so many Jews to perform hard labor, she said. And the *Judenrat* usually designated the Hungarian Jewish refugees first, thereby protecting the local Jews. She also urged me to warn Moshe against registering: the little bit of soup one could get at the *Judenrat* was not worth the risk. "What we will eat, you will eat," she said. "We will share with you." I was touched and moved by such dear kindness, coming from her and both the families.

The next morning, Zvi and I returned to Moshe and related everything we learned. The people where Moshe was staying had provided him with a room, including two beds, a table and chairs. What luxury, compared to what Moshe and his family had lately been experiencing! Waiting here in Dolina, we realized we were only some 50 kilometers from Torun, and we were buoyed with hopes of getting back into Hungary before too long. We still had Hungarian money, so we could buy food. (So close to the Hungarian border, the locals in the Polish Ukraine accepted *pengas*). So overall, our state of mind improved remarkably.

Waiting for our next move, I had the opportunity to get to know my hosts a little better. Conversing with the head of the household about the fate of our Jewish people, I posed the question: "We Carpathian Jews had no choice. But you were here [in Poland] for two years under Soviet rule. Why did you remain here? Why did you wait for Hitler? Couldn't you have run away with the retreating Russian army?" (I have to admit that we had no notion then about the terror Stalin was fostering within the Soviet Union; at that time this to me seemed a perfectly reasonable way to escape the Nazis.)

"Look out the window," he replied. "Do you see forest, all the way around Dolina?[2] All that lumber? Can you believe that last winter we were freezing here in our homes because we had no firewood and we couldn't get any? The Russians didn't allow anybody to take lumber out of the forest. Can you imagine that?" Not too far away were large salt mines, he continued, but the townspeople had suffered without salt rations for the past two years. No one could understand this; nobody could believe such an economic system

---

[2] "Dolina" is the word in Slavic for "valley." The town of Dolina was indeed the central valley around which stretched rich forests in every direction.

existed. And besides, he said, we didn't believe that Hitler was what he really turned out to be, either.

Our stay in Dolina stretched to two or three weeks. We stared up at the Carpathian Mountains, the range that had formed a natural boundary between Poland and Czechoslovakia until 1939, when Czechoslovakia was torn apart. Just over the crest on the other side was Torun. But other refugees like us had tried to enter Hungary near Vishkof (the last village on the Polish side of the mountain), and some returned with dreadful, frightful stories.

At first, Hungarian border police let people cross, taking them into Torun. From there, however, refugees were once again loaded onto trucks and sent *back* into Poland – only this time, they were handed over to the Germans. Before long, the Hungarians themselves learned a new trade: murdering Jews. They killed refugees whom they suspected had money or diamonds, gold or other precious metals. A few of these people managed to escape the Hungarians and find their way back to Dolina to warn us about the impossibility of crossing the border.

This news had an especially depressing effect on us. We were so close to our goal of returning to Torun, yet the rumors and scary tales meant we were as far away as ever. We met a Jewish man who had been a teacher in Torun; he told us that he, his family and some others had been trying to cross the border in Vishkof when they were caught. Of the entire group, he alone escaped. A few were killed on the spot by Hungarian border police. His whole family had been taken to Torun, with other refugees. He implored us not to venture near the border. We believed his story, but were still torn: should we take the risk or not? It was October, and now in the autumn it was not unusual for there to be snow in the mountains. If we were to cross the Carpathians, we had to move quickly because once the mountains were covered with snow, traversing them would be practically impossible. Every day we stayed in Dolina decreased our chances of success. In the meantime, life in Dolina under the Germans and Hungarians was getting harder. They pressured the *Judenrat* for more and more slave-laborers. My friend who was a *Judenrat* secretary told me that the Germans came into the offices almost daily now to conscript workers. One day, they beat up the head of the Jewish council. The local situation was worsening almost by the minute.

Finally, Zvi and I decided to risk the border – without Moshe and Montze and the children. After all, we were the grown-ups, and if we succeeded in getting to Torun, we believed our parents could somehow send a messenger for Moshe and the children, like the one who came for the Munkatcher Rebbe. Of course, everything was possible for money. We talked it over with Moshe, and he agreed that Zvi and I should make the attempt. It was decided that we'd get underway very early in the morning. Leaving Moshe all our money except for 40 *pengas*, we kissed and hugged them all good-bye. With tears in our eyes, we parted.

Upon returning from Moshe's to my hosts' home, we were surprised to find waiting for us two brothers also from Torun: Chaim and Yankele Prizant. The elder one, Chaim, was my friend from yeshiva in Sevlush. I don't know how they found out we were in Dolina, let alone how they knew we were planning to head for the border.

"We heard you are ready to go to Vishkof," Chaim said, adding that they wanted to join us.

We weren't happy with this proposition because we feared a bigger group would draw more attention and be more dangerous. But we could not bring ourselves to deny them a chance to come with us, so we agreed.

Early the next morning, Zvi and I were ready to leave. Suddenly, Chaim came running up to us and breathlessly begged us to delay our departure until the afternoon. Apparently, Yankele could not make it until noon, for what reason I don't recall. We agreed to postpone our journey, but thought it would be safer to wait until the next morning and leave under cover of darkness. Unexpectedly, both brothers came running to us right after noontime, and we changed our plans again: instead of waiting for the next morning, we got underway immediately, hiking the 50 kilometers from Dolina to Vishkof.

We estimated we could cover 25 or 30 kilometers in the afternoon, and by nightfall reach Vigoda, a small village along the way. We decided to walk in pairs, with Zvi and me in the lead. The Prizants stayed approximately 100 meters behind, keeping us in sight. If necessary, we could signal danger with a wave of the hand and warn them off the road. The road cut through fields and small hills; if we saw military cars or trucks at a distance we could dash off the road and into the adjacent field.

Our trek had been progressing uneventfully, when along our route we ran in to some women. Are there any Jews in Vigoda? we asked. They knew we were Hungarian Jews, and told us that lots of "your type of Jews" can be found on these roads. They also let us know that all the Jews from Vigoda were now in Dolina. (Besides Vigoda, there were a few other small villages between Vishkof and Dolina where some Jewish families had lived. When the war broke out, however, they were frightened of their Ukrainian neighbors, and fled to Dolina. They thought it would be safer in the city than in the turmoil surrounding their small villages.)

It got dark early, and quite cold. We came upon an empty, one-story house; the *mezuzah* on the door post told us it had been a Jewish home. Panes of glass in the windows and door had been smashed. Inside, strewn across the floor of every room were dozens of pages ripped out of prayer books and other holy Jewish volumes. Because of the broken windows, the wind howled and whistled through the house. It made a terrifying noise and gave us all an eerie feeling. We found a corner of one room with an intact window and huddled together to protect ourselves from the wind and the cold. I'll never forget that night. Like dogs, we sneaked into this house. The only difference is that dogs have no fear that other dogs will come and kill them. Only we humans, just because we are Jewish, must fear for our lives. G-d forbid that humans worse than animals should find us here and murder us!

In the room, we found a pile of straw. Spreading it on the floor of the one protected corner, we tried to make ourselves a little comfortable. Fearful that even a whisper might be too loud, we fell silent and tried to catch a nap. But sleep was impossible: our anxieties about tomorrow, the unknown, and the incessant wailing of the wind kept us awake. To add to our misery, we all started to become aware of lice, biting and crawling all over us. It was as though they rained on us from the ceiling. We realized at once that resting on the straw was a horrible mistake, but it was now too late. Zvi and I went over to another wall and huddled together. There was no way we could fall asleep. All we could do was sit, our hearts racing, and endure the biting of the lice while we waited for dawn to break.

At the first sign of morning light, we continued on our way. We estimated Vishkof was only a 3- to 4-hour walk. We whispered the traveler's prayer (*tephilat ha-derech*), took up our positions 100-meters apart and, with great anxiety, began walking briskly toward our goal. I regret now that I don't remember what day of the week it was, because this was surely one of the luckiest days of my life. On this particular day, a miracle occurred for us – and we immediately understood that it had.

It was still early morning, not quite full light, when without warning two German border guards, rifles fixed with bayonets, appeared just up ahead. They were upon us so suddenly that we had no chance to slip off the road, as we had planned to do. Without uttering a word to each other, Zvi and I continued walking. We were absolutely numb. I felt the hair on the back of my neck stand up from deadly fear. We came face to face with these German guards. For some reason, Zvi greeted them with a "Good Morning" (*Guten Morgen*). They simply answered, "*Guten Morgen,*" and then continued walking past us, never breaking stride.

Zvi and I just looked at each other. Fear paralyzed us from uttering a single word or even looking back. We picked up our pace and covered another 100 meters or so before we dared glance over our shoulders. There, we saw the soldiers pass the Prizant brothers and allow them, too, to continue in peace. We got off the road and waited for the Prizants. When they caught up, we retreated even deeper into a field, stopping by a small group of trees where we could collect our wits.

Zvi, the oldest among us, tried to cheer us up. "This is our lucky [*mazeldik*] day," he announced. "It will be a *mazeldik* day, and we'll succeed in our quest to cross the border."

After resting a while, we resumed our walk, and we felt lighter now, keeping up a good clip for about two hours. Around nine or ten o'clock in the morning, we reached the outskirts of Vishkof. In the distance, we could see the border mountain. Before us was a farm, with some cattle and sheep grazing out front. We decided to head there.

Chapter 12

'Welcome' Home

OUR PLAN WAS TO FIND A LOCAL PERSONwilling – for a fee, of course – to take us to the border. When we reached the farmhouse we found an older couple there. Right away, they knew who we were: many Hungarian Jews had passed through here, they told us. Speaking in Ruthenian, we offered to trade them soap and matches for something to eat. They agreed, and the wife prepared an oatmeal porridge with milk. It tasted like the best oatmeal ever because we were so very hungry. She also offered us some ham, but we thanked her and said that we didn't eat that kind of meat.

After our meal, we asked the old man whether he knew of someone we could pay to lead us to the border. It was important to have a guide, as the mountain was covered with pine trees and it would be easy to lose our way. (Zvi was familiar with the *other* side of the mountain, the Torun side, and would have no trouble navigating once we got over there.) The old man said that for 50 Hungarian *pengas* his son could take us to the border. It was downright obvious that we weren't their first customers. Not only did the man make a business of it, he also had a set rate! Zvi and I had only 40 *pengas* remaining; the Prizants had none. So we said we had only 30 *pengas*, to see if he'd drop his price. Wait in the stable, he told us, and he'd talk it over with his son when he got back home, later in the day.

Apparently, the farmer had noticed that Zvi was wearing a wristwatch, because when the son returned, they informed us the price would drop to 30 *pengas* – as long as the deal included Zvi's watch. We had no choice but to agree. The son, a young man in his 20s, motioned us to the door of the stable where we could see the border mountain. "Do you see the *prohalina* there?" he asked. At first we didn't understand, but then we caught on: *prohalina* was Slavic for a large patch of grassy land – in this case, a clearing amidst a grove of trees. "Head for the clearing in the afternoon and wait for me there," he said. "I will come by when it gets darker outside and lead you to the border."

He also advised us to stay off the roads. The farm was not too far from the tree-line; from there, an unbroken stretch of large pine trees offered us cover all the way to the *prohalina*. Once we got into the forest, he said, we'd be hidden from view, and it shouldn't take us more than an hour to reach the *prohalina*.

We started toward the woods, walking through the fields by twos. Before long, we were walking faster and faster. Finally, we broke into a trot. We were exposed, out in the open, and trying to close the distance between ourselves and the relative safety of the trees as quickly as we could. At the time, it never occurred to us that this thinking wasn't very smart, because running made us look more suspicious and all the more easy to spot.

Thankfully, it seemed as though we covered the distance of a few hundred yards and reached the tree-line very fast. Instantly, we disappeared into the thick stand of trees. Our hearts pounded from tension, and all four of us slumped onto the pine-needle-covered forest floor to catch our breath. We rested for 15 or 20 minutes before resuming our walk. But which way was the *prohalina* now? It is very easy to lose one's direction in a thick forest and, of course, we didn't have a compass to distinguish east from west. Should we go up to the right or left? Finally we decided. Our climb to the right took us up the steep mountainside and, fortunately, toward the clearing. At last we could see it ahead of us through the trees, when suddenly we heard yelling. Scared to death, we all dropped to the ground, not uttering a sound. With sign language and hand motions, we communicated with each other and tried to determine what the voices were.

It took some time, but eventually we recognized a few Ukrainian words. We surmised that some shepherd boys were probably grazing their flock on the *prohalina*. We began to relax a little and waited there on the ground until they went away. Slowly, the sounds grew weaker and weaker as they withdrew.

Tentatively, we crept to the edge of the clearing and sat down to wait for the farmer's son. We never doubted he'd show up, because of course he wouldn't receive his payment unless he met us there. But we were very nervous and impatient. We kept checking Zvi's watch. It was late in the afternoon and it would get dark early, especially under the trees' dense canopy. Around 4:30, we decided that we would wait no longer than another 15 or 20 minutes. With the *prohalina* in front of us, now we had a reference point to orient us. Zvi and Chaim thought we could cross the border without this man. Both of them felt we needed to climb toward the east. Later we learned that, had we gone that way, our journey would have ended in disaster. The border police were stationed to the east, and we would have walked right into their headquarters.

Close to five o'clock, the son arrived and immediately demanded the 30 *pengas* along with Zvi's watch. We paid him and he started leading us westward – in the opposite direction from how Zvi and Chaim thought we should go. Zvi kept on saying to me in Yiddish, "He is leading us the wrong way. He is leading us the wrong way." But the man was climbing very fast, and there was no time and no alternative but to follow him. The mountain was even steeper there, and we kept climbing until we were only 200 or 250 meters below the crest. Then he stopped and announced he will go no further. "The border," he said, "is right over the summit. On the other side, you will find fields, called the Beskides." The Beskides (pronounced bess-KEED-ess) were actually in Hungary, and Zvi and Chaim were familiar with them. The man then wished us luck and quickly disappeared into the dark.

No sooner had we resumed our climb when we heard dogs barking. We immediately dropped to the ground and held our breath. It seemed that the dogs had gotten wind of something, but here the second miracle of our lucky day transpired. The baying never stopped, so we could guess their distance from the volume of the sounds. At one point, the border guards came so close we could actually hear them talking to one another. We never moved, even as the dogs neared and kept up their howling. In the otherwise still of the evening, their yelps echoed back at us from other mountains in the distance. Finally, the barking began to grow weaker, signaling that the patrol had progressed far past us.

When the sounds diminished to almost nothing and we were certain the guards were quite a distance away, we made a dash for the summit. We climbed with all our strength and started running across the other side. We ran without stopping for 10 or 15 minutes. Then Zvi called to me, his words cheering me immediately: "I recognize this place," he gasped. "I know where we are." This was a great relief to all of us.

It was now totally dark outside and we walked under cover of night for about an hour. The terrain was relatively flat and, at this altitude, grassy instead of tree-covered. We were traveling along the mountain crest when suddenly, in the distance, I noticed a man moving toward us along the ridge. He was striking a match, probably to light a cigarette. This must be a second patrol, I thought, and with lightning speed I grabbed Zvi's arm and pulled him down, off the summit. We started to run down the mountain on the Hungarian side. In the confusion, we never saw what direction the Prizant brothers ran. After five or 10 minutes, we regained our composure and climbed back to the summit. We tried to reconnect with the Prizants, calling for them in whispers, since shouting would certainly attract the patrols. But soon we realized that there would be no finding them.[1]

Not only was our search for the Prizants completely futile, but in our dash off the summit we lost all sense of direction. Wandering around trying to find our way, we happened upon a fence. In the darkness (there were no stars or moonlight that night), we could barely make out that it cordoned off the large yard of a house. Again, someone lit a match to light a cigarette and before we knew it, he was coming toward us.

"Who is there?" he shouted in Ukrainian. We couldn't make out his face in the dark, just the glow of his cigarette when he inhaled. Zvi answered in Ukrainian, "We've lost our way and we want to reach the [mountain called] Yalova. We are Hungarian Jewish refugees."

In a calmer voice, the man explained that we should return to the summit and bear right to get to the Yalova. Zvi called out a thank you. As we turned to leave, the man said, "Go with G-d, with G-d's blessings, where G-d has directed you." Later, Zvi told me that he had recognized the voice, that the man offering this blessing was someone from Torun. I don't know whether the man also recognized Zvi's voice, although it seemed possible, and might have been why he calmed down so quickly.

Following the man's directions, we reached the top of the Yalova in no time at all. Immediately, we recognized where we were and knew that at the foot of the Yalova, to the right, lay Torun; to the left was Lopishna. In a way, we were in fact already home: my father owned a large parcel of land on the Yalova. Once, when I was growing up, my father took me up the huge mountain to show me the boundaries of the tract.

We descended the mountainside. It took about half an hour before we were close enough to see our house and the other homes in Torun and Lopishna, villages built in the valley formed by the Yalova. All the houses in Torun were lit up, and to us it should have

---

[1] Long after we were separated that night, I met Chaim Prizant again – in 1948, at a Displaced Person camp in West Germany. Chaim and his brother indeed had gotten back to Torun, but they were later shipped to a concentration camp. The younger brother, Yankele, did not survive the war. Chaim, like me, was the sole survivor of his family.

been a joyful sight. But we who were born there now had to sneak back into town under cover of night, like thieves, worried for our lives.

Still, with a heavy sigh of relief, Zvi asked me, "Do you hear our lumber mill?" My father had partnered with his younger brother, Zecharia, and brother-in-law Berel Drimmer (my mother's younger brother), and together they operated a water-driven lumber mill in Lopishna. The mill ran 24 hours a day, splitting tree trunks and cutting boards of different lengths and thickness from timber felled in the nearby the Leptitsia Forest. In the quiet of the night, the roar of the mill could be heard all the way to the top of the Yalova.

Our house was in the center of the village. Across the street, the Hebrew school was still being used by the military. We decided against going directly to our house, not even certain whether our parents were still there. Instead, we elected to head toward Lopishna, where we were familiar with an elderly couple by the name of Neiman; we somehow knew that they were among the 17 lucky Jewish souls who were left in Torun and vicinity on the night we were first rounded up.

Dudja Neiman's house was set back from the main road. In the dark, we slipped around to the rear of his home. It was completely dark; not a single light shone from the house. We knocked at a window, tentatively at first, and didn't get an answer. We rapped harder on the glass and called to him in Yiddish: "Reb Dudja, Reb Dudja, open up. We're Avram's children!" Finally the window opened and we started to say, "It's Mechel and Hersch – Avraham Jakubowics' children."[2]

But what a response we got. He groaned bitterly. "Oh my G-d, children, what have you done?" He sounded both scared and shocked. "We cannot let you in."

His words struck me like physical blows. "Why did you come?" he continued. After the horror of what Zvi and I had just gone through, I was devastated at being turned away. Who could have anticipated this bitter welcome in Torun.

Reb Dudja's daughter, a girl of about 18 named Chaya, was at the window, too. I had no idea how she escaped the August

---

[2] The Yiddish form of Zvi's name is "Hersch."

deportations, but she obviously was still with her parents. Chaya told us to go to the nearby *mikvah*. Located in the attic of an empty building, this *mikvah* didn't belong to anybody in particular. If we were found, then the two remaining Jewish families in Lopishna wouldn't get into trouble. Hungarian gendarmes came almost daily to search for refugees like us, Chaya explained, and everyone was very scared.

Reb Dudja finally calmed down enough to say that our father and mother were still in Torun, and that he'd let them know about us. Meanwhile, they gave us a *challah* so we'd have something to eat. (I then realized it had to be either *Shabbos* or Sunday; Zvi and I had lost all track of time.) Then they closed the window.

What was going on here? This "welcome" left us completely bewildered. We walked toward the ownerless *mikvah* building. The door was unlocked, and when we climbed to the attic we found fresh hay on the floor. I couldn't understand how hay got into the attic, unless Reb Dudja had put it there so refugees like us could rest comfortably for a little while. We planted ourselves on the piles of hay. Despite being bone-tired, we couldn't rest. We had experienced two great miracles in the last 12 hours, but we couldn't free ourselves from the terrible sense of irony: finally we had reached our goal, safely and in one piece, but then were turned away.

Zvi and I talked quietly and tried to understand what was happening. It wasn't until a while later that we learned the reasons for Reb Dudja's reaction. Dudja Neiman had a second daughter, Charna. She was married and pregnant when she, her husband, and the rest of Torun's Jews were deported that fateful night. The couple had somehow managed to sneak back (shortly before we had returned) and, of course, they went to her parents' home. By this time, she was late in her pregnancy. When the Hungarian gendarmes found her in her father's house, they literally dragged her out of bed in her parents' house and shot her dead. People found her body the next day, a few kilometers from the Neiman house. Her husband, hiding in the *mikvah* attic, was able to escape.

The Neimans couldn't believe the Hungarians were capable of such an atrocity: murdering a pregnant woman in her home. Now we could understand Reb Neiman's grief and fear, and why he greeted us as he did.

Finally, we fell asleep. When we awoke it was late in the day and our spirits were quite low. Anxiously, we awaited word from our parents, hoping that Reb Neiman had kept his promise to contact them. We also wondered whether the Prizant brothers had arrived safely as well. But we knew that during light of day, there would be no messages coming from anyone. Zvi and I were hungry, having already finished our _challah_, but that did not bother us too much. We were too wrapped up in feelings of fear, depression and helplessness, worried that we wouldn't be able to reach Torun. We both tried to boost each other's mood by recounting the miracles of the previous day. Finally, there was nothing left to do but wait as patiently as we could for a message from our parents.

The _mikvah_ attic was very dark, except for small cracks in the roof that enabled us to see it was still daylight. We no longer had a watch, so it was only when these small streams of light disappeared that we knew night had arrived. Now with no light filtering into the attic, the darkness felt like the impenetrable blackness of the ninth plague leveled against biblical Egypt.[3] We couldn't see each other's face. But after a while, our eyes adjusted and we were able to see a little bit in the dark.

I don't know how late at night it was, but finally we heard the _mikvah_ door opening, and then a voice from below calling us by name. "This is Tovah Godinger," she whispered. The Godingers didn't live too far from the Neimans, and I was happy to find out that they had managed to avoid our lot. Getting left behind during a deportation wasn't necessarily a random event. In Lopishna, when they were rounding up all the Jews, the village mayor saved one Jewish family: the Godingers. The head of the Godinger household was a tailor, the only one in the area. The locals needed a tailor, after all, so they spared him.

I knew Tovah from school and had a special feeling of friendship toward her. Zvi and I moved closer to the attic opening. She came part-way up the ladder and whispered that Reb Neiman had contacted our parents and that my father had a plan. He would travel to Volova tomorrow and try to hire a car and driver to take us deeper into Hungary. We couldn't remain here, she explained, because it was no longer safe. Meanwhile, we would need to remain in the attic, pending further instructions from our parents.

Despite her fears, Tovah became the brave messenger between us and our parents. She brought us enough food to last a few days —

---

[3] In Hebrew: "_Choshech Mitzrayim._"

hard salami, bread and something to drink. It was so dark in the *mikvah* that we couldn't see her at all (of course coming during the day would be far too dangerous). Blindly we reached for the items as she handed them up to us. Tovah was in a hurry to leave, but before going she asked us what else we needed so she could try to bring it the next time. Immediately we both asked for cigarettes. As smokers, our state of tension made us miss the nicotine even more. We thanked her and she promptly left.

On our third night in the *mikvah*, Tovah returned, this time with cigarettes, additional food and, most importantly, news from our father. He indeed had been able to travel to Volova, she told us, and now we had to wait for instructions. In the meantime, we must stay in the attic and hope we remain undiscovered. For the time being, there was nothing we could do but wait and hope for the best.

Chapter 13

My Father's Voice

THE FOOD AND, ESPECIALLY, THE CIGARETTES that Tovah brought us seemed to hold our tensions somewhat in check. But Zvi and I were extremely careful with our smoking. Naturally we wanted to avoid accidentally igniting the very dry hay that surrounded us. On the floor of the attic, we found a plank that we used like a table for our food, but after eating, we'd turn the board over and spit on a certain spot repeatedly, until enough saliva collected so we could be certain we'd be able to extinguish a cigarette butt quickly. We were also worried that the glow from our cigarettes might be seen outside, so at night we refrained from smoking altogether.

This environment challenged both our patience and our vision, but with the passing of the days, slowly our senses were able to compensate: we grew accustomed to the dark, and were able to see pretty well. On the fourth night of hiding, Tovah came by again and brought a letter of instructions from our father.

The plan called for us to wait until the next night, then cross the nearby Rika River around eleven o'clock and proceed on foot to the Pleshiva Forest. From there, we were to walk east, remaining under cover of the forest, toward the Krauss sawmill. After reaching the sawmill, we were to drop out of the forest, cross the Rika again and follow a highway that paralleled the river. We'd stay on this road through the Runyas, a flatland area between the Pleshiva and Smerek mountains. Finally, we'd reach the Smerek Forest, only a kilometer or so from the village of Bistra. All along the highway, at one-kilometer intervals, were whitewashed boulders marking the distance from Chust to the former Polish border. We were to wait in the Smerek Forest from a position where we could observe the highway and the 76-kilometer stone. At exactly midnight, a car would come from the direction of Bistra, stop at the 76-kilometer stone, and turn around. The driver, a Hungarian detective hired by my father, would flash the headlights three times. Then we were to descend from the Smerek to the highway and into the car.

We couldn't read the letter in the dark, of course, but Tovah explained the plan briefly. We barely slept that night, anxiously awaiting dawn, when we'd be able to see the letter for ourselves. As soon as the first rays of light broke through the cracks of the roof, we started reading our father's instructions. The driver, he wrote, would take us to C͟hust, to the home of David Schwartz. Mr. Schwartz was a good friend and business associate of my father's. The letter also revealed that our father would come to C͟hust several days later to give us further instructions. It was a great joy and relief to see our father's handwriting, to have contact with him again after such a long nightmarish time.

As nervous as Zvi and I were, I could only imagine how anxious our parents were, knowing how dangerous it would be for us to leave the *mikvah* attic, cross the river and get to C͟hust without anyone spotting us. Our father later told us he worried whether the detective would come for us, despite being well paid. It also took about three hours to drive by car from Torun to C͟hust. For two days and two nights, there would be no way for our parents to know whether we passed all the danger points successfully. My G-d, how painful it must have been for them!

I didn't know what day it was or the date, as uneasily we awaited the next night. We felt we were as ready as we'd ever be. Tovah had brought a pocket watch from our father, to replace Zvi's, so we'd be able to track the time, and we were very familiar with the area we'd be traveling. In summertime and on Saturday afternoons, we often used to stroll to the Runyas. We were allowed to walk there on *Shabbos* because it was inside the Sabbath boundary that had been erected around Torun, and young boys and girls from Torun and Bistra used to congregate there.[1]

By nightfall, our tensions were extremely high. We smoked even more, partly to ease our nerves and partly so we could check the time. When we'd inhale deeply, we could see the watch face by the glow of the cigarette. We knew the distance we had to cover to reach the Runyas should take us between 30 to 40 minutes, so we had to leave the *mikvah* no later than 11 p.m.

Close to eleven o'clock, we descended from the attic and snuck out. The doors squeaked a little bit, scaring us, so we withdrew as fast as we could. In the dark, we zigzagged our way to the river. In crossing the river we had several options. The river was not very deep, and there were footbridges at certain places. Somewhat further

---

[1] The Sabbath boundary (*t'chum shabbos*) is the distance past the perimeter of a city beyond which one may not walk. Bistra's Jewish community was smaller than Torun's, totaling only about a hundred Jewish families. Bistra also had fewer Zionists, not because the community was smaller but because the village lacked a Hebrew school. In general, the Jews of Bistra were more pious than those in Torun. Only a small group of Jewish youths from Bistra secretly belonged to the Zionist organization.

downstream was a real bridge, wide enough both for people and wagons to cross. Naturally, this bridge would be too conspicuous to traverse, so if we couldn't find a footbridge, we planned to wade across the river barefoot.

To our good luck, we found a footbridge almost immediately, and we speedily crossed the river. About a hundred yards away from the river, we started to ascend toward the Pleshiva Forest, to disappear among the thick pines. We climbed as fast as humanly possible. Once we were inside the forest no one could see us, so we stopped for a few minutes to catch our breath. It was a dark night, and we were almost certain none of the gentile neighbors had spotted us. Not too far from where we crossed the river was the Krauss family's lumber mill. This mill also operated 24 hours a day, as ours did elsewhere along the same river.

Walking in the dark, Zvi and I couldn't help but step on small stones, dried twigs and fallen leaves, and so we were sure we were making far too much noise. In truth, the roar of the two lumber mills, not to mention the river itself, drowned out the little noise we made in the underbrush. It simply was our understandable fear playing tricks on us.

Once again, our journey seemed miraculously shortened, as we quickly made our way to the 76-kilometer stone. We weren't lucky enough to locate a footbridge at this end of the river, so we took off our shoes and waded across. Back on the other side, exactly as the plan called for, we quickly crossed the highway and started to climb the Smerek Mountain, in order to wait out of sight for the car. By now, of course, we didn't have enough light to see Zvi's watch, but we were certain it was no later than 12 midnight.

Our hearts raced as we waited. Our feet were still wet, but we put our shoes back on anyway; this was hardly our main concern. Now, our eyes focused on the darkened direction from where a car was supposed to come. To our good fortune, it was not long before the car arrived. At night, we could see it from a great distance, its headlights two glowing circles of light. With great trepidation, we watched the car approach the 76-kilometer stone and then swing around. A moment later, the car's lights turned off and on three times. We quickly descended the hill and drew near to the car. The driver told us to get inside fast, and then he started to travel in the direction of <u>Chust</u>.

We had been under way for no more than half an hour when suddenly a tire burst. The driver started cursing in Hungarian and told us to get out of the car. Thank goodness the flat occurred in an uninhabited area between the villages of Maidan and Volova. He told us to hide in the nearby field until he changed the tire. This took him only 15 or 20 minutes, but for us it felt like an eternity. Finally, he signaled to us to return and we continued along our route.

Now, we thought, we'd head straight to <u>Chust</u>. But when the driver reached Volova, he drove into a yard and ordered us to lie down on the floor of the car. Zvi and I had to curl into fetal position to fit (neither a comfortable nor an easy feat for the two of us, since we were both very tall), and then he covered us with a blanket. He told us he had to buy a can of gasoline, and that it wouldn't take him longer than 10 or 15 minutes. We lay like that without a peep until he returned – much longer, it seemed, than 15 minutes. The thoughts that crossed my mind were so horrible that, as the old Yiddish saying goes, they should get lost in the wild, abandoned forest. [2]

When he finally returned he told us to remain on the floor, covered with the blanket, until we passed the military post at the outskirts of Volova. That was the checkpoint for all traffic coming in and out of the village. During this portion of our journey, fear completely seized us. My brother and I knew that if we were discovered there, we faced death. Maybe recognizing the dire situation we were in gave us the amazing ability to fold up like worms in that cramped space. (The back seat of my car today is bigger than the whole car we were in then!) Every minute under the blanket felt like hours long. To this day, I have still nightmares about it.

At last, the driver told us we'd passed the military post. Finally we could sit up in the back seat and actually breathe again. Around three or four o'clock in the morning, we arrived at the edge of <u>Chust</u>, without any more dangerous encounters. The driver said he wouldn't take us to David Schwartz's house because it was too dangerous to go into the city. Instead he took us to another place, on the outskirts of <u>Chust</u>. He drove into the yard of a house, got out, and knocked at the door. Quietly he said to the people, "I have brought you two Jews." We got out of the car and he speedily drove off. Despite the hour, the people let us inside. I didn't know these people, but Zvi

---

[2] *"Zol oysgehen oif piste velder."* This expression might translate, in more contemporary slang, as "I wish my worries would get lost – permanently."

told me that he recognized them and that they were familiar with our family in Torun.

The family members led us into a room with one bed and offered it to us. We declined, choosing to sleep on the floor because we were very dirty and still infested with lice. We yearned for a bath, but this was a poor house, and they didn't have an indoor bathroom. They told us that during the day, when the traffic on the street was heaviest and we could blend in with the crowd, they would take us over to the home of Mr. David Schwartz.

And that's how it was. Around noon they led us to Mr. Schwartz's house, whose family received us with kindness and friendship. Although the Hungarian authorities had threatened people with grave consequences for helping deportees like us, they furnished us with a room. This was a wealthy family, and in their home we were able to take a warm bath. For the first time in four months, I felt clean again. After our baths, Zvi and I fell asleep, with a feeling of gratitude to G-d that we were again among friends. We slept for more than 15 hours without interruption.

In the morning, a very good friend (also a distant relative) entered our room. At least I thought he was a very good friend. His name was Herschel Zicherman. He stared right at us, observing us closely without saying a word. Then he walked right out. Zvi and I were both flabbergasted. "Never mind that he didn't say 'Hello' or 'Good morning' to *me*," Zvi said. "But why not to *you*? You are the same age and friends." We didn't understand what happened. Was the situation so dangerous that people were afraid to speak to us? This incident illustrates the truth of Benjamin Franklin's maxim, "A friend in need is a friend indeed." We were welcome guests in the Shwartzes' home, but we were still tormented by Dudja Neiman's words, "Oh my G-d, children, what have you done?" Unable to fathom the changes in people's character, I fell asleep again – despite having just slept for so long.

I don't know how long I was out the second time, but I awoke slowly, still groggy from sleep. Suddenly, I realized I was hearing my father's voice. He was sitting at the table with Zvi, speaking quietly and asking about our brother Moshe and his family. I jumped out of bed and ran to him; we embraced, tears streaming from our eyes. We were drenched with tears of joy.[3] I noticed right away that in the four months since I had last seen him, my father had aged a lot. His beard was now completely white. Yet, horrible experiences notwithstanding, this was a very happy reunion for us.

Two days after Zvi and I began our journey, my father boarded the bus to Chust. Along its usual route, it stopped in Volova for 10 or 15 minutes, and that's when he found out from his contact that we had been transported successfully. From there, he was also able to send a coded message back to my mother in Torun via a trusted gentile employee who had traveled to Volova for supplies.

How did our parents cope with all this pain and anguish? G-d only knows. Our father had already slipped into poor health by then. And at that time, it was fairly dangerous for a Jew with a beard to travel. Yet "as a father has compassion upon his children,"[4] they were sustained in time of danger, drawing from hidden reserves of strength that every human being seems to possess.

The Carpathian region was very dangerous now, Dad told us, and we couldn't remain here safely. He wanted us to go deeper into Hungary, the sooner the better. At that time, the end of 1941, approximately three-quarters of a million Jews still lived in Hungary's cities and villages. With a large Jewish community like that, he reasoned, it would be easier for us to hide.

All over our region, Jews had been shipped out to the Ukraine. But Zvi was overcome with joy when our father confirmed that his wife Piri and their 1-year-old son Baruch were among the few who were still left in the village of Kalin. Piri and little "Buchyk" had been visiting her parents on that Tisha b'Av when the Carpathian deportations began.

My father's plan now was to hire a taxi to transport us (he considered it too dangerous for us to travel by train). He wanted us to go to the town of Sokmar (which the Hungarians called Szatmarnemety, while the Romanians called it Satu Mare). Trying to quiet our anxieties – a bit, anyway – he also assured us that if the Hungarians caught refugees like us, they would just arrest us and send us to a labor camp, but not deport us again to the Ukraine.

Later that same day, my father traveled to his sister, our Aunt Jutta, in the village of Bereziv, only 10 kilometers from Chust. As I mentioned earlier, prior to our deportation we had sent her some valuables and clothing for safekeeping. So my father arranged to

---

[3] "*In treiren hoben ints begossen.*"
[4] "*K'rachem av al banim*" (from Psalm 103:13).

bring us a fresh change of clothes and a shaving razor. By this time, we looked like unshaved wild men, just out of the forest.

He returned the next morning, with our Aunt Jutta in tow. When she saw us, she broke down and cried. I think her tears were as much from relief at finding us alive as they were from the shock of seeing what we looked like after what we had been through. Like many others, she had heard rumors of what occurred after the deportations. In fact, she and our father both pressed us for details about the fate of our Uncle Zecharia and his entire family. Of approximately 100,000 Jews living in the Carpathian region, 40,000 were now in labor camps, and roughly 30,000 were deported to the Ukraine that fateful Tisha b'Av *nidcheh* in 1941.[5] The majority perished in the vicinity of Kamieniec Podolski. Very few managed successfully to sneak back to Hungary. We simply told them that we got separated from Uncle Zecharia. From then on, we said, we'd had no news. Zvi and I didn't have the heart to tell them about the atrocities that took place in the Polish Ukraine. We didn't want to dash their hopes that somehow our family members were still alive.

For three or four days, we remained with our host, Mr. David Schwartz. Using a hand clipper, Zvi and I cut each other's hair, trying to rid ourselves of the third plague of biblical Egypt: lice. We also bathed two or three times a day for the same reason. After a fresh shave, we looked like normal people again. But when we changed into our clean clothes, the suits and pants were too baggy. We realized, then, how much weight we had lost over the last four months.

In the meantime, our father hired a taxi. He paid 300 *pengas*, a lot of money at that time, to take us to Sokmar. The morning before we left, he gave us some more money, so that we'd have some cash. Two of our uncles and a first cousin of my mother's lived in Sokmar at that time.[6] The cousin, Mrs. Rifka Weiss, owned a prominent hotel

---

[5] While writing these memoirs, I looked these numbers up in the *Encyclopaedia Judaica* (vol. 15, pp. 468-471; vol. 8, pp. 1096-1097). My recollection differs with the encyclopaedia's entries. The editors put the total Jewish population at 70-80,000 but I have distinct memories of the Czech parliamentary election from 1935 or '36, in which Jewish organizations put the population at 100,000.

[6] One uncle, Alter Fried, was married to my father's younger sister, Rachael. The other uncle was my mother's younger brother, Zvi Drimmer, whom I mentioned

there called The Victoria; it was decided that that was where the driver should take us. Then, once in Sokmar, we would determine our next steps. We parted with a good-bye and wish of success from our father and Aunt Jutta. Again, we cried.

It was easy to see great worry in our father's eyes. Worse, we couldn't communicate with our mother: there was no one to send a message with back from <u>Ch</u>ust, and we dared not use the telephone to communicate with her, for fear of somebody listening in. She was surely waiting anxiously in Torun for more details since she heard from our father in Volova.

---

earlier had changed his name many years before to the more Hungarian-sounding Armin Darvosh. Because he was a high school teacher in Hungary (a government job), localizing his name was supposed to help in his livelihood.

Chapter 14

A Night at the Movies

THE TAXI DRIVER PICKED UP ZVI AND ME the next morning, as our father had arranged, and by afternoon we were in Sokmar. We entered the hotel lobby and asked for our mother's cousin, Rifka Weiss. They gave us the number of a suite on the third floor. When we got upstairs, they immediately took us to another room, that of Rifka's father, our great-uncle Zalman, who also lived in the hotel. Originally from Torun, Uncle Zalman was already in his 80s and was very, very happy to see us.

Right off the bat, he started asking us about the welfare of his daughter-in-law and his granddaughter. We didn't know, we said. In fact, we *did* know and preferred not to say anything. Along with the other residents of Torun, they had been sent to Kamieniec Podolski. More than that we couldn't say – or rather wouldn't say – since we felt it would be better for him if we were less specific.

A hotel waiter brought food into the room, sent us by Cousin Rifka. We were still hungry all the time and so we consumed it with much gusto. While we ate, great-uncle Zalman told us that his son, Bynish, had already been in a *munkotabor* on Tisha b'Av 1941, and still was, when the Hungarians deported his wife, Hannah, and their only child, a beautiful little girl named Dvorah, who was only two or three years old. Bynish was the same age as Zvi. He was known throughout our region as a genius. A brilliant scholar in talmudic literature, he attended great and famous yeshivas. He also had a phenomenal photographic memory.[1]

Great-uncle Zalman summoned our two other uncles to come see him at the hotel. How he got word to them I don't know; he couldn't have phoned them. He also offered no explanation why he wanted them to come. When they entered the room, they were very surprised to see us. "Here are two of Avraham and Rifka's children," he said. "Divide them between the two of you. Each of you take one to your house." They agreed. Then they asked us all kinds of questions, a real board of inquiry. It was easy to see the nervousness on their faces.

---

[1] He and my brother Zvi died as martyrs, HYD, on the same day in 1944 on the holiday of *Simchat Torah*.

As evening approached, Uncle Armin spoke out: "Who wants to come with me to my house?" Before I could answer, Zvi jumped in: "I want to go with Uncle Alter, and Mechel – you go with Uncle Armin." Later Zvi told me that he volunteered for Uncle Alter's house because it would have been harder for me to cope there. Uncle Alter headed a strictly religious home. Uncle Armin's house, on the other hand, was a more modern Jewish environment. Zvi was absolutely correct in sizing up the situation. Uncle Alter's house was not at all in line with my tastes, and would have been very difficult for me.

Uncle Armin had five children: three daughters and two sons. One daughter, Sharrie, was a pharmacist by profession. Sharrie was married and lived in another city (the name of which escapes me). Neither of the boys were at home anymore either: Lotsy, five or six years my senior, had a job somewhere in another city; and Willy, about a year younger than I, was in rabbinical school in Budapest. Still living at home were his two other daughters, Böske (BISH-keh) and Motzko (MOTS-ko).

At their home, everyone spoke Hungarian, not Yiddish. I knew next to nothing of this language then, but Uncle Armin's wife, my aunt Molvin, spoke a little German, so I could at least communicate with her somewhat. She was very ill, however, and a week after I came to their house, she was taken to the hospital in the larger city of Debrecen. At first the only one with whom I could communicate easily was my uncle. The older daughter, Böske, acted friendly and caring, but the younger one, Motzko, was very cold to me. She was a college student, though, and out of the house for most of the day. In general, I felt good to be in this home.

After a week or so passed, I received a letter from my father, along with a money order made out to Uncle Armin, so that I could contribute toward expenses, since I was an extra mouth to feed and had no ration card. Also he didn't want me to feel as though I was a burden to them. Hungary was then officially allied with Germany and Italy against Russia. Even at this stage of the war, a rationing system had been put in place, so it was hard to obtain food products in the city without ration cards. The alternative was to obtain it on the black market, where one could get just about anything, of course, at usurious prices.

Uncle Armin's house was managed like a train station, with everything conducted in order, and with to-the-minute precision. Breakfast, lunch and dinner were served on white tablecloths, with linen napkins and beautiful dishes. There was no shortage of water –

everyone received a full glass. The portions of food, however, were quite meager. I was 21 years old and still haggard and hungry after four months of a starvation diet; with my ferocious appetite, I looked at how much food was put on the table to feed *everyone* and felt the entire amount might just be enough to satisfy me alone. I resolved to leave a little bit of food on my plate with each meal, so I didn't appear quite so ravenous.

My first week there, I suffered terribly. To try quieting my hunger pangs, I filled my belly with lots of water. When Aunt Molvin left for the hospital in Debrecen, Böske, the oldest daughter, took over the job of preparing the food. From time to time, she would offer me something between the clockwork meals, like a piece of bread with butter or some goodies to nibble on. I felt she must have instinctively understood my plight, because I had never said anything to her about being hungry. Though she knew very little German, she also talked to me constantly and tried to teach me Hungarian.

This entire time, I never ventured outside the house, not even into the yard, for fear of the neighbors. All of them were gentile and I was worried they would report my presence. One day, though, Böske asked me to go to the movies with her. I admitted to being afraid to go out. "Don't be scared," she said. "Just put your arm around me and we'll go as a couple." Despite my sense of the danger involved, I agreed.

I recall exactly what film we saw – *The Wizard of Oz* – and precisely what day it was: December 7, 1941. We left the theater around ten or eleven o'clock. A light snow was falling. On the street corner, Hungarian newspaper boys were shouting the latest news of the war. I could see the banner headline – bold, black letters across the top of an "extra" edition of the paper. I couldn't understand the words, of course, but Böske translated for me: Japan had attacked the United States and declared war on Britain and France.

I was seized with a feeling of great joy. No matter that the Axis powers now comprised Berlin, Rome *and* Tokyo. This would bring America into the war and, I was absolutely certain, would hasten Hitler's demise. It is often explained that movies are entertaining because they enable us to suspend our disbelief, so we can lose ourselves in the unfolding story. For the duration of the movie, we can believe almost anything. Unfortunately, my hope of a quick defeat for Hitler was as real as the movie we saw.

Before I knew it, I had been at Uncle Armin's house for two weeks. Very few Jews had telephones back then, so I had no contact with my brother the entire time. I really wanted to know how Zvi was coping, especially whether he was as hungry as I was all the time. He was staying only 10 or 12 blocks from us, but Uncle Alter's house was in a Jewish neighborhood: police were everywhere and it was especially dangerous for Jewish male deportees like us to roam around. Despite how eager I was to see Zvi, Uncle Armin managed to talk me out of it.

Hunger drove me elsewhere. I knew that another cousin from Torun, Shoshana Chaimowitz, had settled there. She had married a boy from Sokmar and lived not too far from where I was staying with my uncle. One day I got up the courage to walk to her house. Shoshana greeted me at the door with a small baby in her arms, and received me warmly. I didn't know where her husband was – perhaps in a labor camp. I confided to her how I suffered from hunger in my uncle's house. Both Uncle Armin and Aunt Molvin were retired high school teachers, entirely dependent on their government pensions. Especially as Jews, they avoided buying or selling goods on the black market because they feared their pensions would be revoked should they be caught.[2] Since I was staying with them illegally, they had no ration card for me, and had to divide their family's food allotment, already lean by any standard for four people, among five hungry souls.

Without a word of explanation, Shoshana told me to follow her across the street. On the corner was a grocery store. The owner might have been Jewish (at that time, Jews in Hungary could still own businesses). She whispered something to the owner in Hungarian. I couldn't hear what was said (nor could I have understood it even if I had), but he handed me a whole loaf of bread and a jar of honey. I paid with *pengas* that my father had given us in Chust. With my treasure, I returned with Shoshana to her apartment. It didn't take long for me to pack away half the loaf, slopped with honey. For the first time since Zvi and I came back from our dangerous journey, I satisfied the beast gnawing inside my stomach.

Shoshana also listened sympathetically when I related how badly I wanted to see Zvi, though I feared going to his neighborhood

---

[2] In general, Jews who did not rely on government pensions could risk buying food on the black market, and thus supplement the food they were entitled to receive with their ration cards.

against my uncle's advice. She promised to travel to Uncle Alter's herself the next day, and try to bring Zvi back to her place. Uncle Alter owned a soda factory and had a delivery truck, so they arranged to put Zvi aboard the truck and drop him by Shoshana's house along its delivery route. Traveling by truck presented less of a danger, especially when in fact the driver was my cousin Bumy (pronounced BOO-mee), Uncle Alter's oldest son.

Zvi and I talked our hearts out to one another. His situation was almost the same as mine: hungry all the time. Thankfully, he had gotten a message from his wife, Piri, indicating that she and Baruch were okay. At Uncle Alter's, Zvi also had been visited by our cousin Shonie Fixler. Shonie lived deeper in Hungary and, realizing the circumstances, offered to bring Zvi to his village, Mariopoch, permanently. Mariopoch is in the Nyer region, the richest agricultural area in Hungary. It boasted fertile soil and abundant harvests. Residents were free of ration cards, and were able to get whatever food one's heart desired.

No more than a week had gone by when Zvi and his hosts at Uncle Alter's started to receive huge loaves of Hungarian bread, which Shonie mailed to them. In Hungary, farmer's bread was famous not only for its size, but also its long shelf-life. Some ingredient added to the dough prevented the bread from spoiling or growing moldy for an extended period of time. Farmers in Hungary lacked abundant supplies of wood or coal, so they had home ovens that were fired with a mixture of dried manure and straw, in which they baked big loaves that would last two or three weeks at a stretch. In food-rationed Sokmar, these loaves of bread were greatly prized.

My situation began to improve, too. I'd go to Shoshana's corner grocery store where the owner now knew me. If other customers were there, he let me wait until I was the last one in the store. Then, once everybody else left, he'd sell me bread, sardines, cheese, all kinds of food. Then I'd go to Shoshana's apartment and fill the hole in my stomach. Shoshana was very happy that I visited, because I could baby-sit for her while she went into the city. This made me happy, too, because I ate better when I was alone. Truthfully, I was ashamed at how much I wanted to eat, even in front of Shoshana.

After a while, I stopped being hungry all the time. I regained the weight I had lost and began to concentrate on learning the Hungarian language as quickly as possible. Without language skills, I would always be a suspect as a deportee. Uncle Armin used to go out every day between meals; that left me at home with Böske and Motzko, and forced me to start speaking Hungarian. I made great progress in a very short time.

I loved my Uncle Armin very much. His background always fascinated me. His father (my maternal grandfather, Ephraim) had sent him off to the famed yeshiva in Bonyhad, Hungary[3] – the same yeshiva attended years later by my eldest brother, Eliezer. At the time, Armin was friends with two students of this yeshiva who later became quite famous: the noted poet Avigdor Hameiri and the renown Zionist leader, Dr. Josef Pottoi (pronounced POH-toh-ee). They influenced Armin greatly, and he became a devoted Zionist. He once told me that he bought "inherited land" in Palestine, and that he worked for the Zionist ideal.[4]

For a time Armin attended that yeshiva, but after a while he dropped out to pursue secular studies. He managed to complete the eight-year *gymnasium* program, which was mandatory for entrance to college. After that, he attended a teacher's college in Budapest, graduating with honors to become a high school instructor.

My grandfather Ephraim anguished over his son's secular education. Worse still, in college, Armin met a fellow student – Molvin – whom he married. Of course Molvin was Jewish and the two of them were married in a Jewish ceremony, but my grandfather and grandmother were very unhappy with in-laws who were more secularly inclined and less observant. Those of us in the next generation, however, admired Armin's free spirit and revered him. As the Yiddish proverb says, a self-made man is "to G-d and to humanity"[5]: meaning that among Jews he is at home, given his Jewish education, and among gentiles he is at home because of his secular education.

* * *

---

[3] Until the end of World War I, this region was part of the Austro-Hungarian Empire under the rule of King Franz Josef.

[4] The term in Hebrew for "inherited land" (*nachalah*) is based on G-d's promise to Abraham in Genesis XII: 7 – "Unto thy seed I will give this land." Uncle Armin Darvosh bought the land to redeem as *his* inheritance, although life circumstances prevented him from fulfilling his Zionist dreams.

[5] "*Tsu Got in tsu la'at.*"

In early January 1942, we received the joyful news that our brother Moshe, along with Montze and their children, had somehow reached Chust. I didn't learn the details of their border-crossing saga until much later, but I nevertheless appreciated how much effort my parents made and how much pain they must have endured in rescuing their children. My father surely aged 20 years from worry in those few months. Physically, he was completely drained. I am certain he paid with his life, because from the time we arrived in Sokmar, his health declined steadily. He lived only a year and a half longer.

This much I knew: my father had hired a gentile farmer from Torun (and paid him handsomely, of course) to cross the border into Dolina to find Moshe and his family. I was never told how they returned, however – how long it took or how they eluded the border guards. This remained a mystery to me for years. Then, in 1990, during one of my visits to Israel, I had a chance meeting with a fellow countryman (*landsman*) by the name of Chaim Friedman. The Friedmans had lived in Prislip, adjacent to Torun.[6] (We used to call the senior Friedman "*der kutzer*" [which means "the short one"], and my friend became known as "Chaim the *kutzer*'s son"– to distinguish him from all the other Chaims in our community.)

I was happy to see Chaim. I had no idea he survived the war, and now it was pure coincidence that we happened to visit Israel at the same time. While updating each other, I learned he lived in Chicago along with his sister Cayla, and that during the war she had come over from Dolina to Chust – transported by the same man my father sent for Moshe and his family. Chaim thanked me profusely for this, and said my father actually saved his sister's life. When I returned to the States, I decided to call Cayla for more details. When she answered the phone and I identified myself, she was completely overwhelmed. "Oy, Mecheleh," she gasped. "I'm fainting. I'm fainting. I'm so happy to hear your voice." She cried, and over and

---

[6] Essentially, Torun formed one large community with the villages of Prislip, Lapishna and Schora; everyone knew everyone else. Prislip, moreover, was linked to my village by being the site of the only Jewish cemetery for Torun. All my grandparents and great-grandparents (except for my great-grandparents Michael and Malya) are buried there. But this Jewish burial ground was desecrated and, today, for all I know, Ukrainians are planting potatoes on it.

over she repeated, "Your father saved my life. Your father saved my life."

At first, she was too emotional to explain what happened to them. But bit by bit, she gave more answers to my many questions. What time of year did you come over? She didn't remember exactly; it might have been December 1941 or January 1942. Who brought you? A Hungarian driver, a private detective. Undoubtedly, this had been the same detective my father hired to spirit Zvi and me across the border. Just like us, the detective covered them with a blanket before taking them through the traffic checkpoint in the village of Volova. Cayla recounted that Moshe and Montze's two children, Schloimi and Channi, kept completely quiet: not a peep out of them. For the life of me, I couldn't understand how they had room in this car for three adults and two children. But they got through and were brought to Chust.

Chapter 15

The Dream

SOME TIME IN MID-JANUARY 1942, cousin Shonie returned to Sokmar, keeping his promise to take Zvi out of the city. Shonie owned a "mom and pop" grocery store in Mariopoch, where he was very tight with the Hungarian authorities, especially the local gendarmes. He arranged to legalize Zvi's stay by registering him as a teacher of Jewish children in _Chumash_ and Rashi. Zvi was a student of two yeshivas, Nytra and Pishchan, and well qualified for the position. What a great relief this new environment was for him! In comparison to the dangerous and suffocating atmosphere in Sokmar, Zvi felt virtually free. But the biggest improvement for him was the comparative abundance of food.[1]

At the end of that month, two other cousins arrived in Sokmar, this time looking for me. My aunt Etya, my father's sister, and her family lived in Bihor-Dioszeg (BEE-hor-DEE-oh-seg), a small farming village 15-20 kilometers from the city of Nogyvarod.[2] This area was overrun by the Hungarians in 1939, but previously had belonged to Romania. Traveling there from Czechoslovakia required a passport, so we never had much contact with this branch of the family, the Goldbergs. As a result, I never met either one of these cousins: Clarri and her younger sister Piri, both in their 20s. Despite being strangers, they came to me, acknowledging how difficult it was to get food in Sokmar, especially for people like me who lacked a ration card. They said their parents wanted me to return to Bihor-Dioszeg with them and live at their house.

To this day, I don't know whether this was an altruistic impulse on my relatives' part or the result of my father's behind-the-scenes actions on my behalf. Either way, Bihor-Dioszeg was deeper inside Hungary and safer for Jewish deportees like me, so on the whole I was only too happy to go. A day or two later, I packed up whatever belongings I had, said goodbye to Uncle Armin, and departed with my cousins.

---

[1] Piri and Buchyk had been in Kalin all this time, and both Zvi and Piri were afraid to travel to see each other. How it must have pained them to be separated. Thankfully, later in 1942, when we got our Hungarian citizenship papers, Piri, Buchyk and Zvi were able to meet for the first time in over a year, in Chust.

[2] Jews referred to this city as Grossverdein.

Two and a half months in Sokmar had improved my Hungarian language skills adequately enough for me to deal with the challenge of purchasing my own train ticket. Clarri and Piri both felt this would be best: for either of them to purchase a ticket for someone else might have raised suspicions among the authorities. We would travel as a threesome, again to make me look less conspicuous. From time to time, officials would ask people for their identification cards while on the train, but this was not the main danger in rail travel. Far more difficult was getting *off* the train in small towns like Bihor-Dioszeg. Local police always patrolled the train stations for any strange new faces and, on finding an unfamiliar person, immediately demanded an identification card. Making the journey with my cousins seemed to lessen this danger.

Without incident, we arrived in Bihor-Dioszeg, and walked onto the platform; no one stopped us. Moving purposefully, Clarri, Piri and I strode swiftly from the train station and continued on foot to their house nearby. Though it was also my first meeting with Aunt Etya and her husband (also named Alter!), their entire family received me warmly. The language spoken in the home was Hungarian, although everyone knew Yiddish. Uncle Alter produced wine from his own vineyard in Bihor-Dioszeg, and conducted trade in the local wine industry. Apparently he did quite well in this business, because they had a very nice house – it was furnished nicely, and there was no shortage of food or anything.

This close-knit family consisted of two sons and three daughters. The oldest daughter, Ettush, was married, but lived there with her husband, a dentist. Next in line was Mortzi, a young man about 26 or 27, who helped in his father's business. Then came Clarri and Piri and, finally, the youngest brother, who was very sickly (I'm afraid I don't recall his name). I never learned what afflicted him, but everyone in the family had a role in caring for him. (Of five children, three fortunately came through the *Shoah*. Ettush lost her husband, but she, Piri and Mortzi survived. All three of them later settled in Jerusalem.)

My first three evenings at the Goldberg house were delightful. Each supper left me full and satisfied. Then Aunt Etya started quizzing me for details about the family. I tried to conceal as much of the bitter truth as possible, but she was especially keen to learn the fate of my Uncle Zecharia (her younger brother) and family. I was determined to spare her from feeling any more grief. What I *did* tell her was true: we were separated somewhere in Poland; from there, I didn't know what became of them. "What happened at Kamieniec

Podolski?" she kept asking. Information had reached the Jewish community about great atrocities perpetrated there by the Germans and Hungarians upon the Jewish refugees from the Carpathian, Maramaros and Felvidek regions. I had not been in Kamieniec Podolski, I repeated – I didn't know what happened there.

Unlike the big cities, Bihor-Dioszeg had no card rationing system, so there was no shortage of food in the house. I ate well and regained my strength. Aunt Etya's house was situated right on Bihor-Dioszeg's main street, a wide thoroughfare lined on both sides by tall, leafy trees. I was given a room in the front of the house on the first floor, overlooking this avenue. The window was curtained and, in addition, thick foliage obscured that part of the house. From the sidewalk out front, a passerby would barely notice the window, let alone see anything inside. During the day, I was able to stand by the side of the window and watch people come and go along the street, as the house was right on the sidewalk. From time to time, I could see gendarmes, usually patrolling in pairs. These Hungarian "roosters"[3] could be brutal, so people feared them and stayed clear when they could.

The Goldbergs entertained a lot (often, their business associates). Though no one ever told me directly, it was understood that I dared not be seen by any visitors – not even by other Jews. When guests were in the house, I had to remain quietly in my room with the door closed. This room was next to their living room, so the frequency of visitors and the need to stay out of sight resulted in my spending almost the entire day in the room by myself. Like a man convicted of a crime – the illegal offense of being born a Jew – I was in a way also incarcerated.

I passed the time a number of ways. On occasion, I rose quite early in the morning to pray slowly, trying to understand the meaning of every word in every prayer. I also obtained a copy of the _Chumash_ and commentaries from the Goldberg's library.[4] In the solitude of my

---

[3] Hungarians referred to their gendarmes as _kokoshok_ (roosters) or, literally, "the feathered ones" because of the signature feathered hats they wore with their uniforms.

[4] The Goldberg's had none of the secular books (_seforim chitzonim_) in Yiddish or Hebrew that my family had in Torun. Along with the religious books found in every Jewish home, they owned only a few Hungarian books. While I appreciated

quarters, I focused on studying the weekly Torah portion and rabbinic discussions. I also started keeping a journal of everything that had happened to us in the Ukraine and Poland. I corresponded regularly with my brother Zvi (by then safely in Mariopoch). When I mentioned to him that I was chronicling our history, he wrote back with encouragement. "Write everything, from Egypt until now,"[5] he said – meaning to record all of our travails. Zvi seemed to sense our troubles were not over, and that capturing the story for posterity was important. It took some doing, but by the time I left Bihor-Dioszeg in the spring, I had compiled a complete account of what we went through. At that time, it was all fresh in my mind: dates, places, people's names, everything. But later on, in Debrecen, this journal was lost, and with it, all these details.

For me, the hardest part of my stay at the Goldbergs' house was getting through the long winter nights. After dark, I could not read. A light bright enough to read by would have illuminated my room, and chanced revealing it to anyone passing by on the main street. I could rest, of course, but I found it difficult to sleep; news of the war often kept me awake. On my uncle's radio, we listened to painful broadcasts from Budapest: reports from the eastern front, where Hungarian and German forces celebrated their triumphs deep inside the Soviet Union. Even more than the local Jews, I was terrified and very affected by it. I lived in fear because I believed that when a non-Jew tells you that he is going to kill you, believe him. When Hitler, YS, started to threaten the German Jews in the early 1930s and pronounced intentions to kill them, I wish they would have believed him. Many would have saved their lives.

To try calming my nerves and to get some sleep, I pictured the map of Europe: England, France, Belgium, the Netherlands, the Scandinavian countries. Some of them were still free, as of yet unoccupied by the Nazi armies. I also reminded myself that the United States was on the side of the Allies. Through gathered facts and reason, I struggled to control my emotions. I was almost positive that the Devil would be defeated.[6]

---

having these to read, I missed my own copy of the *Tanach* (the acronym for the Torah [the Five Books of Moses], *Nevi'im* [the Prophets], and *Kesuvim* [the Writings, i.e., the *Hagiographa*]). I had purchased a special edition when I was 14 or 15 years old, with complete commentaries, like Rashi, *Perush Radak* and *Siphsay Chachamim*, as well as a Yiddish translation, making it easier for me to understand. Unfortunately, those volumes and all my family's other books were left in Torun.

[5] "*Farshribe alles, 'mi Mitzrayim v'ad heina'*" – Numbers XIV:19.

[6] As Professor Shimon Dabnof, a famous Jewish historian, once said: "knowledge always bends toward the will (*ha-da'at noteh l'ratzon*)."

The Jews of Hungary *en masse* participated in a similar mental exercise. Hungarian Prime Minister Kallay (pronounced KAH-lo-ee) enacted a series of laws against Jewish citizens, each one harsher and more restrictive than any that came before. Jews listened to his anti-Semitic speeches, broadcast from the Hungarian Parliament, but excused his rhetoric. "The Prime Minister doesn't really mean that stuff. Kallay is trying to appease Hitler; in reality, he won't apply these laws. You'll see, he won't harm the Jews." In the Hungary of the 1940s, Jewish citizens had no trouble deluding themselves with this kind of logic. They still owned their businesses – unlike Jews in Poland whose businesses had been seized. In general, Hungarian Jews were very assimilated (most adopted the country's language and culture), and were convinced that, as *mammalandische Yidden*, they would be spared the destiny of other Jews in Europe. "Everything that happened to the Carpathian Jews?" they thought, "well, that's only what happened to the Carpathian Jews."

All around them, however, was a prescription for genocidal disaster. As I mentioned earlier, laws establishing labor camps (*munkotabors*) for Jewish men aged 20-50 were already in force, and the Hungarian fascists divided these conscripted men into work units (*munkoszazods*) of 220 or 230 souls. Each unit operated under a company commander, the *Szazod Poroncsnok* (pronounced POH-ronsh-nohk); this was usually a lieutenant or captain in the Hungarian army), and a dozen or so Hungarian soldiers. This armed contingent was called the *keret* [KEH-ret] – literally, a frame or fence – which in fact did serve as a sort of human corral to confine and monitor the Jewish laborers.

The welfare of individuals in a unit depended entirely on their commander. If he was essentially a passive person, their situation could be more or less bearable. But if the commander was a pathological anti-Semite, then people under his command suffered greatly from humiliations and beatings. Later, in 1943 and '44, the life or death of a Jewish man was, in no uncertain terms, in the hands of his work battalion commander.

Near the end of April or early May 1942, I was entering some thoughts in my journal about Uncle Zecharia and his family. I had been very close with all of them, and my mood was exceptionally low. Eulogizing their untimely deaths at Kamieniec Podolski, I compared the loss of my two young cousins, Yoseph and <u>Ch</u>annah, to a pair of thriving trees being cut down while in full bloom. I glanced up from my writing and realized that the tree hiding my room had just started to bloom. Its leaves shaded my window and protected me from nosy eyes. I noted this luck in the journal and wondered, What would I do if someone cut my tree down?

That very night, when I finally dropped off into a restless sleep, I dreamed that someone chopped down my tree. The dream was terrifyingly real, and I felt exposed and in extreme danger. I awoke with a start, my heart racing, my mind filled with fear. It was dark, but I rushed to the window to make certain the tree was still there. It was, of course, and I tried to calm myself, to dismiss the whole thing as a nightmare brought on by stress. No matter how I tried, though, I wasn't able to fall back asleep.

There's no way I could have imagined what happened next. Around 8 a.m., after daylight had broken, village workmen arrived and, to my utter amazement, *cut the tree down*. Nothing was left but the freshly sawed-off stump! Other than my dream, nothing had foreshadowed this event. I hadn't noticed surveyors measuring tree trunks (or seen anything else like that), which might have subliminally inspired my dream, nor had any of the Goldbergs known about it, because surely they would have told me (they were just as happy as I was that this tree helped obscure my presence in their house). Evidently, some town official determined the foliage on the street was too thick or too close to the buildings. And now, with the tree completely gone, my window was exposed. My fearful dream had come true.[7] The workmen continued down the street, either cutting down every other tree, or thinning them out. With no tree concealing my window, protecting me, my fear – already heightened – grew greater day by day.

Soon after *Pesach* (which began in early April 1942), it was evident that I wasn't the only anxious one in the house. From time to time I caught my cousins in tense, whispered conversations. They couldn't hide their nervousness. Later, I found out why: Uncle Alter had run into a business problem with a fellow Jew (a neighbor, in

---

[7] Years later, after I had emigrated to the United States, a well-known Yiddish and Hebrew poet, Aaron Tzeitlin, authored a book entitled *The Other Reality* (written in Hebrew and published in Israel under the title *Ha-Met<u>z</u>iyut ha-A<u>ch</u>ere<u>t</u>). It dealt with the subject of telepathy and extrasensory perception. While researching his subject, Tzeitlin invited readers of the Yiddish daily *Der Tag* to write him about such experiences. I submitted this story of my dream and Tzeitlin included it in his book.

fact, who lived on the same street), and unfortunately I stumbled into the middle of their conflict. The village synagogue was just a few houses away from the Goldberg's. One Friday night after dark, I sneaked into the synagogue. Apparently, this business associate was there that evening also, and he inquired about the "strange face" attending services. Uncle Alter worried that this man would inform the authorities that he was hiding a Carpathian Jew in his house.

Their business conflict occurred around the same time that my dream came true. Maybe this stoked my imagination and magnified my fear, but in any event, I felt increasingly unsure of my safety, and decided I had better scram, fast. The invisible hand prepared to move me again.

Chapter 16

Debrecen

WHEN THEY DEPORTED MY FAMILY that Tisha b'Av *nidcheh* night, my eldest brother Eliezer, HYD, managed to escape to reunite with his wife and children in Debrecen. I longed to see him, so, from my uncle's home, I sent a postcard informing him that I'd be arriving on Tuesday. On the bottom I added a Hebrew acronym – *v'dal* – meaning "the wise will understand."[1] Where else could I have gone if not to my brother? Debrecen was a big city and though I knew it would be difficult to obtain food there without a ration card, the fear that engulfed me was very strong. My intuition told me that I must leave Bihor-Dioszeg as quickly as possible. This was the real curse: I was driven by fear, even though I couldn't see my pursuer.[2]

That Tuesday, Clarri and Piri escorted me to the train station, and to my good fortune, I did not rouse any suspicion. I bought a ticket and the train arrived promptly. With a hug and a kiss, we parted, and, with great trepidation, I entered the train. I'd never been to Debrecen before, and although I now more or less spoke the language, I still didn't have an ID card if anyone asked me to produce one. Moreover, my accent would have given me away immediately. But I arrived safely, and nobody stopped or questioned me. I hired a taxi and reached Szepesegi (pronounced SEH-peh-shehg-ee) Number 44, where my brother Eliezer and his family lived. They had two rooms – a kitchen and one additional room – in a house they rented from an elderly couple. After being separated for almost 10 months, we were so happy to see each other and be together. We were especially grateful knowing all four brothers were back in Hungary, even if scattered in different places. We were also thankful that our destiny turned out to be better than the rest of our extended family.

Living in their two small rooms were Eliezer, Shari and their sons Berzi (aged 11 or 12) and Willi (about 7 or 8). And here I came to fill their small quarters even more. I told them why I couldn't stay any longer in Bihor-Dioszeg. To make room for me, they sent the

---

[1] "*V'dal*" stands for "*v'dai l'chochem*" (literally, "enough for the wise) and is used like an ellipsis.

[2] "… and ye shall flee when none pursueth you" (*v'nastem v'ain rodaif etchem*) – from Leviticus XXVI:17. The Hebrew name for this particular chapter is *Tochacha*, meaning "warning" or "admonition."

children to Shari's sister, who also lived in Debrecen. Eliezer explained that this was a Jewish neighborhood and the local authorities very frequently conducted *rozias* (the Hungarian term for round-up or random search). Without warning, police would suddenly close off a street and search house to house, room to room, for Jews like me: anyone without local identification cards.

Considering this, therefore, Eliezer said he'd try to find me a place in a safer neighborhood. Meanwhile, he told me, "Let's find a spot here for you to lie down." When I saw the poverty of his apartment, after what he had in Torun – a big house with six large rooms – I felt awful. I was very depressed that my brother and his family lived under such conditions; I didn't know what to say.

A few days later, Eliezer found a room for me in a completely gentile neighborhood. The house belonged to a man who was a former neighbor of my sister-in-law Shari's mother, and they were on friendly terms. He was a veteran and invalid dating back to World War I. Around his house was a high fence, and the entry gate bore a plaque noting the person's name and his status as a war hero.

The edict at the time was that anybody who entered the city for longer than 48 hours had to register with the police. Anyone's house guests also had to be registered. Of course, hotel guests had to register immediately, but this law applied to people staying in private homes. This man agreed to rent me a room without registering me, and said that in case I got caught and was asked for identification, I should tell the police that I just arrived in the city that day. Naturally I was happy to agree to this condition.

While my situation had somewhat improved with my arrival in Debrecen, I learned that my parents' circumstances around the same time had worsened. It was at the end of February or early March 1942, after they successfully managed to sneak my brother Moshe and his family back to Hungary from Dolina. One day, Hungarian soldiers stationed in Torun rounded up three of the town's remaining 17 elderly Jews. The next day, these people were found dead not too far from their homes. The soldiers simply murdered them for their money and whatever valuables they could ransack from their houses. Such was the value of Jewish life.

When my parents heard of this atrocity, they immediately decided to run. My father had a sister who lived in Volova, 20 kilometers from Torun. After the deportations, a few elderly Jews remained in Volova, as well as my father's sister, Byla, and her husband Isaac Zoldan. They were only in their 60s, but Uncle Isaac was a World War I veteran and amputee from the days of the "dual monarchy" of Austria-Hungary. Even the Czechs honored these World War I invalids. For example, the Czech government only granted liquor licenses to World War I veterans; that was how Uncle Isaac owned a special wholesale store for selling whiskey. Right after the Hungarians marched into the Carpathian region in 1939, Isaac applied for his Hungarian citizenship papers, so he could continue his business. It was thanks to this bit of paperwork – his having citizenship papers – that he and his family were not deported in 1941. (In 99 percent of the cases, deportation orders were issued and carried out on the grounds that people "lacked citizenship papers." These were people who were born in their respective communities in the Carpathian – descendants of native-born people who had lived there for generations. In other words, deportation was an outrageous pretext to camouflage murders the Nazis perpetrated.)

Until I arrived in Debrecen, I didn't know about my parents' situation. I thought they were still in Torun, but Eliezer filled me in with the distressing details. My parents were able to have more contact with him because he was more or less legal – his name wasn't on the list of deportees.

The news devastated me. Here we were, four children, three with families, on the run. Now, my mother and father also were refugees. When we left them in August 1941, they still had money and seemed to be in a relatively safe situation. Now they had to flee Torun at their advanced ages, were homeless, and for all I knew penniless. How were we all going to cope? It was terrible news.

Eliezer got a job engraving tombstones. The work was physically hard and dirty. Having been in business with our father, he never in his life had done such heavy labor. I asked Eliezer if he could help me find some kind of work, so hopefully I could lessen the load on our parents. I even hinted at my intentions in a note to my father. He replied quickly, quoting from the blessing that serves to call Jews to a house of prayer: "Praiseworthy are those who dwell in Your house."[3] I understood immediately what he was implying: sit tight and don't worry about a job. And, he added, "G-d will give us as much as we will need. Stay off the streets."

---

[3] *"Ashrai yoshvai baitecha."*

After some time in Debrecen, I settled down, and my case of nerves did, too. I had some help in that regard. My mother's cousin Kylah lived in Debrecen, my great-uncle Zalman's daughter. She and her husband had three grown children: a son named Shulie and two daughters – Marta and (the youngest one) Klari, who was 16 or 17 years old. Marta was about two years younger than I, and she always invited me to go places with her. I was often nervous and didn't want to go out, but she would laugh it off and say, "Don't be afraid. Come on." Obviously, in the prime of youth, as we were then, common sense doesn't always prevail.

I would rise at eight in the morning, and rarely left the house before ten or eleven. I felt that this was a safer time of day to walk the streets. I often visited Kylah, who lived in an apartment complex where there were 10 or 12 apartments, and a courtyard under that one street number. I always felt good at their place. Shulie was out working somewhere during the day, and Kyle's husband was out, too, working in a kosher wine store, selling wholesale. Klari was still in high school. Already done with high school, Marta had bought a sewing machine and took in work sewing collars and cuffs on men's shirts. So during the day, Marta and her mother Kylah were always in the house.

A stroll that Marta and I took one sunny day turned out to be quite comical and embarrassing. We were headed to Eliezer's place a few blocks away and were about to cross the street when we passed a strange, small alley that neither of us had noticed before. Little did we know what kind of a street it was: Debrecen's red-light district. Since it was summertime, windows up and down the cramped alley were open, and prostitutes sat in each one looking out onto the sidewalks. As we passed one house, a prostitute called out to me, "Hey you, long one, why don't you come in?" Marta's face turned beet red, and I, not knowing how to react, was speechless. When I regained my composure, I told Marta that usually prostitutes were very careful not to embarrass their "regulars." I hoped that she accepted my explanation and didn't think that I was ever a customer in one of these places. After that incident, we never walked by that area again. End of story.

* * *

In June 1942, Moshe, Montze and their children wound up in Sokmar, because it was considered a safer place than C̲hust. There, they rented one room in a Jewish house. After nine months since we last saw one another in Dolina, I yearned deeply to see them again. Gathering my courage, I bought a train ticket. I didn't notify my parents about my trip for I was certain they'd tell me not to go. They were always worried about our safety.

Debrecen had two daily newspapers. One paper in particular distinguished itself as a pathologically anti-Semitic paper. It simply appealed to the lowest instincts of the mob to incite pogroms. Called *Magyar Nemzet* (*Hungarian Nation*), the newspaper was almost a carbon-copy of the German *Stürmer* that Streicher and Goebbels published. In the *Magyar Nemzet,* they serialized a so-called novel in daily installments. The novel was called *Tarnopolbul El-indult,* which means "He Who Came From Tarnopol." Of course, Tarnopol was a city in Russia, and the title implied that all the Jews in Hungary were aliens and came from the communistic Soviet Union. At the head of each chapter was a caricature of a hunchback Jew with long *pais*, a long, crooked nose and the fringes adorning his prayer shawl hanging out of his trousers – a typical Nazi style caricature. This literally illustrates the kind of atmosphere Jews had to cope with in a Hungarian city.

Naturally, Jews didn't read this paper. But I often bought it when I had to ride a streetcar or be in a public place like a train station waiting room. I'd pretend to read it or keep it in my pocket so the paper's masthead showed. This was my precaution to avoid looking suspicious. Who knows whether it really helped, but I was never stopped and asked for identification.

For this trip to Sokmar, too, I bought the paper, and after a train ride of about three hours, arrived without incident. I didn't know the address of the house where my brother Moshe and his family were staying, so I went directly to the apartment of my cousin Shoshana Heimowitz, in the hope that she knew where they were. What a happy surprise I had, finding Moshe there! We fell all over each other, hugging with tears of joy. I noticed immediately that Moshe had aged a lot in less than a year. Montze and the children weren't there. Really, it was no wonder that pain showed deeply on his face. Obviously, the strain on a father and husband in fear for his family took a greater toll than someone concerned about only himself. When we had been together in the Polish Ukraine, Zvi and I could help him very little. The only real help we provided him was after Zvi and I left on our precarious journey back to Torun. We managed to let our parents know Moshe's whereabouts, and this resulted in my father arranging for a messenger to bring them back to Hungary.

We told one another all the miracles that G-d showed us on our way back to Torun and all those we experienced since we parted in Dolina. To get a chance to see their children, Shloimi and <u>Channi</u>, I stayed two more days in Sokmar, and then returned to Debrecen. Those were a memorable two days I spent with Moshe and his family. It would be the last time I saw the children and Montze before they perished in the fires of the *Shoah*. Later, I saw Moshe one more time.

Oh G-d, you are the Merciful Father. But where were you when the German *Ashmedai* butchered all of the suckling babies? I will never understand this. And yet you are also the Judge of Truth.

I took the 10 p.m. train back to Debrecen. It usually took about three hours by rail from Sokmar to Debrecen. At night during wartime, the trains traveled without lights. Tiny, red lamps inside the cars provided the only illumination, and the curtains were tightly drawn over the windows. I had bought a first-class ticket because I thought this was another way to avoid looking suspicious. The first-class compartments had room enough for four people, and had plush seats; when I entered my compartment (they were numbered and assigned by ticket), it was empty.

At the next stop, a man entered my compartment and sat down without saying a word. For quite a while, we eyed each other in the dim light. I spoke Hungarian pretty well by this time, but it was with an accent – so I hesitated starting a conversation. From time to time I lit a cigarette, to catch a glimpse of my neighbor and to try to see if he was Jewish, but I couldn't tell. I didn't expect him to be a Jew, but I was hoping. By and by, the conductor entered and greeted us with a "Good evening." We each handed him our tickets; he punched them and then moved on to the next compartment. (His leaving didn't make me any less anxious, because during the war, conductors often acted as informers. If they thought someone looked suspicious, they informed on him at the next station; Secret Police would then show up and confront that person.)

After almost three hours of silence, I took courage and asked the man where he was traveling. This particular train was headed to

Budapest, through Debrecen. He told me that he was getting off at the next stop – Debrecen.

As he spoke, I detected an accent that indicated he also wasn't Hungarian-born. "Where in Debrecen are you headed?" I asked. "Maybe we can take a taxi together." He handed me the street name and number; I recognized the address to be in a Jewish neighborhood.

We got off the train together. The station platform was better-lit, now giving us an excellent look at one another. He was a young man, about my age, in his early 20s. I took a chance and asked him whether he spoke Yiddish.[4] He instantly nodded. A heavy weight fell off our shoulders. It was as if two brothers in the same predicament recognized each other. He told me that he was a refugee, like me, from Slovakia, and that he was wandering from city to city now. I shall never forget the sad irony of this encounter: we sat in the same compartment for hours, silent, in unwarranted fear of each other.

We bade each other good-bye and parted. I headed by foot to my room because it was close to the station; he took a taxi because his destination was further away. A few weeks later, we met again on a main street in Debrecen, but we purposely didn't acknowledge each other, because there were police or detectives on almost every corner.

In 1942, the Jewish community was functioning more or less normally. Hungary's Jews still hoped and believed the fate that befell the Carpathian, Slovakian and Polish Jews would bypass them. Had the Hungarian Jews really felt they'd meet the same fate as the Carpathian Jewish refugees, I was certain they would have made a greater effort to save themselves.

A few days after I returned from Sokmar, the detectives, with the cooperation of the local police, made a round-up. They cordoned off blocks of the city; even the city traffic of trolley cars, buses and taxis was stopped, and a horde of police and detectives checked every person for identification papers. If they had an iota of suspicion, they detained those people. They rounded up hundreds and took them to the police station. It was clear that they were looking for Jewish refugees, like me, who were hiding out in the city. Round-ups like this lasted for a few hours. Nobody could escape from inside the cordoned off area.

By bribing the local officials, leaders of the Jewish community could get advance warning that a round-up was to occur at a certain time and place. They would then tip off many of the refugees,

---

[4] *"Mir kennen redden Yiddish?"*

enabling them to skip town or hide in safer places. But this time nobody got advance warning. It was the first round-up I escaped.

The Hungarian World War I veteran who rented me a room also had a daughter, and she lived at home with him. She was quite a few years older than me, but one time when she needed an escort, she invited me to go with her to the theater. I confessed I was afraid to go, but she reassured me I had nothing to fear. "When you are with me," she said, "no harm will come to you." This turned out to be true.

The morning of the round-up, she happened to be outside and spotted the police activity a few blocks away. Rushing home, she entered my room, instructed me not to go out, and explained why. She brought me breakfast and said she'd let me know when it was clear. I thanked her profusely. Until that moment I had no idea she had a crush on me. I realized then, as the saying goes, that I had found favor in her eyes. My good luck at staying in this house was also due to the war-veteran plaque affixed to the front gate. No one ever entered the house during this particular round-up, nor when any others were staged. I felt fortunate to be in this war hero's home, and thus more or less safe.

Weeks stretched on like that – we were always on edge, wary of round-ups or informants. At the same time we Jews hoped that a sudden miracle would reverse the circumstances that had turned our lives upside down.

One day I decided to visit my brother Zvi in Mariopoch, which wasn't too far from Debrecen (about a two-hour train ride). Eliezer lived near the train station, at which an electric train stopped on its way to the city of Nyearbator. From Nyearbator I had to transfer to a regular train that made its first stop in Mariopoch. At Nyearbator, I had to wait approximately 30 to 40 minutes for connections. As usual, I took a seat in the waiting room and began to read my newspaper, the anti-Semitic *Hungarian Nation*. Suddenly a bunch of loud hoodlums rushed in to the waiting room, dragging a young yeshiva student by his *pais*, pushing him around and laughing wildly. They ripped his hat off his head and threw it on the floor. The poor boy was terrified. He couldn't have been older than 15 or 16. The entire waiting room of people all laughed loudly, greatly amused by the sight of that frightened boy. I didn't laugh, but, fearing for my own life, neither did I dare to intercede. In the end, no one tried to stop this mob of wild beasts; no one came to the boy's aid. I couldn't bear to watch this cruel orgy, so I slipped out quietly to another waiting room, and, to my good fortune, my train arrived a few minutes later. Boarding the train, I promptly sat down and continued to read my paper.

Wild laughter from that waiting room still rang in my ears — exactly like hyenas fighting among themselves over a kill. I was amazed how much courage the boy displayed by braving the streets in his black brimmed hat, long coat, black pants and long side locks.[5] It was a measure of his conviction to his beliefs. And here I was, 22 years old, six-foot-two-and-a-half, and didn't have the courage to help him. Of course I'm certain I was not alone. Surely there were other Nyearbator Jews in the waiting room, without *pais*, like me, but they, too, were afraid to lift a hand. Unlike me, they may have had citizenship papers and the lawful right to be there, but they also remained silent.

Although it didn't relieve my conscience, I came up with a possible explanation why neither they nor I tried to help our Jewish brother. I think it dates back to the Bar Kochba rebellion in 135 CE, when we Jews lost our homeland. Since then (and before 1948), we hadn't had the national zeal that people have when they dwell on their own land. It is very hard to be a hero when you're a refugee.

The train stopped in Mariopoch. I got off and started to walk toward the village. I had never been there before, and it was quite a distance to my cousin Shonie Fixler's place, but it was hard to get lost because there was only one long street, and Zvi had written me directions. From a distance, I saw a patrol of two gendarmes, the "roosters," coming toward me. The sight of them filled me with terror and anxiety, but I had no choice other than to keep on walking. I came face to face with them and said hello. They asked where I was going. I told them that I was coming from Debrecen to visit my cousin, Shandor Fixler. As I mentioned the name Fixler, I felt their questions become less harsh. They asked how long I was going to stay there. A few days, I said. Then they let me go. I breathed a little easier and picked up my pace. Soon my brother Zvi

---

[5] One could ask why this young man – or any of Europe's Jews – would draw attention to himself by continuing to dress or act differently than the rest of the population. A Midrash by 11th century commentator Rabbi Tuviah Eliezer may shed some light on this choice. He concluded that the Jews merited liberation from slavery in Egypt for three reasons: they did not change their names, their language or their national clothing.

came toward me. When we met, we embraced and he noticed that I was nervous. He asked me why, and I told him about my encounter with the authorities, but he calmed me down and assured me that I had nothing to fear, because our cousin Shonie was very friendly with the commander of the gendarmes.

It was a great joy for Zvi and me to be together for the first time since we parted in Sokmar. I told him why I had to leave Bihor-Dioszeg; I also described the so-called apartment where Eliezer was living; mainly I told him that I saw our brother Moshe and the children. We were very happy that all four brothers were back in Hungary, finally, and not in the hell of Poland. Zvi told me that he was teaching Jewish children _Chumash_ and Rashi every day, and that in Shonie's house they set aside a special room for his class. He also said this village was in a rural area, and that there was no shortage of food whatsoever. (Mariopoch is within the Nyear area, which is considered to be the bread-basket of Hungary. From this area, Hungarians supplied bread for the entire German _Wehrmacht_ during the war.)

In Mariopoch lived another of our cousins, Shonie Fixler's older brother Shmuel. He was a land owner, a farmer. (At that time Jews still had land ownership rights.) And in his house there was also an abundance of food. Zvi and I were both invited there for _Shabbos_. We had a great time for the few days that we spent together.

Our cousin Shmuel survived the _Shoah_ alone, losing his wife and their three children. After the _Shoah_, under difficult conditions he emigrated from Hungary to what was then Palestine. There, he returned to agriculture, joining an agricultural collective (_moshavah_) to farm and raise cattle. This was the same kind of work he had done in Hungary, and he loved it. One morning in 1950 when he got up before dawn to tend to his cattle, an Arab killed him, HYD – another _Shoah_ survivor slain in his own land.

I told Zvi that Eliezer received a letter from the lawyer from Budapest whom our father had hired to work on our citizenship papers. The lawyer assured us that we'd receive these papers shortly. We believed and hoped that this would protect us and that, even though we were Carpathian-born Jews, we would have the same freedom to come and go and the same destiny as the Hungarian Jewry. Eliezer was supposed to travel the following week to Budapest and bring a certain amount of cash to the lawyer, who wrote that he had to "grease the government wheels" in order to get our papers faster. This was another way of squeezing the last drop of blood from the Carpathian Jews. How much aggravation, heartache and financial demands afflicted our father. We who lived in Torun for generations and generations suddenly had to go through all this.

Later, we encountered another obstacle. In the ministry in Budapest that issued the citizenship papers, the official insisted that the papers had to be sent by certified mail. This official said he could not just hand it over to the lawyer, but rather he had to send it to the local government official in Torun for authorization. Naturally, we could not travel to Torun – it would have been like going straight into the lion's den. Zvi and I discussed this situation that *Shabbos* with our cousin Shonie, and he came up with the idea that maybe the lawyer could persuade the official in Budapest to mail the papers to the local official in Mariopoch. With Shonie's influence, Zvi and I would then be able to sign for our papers right there. For a great sum of money, the official in the ministry agreed to these terms, and mailed the citizenship papers in our names to the local city hall in Mariopoch. Thanks to the clout that our cousin Shonie Fixler had, a few months later Zvi and I finally got our citizenship papers.

In the meantime, after staying just three or four days with Zvi and Shonie, I traveled back to Debrecen, optimistic that we'd soon get our papers and perhaps I'd also be able to get some kind of a job, in order to ease the financial burden on our parents.

Sometime later, cousin Shonie and my brother Zvi came to Debrecen for the day to see Eliezer and his family. On their way back to Mariopoch, however, they were trapped in a round-up. Because Shonie was a resident and could show his identification papers, he was let go, but Zvi was jailed and taken to Nyearbator. Eliezer and I didn't even know what happened to him until later. What little joy Zvi and I had in being together with Eliezer, whom Zvi hadn't seen in such a long time, quickly evaporated when he was detained and taken to jail. He certainly didn't know how soon, if at all, Shonie would be able to get him out. Zvi was lucky that Shonie knew where they were taking him. The next day he traveled to Nyearbator, and I guess through his pull (and surely some money) he got Zvi out of jail and back to Mariopoch. Our cousin Shonie was a real angel.

The ensuing weeks were full of strain and tension. News from the eastern battlefront was very depressing. The Germans and their allies, the Hungarians and Italians, recorded one victory after other, deep inside Russia. The situation seemed hopeless. But in September

1942, I received good news that my citizenship papers arrived in Mariopoch. I traveled there shortly and, with Shonie's help, I finally had the document in hand. It gave me a little lift and some hope. At last, I thought, if I were asked for identification, I'd have something to show. Right away I had two copies made of my document in Debrecen. At that time, of course, there were no copying machines; in order to make copies, a photographer secured the paper with thumbtacks at all four corners and literally photographed it. This left four tiny holes in the corners of the paper – a detail that proved important to me later.

At the beginning of October 1942, now that I had my citizenship papers, I decided to travel to see my parents. I had received a letter from my mother, who hinted that my father was seriously ill. They were in Volova with my uncle Isaac Zoldan, so I boarded a train to Chust, and from there took a bus. Naturally I left the copies of my citizenship papers with Eliezer in Debrecen, and took the original with me. When I boarded the bus in Chust, a strange feeling came over me. I couldn't have known then, of course, that this would be my last time in the Carpathian. But I had a kind of premonition, a feeling that something very bad might happen, and my pulse raced terribly. Just before Volova, I began to think about how close I was to my birthplace, Torun.

As soon as my bus arrived at the terminal in Volova, two detectives came over to the door and started to ask everybody for identification. All of the passengers in front of me got out, but when it was my turn to get off, they told me to wait. They detained two more men and let the rest go. The detectives took me to one room (they brought the other two men to another room) on the second floor of a nearby building, on the main street of Volova. In the room where I was, there was only a desk and two chairs, one in front and another behind the desk. One detective told me to sit down and then he said, "Now, tell me straight. Right away. You were born in Torun. And how did you get this citizenship paper? You were deported to the other side." I denied this, naturally, insisting that I had never been deported, that I'd been living in Mariopoch for a long time now.

He examined my citizenship paper closely and noticed that it had a tiny hole on each corner. Then he yelled at me: "You made a copy of this paper!"

"Yes I did," I said, trying to maintain my composure. "I left a copy in Mariopoch."

"But you were deported to Poland," he started to scream, and he looked at the list that he pulled out from his desk. "Tell me the truth," he yelled. "I know you were there!"

Still I insisted I was never deported, and he yelled back, "You were in Poland!"

Then, from a drawer in the desk, he pulled out a snake-like leather cudgel and started hitting me over the head. I fell off my chair. Then the second detective came into the room and he started to kick me in the head while I was lying on the floor. Both started to curse, "Dirty Jew! Tell us the truth now!"

Rising from the floor, I still didn't answer their question. So again they struck my head with their leather clubs. Again they demanded, "You were on the other side of the border, yes or no?" I kept on denying it, and a hail of blows rained down on me from both sides, from both of them. Blood started to run from my head and my ears. As I slumped to the floor, they shoved me one to the other and at the same time lashed me with their sticks. I tried to protect my head with my hands, but when they hit harder and harder, my hands dropped and I fell to the floor again. Then they started to kick me in the head with their shoes. I realized that if I didn't admit that I had been on the other side, these beasts would kill me. On the floor, I moaned, "Yes, yes, I was on the other side." Then they lifted me up and, with a Hungarian curse, they escorted me out of the room to the steps, gave me a good shove, and I half-fell, half stumbled down the stairs like a dead weight. That I didn't break any bones was a miracle. "Scram," they yelled. "You dirty Jew! We don't want to see you in front of our eyes anymore."

It was dark, and I lay on the floor until I mustered strength to get up and leave the building. I realized I didn't have my hat (it flew off when they started beating me over the head), and, of course, my citizenship paper was back in the room, too. My Uncle Isaac's house was not too far from there. With my last ounce of strength, I managed to drag myself to the house. There, my Aunt Byla let me into the room where my parents were. When they saw me, they almost fainted. My eyes were almost completely swollen shut; I could barely see. My whole head was bloody. My mother washed me, and applied cold, wet towels to my swollen and discolored face. Shocked and aggrieved, my father barely spoke a word to me. Both of them were in great pain to see me this way. I tried to reassure them that I was okay.

In truth, I regretted that I came, not because I got a good beating, but because I realized then that I caused my parents great emotional anguish. My dear mother Rifka was always the strong one in my family, courageous and optimistic. No matter how I looked, she was only too happy to see me – especially after a year's lapse – but seeing me this way really distressed her. The last time I had seen my father was when we reached <u>Ch</u>ust near the end of 1941. Of course we were hoping for a happy reunion after a year, but this horrible incident marred it. My mother kept on changing the cold, wet towels on my face and head all night long, and around the morning-time I fell asleep.

I was 22 years old; never before in my life had I ever been beaten up like that. I am convinced that when the goon detectives spotted the tiny pin holes in my document and realized I had copies, I was spared from being deported again – or worse. (A year and a half or two years later, in 1944, even citizenship papers didn't help people anymore.)

Because my citizenship paper was taken away from me, my father went next door the following morning to a old friend, Yosel Steinberg, to ask his help in retrieving it. Yosel was in the printing business, and his was one of the few Jewish families left behind in Volova. Calming my father down, Mr. Steinberg said that his daughter would be able to get my citizenship paper back. He also advised my father to tell me to lay low for right now, but that I should get out of Volova and back to Debrecen as soon as she retrieved it for me.

I awoke late the next morning, my body aching, and tried to downplay the beating episode, certainly not wanting to cause any further anxiety to my parents. My father told me all of Mr. Steinberg's advice. A few days later, Miss Steinberg succeeded in retrieving my citizenship paper. She was an angel who was especially helpful to my family, as she had some kind of access to the head of the police department and other Hungarian officials in Volova. She was the person who, with my father, arranged for the detective and his car to smuggle Zvi and me to <u>Ch</u>ust.[6]

---

[6] Years later, in the late 1960s, I saw Miss Steinberg in Brooklyn, at a Bar Mitzvah arranged by my cousin Moshe Zoldan. I was very happy to see that Miss Steinberg

Though I was recovering from the beating, my face was still black and blue. My main concern, during that time, focused on my parents' grief over the matter and the situation they were in. My father had gotten so old and gray. He had also lost a lot of weight. And he coughed a lot, despite his having given up smoking nearly a year or so earlier. (I gave up smoking many years ago, in the late 1960s, and it was none too easy; having been a smoker myself, I understand how hard it must have been for him to quit back then, particularly in such a tense situation and environment.)

In the morning of the third or fourth day of my visit to my parents, I left Volova. I went to the bus terminal, hoping that I wouldn't run into a round-up, let alone the detectives who beat me. I didn't. I was very happy that I didn't have to look at their faces again. There were only a few soldiers. They allowed me to pass, and I boarded the bus. Arriving in Chust, I immediately went to the train station. To my good fortune, I didn't have to wait too long for a train connection, and I arrived uneventfully to Debrecen. Then, I went directly to my residence. For several days, I didn't go to see Eliezer, or even inform him that I had returned, because I wanted to wait till my face healed a bit more. Several days later, I did go over to Eliezer's place, but he happened to be out. Only my sister-in-law Shari, HYD, was there. When she saw my face, she plied me with questions, wanting to know what had happened. When I told her, she broke down in tears. I did my best to calm her, saying that other than the black-and-blue patches under my eyes, I felt fine, and in a few days these marks would also disappear. Finally I confided to her my main concern: that my father looked very ill.

For the first time in my life, very sad and troubling thoughts entered my mind that, G-d forbid, I might lose my father. The *tsuris* he went through and was still going through was taking its toll. On that Tisha b'Av *nidcheh* of 1941, he lost his younger brother Zecharia and his entire family. He lost his older sister Sara Chaimowics and half her family (half escaped the Holocaust because they emigrated to Palestine in the late 1920s). His brother-in-law, my mother's younger brother Berel Drimmer's huge family was also wiped out. And now, all of us, my father's own family, were in a dire and terrible situation as refugees.

---

survived the *Shoah*, so I could personally thank her for her acts of kindness (I had never had a chance to thank her for her help back in 1942).

Chapter 17

The First Memoir

THE SUMMER OF 1942 PASSED FAIRLY UNEVENTFULLY for me. I spent my days in Debrecen, reading a lot and writing about my experiences in the Ukraine. Life became a little easier for me because of my citizenship paper, and I grew a bit more courageous about walking around the city. But still, after my experience in Volova, I understood that it was advisable for me not to rely too much on this document. I still felt like a hunted person.

It worried me sick that my father and mother were refugees and homeless, and even more that my father was seriously ill. But my mother's cousin Kylah encouraged me to go out, to be happy and joyful that all of my brothers were now safely back in Hungary. So, from time to time, I went out with Marta, Kylah's daughter. This little bit of social activity was what I needed to keep from falling into depression or despair.

Kylah's husband, whose name I don't remember, was a very observant Jew. A great man of faith, he'd tell me all the good and hopeful news. In Hebrew, there's a saying that "a good person spreads good news."[1] According to him, Hitler soon would be defeated. Who knew if he believed that, or whether he was just trying to lift my spirits.

Of Debrecen's two daily newspapers, Jews naturally read the more moderate one (not the anti-Semitic *Hungarian Nation*). In it was a column that dealt strictly with current military strategies. The columnist was a military man – a colonel, I believe – who hinted between the lines that Germany's pronouncements of battle victories were not all that they said they were. Jews in Debrecen extrapolated optimism and hope from this. They'd discuss this column and parse every word, "to make a thousand distinctions"[2] – like the great commentator Rashi interpreting the _Chumash_. This serves as another example of how knowledge bent toward desire: we always found good news in the deplorable newspaper headlines.

In the beginning of December 1942, we received a letter from my mother in which she informed us that my father was very sick and that she was taking him to _Chust_ to a lung specialist. Eliezer and

---

[1] *"Ish tov m'vasair tov."*

[2] In Hebrew, *"L'havdil eleph havdalot."*

I contacted Zvi in Mariopoch. We decided that he should come to Debrecen, and that all three of us would travel together to Ch̲ust to check on our father. (This was the first time in almost a year and a half that Zvi would get to see his wife Piri and son Buchyk, who were in Kalin and were able to come visit him in Chust.) We also notified Moshe in Sokmar to come to Ch̲ust as well.

As soon as we got off the train in Ch̲ust, we spotted a group of Hungarian gendarmes stopping every Jew. Surrounding my brothers and me and about thirty other travelers, these gendarmes pointed their bayonets at us as if we were dangerous bandits and led us to some kind of military barrack in the city. It was around six or seven o'clock in the evening, and the streetlights were on. People on the sidewalks looked at us. I overheard them speaking, one saying to the other, "Those are just *Zhiddes*" (Jews, in Ukrainian) – meaning that this round-up was a non-issue as far as they were concerned. The gendarmes brought us into a large hall and then called us in, one by one, to a side office. There, an officer interrogated everyone as to where he was going, where he was from, and he checked our papers.

One young Jew among us was from Poland and had escaped a Polish ghetto during liquidation, only to wind up in Hungary. He didn't speak a word of Hungarian, and of course had no papers. Since he didn't know the language, he was particularly suspect.

This poor fellow was extremely nervous, and asked me, "What do you do here? What do you do now? What shall I do?" With a look of great despair on his face, he kept on praying, "Oh G-d, oh G-d, let this gendarme get a *g'derrim farknipung*." This was a term I'd never heard before. When I asked him what it was, he explained that it meant an intestinal knot that comes on very suddenly and immobilizes a person.

Suddenly this Polish Jew made a bold move: dashing to the door, he fled the barracks. When the gendarme noticed that the door was shut, he chased after him. We heard a few shots, but we never found out what happened to him – whether he was shot and killed, just wounded or escaped.

When our turn came to enter the office for interrogation, we told them the truth: that our father was in Ch̲ust for medical treatment by a local doctor, and that was why the three of us came there. The gendarme examined our papers and, thankfully, let us go.

From there we went to the house where we knew our parents were staying – a small hotel set up like a bed-and-breakfast. The owner knew our family, and when we arrived he told us that our parents already were aware of our being detained. Again, my sick father and my mother had to go through the agony of worrying about whether something terrible had happened to us. (It was fortunate that Moshe was not with us; that would have made them worry even more. Moshe arrived the next day.)

After giving our father tests over a few days, the doctor in <u>C</u>hust told Eliezer that Dad's condition was very grave. We were all shocked by this terrible news. Then Eliezer said that he wanted us to take our father to Debrecen. It was a bigger city and had better doctors and hospitals. Naturally we all agreed, hoping that maybe in a hospital in Debrecen they would find a cure for him.

But before we could leave, my father had some business to attend to. At that time a German gentile by the name of Schrammel lived in <u>C</u>hust. He was an employee at a Jewish firm in Budapest called Holas, one that dealt in lumber. Since my father had been in the lumber trade and done business with this firm, he knew Schrammel. One of the first laws that took effect when the Hungarians occupied our part of Carpathia was that Jews were prohibited from trading in lumber. So in <u>C</u>hust, Holas kept Schrammel as a "*Strohmann*" – a quasi-executive officer who would sign all official business documents.

My father owned close to 500 acres of forest in the early 1930s. (Each forest in the area had a name, and my father's was called the Leptitsia.) During the Great Depression our family went through financial hardship and also suffered from what we now call a cash-flow problem. My mother had urged my father then to sell the lumber in the Leptitsia, and not be so tight-fisted. But my father told her, "The Leptitsia is still too young to cut now. We have to wait about 10 or 15 years." Now of course he needed to get some money, whatever was possible, so he asked us to accompany him to see Schrammel and try to sell him the lumber from that forest. Schrammel wouldn't have any problem obtaining a special permit from the ministry to cut the lumber.

Our father proposed that Schrammel give him 10,000 *pengas* as a down payment now, and pay the rest after he finished cutting. He knew how many cubic meters of lumber he had there. All Schrammel had to do was tell Dad how much he cut and he would take his word for it. Of course, Schrammel agreed to a deal like that. He suddenly became the owner of the whole forest, and there was no way that my father could have somebody check it out. So Schrammel gave my father the 10,000 *pengas*, even though we all knew that there was enough lumber for 20 times that amount. But I think Dad also realized the dire situation he was in and that this exchange was in effect a fire-sale. It was also evident to me that Dad took us along to witness the deal with Schrammel because he knew how seriously ill he was. Perhaps he had hoped that something would happen soon to defeat Hitler, and that he wanted us to know what the deal was for after the war. I can only imagine how painful his decision was: the Leptitsia was the crown jewel of his achievements as a forest owner.

My father often told me the story how he bought the Leptitsia. Somehow he found out that a baron wanted to sell his forest. This baron owned thousands and thousands of acres, all around our area. Contacting the baron personally, Dad asked him if he wanted to sell the Leptitsia, and the baron asked right away, "Who is the buyer? Who wants to buy it?"

My father realized immediately that if he said he wanted to buy it, the baron would refuse. Why? Because Dad was too young then, only in his 20s. So my father claimed his uncle wanted to purchase it. The deal was made. Uncle Zalman bought it from the baron and then later transferred it to my father, as a resale.

By the end of December 1942, with heavy hearts we parted from our mother, who returned to Volova. Moshe went back to Sokmar, and Zvi traveled back to Mariopoch. Only Eliezer, Dad and I went to Debrecen. We were traveling in the evening and were fortunate to find an empty seat for our father; the train was overfilled, with people standing in the aisles. Certainly, Dad would not have been able to stand for the four hours it took to get from Chust to Debrecen. We regretted that we hadn't bought first class train tickets, which would have guaranteed each of us a reserved seat. But it was too late now to change.

As usual, the train we traveled on had dim lights in the coaches; our particular coach had only one tiny red light. The dark hours in the train stretched on for an eternity, and I was filled with sober thoughts. As a young single man, I had no worries in my life until the war started. And even when it did, I felt protected under the wings of my dear parents. Things drastically changed Tisha b'Av of 1941. Suddenly I was thrown into a situation where I had to fend for my life, yet still I felt reassured that my caring parents would be there for me whenever they could. Now, in this coach, it hit me: I was on the verge of losing my father forever, and I was gripped by terrible fear and pain.

Every so often, we asked Dad how he felt, and he tried to reassure us that he was okay. This long trip had to be very hard on him, in his weak condition. Finally, we arrived safely in Debrecen. We hired a horse-drawn coach and driver and he drove us to Eliezer's tiny apartment, which consisted of one room, a little corridor and a kitchen that served as home to him, Shari and their two children.

Shari had no idea that Eliezer would bring Dad to Debrecen; he hadn't notified her. We made an on-the-spot decision to bring him, and telephones at that time were not as common as they are now. Nevertheless, Shari received her father-in-law with great love and care. She acted like she was a daughter to our parents, and they reciprocated.

How did they arrange the first night's sleeping conditions in that one room? I don't know. Not to be in the way, I departed to my room at the Hungarian veteran's home. Later, the next day, Shari arranged to send the two children, Berzi and Willi, to stay with her sister who lived in Debrecen. She also had a brother and an uncle who lived there. I doubt very much if today's children and in-laws would behave towards their parents as Eliezer and Shari did in 1942.

Soon Eliezer contacted the Jewish doctor, a friend of the Krauss family. He came to us at the apartment. After examining our father, he told Eliezer to bring him to his office. Not only did the doctor want to take some more tests, but he also wanted to inspect Dad's lungs under what he called a Roentgen machine. We had never before seen or heard of an X-ray machine, and the concept of the doctor being able to see inside the body to examine the lungs with this device amazed us. Meanwhile, the physician also wrote out some prescriptions for medication: by then, Dad was breathing very heavily and coughing a lot.

One week later, this doctor contacted another Jewish doctor, a lung specialist who still worked in the city hospital. With the other physician's help, he tried to hospitalize Dad. But it wasn't a simple thing at that time for a bearded Jew to be accepted by a city hospital. Still, the doctor succeeded, and Dad was admitted. He was able to stay in the hospital for about a week or ten days (until sometime in the middle of January 1943), after which they discharged him, with the excuse that he didn't need special treatment, only lots of rest.

The family doctor came almost every day to see Dad in this one-room apartment. And he kept on trying out all kinds of medicines to lessen the pain and the cough. Dad had lost a lot of weight, and in a very short time he complained that all the bones in his body hurt him. The doctor didn't paint a rosy picture for us. He told us the truth about our father's condition: he had TB, but he also had a very strong heart, and his blood pressure was good, so that's why he was holding up the way he did.[3]

From time to time, Shari's uncle Romi would come to visit Dad. Romi was a very respected personality among the Jews in Debrecen, the leader of the Orthodox Jewish community. Debrecen was one of the few cities besides Budapest that had two congregations. One was the Orthodox congregation and the other was called the neologue congregation (comparable to the Conservative movement in the United States). Romi had rabbinic ordination, as well as a degree from a secular university, although I never knew what area his degree was in. Dad enjoyed Romi's visits very much. Among their many topics of conversation was, inevitably, the subject of the war. When my father asked him how the fight against Hitler was going, Romi would always be very optimistic and say, "The defeat is coming very soon."

At the beginning of February 1943, new persecutions and terrible edicts afflicted the Jews in the Debrecen area. Suddenly one morning I spotted along the streets placards plastered with new laws against us: "Attention Male Jews! Every Jew between 18 and 50 must register for the *munkotabors* at such-and-such locations. Failure to register is punishable by death. If the police and the gendarmes find a Jew between these ages, he will be executed." Whereas in 1939 or '40, you received your draft notice for service in the *munkotabors* by mail, now these placards essentially announced the Hungarians' means of rounding up all Jews, regardless of their physical condition, for forced hard labor. What it amounted to was that we Jews again were further stripped of our rights.

According to the records on my date of birth – 1920 – I was supposed to register on February 21, 1943, in a city in the area of

---

[3] As a heavy smoker, my father could have had lung cancer as well, although I don't remember the doctor saying as much.

Zimbürgen, formerly in Romania. I don't recall the city's name. But the tremendous panic that suddenly seized the Jewish community in Debrecen especially hit home with Jewish refugees from the Carpathians and Slovakia, who were then hiding out in Debrecen and didn't have papers. They fled the city and sneaked into Budapest, where the decrees were at least a bit milder.

I decided that I would not hide out any longer, in order not to place any more burdens on or worry my parents too much. Then, too, I decided that whatever happened to the "community of Israel"[4] should happen to me. I would share my people's destiny. Hiding was difficult and dangerous, as the incident in Volova proved, and I was tired of it. I would take my chances in the *munkotabor*.

This was not an easy decision to make, since the climate in 1943 for Debrecen's Jews could be ugly. For example, my father's younger sister Jutta called from Bereziv to inquire about his condition. Since in those days not everybody – especially not Jews – had telephones, when someone wished to make a phone call, he or she went to the local post office and ordered a telephone connection; usually it was arranged for two or three hours later. The local post office clerk would phone a post office in the city of the person to be reached. Then a postal deliverer would be sent out with a message notifying the other person that so-and-so was calling him from such-and-such place, so he should come to the post office by a certain time to receive the telephone call. The person would then come at the designated time, with this notice in hand, to the post office, where there were seven to 10 phone booths. A clerk would make the phone connection, and then direct the person to pick up the receiver in one of the booths.

We received such notification of Aunt Jutta's call at Eliezer's address, and I was chosen to go to the post office to receive it. When I arrived at the main post office in Debrecen and handed my notice to the clerk, he asked me to sit down and wait until he would tell me in which booth I should pick up the call.

A policeman was on duty in the main lobby of the post office all the time, and as soon as I sat down I noticed in my peripheral vision that he was eyeing me suspiciously. Newspapers were sold in the lobby, so I picked one up and tried to make myself inconspicuous by reading it. But he came toward me anyway, just as the postal clerk called over to me and told me to go to one of the booths. I stood up and went in, but the policeman followed me and didn't allow me to

---

[4] In Hebrew, "*klal Yisroel*."

close the booth's door. In the booth were two tiny receivers, one hanging on either side of the walls. I was supposed to put both receivers to my ears. (For people who grew up with telephones everywhere, this might sound strange, but that's the way it was.)

As soon as I picked up one receiver, the policeman picked up the other one and listened in on my conversation. My Aunt Jutta spoke in Yiddish and asked, "How is your father's condition?"[5] But I answered her in Hungarian. To whatever questions she asked, I kept replying in Hungarian. Finally she asked me why I wasn't speaking in Yiddish, and I explained about the policeman. When she heard that, she got terribly worried that she'd caused me a lot of trouble by phoning.

When I finished this conversation with Jutta, I plucked up some courage and asked the policeman a question. "Do I look suspicious to you? Like some kind of a suspect?" And at the same time I pulled out my citizenship paper.

He examined the paper and asked me where I lived. I told him. Then he asked me how tall I was. I told him I was a hundred and eighty-seven centimeters (6-foot 2-½-inches), and then he gave me back the paper and let me go.

This was the only time during my stay in Debrecen that I was checked, in spite of having my citizenship paper stamped by the interior ministry in Budapest. But it shows how Jews were persecuted and oppressed merely because we were from Abraham's seed.[6]

---

[5] *"Vus macht der tateh?"*
[6] In Hebrew, *"Mi-zerra Avraham."*

Chapter 18

Avraham Zalman

I PREPARED TO REGISTER FOR THE WORK CAMP on the evening of Friday, February 21, 1943. It was a cold winter day, so I dressed in warm clothing, and trekked off to the train station.

Parting from my father was especially painful. His eyes filled with tears as I tried to calm him and tell him it wouldn't last too long. I felt reason for hope because at the beginning of that month, the Russians broke through the lines in Stalingrad, and the German General Paulus, along with his 250,000 German soldiers, surrendered to them. This was a very great victory – the whole course of the war changed at that time in favor of the Allies. Military historians agree that this date was the beginning of the end for Hitler. Regretfully, it took two more bitter and bloody years for the world and especially the Jews to see the end of this nightmare.

At the station was a special train that awaited all the young male Jews from Debrecen. That evening we departed, traveled all night, and arrived early in the morning at a city whose name I can't remember, but it belonged formerly to Romania, in the region that was called Zimbürgen. The city was covered with a white blanket of snow, and it was extremely cold, even though the sun shone.

We inquired about directions to the military barracks. When we got there, we said to the commandant: "We are here, according to the orders of the Debrecen authorities." The commander of these barracks was totally surprised and told us that he had no orders to accept us – nor had he room for us in the camp. One of our head spokesmen then asked the commandant to give us a letter attesting to as much, since without such a document we would have been afraid to travel back to Debrecen. Thankfully, this officer was a decent person and he obliged us.

Our spokesman had an acquaintance, a lawyer in this city; he went to him and somehow made a few hundred copies of this paper and distributed one to each of us. We were very happy with this set of circumstances, of course, and were ready to travel back to Debrecen, but the train was scheduled only to leave in the evening, so we had to wait half a day in the city. I went over to the post office and posted a telegram with these four words in it: "I'm coming back tomorrow." Actually, I didn't want to give the reasons, but just wanted my father and Eliezer to know that I was returning. I knew that this would give my ailing father pleasure – the best medicine in the world.

One group of Jewish boys decided to stay overnight in that city and travel the following day, but another group of us went to the train station around 6 p.m. to wait for our train. I became acquainted with a fellow in this group by the name of David Weingarten who lived very near Debrecen, only one stop before mine. As we arrived roughly around midnight at the train stop before Debrecen, we noticed some turmoil at the station. Local gendarmes were detaining all the boys on this train. They ordered all of them to get off, even though most of them were traveling to Debrecen. I didn't realize what was going on, but David Weingarten grasped it right away, and he said, "Just come with me. We'll go across the tracks, not to the waiting room. Just the opposite." He knew the place well, being a native, and his parents lived very close to the station. I followed him and we jumped off the other side of the train, crossed some tracks, and soon safely arrived at his parents' house.

His parents rejoiced at his return, and we told them what had transpired. They were very friendly toward me and I stayed there overnight. The next morning we found out that all those other boys were detained, so I was afraid to travel by the same train to Debrecen. David's parents suggested it would be safer to take an electric trolley car instead that traveled from there to Debrecen. I heeded their advice, and arrived safely.

My family and I had a joyful reunion. Interestingly enough, the mood in the Jewish community in Debrecen at the time was upbeat, in spite of the recent labor camp edicts. By then, everybody had heard how the war was turning against the Nazis after Stalingrad. Every Jew took comfort in believing Hitler's end was near. And Hungarian Jews still thought that they'd escape the fate of the majority of the Polish Jews in eastern Europe. Such is faith, a great medicine. I know it was the greatest medicine for my father.

Dad was constantly asking for news from the battlefield. He was obsessed with it. He knew that our lives depended on it. And his great hope and faith that Hitler would soon have a bloody demise gave him the strength to wrestle with his ever-worsening disease. (I should say here that the human instinct for revenge, retribution for the great injustice inflicted on us, is a natural instinct.)

In the coming wintry days and weeks of February and March, good news reached the Jewish community in Debrecen. On the eastern front the Russians were pushing back the German hordes from the great Russian expanses that the Nazis had occupied. Of course the Hungarian media toed the German line of propaganda by announcing that the retreats were tactical. But the truth was that a very cold winter was aiding Russia's armies, as it had in years past: the Russian winter also had defeated Napoleon's armies.

Every week, Zvi came from Mariopoch to see our father. Sometimes he would come even just for the day. Where Zvi lived there were no placards all over the place ordering young Jewish men to labor camps. Once he saw our placards, he was afraid to be in Debrecen, yet still he came. For Dad. Zvi and I would get him out of bed, dress him, and help him sit up in a chair. After being in the chair for half an hour, though, he complained it was too much for him, and we put him back to bed. He was weak, and his health was deteriorating rapidly.

In the beginning of March, our mother came to Debrecen from Volova. She saw the sad situation there – Dad's poor physical condition and the desperate financial situation. She realized of course that we needed a lot of money for doctor bills and medication. Moshe and his children also had to be supported, and I needed money for rent and food. Zvi more or less supported himself as a teacher in Mariopoch. Eliezer was holding down a job, but his wages were very lean, and he also needed financial help.

Our mother now took all this responsibility on her own shoulders. She told Zvi and me that she would sell all their jewelry. My father owned a big, heavy golden chain, and she had some diamonds, gold chains, rings, and watches. "In such a time," she said, "who needs jewelry?" Around July 1941, just before that fateful Tisha b'Av *nidcheh*, my parents had sent their jewelry for safekeeping to my Aunt Jutta in Bereziv. My mother now asked me to travel there and bring back these belongings.

I left Debrecen for Bereziv around the tenth or eleventh of March 1943, on a Tuesday. I arrived safely to Chust by train, where I boarded a bus that continued in the direction of Bereziv. The day was very cold and the ground covered with snow, a real Carpathian winter. From the bus stop to Aunt Jutta's house was a good distance, so I walked briskly to keep warm. The snow crackled under my feet with every step, that's how bitterly cold it was. By the time I reached her house, it was dark outside. Once inside, I warmed up quickly. Of all my aunts and uncles, I had always loved my Aunt Jutta, her family (her husband Zisya and their children) the most.

Aunt Jutta was one of Dad's eight sisters. She had a full house of children, seven in number. The oldest one of the children was a boy named Moshe, about 19. Then there was a daughter a year or so younger; another daughter, named Basya, about age 15. There was also a set of twins, boys, and two more children; I can't recall all their names now. Uncle Zisya Nojovich was well-to-do, owning a lot of land. He was also a fairly modern Jew, not a religious fanatic,[1] and because of that I felt very good in his house. The oldest girl, Rifka (we called her Rifkila, as an endearment), was very pretty, with big, brown eyes, very smart and full of life. For all these reasons I felt very comfortable in their home.

It's precisely my feeling of contentment there, however, that led to my lifetime of guilt about staying in Bereziv longer than I should have. I was supposed to pick up the jewelry and return the next day. I knew my father was very ill and that my mother was with him and needed my help. And yet I tarried longer because my good Aunt Jutta, who certainly meant well, literally begged me to stay over at least for *Shabbos* and to return to Debrecen on Sunday. Although I told her that Dad's condition was very serious, I agreed to stay over. I can't forgive myself for my irresponsible decision, knowing how gravely ill my father was, possibly that his days were numbered. To this day I still regret that I didn't take advantage of every minute I could to be with him.

Directly across the street from Aunt Jutta's house was the house of my mother's sister, Yenta. She had died years earlier, leaving four children: two boys who were about my age, and an older and a younger daughter. After Yenta died, their father remarried, but he had no children with his second wife. I felt a kinship to the cousins, but not too close a kinship to their father and stepmother. That's why I had never stayed in their house when I visited Bereziv before the war.

That *Shabbos* my cousins popped over at Aunt Jutta's house and we spent a very pleasant and joyful afternoon. Such is the nature of

---

[1] In Yiddish, he was not "*farchnyoket.*"

young people. Terrible conditions notwithstanding, we tried to forget and have fun.

That evening, we received a telegram from Eliezer: "Dad gravely ill. Come back immediately." As I later found out, Dad had fallen into a coma and everyone thought this was the end. Eliezer also telegrammed Moshe in Sokmar and Zvi in Mariopoch. When we received our telegram, Aunt Jutta felt very bad for asking me to stay over *Shabbos*. I shivered, dreading that when I will reach Debrecen, my father would no longer be among us.

Aunt Jutta decided she'd accompany me to Debrecen. Right after *Shabbos* we hired a horse and sleigh to take us to Chust and then, with luck, catch the nine o'clock train. We could barely wait until it got dark.

As *Shabbos* ended, Aunt Jutta, carrying my parents' jewelry, and I left for Chust. It was very cold, so Aunt Jutta took along a woolen blanket for us to bundle up in. Our journey was successful: we made the nine o'clock train connection in Chust. The ride took approximately four hours, and we arrived after midnight in Debrecen. The entire train ride, I was filled with remorse for staying so long at Aunt Jutta's, but said nothing about it to her. I was just terrified that my father may already have passed into the World of Truth.[2]

With great trepidation we entered Eliezer's apartment. Fortunately, Dad was just asleep. Eliezer informed Aunt Jutta and me that our father had fallen into a coma 24 hours earlier, and naturally they thought this was the end. But then he awoke and started to talk. He told Eliezer and Mother that he had had a very frightening dream, and that he felt much better and relieved now that he was no longer dreaming. Jutta and I thanked G-d that he was still with us. The woolen blanket that Aunt Jutta took along came in handy now, because she'd have to sleep on the floor in this one room. It's true that the room was fairly large, but five people were sleeping in it. But in times of trouble or calamity, there is no such thing as being too crowded when you're among your loving family.

Aunt Jutta stayed until the next day, and then returned to Bereziv. I'm sure she would have preferred to have stayed longer with her brother, but she saw that we were all crowded at Eliezer's. When I took her to the train station, she was close to tears about our whole situation. "Your Dad has such a big, nice house in Torun," she

---

[2] In Hebrew, *"Olam ha-Emmet."*

lamented to me, "and Eliezer has one too, and now you have to be squeezed into this one room."

At noontime Sunday, Zvi arrived from Mariopoch; Moshe appeared on Monday morning. I sneaked Zvi into my place with the Hungarian invalid, so he bedded down there with me. (I wasn't allowed to have guests, but I had to take the chance.) Moshe found room at my mother's cousin Kylah who also lived in Debrecen. (I mentioned earlier that Eliezer's two children had been sent away to stay with Shari's sister.) In this way we brothers could all be with our father during the day, except for Eliezer, who was working. Dad, I could only imagine, might have been frightened when he saw us all there, realizing we were together because we thought he'd die soon. But I prefer to believe that he took comfort in seeing all his children together and safe. He knew very well that his brother Zecharia, his sister Sara, his brother-in-law Berel Drimmer, the other brother-in-law Eliezer Jakubowics who lived in Mydan, and their entire families were no longer among the living, except for one soul who survived that time from the Drimmer family and one from the Jakubowics family. (My father's brother-in-law Eliezer Jakubowics who lived in Mydan shared our family name, but weren't related to us on the Jakubowics' side. Our region was home to many Jakubowics families who were not directly related.)

We all tried to talk optimistically about the course of the war. This was the medicine that lifted our father's spirits. At that point in 1943, the Russians were pushing the Germans back and inflicting heavy losses. Sadly, the two additional years it took to annihilate Hitler would cost most of Europe's and Hungary's Jews their lives.

It was almost time for a joyful Jewish holiday, Purim, celebrating the demise of another Hitler – Haman, YS – who lived almost 2,500 years ago. Back then, our people were saved from destruction, but not this time. Still, Purim spirit helped somewhat to lighten our heavy hearts.

Moshe traveled back to Sokmar on Purim day. There was simply no room for him to stay. Our sages tell us "it is enough for a guest to stay three days,"[3] meaning that one should not overstay one's

---

[3] In Hebrew, "*Orech dy l'shloshah yammim.*"

welcome. I think Moshe understood that, and that's why he left our cousin Kylah's.

A few days later, my mother, Shari, Eliezer, Zvi, my father and I were all in the apartment when Zvi and I decided to go out to the courtyard to smoke a cigarette. Of course we never smoked inside. We weren't outside very long, when suddenly our mother rushed out and sobbed, "Cry children, cry. You had a good dad, a devoted father. He is no more." Both Zvi and I began to cry and rushed into the room. Our father lay in bed as if in a deep sleep. His face looked contented. No more pain.

"May His great Name grow exalted and sanctified in the world that He created as He willed."[4]

My father died around noontime on a Thursday, the 18th day of the Hebrew month of *Adar Beth* in the Hebrew leap-year 5703 (*taph-shin-gimmel*). According to the Julian calendar, it was Thursday, March 25, 1943. His life was extinguished at 67, considered a young age for our family. His mother died at the age of 96 or 97. His father died in his late 70s. All the *tsuris* of the last two years had broken him physically, but not spiritually. He believed to his last breath that Israel is eternal and won't be defeated,[5] that we would prevail and that Hitler would suffer a crushing defeat. My father had the great merit of being interred in an Orthodox Jewish cemetery in Debrecen, an honor regretfully not bestowed upon the rest of my family.[6]

My father Avraham Zalman was a pious and gentle man. When I was in my early teens, I wanted to have a dog, but he explained that we couldn't have one in the yard because a lot of poor Jewish families, as well as volunteers collecting for various Jewish causes, often came to our house, and he was concerned that a dog might scare them off. He also told me, "Remember, never refuse a hand that is outstretched to you for help." He was a man who gave charity anonymously. He was considered a wise, intelligent person, often sought after to arbitrate disputes. For years, he served as the president of the congregation in Torun. Maybe for these reasons he merited being buried in a Jewish cemetery.

---

[4] These are the first words of the *Kaddish*, the prayer of mourning: "*Yitgadal v'yitkadash sh'mei rabba.*"

[5] In Hebrew, the phrase is "*Netzach Yisroel lo y'shakair.*"

[6] Long after the war, a cousin of mine who remained in Budapest was able to locate this cemetery and determine that my father's gravesite and headstone had been spared desecration. In April 1982, my son and I visited Debrecen, where we went to this cemetery to chant *Kaddish* and place stones on the grave marker to record our presence.

We notified Moshe by telegram on Thursday about our father, and he came immediately, so all four of Avraham Zalman's sons were together on Friday to mark his eternal sleep in the Garden of Eden. The traditional Jewish condolence goes like this: "May the Omnipresent console you among the other mourners of Zion and Jerusalem."[7] When I was younger, I often wondered why, of all G-d's many different names, why in this particular phrase do we refer to G-d as "the Omnipresent" (in Hebrew, "*Ha-Makom*," literally, "the place"). But how can a place console you? Now I believe I understand why: if people know the place where their loved ones rest eternally, the family can go there and cry their hearts out to relieve their grief. And this is why the grief I feel for my mother and brothers has never left me. G-d only knows where their lives ended. I just pray that since they gave their lives in sanctifying G-d's holy name they are also resting eternally in the Garden of Eden.

All of us mourned together in Debrecen. After the *shiva*,[8] Zvi went back to Mariopoch, Moshe to Sokmar, and my widowed mother to Volova, to live with her sister-in-law Byla. Little did my mother and I know that this time in Debrecen was to be the last we'd ever see each other. All she was concerned about was my safety. I was to leave for Mariopoch a few days later, having been invited by our cousin Shonie. It is a Jewish custom that male children go 30 days without shaving as a sign of mourning,[9] but she worried that it would be easier to recognize me as a Jew if I traveled to Mariopoch this way, so she advised me to shave. I did, and later left for Mariopoch.

I didn't have any problem getting there, and felt very comfortable in that small village. I felt relatively safe being with Zvi and Shonie. Zvi kept asking me, "Do you remember the patrol, the

---

[7] "*Ha-Makom y'nachaim et'chem b'toch sh'ar availai Zion v'Yerushalayim.*"
[8] From the Hebrew word for "seven," *shiva* refers to the seven solemn days of intense mourning for the dead, beginning immediately after the funeral.
[9] In Hebrew this is called the "*shloshim*" (thirty).

two Germans who let us pass?" I agreed, it had been a miracle. Zvi kept reminding me of it to buoy my courage.

Chapter 19

Szazod 104/108

DECREES AGAINST JEWS that, prior to May 1943, had applied only to selected areas now were in force all over the country. Jews had to register in labor camps in different cities. I had to register in the former Czech city called Kosice (the Hungarians called it Kasso); I believe I registered on May 25. Two or three thousand Jews must have been registered already by the time I got there. Everybody had to have a medical exam; if people were ill or crippled, they were supposed to be let go, but we got wind that the captain of the camp in Kosice was a wild beast. Nobody who survived that camp could ever forget his vile name: Milakovich. He was probably Hungarian since a Slav wouldn't have been made an officer by the Hungarian military. He was a terrible enemy of the Jews. (I found out after the war that he was caught and hanged: "Thus should all enemies of the Jews meet their end!"[1])

Milakovich ordered the doctors not to release anybody – not the crippled, the sick, no one. When my turn came, I told the doctors that I was fine. I didn't want to undress, but they insisted. For the so-called medical examination, the doctors looked me over and felt certain parts of my body. This took place in an open field and thousands of us were examined there. In one area there were two long tables, at which military doctors sat in chairs. Each person was "examined" for 10 or 15 seconds, then the doctors wrote down the name, age, and that was it. From there we were taken to a second area in a huge football field, enclosed by a tall fence. Hungarian soldiers were posted on guard along the fence's perimeter. My group consisted of 230 or 240 young men. In Hungarian this group was called a *szazod* (pronounced SAH-zod). We were assigned the number 104/108, and we all had to wear yellow armbands on our left arm with this number printed on them. We were also each given a military identification card; the only difference between our I.D. cards and those of the soldiers was that ours were marked with a big, red "Z" across the front – "Z" for "*Zhido*": Jew. *Szazod* 104/108 was my address for the next year and a half – until December 1944, when we were shipped to the concentration camp in Flossenburg, Germany.

---

[1] "*Kain yovdu kol oyvai Yisroel!*"

My extended family, in a photo taken in Torun around 1934. (1) Bumy Popper, who shot this picture with a timed camera (and son of Itzchak Popper); (2) Eliezer, my oldest brother, in one of only two surviving photographs I have of him; (3) Zecharia Heimowitz (legend has it he survived the war, returned to Torun and was murdered there); (4) Zvi Heimowitz; (5) Joseph Meir Heimowitz, Chaya Yudenberg's youngest brother (he later changed his name to Alex Coleman and lives in London); (6) my Aunt Baila's daughter, Chanah Zoldan (Moshe Zoldan's older sister); (7) me, towering above most of my relatives at age 14 or 15; (8) my father, Avraham Zalman Jakubowics; (9) Shoshana, daughter of my paternal Aunt Sarah Heimowitz; (10) Eliezer Herz, who married into the Popper family; (11) my father's only brother, Zecharia Jakubowics; (12) Faiga, Rivkah ('Rifchew') Popper's mother, with Baila's grand son on her lap (I stayed with her family when I went to Yeshiva in Sevlush); (13) my father's eldest sister, Sarah, who married Moshe Leeb Heimowitz; (14) my mother, Rivkah (Drimmer) Jakubowics; (15) my father's next sister, Baila (Moshe Zoldan's mother).

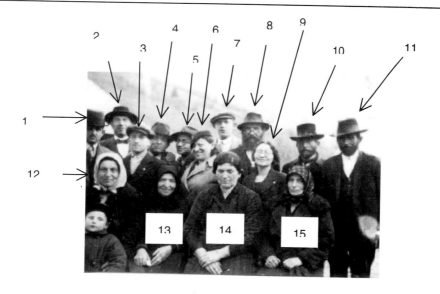

Back row, left to right: Eliezer; his wife, Shari; Shoshana; Bumy **Popper**; Chanah Zoldan (Moshe Zoldan's older sister); Chanah Jakubowics, my Uncle Zecharia's daughter to whom Zvi had been engaged; Uncle Zecharia. Middle row: Aunt Faiga Popper, my father's sister (and mother of my cousin, Rivka ['Rifchew'] Popper; my paternal grandmother, Miriam Dvorah **Kirzner** Jakubowics (who died in 1938); my Aunt Baila, another of my father's sisters; Zecharia's wife, Sarah. Front row: both boys are Baila's grandchildren (2 of 4 children of Michael Zoldan, Moshe's older brother); I've forgotten their names.

My brother, Moshe, and his wife, Montzi; undated picture.

My brother, Zvi (center), around 1926 or 1927 with fellow troopers in the Czech military. He was drafted at age 20 for 18 months of service. This picture is actually the front of a post card I located with relatives in Israel in 1966.

Zvi and kids from the Hebrew Day School (<u>*Cheder*</u>) lined up in front of our stone and masonry house. The girl standing second from the right is Zipporah (Drimmer) Goldhaber, my cousin who lives in Israel. To the left of Zipporah is <u>Ch</u>aya Neiman, who lives there, too.

My Aunt Molvin's family, with whom I stayed for a time in Sokmar. This photo was taken many years earlier, for when I lived with them, three of the five kids had already left home. From left to right: Böske, Moçko (the only one still alive today); Lotsy, Sharrie; Aunt Molvin (Reich) Darvosh; Uncle Armin Darvosh; and Willi, on his father's lap.

Zvi's wife, Piri (left), and a friend in an undated picture. This was given to me by the friend while I was in Geretsried DP Camp and she was passing through (June or July 1947).

D

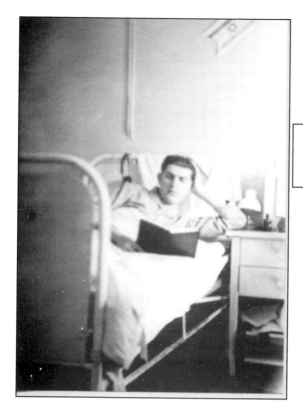

Reading in my hospital bed in Gauting, at the end of 1946.

Still at the head of the line, during a Zionist rally on May 14, 1947. The partially obscured banner reads in Yiddish: 'Testament left by the Six Million is the creation of the State of Israel.' I am wearing the one and only suit I owned.

E

Addressing the same May rally.

Speaking at another rally in Geretsried -- on the day statehood for Israel was declared in 1948. (I'm wearing a much better suit by now!)

F

Nina's and my wedding portrait.

Two of us relaxing at a party some time after we married. I couldn't afford an engagement ring, but Nina said what she *really* needed was a wristwatch, so I bought her a Swiss watch ($20 American) and a $10 wedding ring.

I'm watching the Rabbi fill out our marriage papers in the town of Wolfratshausen, where Nina and I were married on July 18, 1948.

From the ashes of the *Shoah*, new generations have flowered. My son, Jack, holding our first grandchild, Daniel (8 months), in Allentown, Aug. 1986.

Our growing family, Aug. 1998, in our backyard to celebrate our 50th anniversary. From left to right: Renata; Nina, hugging Julie, 7; me; Daniel, seated in front of me, 12; Cindy (Lewiton) Jackson, hugging Eric, 9; and Jack.

H

When they put together our *szazod* in Kosice, I rejoiced to find out that my buddy from Torun, David Godinger, was also assigned to the same one. Both of us were very happy to be together – it was like finding a long-lost brother to share the same destiny with. Many in our group hailed from the Maramaros region of the Carpathians; there also were those who considered themselves from the "motherland" of Hungary. Most of these fellows barely spoke Yiddish, and most of the Carpathian boys didn't know Hungarian, but it didn't take them very long to master it (I already knew quite a bit of Hungarian by then). I can't remember exactly how long we stayed in Kosice – for two or three more days – without being given any food or water, and sleeping out in the open field while we were guarded by Milakovich's soldiers. We were lucky that it didn't rain. Being with my old friend David made this hell slightly easier to bear. Finally we were loaded onto a freight train and shipped to a small village near Sighet in the Maramaros region. The name of that village escapes me, but among ourselves we referred to it by an epithet in Yiddish meaning black and impure: "*Schvartz-tummah*."

Each *szazod* was considered a full labor battalion, with a commander who was inevitably a Hungarian military officer of varying rank. The commander had a *keret* consisting of a sergeant and 13 to 14 Hungarian soldiers under him whose job it was to guard the battalion of Jews. Naturally, they had weapons. Our well-being – or our demise – depended upon the mercy of this battalion commander. Luckily the commander of Battalion 104/108 was a decent person, and he ordered the *keret* to be treat us humanely. G-d forbid if he had been a sadist and an anti-Semite. We had no work chores in *Schvartz-tummah*. Instead, we conducted regular military routines: marching drills and so forth. This commander also informed us that we were allowed to write two postcards home a month, but of course it was prohibited for us to identify the places where we were stationed; we could only put 104/108 as the return address.

One time our commander took our battalion to the city of Sighet so we could go to the ritual bath and bathe. By chance while I was there I ran into our rabbinical judge from Torun, Rav Yitzchak Gross, HYD. He was a Talmud scholar who, by divine providence, wasn't at home on Tisha b'Av *nidcheh* in 1941; he thus escaped being deported, but survived only a few more years. Of Rav Gross's beautiful family – a wife and seven children – only one child, a girl named Shifrah, no more than age 15 back then, escaped the holocaust in Kamieniec Podolski; she now resides in Israel. Rav

Gross's eldest son also perished; he had been my tutor in Talmud during 1933-'34.

We remained in *Schvartz-tummah* no more than 10-12 days. Then the order came that we were to go to the area of Dunantul. Exactly where we didn't know, but we knew that this meant somewhere behind the line of the Danube River, close to Yugoslavia. Again, we were loaded onto a freight train. It was summertime, and the doors of the boxcars were kept open so that we could breathe fresh air. In every boxcar there were at least thirty or forty of us, guarded by an armed soldier. We had practically traversed all of Hungary from one end to the other. In a few days, we reached a place called Zombor, which was annexed by the Hungarians from Yugoslavia. There, we were put up in stables and barns owned by the local farmers, who were friendly and rather sympathetic towards us. What impressed me was that all the barns and the stables were very clean. The farm house windows were spic and span, sparkling.

When we arrived in Zombor, our whole *keret* and battalion commander were changed. We got a new commander, an elderly person with the rank of *oberleutnant* (first-lieutenant), and another *keret*. We were terribly worried about what kind of changes we'd see. The next morning the *oberleutnant* marched us onto a big field and told us all to sit down in a circle.

He addressed us: "I am an old soldier from World War I. You Jews were sent here to do a very important job. You will work here to complete an airfield. It has to be completed by a certain time. If you work diligently and aren't lazy, not even a hair from your heads will be missing. We shall supply you with decent meals. You won't be hungry or thirsty. I hope you understand that. I'm an old, smoked-out pipe," he added. "I know what work is. Those who dilly-dally will be dealt with mercilessly." And then he said to the *keret*, "You have to treat those people with respect. Same as soldiers. You have to see that every individual does his job right." And then he asked if there was somebody in our group who played a musical instrument. "He should register." He didn't want us to be gloomy and depressed. He wanted us to march to and from work singing and playing instruments. There were a few among the fellows who played the accordion and balalaika, so he organized a little make-shift band from among our battalion. We all breathed a sigh of relief after this lecture and felt more at ease. Even the heat was easier to bear. Until then, I'd never experienced such a warm climate; the ground was even too hot to walk barefoot.

There were eight or ten *szazod*s, maybe even more, in the vicinity of Zombor assigned to build the airfield. They handed us shovels, pick axes and wheelbarrows to level the area; we had to dig up entire hills and fill in valleys. This slave labor began early morning and halted late in the evening, eleven hours a day in this hot climate. Hungarian engineers oversaw our work.

One day, I learned my brother Zvi was in one of those other *szazod*s. Like the Biblical story of Joseph looking for his brothers,[2] I asked permission from one of my overseers to find him. He gave me one hour, and I ran like the dickens. In this huge area, people working in the distance looked tiny. I didn't know the *szazod* number that my brother was in. Finally, somehow, I found him (I think he was in 104/109). Our joy was indescribable. The first question he asked me was what kind of a commander I had. He seemed to be a decent person, I told Zvi. That made him very happy because he knew too that everything depended on what kind of commander we had. Even under these circumstances, he was looking out for me as his younger brother.

On the other hand, unfortunately, Zvi's unit commander was a virulent anti-Semite and people in his *szazod* had to be very careful because he brutalized and punished people for the slightest infraction. Zvi couldn't even leave his work detail for a minute, so I told him that after work in the evening I would come to visit him.

Quickly he informed me that our cousin Bynish was also in his battalion, working with a different group. I told him that David Godinger from Torun was in mine. We parted sorrowfully – my one hour's time was about up. When I returned to my unit, I updated David Godinger about my brother and Bynish. He knew them both; all of us Jews from Torun knew each other.

For a few weeks, we worked on the airfield, during which time I visited my brother and Cousin Bynish a number of times. They lived under a lot stricter conditions than I did, and it pained me to see this. Although Zvi was happy that I had it easier than he did, he was also afraid that he might get into trouble by my coming to see him. We could easily spot prying military people, who wore uniforms. But there were many spies in civilian clothes, too – Hungarians who

---

[2] "It is my brothers for whom I search" (*"Et achai ani m'vakesh"*), from Genesis XXXVII:16.

would rat to the military and cause us to be punished severely for our "crimes." So we had to watch our step at all times.

We workers developed a secret code. If we spotted somebody we didn't recognize, we'd alert each other by whispering the Hebrew word for rain (*geshem*) and pass it from one to the other. The *geshem* signal, which we all understood, traveled in minutes from one end of the airfield to the other. It meant somebody was watching us. If anyone spotted something threatening, he'd cry out "*Geshem,*" so everybody would get busy and not stand idle.

We stayed in Zombor until the middle of July 1943. Then an order came to move on. Of course we never knew ahead of time where we were going. As it turned out, we were sent back to Hungary in the area between Pispiklodany and Budapest. Our work there was laying a new rail line between those two cities. Before we left, I went to see Zvi and told him that we were ordered to leave the next day. We were both pained about parting, but we had no way to prevent it.

One good thing: Zvi and I had time to arrange another secret code between us. As I mentioned, we were allowed to write two postcards each month. One entire side, of course, was for a text message; on the front of the card, half was reserved for the address and the other half for any remaining portion of the message. Our sign was this: if we started writing on the full, non-address side of the card it meant the situation was more or less bearable. If we started on the other, half-side of the card, then times were very bitter.

When we prepared to march out the next morning, I was in my usual position, at the head of the line, with workers falling in from tallest to shortest. From far away I saw Zvi working on the airfield. He dared not come over to me and I couldn't leave the ranks either because we were already set to march. Had I not been at the front of the formation, he might not have spotted me, and I might not have seen him from across the field.

My eyes were filled with tears. That moment in July 1943 was the final time I saw my brother Zvi. Naturally, we didn't know then that our glances at each other were our last. Those few seconds occurred more than five decades ago. Yet even now, as I write these lines, I still see him through my tears. HYD. "Oh, for those who are gone and cannot be replaced!"[3]

---

[3] Hebrew: "*Chaval al di-abdin v'loh mishtakchin.*"

Chapter 20

Yom Kippur 1943

WHEN WE ARRIVED IN THE AREA OF PISPIKLODANY, we stayed in a small village surrounded by farm area. Luck was with us because David Godinger and I were put up in a farmhouse room with two beds in it. Sleeping in beds was a great privilege for us at this point. We all had to assemble at 5:30 a.m., at the local train station. From there, we were loaded into a freight train, and traveled more than a half hour to a place where we were assigned to work on the same railroad. The work consisted of replacing the old rails, which were thinner and a lot weaker, with new, heavier ones.

This was also a main line that carried freight and war materiel to the eastern front. The Hungarians didn't want to hold the civilian traffic back on that line, so we had to work around that schedule. We worked in pairs, with each pair given six ties. It was really backbreaking labor. Using shovels, we quickly dug all the stones out from beneath the ties; after we removed the stones, we placed small support logs under the rails. Around ten o'clock each morning, a civilian train passed in the direction of Debrecen, slowing down considerably as it passed the work area. It took almost a quarter hour to pass. Those were the only few minutes we were able to rest and catch our breath. After the train passed by, we had until 3 p.m. to lay and secure the new rails.

All this we did with our bare hands – we were given no heavy machinery – while being directed by the experienced Hungarian foremen. Standing by, the soldiers watched us. Everything was done on command. So many hands had to grab the rail; with a command we lifted it up, and with another command we put it down on the ties. There were also engineers supervising the work. In my entire life, I have never worked as hard, before or since. Everything had to be done exactly on time. Fortunately, our work unit was given enough food so we weren't hungry. The commander of our *szazod* ordered the kitchen help, Jewish boys who were the cooks, to buy pigs and calves and slaughter them for meat. He told the cooks that because we were doing very important work, we had to be well fed. Most of the Hungarian Jews continued receiving food packages from home, and thus were able to observe Jewish dietary laws. They didn't eat from the kitchen at all, except to drink coffee. We Carpathian Jews had no homes anymore, though, so either we ate what they cooked or went hungry.

We who were from the Carpathian region, whenever possible, tried to slow down the progress of work on the railroad. The Hungarian boys, however, gave it every last ounce of strength they had; that's why we called them the *mammalandische tipshim* (stupid mamma's boys). They really believed that by doing this hard work they'd be spared from being shipped out to the Ukraine, where the war was in full swing.

We went on for weeks doing that excruciatingly hard slave labor. There were many weak and sick among us who could in no way fulfill their portion of digging out the stones from under the railroad ties. To our merit, we helped one another, and saved the weaker ones among us from a lot of trouble.

One such person was a yeshiva scholar from Sighet. His name was Israel Katz, a gentle young man with a very fine sense of humor. We often helped him cope every day while we worked on the railroad and also later in the Ukraine. Many times, we saved him from *tsuris* and from beatings. He survived the war and emigrated to the US, living his last years in Kingston, New York. Often over the years, we'd talk over the telephone, and we also met a couple of times. He had a phenomenal memory. We would inevitably discuss our time together during the *Shoah*, and he always astonished me with his total recall of names, dates and places. (Israel Katz passed away during the mid-1980s. I still miss him very much, blessed be his memory.)

The hardest thing for me at that time was to get up at four or five o'clock in the morning. Yet I had to. I told myself, if I survived the Holocaust and G-d granted me many years, my greatest pleasure would be to sleep way past 5 a.m.

In the morning we went to the kitchen for coffee; that took about fifteen minutes, standing in line. So David Godinger and I arranged that one day I'd line up and fetch his coffee and the next day he'd grab mine. In this way, on alternate days we were able to catch a few extra minutes of sleep. We were so tired from the backbreaking work that every minute of rest was more precious than gold.

Since it took over half an hour to travel to and from the workplace, we had two opportunities a day to make a *minyan* and say *Kaddish*. There were many of us who were in a year of mourning, as I was, so we were able to say *Kaddish* in the boxcars as we traveled back and forth.

The whole summer we worked on the railroad tracks between Pispiklodany and Budapest. Soon our High Holidays came. Rosh Hashanah in 1943 fell on October 1, and Yom Kippur October 10. All the fellows with families close by, those who could make it back and forth in a day's time, received 24-hour passes. Thank G-d, I was fortunate to have my brother Eliezer in Debrecen, only a few hours away by train. So I asked for a 24-hour pass.

Naturally, the day before Yom Kippur we had to complete our work quota, six ties. A train was passing through to Debrecen around 3 p.m. So I worked my tail off to finish and bribed one of the Hungarian civilian overseers. I paid him with *pengas* and he helped me complete my quota. The sergeant who handed out the papers was the problem. Those papers were first signed by the commander and he handed them to the sergeant, who was supposed to give them out to us. But he was a terribly evil person, an anti-Semite, and he held them back. When I asked him for my papers he replied that he couldn't give them out before four o'clock. So naturally, I had no alternative. I watched the three o'clock train pass by: it was an express, and would have gotten me to Debrecen before sundown, before Yom Kippur began. There was another train, a local, that would go in the direction of Debrecen at 5:30. When I finally got my pass after four o'clock, I went to the train station. Nearby there was a store, where I bought a loaf of bread and half a kilogram of fresh grapes. Then I sat in the station's waiting room for the train. There, I had my feast before Yom Kippur; after that I was ready for the Yom Kippur fast.

The train arrived promptly at 5:30 p.m. Boarding it, I sat down near a window and gazed out at the disappearing panorama. My thoughts shifted to previous High Holy Days, at home, when the whole family partook of the feast, and I recalled the past year's Yom Kippur which we spent together with Moshe and Montze in Horodenka. I immersed myself in such bitter-sweet thoughts. All the while, the train kept stopping at every small village. At one stop, I suddenly noticed a Jewish man with his young son, maybe ten years old. The father was carrying a *tallis* and they were heading to *shul.* Suddenly a thought came over me: I'd be ashamed to arrive at my brother's late on Yom Kippur night, because in doing so I would desecrate the holy day. On the spur of the moment, I decided to leave the train and stay in this village for Yom Kippur. Obviously it had a Jewish community. Outside, I saw another man going to *shul*. Going over to this Jew, I asked him whether he had room for me to stay overnight. He saw I was a Jewish slave laborer because of my yellow armband. I added that I have already eaten my pre-Yom Kippur feast. Then he took me to his house, where I left the little backpack I had with me; I washed up a bit and we went together to services.

By the time we entered the *shul*, it was already after Kol Nidre, the prayer that ushers in the holiday. I'll never forget that Yom Kippur. The *shul* was very well lit, full of people praying, and the women's section, usually an upstairs balcony in European synagogues, brimmed with women and little children. In 1943 in this area of Hungary, families were still relatively intact, except for young Jewish males like me, who were in labor camps. I was probably the only young man in this *shul* who suffered the Carpathian Holocaust in 1941. The rabbi gave a moving sermon. He spoke of the destruction of the Carpathian Jewish community and of the horrible news coming out from Poland, the destruction of the greatest Jewish community in Europe. He spoke about the ghettos into which Jews were herded in 1943. And when he mentioned specific crimes perpetrated on the Polish Jews, he cried. He beseeched the congregation to pray to G-d to save *their* community, that they shouldn't share the same destiny as the Polish and the Carpathian Jews. I listened to that sermon on Kol Nidre night, and my tears wouldn't stop flowing.

It felt like every one of these hundreds of worshippers breathed in unison. From the women's section, I could hear groans, moans and occasional cries. Before my eyes, images of my own synagogue in Torun on past Kol Nidre nights appeared. But I knew that those days were no more and would never be again.

When my host and I returned to his home after services, I went straight to bed. Though I was very tired, I couldn't fall asleep all night. The next day, Yom Kippur, we rose early and we went to *shul*. I spent almost all day there. During the break before afternoon services, I strolled around the town (I can't recall the name of this place). It was a nice, sunny day, yet I was nagged by thoughts: "Where am I? Why am I here alone on this High Holy Day when I should be with my family? My father's gone. My mother's alone. My brothers and I are scattered all over the place."

When the Yom Kippur services ended, my host invited me to break the fast with his family. At the meal he asked me what family I was traveling to in Debrecen. I told him I have a brother who is married to a granddaughter of Benjamin Ze'ev Krauss, who was a very prominent rabbi.

Before too long, I bid them farewell. I was treated very cordially and they saw me off with the customary Hebrew greeting of the day: "Your destiny should be sealed for the good."[1] I thanked them for their hospitality, and walked the short distance to the station to catch the next train for Debrecen.

I arrived at my brother's place around eleven o'clock in the evening. In those days there were no private telephones, so I couldn't notify him. Surely I surprised them with my appearance. I related my adventure, where I spent Yom Kippur and why. At 3 a.m. there was another train going in the opposite direction toward Pispiklodany and Budapest, and with that train I could safely reach my destination on time, within the limits of my 24-hour pass. I knew if I returned before our unit left for work, I wouldn't be punished. Eliezer and Shari stayed up with me the next four hours of the night. All we talked about was the fate of our family.

As I write these lines, I'm still puzzled and cannot forgive myself about the choices I made that Yom Kippur. Those few hours with Eliezer and Shari would be the last time I saw them. Of course we couldn't have known that then. But if I hadn't worried so much about reaching their home after Yom Kippur began, I might have been able to spend all day with them, instead of with strangers. Even if I had arrived in Debrecen an hour after Yom Kippur began, I'm sure Eliezer would have understood. How much better I would feel today, knowing that we prayed together on this holiest of holy days. Sadly, I can't change the past.

I returned to my work camp just in time to start another day of backbreaking labor. I was terribly tired from not sleeping two nights in a row, but there was no alternative. Fortunately, when you're young, you can bear even the unbearable.

---

[1] *"Chatimah tovah."*

Chapter 21

'I Believe'

WE TOILED ON RAILROAD LINES until November 1943. Then we were ordered to pack up because we, the Carpathian and Hungarian Jews, were being shipped out to the eastern front in Poland and the Ukraine. For us, this was a very heavy blow. We'd heard that the conditions for the Jewish labor camp work units were much harder and more dangerous at the eastern front. Lately, terrible news had seeped through about the conditions of the Jewish labor battalions there, and unfortunately we were told we were to replace them.

Despite all this, we Carpathian Jews couldn't resist having a little fun with the Hungarian Jews. In a teasing way, we asked them why they worked so hard and so quickly to finish the railroad. As the Yiddish saying goes, "Revenge on the bedbugs when the house is on fire."[1] In other words, we were really all in the same boat. They thought their hard work would save them, but it didn't. Of course, our sarcasm didn't do us any good either.

We loaded up as always on a freight train. Typically, it was a very cold day, and it goes without saying that the freight coach boxes weren't heated. When we reached Sevlush – approximately 100 kilometers from the former border of Poland in the Carpathian – we were suddenly and unceremoniously unloaded. To this day I don't know why they stopped there. All of us kept hoping we wouldn't have to enter the war zone, after all.

In Sevlush was my alma mater, Yeshivas Yitzchak Bais Yoseph, where I had spent two semesters in 1932 and 1933, so I knew the city well. My father's married sister Faiga lived in Sevlush, as did my brother Moshe with his family; he'd moved from Sokmar. In Sevlush, Moshe obtained work in a barrel factory, although exactly what he did and how he landed this job, I don't know. Barely did he scrape a living together from the job. Sevlush was a wine-producing city and there was still a small Jewish community at the time.

We remained in Sevlush for four or five weeks. We did no work, but the *keret* marched us around like soldiers, back and forth every day for about 15-20 kilometers. I received permission for a few hours' leave, so I went to visit my brother Moshe, Montze, their children, and also my cousins, the Poppers.

---

[1] *"A n'kumah di vansen brennan."*

Every day, news reached us from the eastern front that the Russians continued pushing back the Germans and their allies, the Hungarians and Romanians. That December, they suffered bitter defeats. The Russians broke through the lines at the Don River and later at the Dnieper River; they were more accustomed to the cold winters than the Germans or Hungarians.

Atrocities the Hungarians perpetrated against Jewish *munkoszazod* units started right after January 1943 when the Soviets dealt a crushing blow to the Hungarians at the Russian city of Woroniesh. A total disaster for the Hungarians, it also spelled catastrophe for the Jewish labor units, because the Hungarians vented their frustrations on them. Inside Hungary, we weren't aware of these atrocities right away. Only in the summer of 1943 did news gradually filter through from some soldiers who were wounded or sick and sent back to Hungarian hospitals. From them, we learned what was happening to our Jewish *munkoszazods*.

The Hungarians made us their whipping boys.[2] Almost a hundred thousand young men, the cream of Hungary's Jewish youth, were subjected in 1942-'43 to hard and dangerous work, such as digging trenches on the front lines, building bunkers, repairing roads, and loading and unloading war materiel.

Terrible reports reached us of *szazods* in which commanders starved the Jewish men to death. In one *szazod* a great proportion of the boys became very sick from typhus and other illnesses. They were kept in an unheated barn in the dead of winter. The commander ordered the *keret* to torch the barn, and hundreds of Jewish boys were burned alive. Those who tried to flee the barn were gunned down by the *keret*. All such commanders made every effort to erase any traces of their crimes by ensuring that no witnesses would survive to testify against them.[3]

When these reports reached our labor camp, fear and anxiety engulfed us all. We continued to hope our own commander would remain a reasonable person, which he seemed to be. We knew that

---

[2] *Kappoorahindl.*

[3] One lucky survivor of this massacre lives in my adopted home of Allentown, Pennsylvania. Bélo Roth managed to avoid being hit by gunfire when he ran out of the burning barn. His personal tale about this atrocity was published some years ago in our local newspaper, *The Morning Call.*

we were going to the war territory where the situation was "without justice or judge.[4]" Moshe tried to comfort me by saying that the war would soon end, that by the time we'd get out to the battle lines, it would already be January 1944, and that salvation would soon arrive. That Hitler would soon be defeated sustained us during those frightening days and nights.

Anxious as we were, we were proud that we were spiritual heroes, and in some cases spiritual heroism is of greater merit than physical heroism. At the end of December 1943, one week before we were to be shipped out to the war zone, two messengers arrived from Budapest for us. One was a Jewish *meshumid*[5] and the other also a messenger from some other kind of church, with a proposition that if we'd convert to Christianity – heaven forbid! – we would be removed from our *szazod* and transferred to a convert *szazod*. There, people wore white armbands (not the yellow bands identifying us as Jews), and, the messengers contended, they wouldn't be sent to the war zone in the Ukraine and Poland. In spite of our great anguish, only one boy out of the 230 fellows accepted the proposition, at the urging of his sister who had come from Budapest to convince him to convert. Of the 230 boys in our *szazod*, half of them hailed from around the Carpathian, Slovakian region, the other half were Hungarian. According to Maimonides, even under penalty of death, a Jew must not convert.[6] With great scorn and contempt, we rejected their proposition, and bade good riddance to the one who accepted it. The rest of these young men, in my opinion, were spiritual heroes.

On a very cold day in January 1944, we were again loaded on a freight train and boxcars. This time there was a little coal oven in each car. The oven was put in there not for us, but to warm the soldiers, who were on board to prevent us from jumping out of the car and fleeing. In each car were 25 to 30 fellows. Inside were long benches, so we could sit. Expecting the worst freezing scenario, we brought along good woolen clothing and winter shoes. (My mother was still in Volova at the time, so she was able to send me shoes and 100 percent woolen pants.)

My fear and anxiety were unbearable. Since I'd been in Poland, I knew first-hand what was going on there, but now we were heading into the unknown. My cousin, Esther Popper, came to the station to say goodbye. She already had one brother and two brothers-in-law who were in the Ukraine for more than a year, with no sign from

---

[4] *"Lais din, v'lais dayin."*
[5] A Jew who converted to Christianity.
[6] *"Y'herog v'al ya'avor."*

them for a long time. As it turned out, we learned later that they perished during that winter of '43 when the atrocities directed at the *szazods* took place. Esther was very worried about me; she'd heard in the summer that something very bad was going on and that her family had not been getting any postcards. Around her neck she wore a silver chain with a Star of David; suddenly she took it off, gave it to me, and said, "I'm giving you this necklace for a good luck charm, and it will protect you from trouble. But I want it back. You will come back and give it back to me."

We kissed each other good-bye; both our cheeks were tear-stained. Thank G-d Esther survived the *Shoah*. Today she lives in Israel and established a fine family there. But I couldn't keep my promise to return her necklace because when I got to the concentration camp in Flossenburg at the end of 1944, we had to undress completely and jump out through a window. This way, the Nazis could see whether we hid something in the most intimate places of our body.

Although it wasn't very far from Sevlush to our destination in Stanislov, Poland, the journey took several days. During the war, trains never ran on schedule. Along the way, we stopped at various small stations for hours and hours at a time to let other trains, carrying more important war materiel, along the rail lines. In the meantime, we ran out of coal, so we froze. In our boxcar was a man named Bardosh. He had been a taxi driver before in his native Budapest and was already in his 30s. Very assimilated, he barely knew he was Jewish, and didn't want anything to do with those of us from the Carpathian region (though later, at the front in Poland, he ended his self-imposed isolation and tried to reach out to us). At one of the small train stations where we'd stopped, he boldly asked the Hungarian guard whether he could go and find some coal to bring back to the train. Surprisingly, he was let out and he did bring us more coal to last a while. Most probably the soldier let him go because he himself was freezing.

We were all sitting silently in the box car, everyone submerged in his own thoughts and fears, when suddenly a cantor from a small town in Hungary, who was in the car with us, started to sing "I Believe" (*Ani Ma'amin*). All of us spontaneously joined in this song, which begins, "I believe with perfect faith in the coming of the

Messiah." The Hungarian soldier who was guarding us couldn't grasp what was happening to us, but he didn't prevent us from singing. Slowly, with the *Ani Ma'amin*, we tried to lessen our state of depression.

Chapter 22

Malarita

WE FINALLY REACHED STANISLOV, where our train remained on a side track. A Jewish *szazod* was there, from before, and they were working at the station, loading and unloading cargo. Somehow they found out that a fresh train of Jewish slave workers *(munkotabornikas)* had just arrived from Hungary. Some of them came over to us and pried us with questions about the situation of Jews in Hungary – especially any news concerning their families. By then, they'd been in the Ukraine a year. Exchanging information, we wanted to find out the situations with Jewish *szazods* here. They told us everything depended on the individual commanders of *szazods*, and further filled us in about the atrocities that took place right after the Russians broke through the city of Woroniesh. But it all depended, they said, where a *szazod* was at the time, and on fate. In January of '44 Stanislov was still quite a distance from the battle lines. We had no idea where our final destination would be. For two days and a night (or two nights and a day) we remained at that station. Then, during daylight, we were ordered off the train.

Once off the train, the *keret* marched us into the former Jewish ghetto in Stanislov. We had no idea at first where we were headed, although we realized as soon as we arrived. No Jews lived in this ghetto any longer. It was now a collection of empty houses, with *mezuzahs* on the doorposts showing they had been Jewish homes. Many windows were broken. Ripped-out pages and torn up sacred books were scattered all over the street – the usual picture of desecration. We settled in two of these buildings. We cleaned up some of the empty, unheated rooms as best as we could and made our beds on the floor; each room housed eight to ten fellows. Most of us had a close friend with whom we'd share the woolen blankets we had. My good friend David Godinger and I tried to keep each other warm under our double blanket.

Despite our fatigue, we could not fall asleep because of the destruction all around us. We knew that Stanislov once had a large Jewish community, but here we were in deserted houses, right in the heart of the *Emek ha-Bachah*, The Valley of Tears. At first we weren't allowed to leave the premises, but a day or two later, the commander started sending groups from our *szazod* to do all kinds of jobs. A few of the groups managed to contact some local people, and they found out that no more Jews remained in Stanislov at all.

One group from our *szazod* was assigned to a slaughterhouse for all kinds of farm animals. These boys had to sort the hides from cattle, pigs and horses – dirty and hard work. Their supervisor, a Ukrainian local, kept screaming at them to work harder. He threatened he'd do to their hides what had been done to the Jews in Stanislov.

One day I wound up in a group of five and a soldier from the *keret* who escorted us to a four-story building. This building in Stanislov was a "club" for Hungarian and German officers. It had no elevator, only stairs, and our job was to wash and clean the stairway and some floors. When we reached the top floor, we saw many young women in the rooms, but we had no idea right away what was going on. We Carpathians spoke Yiddish among ourselves. When one of the girls overheard us, she broke into tears and told us that they were kept there solely to be raped by the Germans and Hungarians. G-d in heaven, I shall never forget the face of that one Jewish girl, or the deep anguish and pain I saw in her eyes.

These girls were not even allowed to go down to the third floor. This Jewish girl told us that, after being there for some time, some of the others threw themselves out of the windows of the fourth floor. After that, the Germans secured the windows so that they could not be opened, and put a 24-hour guard on the floor. This poor girl cried bloody tears and said, "If you survive the war, tell our story, tell the world what these beasts did to us."

My dear Jewish sister, I am fulfilling your request now. I still feel the pain I felt when you cried to me. As long as I will live, I will never forget you. And I pray to G-d that the G-d of anger will avenge your pain and your grief.

For almost four weeks, we remained in Stanislov. Every day groups of our *szazod* were taken out to do all kinds of work. The hardest labor was in the railroad yard, where we loaded and unloaded heavy crates of war materiel that had been shipped there and were bound for various places on the battle lines. We didn't have mechanical lifts – only our hands (Jewish hands came very cheap), so we had to use brute force to lift and load.

Then after about a month in Stanislov, we were again loaded onto a freight train and traveled in the direction of the River Bug (pronounced "BOOG"). In about a day we crossed the river and arrived in the city of Brestlitowsk. The Poles called it Brzestnad Bugem; I believe this was the former border between Poland and the former Soviet Union. (By the way, Brestlitowsk is the birthplace of the late Israeli Prime Minister, Menachem Begin.) In Brestlitowsk's train station, we remained aboard our train for two days. We had no more coal; the cars were ice-cold and we were freezing.

The war line at that time was in the area of the cities of Kovel and Kobrin, in Bieloruss, that is, White Russia. Finally, after two days and nights on the train, we finally were let off and marched to the area of Malarita in Welkarita. Of course, we had to carry all our belongings, but we each had a backpack, which made it easier for us. The distance was approximately 20 kilometers, and when we arrived we settled in barn stalls. The local population in the village of Malarita were members of the Subotnik religion, which I believe is a form of the Russian Orthodox church. (Even though religions were prohibited in the Soviet Union, some still observed their beliefs.) These locals knew we were Jewish and their attitude was very friendly.

Now we weren't more than about 50 kilometers from the city of Kovel, which had changed hands a few times between December of '43 and January of '44 as the battle front shifted back and forth. This whole region was a pine forest, with very soft, sandy, swampy soil. A rail line through the forest, called the Pinsk marshes, extended all the way inside the Soviet Union to the city of Pinsk. Russian partisans who operated in these forests constantly blew up these rail lines. It was very easy for them to plant explosives under the ties because the ground was so soft. The partisans would hide in the thick forest and when the trains passed over them, they'd detonate the explosive by wire. This would send the whole train flying through the air, destroying its cargo of vital materials to the battle lines. The Germans in the beginning suffered great losses at the hands of these partisans. Later they'd load up train cars with several wagons of heavy stones, in the front of the locomotive, to minimize their losses. These wagons with stones would then blow apart, but they'd save the locomotive and the rest of the train from destruction. Soon the partisans also became more sophisticated and let the first few cars with the stones roll through. Then, by remote control, they'd detonate the charge when the train reached the point they wanted. The Germans suffered greatly because the line was no longer safe to use.

The Germans were desperate to do something about this. They decided to level the forest, cutting it back half a kilometer on each side of the line so partisans couldn't easily take cover in the thick woods near the tracks. The railroad that passed through this forest stretched for a few miles, so they asked the Hungarians to do this job, who in turn had its *szazods*, roughly 1,000 Jewish boys, do the work. When we arrived there, there were Jewish *szazods* already working.

This was in the winter of 1944. The ground was covered with snow, and as long as it was frozen it was not so bad. But when the temperature was above freezing and the ground started to thaw, we were in a swamp – all mud and marsh. It was simply hell. All of us wore good winter shoes, but the main problem was that we had no place at night to dry or clean our clothing. Even more terrible, most of us had never done this kind of work, so we sustained a lot of accidents with the handsaws and hatchets. (I was in a little better situation because my father had been in the lumber business, and I'd observed this kind of work in the Carpathian mountains.)

We chopped up the small logs and left them on the ground, but the big ones we dragged with chains to the tracks where we loaded them on open wagons. They shipped these logs to I don't know where. For days we waded through this swamp, and worked in wet shoes and wet clothing. We prayed it would be very cold and that everything would freeze up again. Some boys in the *szazods* had shoes with holes, but they were forced to work outdoors. The Hungarians wouldn't give them new shoes.

With the barns we slept in unheated, with wet, dirty clothes and shoes, and with the wet pieces of linen we wrapped around our feet instead of socks, we faced terrible conditions. At night, we had no choice but to wrap our feet with the wet linen to try and keep them warm. Once, I managed to speak with a friendly owner of my barn stall, asked him to sell me some 15-by-20 inch squares of linen so I could change to a dry one every day. He was generous enough to give me some without charging me. He told me to give him the wet ones and he'd dry them in his house. I was lucky that I was able to speak his language, for most of the Hungarian boys could not.

We remained there almost nine weeks, to the beginning of April 1944. A great number of our boys became very sick with pneumonia and other illnesses. If one had a fever over 40 Celsius, he was allowed to remain in the barns and not go out to work. Many boys were so sick that they were sent away to a so-called military hospital, farther away from the battle lines. We never heard from them again, nor did we ever learn what happened to them.

Each of the *szazods* had one or two Jewish doctors assigned to it, although they were also considered inmates. (Our *szazod* happened to have three doctors.) These doctors also wore yellow armbands, but had an additional band that was white with a Red Cross emblem on it. They were supposed to be our first-aid helpers, and didn't have to work. Yet they had to escort us every morning to these terrible places in the marshes. That they didn't do any labor, but just stood around in the cold and wet, was even worse for them. If one of us became sick with a high temperature, the Jewish doctor had no authority to let him stay home and not go to work. He had to accompany the patient to the Hungarian doctor at the military garrison close by. It was up to the Hungarian military doctor to decide what the Jewish doctor could do with his patient. The Hungarian doctor generally allowed a sick Jewish worker two days maximum to stay home from work; after that, the Jewish doctor would have to bring him back to the Hungarian doctor. The patient might have been very sick, but if he didn't have a temperature above 40 degrees Celsius, they sent him out to work.

The first one to get sick was one of our doctors, Bernard Schwartz. He was from Budapest, and I didn't know him very well. When he became very ill, they shipped him to a military hospital. Before he left, he said goodbye to each of us; he seemed very worried about going to that hospital. When he said goodbye to me, he started to recite these Hebrew words from the Psalms: "Even as I walk through the valley of the shadow of death, I fear no evil because you, G-d, are with me."[1] I was very surprised that he knew Hebrew. Sadly, we never heard anything more about him after he left us.

In Malarita, the Germans tried a new measure to find out if there was a bomb hidden under the track ties. They'd order two members of the Jewish *szazods* to hop from tie to tie for one or two kilometers. We weren't allowed to step in between the ties. If there were a bomb underneath, it would explode. In other words, we were to be cannon fodder for the Hungarians/Germans. Two Hungarian soldiers always walked about twelve ties behind us with loaded weapons in case we

---

[1] *Tehillim: "Gam ki ailech b'gai tzalmavet, loh irah rah ki atah imadi."*

tried to run away to the partisans in the surrounding forest. One day, I was elected to make such a walk with another fellow in my *szazod* who was from Kositseh. We stepped from tie to tie as lightly as possible. One time such a walk resulted in an explosion, but miraculously it was seconds after the Jew passed the tie. It also resulted in injuries to the Hungarian soldiers, but no fatalities.

In April '44, we were ordered to pack our belongings again and leave Malarita. Naturally, we never knew where we were going. Our *szazod* had three horse-drawn wagons, two horses apiece. These were military wagons owned by the Hungarian army; one of them served as a field kitchen for our *szazod;* two other wagons hauled the belongings of the *keret* and their weapons, including machine guns. There was a master, in Hungarian *örmester*, who was the highest ranking in the *keret*. Next to him was the sergeant and then a corporal. The rest were all privates. Each wagon was driven by one of our men, who also cared for the horses. We always envied those fellows because they didn't have to walk and they didn't have to carry the heavy belongings we had to lug. There were also two more Jewish boys who were rather privileged in our *szazod* – the cooks who manned the field kitchen. Though they cooked for us, they'd prepare special foods for the *keret*.

During our last week in Malarita, we received no rations. Usually we got half a loaf of bread for two days. Supplies for our *szazod* came from the city of Brestlitowsk. Every week, the men with the horses and wagons would travel there, with two Hungarian soldiers escorting them. They'd bring back supplies for the cooks – enough for a week or 10 days. But during those last days there, we received nothing. Our two cooks still had potatoes, fat, flour and some other supplies left over, so they fixed whatever else they could: they cooked the potatoes, and from the flour they prepared noodles. But we didn't have any bread. I remember it was Passover time, and we agreed among ourselves that since we were not allowed to eat bread anyway, we might as well be without it.

We finally arrived at a small village in the vicinity of Bialapodlaska, a city on the other side of the Bug River. When we reached the village, we found it completely deserted. All the houses were bombed. Next to the houses were huge craters in the ground. Only a few skeletons of single rooms survived these bombardments. Later I found out what happened there. Apparently there was a bridge nearby and the partisans who operated in this area dynamited that bridge as German units were passing over it; many German soldiers and civilians died. The Germans suspected that this village was harboring the partisans, so for punishment they bombed the village without warning in open daylight. When they saw what the Germans were up to, all the inhabitants of the houses abandoned them.

Chapter 23

Food for the Taking

PRIOR TO BEING ATTACKED, village farmers had dug huge storage holds in their yards where they kept their produce for the whole year. These were roughly 6 to 7 feet in diameter and just as deep, or deeper, lined with straw and filled with potatoes, corn, wheat and other vegetables. Over the top they built 6-foot high sheds with straw roofs to protect them from the cold and rain. They had ways of entering and exiting each storage place, which I later learned was called an *oborokee*.

The bombs fell about a week before we arrived. When many *oborokees* were burned down, vast quantities of food were exposed. In the village, we found one house that had a good room left, with doors and windows intact. In that room there was also an oven in which the farmer's wife would have baked bread. Right away we realized we would not have to go hungry; everything was there for the taking.

We found all kinds of cooking and baking utensils. Obviously, the farmers had left in a hurry. Twenty of us settled in this one room, and the rest of our *szazod* found single rooms in different houses that were still inhabitable. To make a fire in the oven and heat our room, we ripped off doors and window frames from the rest of the house. This was the only dry lumber we could find, and it would burn right away. In a way, we took great pleasure in doing this, having seen decimated Jewish houses all over Poland and knowing that the Poles were Hitler's helpers in persecuting the Jews. As we lay on the floor that night – in a warm room for the first time in a long while – pieces of wood from doors and windows burned in the oven, illuminating our room. We talked among ourselves: Passover would start in a couple of days and we should take some wheat out from the *oborokees* and bake matzos in the oven. Our only question was how to grind the wheat into flour.

The next morning, as we went out to repair the road, we learned from civilian passersby that one old man still lived in a partially bombed-out house and that he had a hand-mill to grind wheat into flour. On our second day in the village, a sergeant allowed one of us to stay behind; I was chosen because I knew the Slavic language. Instead of going out to work, I planned to go to the place where the old man lived. Neither we nor the *keret* had any bread then, so the *keret* was anxious to have me grind some wheat for bread also. (Of course, the *keret* already had been in contact with local people, so in no way were they hungry. We, on the other hand, had no contact with the locals except by happenstance.) Inside our bombed-out house, I found an empty sack, filled it with wheat, and went off to find the old farmer. When I located him, I addressed him in Ukrainian and asked what had happened to the village. He told me the whole story of what the partisans had done to the bridge and the Germans' retaliation that killed scores of people.

I handed the farmer the sack of wheat and he soon handed me back a sack of flour. Now the question was how to knead it into dough. A young man in our group from the former Romanian area, near Sighet, took over the whole project. He found the necessary utensils and a large wooden bowl, and he kneaded a flattened dough for matzo.[1] This could hardly qualify as matzo prepared under careful Rabbinical supervision,[2] but to this day whenever I celebrate Passover, I always recall those matzos we baked in 1944 on April 15 and 16.

One day we were ordered to march back to Brestlitowsk. Again we dragged our belongings with us and settled in a big barn. There the Germans wanted to fortify their positions, to stop the Russian advances by the River Bug. In 1941, the Germans encountered very stiff resistance from the Russians in this area. Now they were busy building new fortifications around the city, in trenches and bunkers, making iron and cement tank obstacles, and laying mine fields.

The German military also had their own professional civilian workers assigned to work for them – called the SA. One day I was among a group of 20 men from our *szazod* assigned to dig trenches inside the famous Brestlitowsk citadel. In this citadel, the Germans and Russians signed a peace agreement in 1918, known as the Brestlitowsk Treaty. It was a huge two-story fortress, and two armed Hungarian soldiers from our *szazod* escorted the 20 of us into this structure. German soldiers manned the fortress gates. As we entered, the Hungarians handed us over to a German soldier, the overseer. The yard inside the fortress was huge, built like a Latin "U." The

---

[1] This unleavened dough is known as a *myra*.
[2] *"Shmurah matzo m'hadrin min ha-m'hadrin."*

Germans then ordered us to start digging a trench from one side to the other and also across the middle in this huge yard. The trench had to be two meters deep and three-quarters of a meter wide. We worked a full day, and in the evening the Hungarian soldiers escorted us back to our *szazod*.

On the second day we again were sent to this fortress to continue working on the trenches. It was April 20, 1944, Hitler's birthday. We didn't know that then, but later we found it out because all the German officers and soldiers around us got extra rations of alcohol or wine. They carried on like real drunkards. From the three-sided balcony on the second floor of the citadel, they had fun aiming and shooting at us, over our heads, as we dug trenches. Quickly we took cover in the trenches. Several young officers sang and laughed at our predicament. But it wasn't fun to us. We were sure that we'd never come out of those trenches alive. To our great *mazel*, an elderly German officer, having heard the commotion, emerged from the first floor area and approached us. He demanded to know why we were lying down rather than working. We managed to explain, even though we were frightened to speak. Quickly he yelled up to the drunken soldiers on the balcony to cease shooting. They did, and that is how we were saved on Hitler's birthday.

We continued working in the citadel for another four or five days; after that we built cement tank obstacles. Then we moved on elsewhere.

In the beginning of May '44, we returned to Bialapodlaska, still carrying our heavy belongings – woolen blankets, winter clothing and heavy coats. Many among us thought the war would end before the next winter set in. And many thought that it was time to throw our winter clothing away; they wanted to make it easier on themselves, as it was too warm in the summertime to carry these cumbersome woolen blankets and backpacks.

We remained in Bialapodlaska for a short while. There we were put up in empty Jewish houses again. On many of the doorposts there were still *mezuzahs*. It was terribly depressing for us to stay in those houses, yet we still hoped that by some miracle Hungarian Jewry would be spared. That's the way human nature is: to go on struggling and hoping and continuing with life, for without hope there is no justification for one's existence.

A large contingent of German soldiers was also stationed in Bialapodlaska. Every morning, they'd come to our *szazod* and demand so many men to load and unload all kinds of materials and to do all sorts of other jobs. The Hungarians of course always obliged and delivered the Jewish slaves. There was also a German cavalry unit in Bialapodlaska with many horses. They cleaned their horses in steel disinfectant chambers. One horse at a time would be pushed into a chamber, which had a hole in the front for the horse's head. After locking the door, they piped in steam, mixing it with a chemical to wash and disinfect the horses for a few minutes. The horses were infected with something because they had many blisters, blotches and scars, probably very contagious to humans, too. Our job was to steer the horses into those cages and to clean and wipe them off. We were dumb enough at the time not to be concerned, so we didn't think or speak about it. The work was not really very hard labor, but it was dirty.

There were also disinfectant shower stalls for humans, the *entlausungsanstalt*, and huge laundry machines for the military. In these, we washed and dry cleaned blankets or uniforms. Once they were dry, we folded and sorted them. Again, this was not heavy work, but possibly contaminating.

After two weeks in Bialapodlaska, we were ordered to shoulder our backpacks again and march toward Warsaw. Along the way, we halted in a little town called Mezeritch,[3] approximately halfway between Brestlitowsk and Warsaw. There again we were put up in shattered remnants of Jewish homes. As we later found out, this small town once had a vibrant Jewish community life before Hitler's cohorts arrived in 1939. Exactly how many Jews resided in this town we never knew precisely but, from the look of it, surely a few thousand must have lived there. I later found out from a gentile resident that they even had a Jewish hospital built by a wealthy Jewish benefactor. Naturally, the Germans turned it into a military hospital for their own soldiers. This gentile told me that the hospital's patron managed to emigrate to the United States before the Holocaust decimated Mezeritch.[4]

---

[3] The town's Yiddish name. In Polish it was called Miendziczecpodlasky.

[4] I recall the surname the gentile man mentioned because a fellow by the same name, Moshe Shertok, was very well known in the Zionist movement. Moshe Shertok later became Foreign Secretary of Israel, so I don't believe he was related to the family that built that hospital. More recently, from a book published by survivors of Mezeritch, I read that the town in fact had been a thriving community of 18,000. The city's mayor, police force and fire brigade were Jewish. And the man

Two brigades or battalions of soldiers were stationed in Mezeritch, one German and one Hungarian. Later, they were dispatched to the battlefield. Before they left, I overheard their commander giving them a pep talk.

We worked unloading and lifting heavy crates of munitions: back-breaking work even for two men. One day as we were loading these heavy boxes and crates onto the military trucks, I wasn't feeling well at all. When we returned to the *szazod* where we were stationed, I went straight to my so-called bed (we slept on the floor). From somewhere we had found some straw that we spread out and used for a pillow. Suddenly I blacked out. David Godinger quickly called Doctor Ecker, one of our *szazod* doctors who was friendly with me. At one time he was a student of my Uncle Armin Darvosh in Sighet. When I awoke, Doctor Ecker stood over me and took my pulse, checked my temperature, and listened to my chest. After his examination he told me that I had pneumonia. Luckily he had a few aspirin that he gave me. He told me to put some wet, cold towels on my head to cool the fever. He also said that he'd bring me to the Hungarian battalion doctor the next morning, to get him to excuse me from work since he himself had no authority to let me remain.

David went down to the street (we were on the second floor) and by pure chance a Polish woman had a pitcher of milk that she hoped to barter for soap. He ran upstairs again and picked up a bar of soap and exchanged it for the milk, which he then brought to me. It was a miracle. As the folk saying goes, "G-d supplies the medicine before the illness."[5] I was burning up from high fever and we hadn't seen milk for a long time. That was my best medicine.

The next morning Doctor Ecker took me to the Hungarian doctor, one block away. I felt so weak and sick that I could barely walk with him. Doctor Ecker told the Hungarian doctor that I had pneumonia and a temperature of 41 Celsius. The Hungarian doctor didn't bother examining me. He just told Doctor Ecker to bring me back to him in 48 hours. That meant that I didn't have to go to work and could rest. We went back to our *szazod* and Doctor Ecker reported to Socorowsky, the *szazod* sergeant in the *keret*, that I mustn't go out to work for the next two days. The doctor didn't have any more aspirin so I remained in my "bed." Downstairs on the first

---

who founded the hospital had the family name of Sayetta, not Shertok. Sayetta emigrated to the United States. It's possible that this was the same man, but that he'd changed his name, since "Shertok" means "devil" in Slavic, and "Sayetta" in Hebrew means "help."

[5] Hebrew: *"Refuah lifnai ha-makah."*

floor was our field kitchen. The two cooks, Jewish boys from our *szazod*, brought me coffee and two slices of toast spread with margarine. They did that without authority, an act of true kindness. These cooks also did their best to help others in our *szazod*. Most of the time I wasn't hungry, only thirsty, because of my high fever. But I ate the bread. I knew that this would be the only nourishment I would get.

The 48 hours passed, and I still had a high temperature. Again, Doctor Ecker took me to the Hungarian doctor. He asked how high my temperature was. After being told, he gave me another 48 hours. I was fed again and allowed to lie on the floor and rest for two more days. On the fourth day, my temperature broke, but Doctor Ecker requested at least another 48 hours because I was still very weak. The Hungarian doctor refused, saying that he could not allow me to take time off, and since the fever was gone, I had to go back to work.

Doctor Ecker knew very well that I was incapable of doing work, especially hard work. But he had to report to Sergeant Socorowsky what the Hungarian doctor's decision was. (I'll never forget Socorowsky's name because he was sympathetic to us, and helped out whenever he could. He later deserted and joined the partisans.) Ecker told Sergeant Socorowsky that although my fever was gone I was very weak, that he should keep me back and not send me out to work. He told him that after a bout with pneumonia, I would need at least ten days to recuperate. The sergeant told Doctor Ecker that I should remain in the kitchen for now and peel potatoes. And he said tomorrow he'd see what he could do for me. The rest of the men continued to march out to do different kinds of work.

My friend David and I parted company in Mezeritch. The Hungarian brigade stationed there was in need of a tailor, and so they asked if there was someone in our *szazod* who could sew. David was a tailor, so he registered for the job. Of course this work was a lot easier for him than loading heavy equipment. He would report to the brigade every morning to work, but he returned every evening to sleep in our *szazod*. He'd bring me all kinds of conserves and, most importantly, cigarettes that he got from the Hungarian officers' "station," headquartered in other empty houses. He didn't smoke, but I did, and we couldn't get cigarettes anymore. Cigarettes were a very valuable form of currency: with them one could buy almost anything from a farmer – bread, butter, milk, etc.

One evening, David returned as usual and told me that the officer for whom he worked had confided to him that his Hungarian brigade was being sent back to Hungary. If he wished, David was told, he could accompany them as the brigade's tailor. This was either in May or in the beginning of June, 1944.

Asking me for advice, he said, "I don't want to part from you. We're both from Torun, we've been together a whole year. We practically sleep under the same blanket. What should I do? Whatever you advise me I'll do."

Of course it was very hard for me to separate from David, but I told him, "My advice to you is to go with this brigade. You have a chance to make it easier on yourself, so grab the opportunity! If it's destined that we should survive the war, we will survive it, and maybe reminisce about it in a more joyful time. But now, go, and don't think about it anymore. May G-d help us both to survive."

The next morning, with tears in our eyes, we said goodbye to each other. David, thank G-d, survived the war and now lives in Eshkalon, Israel. In fact, he was liberated four months earlier than I was.

Chapter 24

Learning a 'Trade'

OUR SAGES TAUGHT A PRECEPT that I didn't quite understand for a long time: "It is incumbent upon parents to teach their children three things: Torah, a trade, and swimming."[1] Torah guides Jewish children in a way to live that brings them closer to G-d. As for a trade, I saw that David's having one probably saved his life because he was able to work as a tailor for six of the most terrible months of the war, rather than suffer through hard labor. But the third admonishment, "swimming," used to puzzle me. "What is so important about swimming?" I'd ask myself. But I see it now: swimming is a metaphor for swimming through life's challenges to save yourself from "drowning."

I experienced the difficulty of trying to make a living without knowing a trade when I emigrated to the United States. When I speak of plying a trade, I mean someone like a tailor, a shoemaker, or watchmaker – people who can do their work and earn a living wherever they must go, whatever the country, whatever the language.

Precisely after David left, our biggest problems began. That day, I was in the *szazod* kitchen. As long as there was no one from the *keret* around, the cooks had me do light work. But the next day, Dr. Ecker got a transfer for me to work in the barn, taking care of the horses. This would be easier work for me, and I could recuperate from pneumonia more quickly. In the barn, there were six horses and three wagons, with one of our boys assigned to each wagon. While we had to carry all our heavy backpacks in the rain or heat and walk, these boys sat atop the wagon and drove the horses. Again, because they had a trade – skill at handling a horse-and-buggy, how to care for horses, how to fix wagons – their lives were easier.

Supervising these three fellows was a Hungarian soldier who not long before was promoted to the high rank of *tizedes*. In Hungarian, *tizedes* means ten; that meant he was the lofty commander of 10 soldiers. Not even a general had his bloated ego.

His name was Kish – I'll never forget it. When I arrived in the barn, I had to report to him. Of course I had a written order with me from Sergeant Socorowsky. When I reported to him, he gave me what we call in Yiddish "a *finster baruch ha-bah*" (a nasty welcome).

---

[1] *"Shloshah d'varim chayav adam lilmod et banav–Torah, m'lachah, s'chiyah."*

"You," he screamed, "What do you know about horses? Let me see what you know."

Pointing to one horse, he ordered me to clean and comb it right away. He knew that this was a nervous horse that kicked and bit. As I approached the horse and started to comb him on the rear, Kish yelled even more.

"Never start combing a horse from the rear, only from the neck down." Then he barked, *"Fakutch, fakutch,"* the punishment of falling to the ground and doing 100 push-ups, without touching the floor with one's belly. A person in good physical shape might do that 20 to 30 times at the most, but I was weak and managed only five before collapsing on the floor. Kish grabbed his rifle and with its butt struck my back numerous times, screaming, "You dirty Jew! *You* know how to take care of horses!" He worked himself into a frenzy.

I couldn't get up from the floor, and he continued to kick and hit me with his rifle butt. One of our boys couldn't hold back anymore when he saw the beating I was getting. He rushed over, begging Kish to stop, and tried to calm him down. Kish was in a rage, but he couldn't punish me by overriding the sergeant's order and sending me back to the *szazod* to do hard labor. Finally, he calmed down and left when he had satisfied his sadistic urges.

The Jewish boys later tried to reassure me by telling me not to worry, that they'd help me. They showed me how to harness the horses, how to put on their reins, how to hitch them to the wagons, and how to communicate with them and keep them calm. I never did learn how to speak to the horses. I guess that's a secret part of the trade of a horse and buggy man.

Sometime in early June 1944, I was ordered to take two sick horses out to a field that was at the edge of Mezeritch. Close by there was a small stream. The field was covered with new grass. The road that led to this field passed through the Jewish section, now completely deserted. Suddenly, as I was riding on one horse and leading the other with a rope (fortunately neither horse was the nervous type), a terrible scene unfolded in front of me, and I realized I was passing through a Jewish ghetto. The streets were littered with pillow feathers and torn pillowcases. Cooking utensils, spoons, forks and dishes were thrown all over the place. Many stray leaves from sacred Jewish books were strewn on the streets. It hit me hard. As I slowly rode by, I peered into the houses. Every room was divided with plywood into two or three rooms. It was evident that many families were crammed into each house and that the poor souls divided their rooms for a little privacy. Although I saw empty Jewish houses in Stanislov, Bialapodlaska and other places, nothing made a more terrible impression on me than this. I've no words to describe its destruction and the obviously savage rape of our people. I learned later that this ghetto was emptied out not long before I saw it.

When I reached the nearby field, I dismounted my horse and sat on the grass to rest. I couldn't erase the nightmarish sight from my mind. It reminded me of the famous poem that Chaim Nachman Bialek wrote after the Kishiniev pogrom, entitled "City of Slaughter." To translate one verse of it loosely: "The sun was shining, and the knife was gleaming and the slaughterer was slaughtering."

While I sat there, dazed, the horses quietly grazed on the fresh grass. My body rested, but my soul ached. No more did I feel the pain of Kish's rifle-butt jabs. This gruesome scene in the Jewish ghetto had me asking G-d just one question: "Why did You allow this to happen?"

Suddenly, I awoke as if from a slumber. It was time to take the horses back to the barn. When I returned and told the other fellows what I saw, fear overcame us, yet we had to go on; we tried to convince each other that this wouldn't happen to the Hungarian Jewish community, that we would be spared.

On my second day I was sent out again to tend to the grazing horses. Riding a horse through the ghetto, I passed by an unfamiliar alley where I noticed an open book lying in the middle of the road. I dismounted and picked it up. As I started to read, I was astonished to find that this was a *Chumash* opened to Deuteronomy. The open pages were from the *Tochacha* (which means "punishment"). A shiver came over me as I read: "And He will bring upon thee all the diseases of Egypt which thou was in dread of, and they shall cleave unto thee. Also every sickness and every plague, which is not written in the book of this law, them will the Lord bring upon thee until thou be destroyed" (Deuteronomy XXVIII:60-61).[2]

"What a frightening coincidence," I thought to myself. I brought the *Chumash* along with me to the field and, while the horses grazed, sat down to re-read the entire chapter. The most troubling verse for

---

2 *"V'haishiv b'chah et kol madvai Mitzraiim asher yagorta mipnaihem v'davchu bach. Gam kol choli v'kol maka asher loh katuv b'sepher ha-Torah ha-zot ya'alaim Hashem alechah ad hishamdach."*

me was the passage saying that upon us would be delivered punishments that are not even described in the Torah.[3] This disturbed me greatly. Verse 34 also troubled me: "You shall be driven mad from what your eyes shall see."[4]

It was a day of difficult experiences. The field where the horses grazed was very large. As I sat on the ground, deeply immersed in my thoughts, my two horses moved quite a distance away from me. As I walked toward them, I noticed a big tent in the distance, with small children playing near it. As I approached, I couldn't believe my eyes. The entire tent was made out of Torah scrolls. "G-d in heaven, what is going on here?" I said to myself. If we Jews saw the Torah accidentally drop to the floor, the whole congregation would fast in remorse. And now, my G-d, look at what the *goyim* are doing with your Torah! Is this why we are guilty *ad hashmadah*, until total destruction, as it is written in the *Tochacha*?

An elderly gentile approached and began to speak to me. Perhaps he could see by the look on my face that I was Jewish. "Where did they get all these Torah scrolls to make a tent?" I asked. He then told me that he was a watchman in a nearby lumber mill, and in that mill were many more Jewish scrolls, which had been removed from the ghetto. He told me that not too long ago the Germans had emptied the ghetto out. A lot of Jews were killed, buried not too far from there, on the same field. Many other Jews were sent somewhere, but he didn't know where. It seemed that he was telling me all this with a feeling of sorrow and pity. He was also the man who told me about the rich Jew, Shertok, who had built the hospital in Mezeritch. He claimed that Mezeritch had been filled with many wealthy Jews who owned a lot of brush factories and other businesses. What he said sounded like the typical anti-Semitic belief that all Jews are rich – obviously an expression of jealousy and hatred.

I returned the next day to the same field, and this Polish man again came to talk to me. I soon realized the reason why he spoke to me in a tone of sympathy about the Jews. He told me that the previous Sunday, the Germans executed forty young Poles from Mezeritch and its vicinity, young men whom they accused of taking part in partisan actions against the Germans. That is why he spoke with hatred against the Germans. I listened to his ramblings, but I didn't make any comments because I didn't trust him. I remembered

---

[3] *"Asher loh katuv b'sepher ha-Torah ha-zot."*
[4] *"V'hytah meshugah mi-marai ainecha asher tireh"*

what we found out in Malarita. There, the partisans were very active, and we in the Hungarian *szazod* thought of running away and joining them. But even though the partisans fought the Germans, they were also known to rob and then murder Jews who wanted to join them. Joining the partisans was not an option for us anymore. The hatred of the Poles toward Jews was then and is now still very strong. Many times I heard Poles say to me. that they were grateful to the Germans for one reason: they cleaned the Jews out of Poland.

One day as I rode my horse through the ghetto, I passed a low-built house. I was able to look into the attic and see a pile of books. Through a window, I reached in with my hand and pulled out two of them. To my astonishment, one was an anthology of poems by Chaim Nachman Bialek, which included "City of Slaughter"; the other was *All Quiet on the Western Front* by the German author Erich Maria Remarque, translated into Yiddish.

The attic was filled with a treasure of Yiddish and Hebrew texts by some of our greatest writers: Mendela, Peretz, Shalom Aleichem, Sholem Asch and others. Although I'd read Bialek's book before the war, I wanted to read it again. And as for Erich Maria Remarque's *All Quiet on the Western Front*, I remember my brother Eliezer often spoke about it. Eliezer knew the famous Hebrew poet Avigdor Hameiri (they attended the same yeshiva at the same time) who also wrote about World War I. His book was *The Great Insanity*.[5] It is hard to say whether Eliezer was biased, but he felt that had the Nobel Prize Committee not been anti-Semitic, Avigdor Hameiri would have gotten the Nobel Prize for his book on World War I instead of Remarque.

Over the next few days I had time to finish reading *All Quiet on the Western Front* and also to scan through the pages of *City of Slaughter*. Bialek's words troubled me: "They had no 'flavor' in their lives, and neither did they in their deaths."[6]

Where could we flee now? Like many other Jews, I blamed myself that we didn't flee when we'd been warned. But we were in the deadly grip of the Germans, the mightiest power in Europe, and entire populations – Poles, Ukrainians and all the rest – were against

---

[5] In Hebrew, *Ha-Shigaon Ha-Gadol.*
[6] *"Lo hayah lahem ta'am b'chayehem, v'lo b'motam."*

us and assisting the brutal savages. The revolt in the Warsaw ghetto that took place in 1943 around Passover (in April or in early May) was a heroic resistance, but it was also a suicidal act. The Jews died along with their oppressors, as Samson died along with the Philistines when he pulled the pillars down around him.[7]

It was during this time, while walking through the ghetto, that I spotted a letter with a Palestine postage stamp on it. Picking it up from the ground, I saw the letter was written in early 1939 from a son to his parents in Mezeritch. From this letter it was apparent that his mom and dad had experienced some domestic discord, and the son expressed his happiness that peace and tranquility had returned to their home. But the part of the letter that still haunts my mind was the son beseeching, "I beg you, dear parents, sell the brush factory and come to Zion. The heavens over Europe are filled with black clouds. Come, join me and let's all be together. A terrible hurricane is on the way to destroy the Jewish people." When I finished reading this letter, I wondered if the parents heeded their son's call.

---

[7] *"Tamut naphshi im Plishtim."*

Chapter 25

Retreat

I RECUPERATED FROM THE PNEUMONIA over a span of two weeks. During that time, I did no hard labor, and watching the horses was so easy and restful that I could read. I owe many thanks to Doctor Ecker and mainly to the *szazod* Sergeant Socorowsky, who, realizing by then that the Axis would lose the war, was sympathetic toward us.

Around the middle of June, a member of our *szazod* got hold of a Polish newspaper. This was how we found out about D-Day. American and English troops landed on the coast of France on June 6 and opened a second front. Naturally, the paper headlined the American and British defeats and losses, but we read between the lines and again felt a glimmer of hope that the war would end soon.

At the end of June 1944, we were ordered to move again. Only the commander knew ahead of time where we were going. This time we moved closer to the front lines, closer to the River Bug. As we arrived at the small village called Janof Litowsk, we were ordered to sit down on a field near the main road. In the center square of the village, we saw tables on which a German general and his many other officers spread out maps and studied them. The day was warm and sunny, and we remained on the grass quite a few hours.

To *munkotabornikas* like us, it seemed that we were surrounded by the Russians, and that the Germans and Hungarians didn't know which way to go. Quietly, we spoke among ourselves, hoping our speculation was true. We also hoped that if the Russians captured us, they'd liberate us immediately. Who knew then what we now know: that when the Russians captured some of our Jewish *szazods*, they treated them the same as enemies. Hundreds of our Jewish boys died in Russian war prisoner camps, among them my cousin Abraham Popper.

So we sat on that field and waited for salvation or rescue. The local people from the village freely mingled in the streets with the soldiers. From the locals, we found out that the Russians had broken through the German lines, and the Germans and Hungarians were in retreat. Locals usually were looking to barter for cigarettes and soap, both of which were scarce. We didn't get any food that day at all, only what we had in reserve or were able to buy from the locals. Around 4 p.m., we were ordered to line up in the normal marching order. Organized by height, I took my place at the front and waited. Soon enough a whole battalion of Hungarian soldiers came running in retreat with German soldiers. We marched back this time in the direction of a town called Wengroff.

All kinds of Hungarian and German military units were on the run, and what a beautiful sight that was. It gladdened our hearts to see the Germans running like poisoned mice. The Germans rode on motorized vehicles, while the Hungarians used wagons and horses to carry their military equipment. Naturally, all this traffic created a bottleneck. In such a great hurry, the Germans literally pushed the Hungarians off the narrow road, cursing them as they did. As the Germans ran helter-skelter, we hoped that this signaled the war's end and our imminent "liberation" by the Russians.

Behind these fleeing military units, a few young SS soldiers combed the area on motorcycles. Back and forth they drove to see whether any German or Hungarian soldiers lagged behind or stayed behind voluntarily. Their orders were to shoot to kill any such straying troops on the spot.

When we saw those SS on the motorcycles combing the area for the deserters, those of us who thought of escaping realized it was impossible. The Hungarian *keret* maintained a strict watch over us. With loaded rifles, they marched alongside us, but when they saw Germans shove the Hungarians out of the way they didn't like it at all, and seemed to become a little kinder to us.

We marched like that behind the retreating military units until dark. Then we were ordered off the road to rest in a field until the next morning. It was June 1944, and the weather was mild. We made our makeshift beds – our backpacks became our pillows and we wrapped ourselves up in our warm woolen blankets – and everybody tried to doze off. Then suddenly, around 11 p.m., the roar of airplanes woke us, and very soon the whole area was lit up like midday. Russian planes illuminated the area with flares. Then bombs fell and exploded, the ground shaking a short distance from us. But we were so bitter about our oppressors and so wanted their destruction that we totally lacked any fear of being bombed from above. To us the exploding bombs were like *manna* from heaven.

This bombardment lasted about 15 minutes. Afterward, I couldn't fall back to sleep. Although we were all exhausted, a ray of hope that we'd soon be liberated gave us the strength to cope. In the morning, we marched on again and arrived in Wengroff. There we saw a "beautiful picture." The streets were clogged with broken cars and wagons and dead horses. The human casualties had already been cleared out, but still strewn all over the main street were various kinds of military supplies and provisions. In the midst of the smoke, we could see bombed-out houses, shops and some buildings still burning. On the main street store-fronts had been bombed and policemen were guarding them against being looted. On some of them I could still see *mezuzah* marks, which I always looked for. This little town must have had a Jewish population, but there were no longer signs of any community (neither here, nor, for that matter, in any Polish town by June 1944). Last night's bombardment wiped out the last vestiges. After passing through Wengroff, we reached the town of Sokoloff. On the way there, we encountered more broken vehicles and cars abandoned on the road. But we didn't see any German or Hungarian units again.

Sokoloff also once had a Jewish community, like many small towns near the big city of Warsaw, the heart of Polish Jewry. We stayed in Sokoloff a few days, waiting for orders to march elsewhere, and in the meantime we occupied former Jewish homes. In the neighborhood where "my" house was, there was a bakery. For the first time in a long while, I was able to buy a whole loaf of just-baked warm bread for Hungarian money. I can still taste that baked bread in my mouth. I wolfed it down practically whole.

From Sokoloff we marched off again in the direction of the city of Modlin. Needless to say, we still dragged our heavy winter clothing along. At one point we had to cross over a long bridge where German soldiers at each end and in the center were posted as guards. Again, I marched at the head of our *szazod* due to my height. (Depending on where we were, we lined up either by two, three or four, according to our immediate circumstances. Military strategy dictated that in proximity to enemy troops, it made more sense to march by two or in single-file, since a column of three- or four-across was an easier target for a spray of bullets.) In the summertime especially it was advantageous for me to be up front because most of the roads we trod on were unpaved dirt; those bringing up the rear had to swallow the clouds of dust we kicked up in front.

When we reached the bridge, I boldly asked the German soldier standing guard, "*Wie heist der Fluss?*" – What is the name of this river? He didn't answer me. Was it because I was Jewish? I didn't get a chance to find out because a Hungarian soldier from our *keret* suddenly rammed my back with his rifle butt so hard that I almost fell over. In Hungarian, he barked at me, "This is for your audacity for talking to the German."

After we crossed over the river, we marched till it got dark; then we were ordered to rest in a field overnight. The next morning we started out for Modlin. When we reached our destination, we were put up in a barn on a wealthy farmer's estate.[1]

Near Modlin, three rivers flowed into the Wisla: the Bug, Narew and Wkra. The Germans planned to stop the Russian advances there. They were laying minefields, building bunkers and trenches, and using cement and steel defensive barricades, which would stop even a tank. To get the jobs done right, they utilized a unit of the German SA, civilians who were experts in building projects. Our *szazod* was assigned to help the SA with all sorts of work, including digging trenches along the Wisla River.

A group of us were assigned to chop down all the young pine trees in a nearby forest. From these young pines, we cut off the branches, leaving branch stubs about 12 inches long, up and down the trunk. Then we took three of those trees – really young trees whose trunks measured only 4 or 5 inches in diameter and six meters in length – and secured them together with barbed wire. We then placed them along the banks of the river.

One day I was walking near that forest with a close friend and others from the Carpathian region, when a young man approached us. He spoke to us in Polish and asked us whether we had cigarettes to sell. Even when we told him that we had none, he insisted and became very persistent. In Yiddish, I said to my friend, "Look what a stubborn Polish pig he is!"[2]

Hearing my comment, the young man gasped in astonishment, "Are you Jews? I, too, am a Jew, not a Polish pig!"[3] He started to weep and continued speak to us in Yiddish.

This was the first time we met a Jew in Poland. When we asked him about other Jews in the area, he told us about the Warsaw ghetto uprising. This was the first time that we heard about it. It took place more than one year before, in April 1943 (now we were at the end of June or the beginning of July 1944). He told us of the horrors of the burning ghetto, how he escaped through the sewer canals, and that he was now living in Modlin with a gentile college friend. They had both studied engineering, and he was living there on false Aryan

[1] In Polish, a *filvaruk*.
[2] *"Gib a keek – vus ein eingeshparter Poilische chazzer ist"*
[3] *"Ihr zind Yidden? Ich bin auch a Yid, nicht kein Polische chazzer!"*

papers. Both my friend and I were happy to hear that there was at least one righteous person in "Sodom."

We gave him two cigarettes, which were a precious commodity to us, too. We asked him to come the next day and we'd give him more cigarettes from other *szazod* members. We longed to hear more about what happened in the Warsaw ghetto on Passover 1943. That evening in our *szazod*, we informed the others quietly and secretly what happened to our fellow Jews in Warsaw. All of us were devastated by the news. All night I stayed awake haunted by visions of the burning Warsaw ghetto. I knew that before the war it was the most vibrant and intellectual capital of Jewish thought, superior to all the other Jewish communities in Europe. This tremendous spiritual source produced great rabbis, religious leaders, great poets, literary giants, Jewish historians and Zionist thinkers. The *Kabbalah* scholar Hillel Tsaitlin once lived in Warsaw. Jewish leaders from all over Europe – Jabotinsky, Nachum Sokolov, Chaim Weitzman, Doctor Joshua Tohn, the historian Balaban, Chaim Nachman Bialek, father and son Priluski, and many others – had the fruits of their intellectual labors published in Warsaw. There were at least a half dozen Yiddish daily newspapers published there, and numerous weeklies in Yiddish, Hebrew and Polish.

The next day this fellow tried to visit us, but we couldn't meet him because the Hungarian soldiers had us loading the barbed-wire trees onto their wagons. From afar, we saw but were unable to speak with him. This same day two Russian planes flew overhead, spotted the activity going on near the forest, and descended almost directly over us, firing a hail of bullets. We barely managed to flee unscathed into the forest, when the shooting stopped and the planes flew away. Although terror-shaken, luckily none of us was injured.

For more than a month, we remained in the Modlin area. The Germans and the Hungarians were very busy building fortifications around there and along the length of the Wisla River. One day in July we were ordered to move again, this time to a place called Wizhgorod and Zhelazhna Wola, where we stayed for a short time. There we repaired small wooden bridges along the road. We were usually put up in barns, or if there was no barn, in a field. (The *keret* usually didn't appreciate bedding down in a field, as they had to guard us.)

One day we were working on the unpaved gravel road, scattering stones. Our *szazod* then consisted of about 200 men, working over one kilometer of land. Suddenly, German soldiers on horses rode by with hundreds of cattle, cows, calves and oxen. The Germans rode on all sides of the cattle, driving them away from the battle lines, away from the local population. Maybe they hoped to ship this cattle by train to Germany or drive them somewhere and slaughter them for meat for the German military. We knew that it was a good sign that they were retreating and running from the Russians, looting from the local population as they went. We got off the road and stood aside as the cattle passed.

One mounted officer said to us repeatedly, "Hitler is *kaput*, Hitler is *kaput*." We couldn't believe our ears and wondered if he were drunk or speaking the truth. Naturally, we were too flabbergasted and said nothing. When we returned to that road the next day, two German planes flew very low overhead and dropped leaflets to the ground. On those leaflets was the news that an attempt was made on Hitler's life, but that the Führer had survived and all was well. It seems the Germans feared the local population would contemplate revolting, so they wanted to let them know that Hitler, YS, was alive and well.

Hitler's life was spared on July 20, 1944. As I write these lines, I still wonder, *Oh G-d in heaven, why did you spare him?* Surely more than a million Jews would have been saved had Hitler been finished off and the war ended at this point. Almost all of the Hungarian Jewish community was still intact. My whole family, my mother and my three brothers and their families, I believed, might still be alive.

Of course, I didn't know then that my mother, Eliezer and Moshe and their families, as well as Zvi's family had already been shipped to Auschwitz. In fact, I didn't know about this concentration camp at all at this point. It was only later that I learned the Nazis herded our people into ghettos on *Shavuot*, the Festival of Weeks (May 28, 1944); thereafter they shipped them to Auschwitz. My own family had been deported near the end of May or beginning of June 1944. Who knew whether any of them were still alive by this point in July?

The Russians, still pushing the Germans and Hungarians back, were nearing the Wisla river. Abruptly, we had to move on again. The Hungarians, it seemed, were in a great hurry to flee because we were ordered to cease work in the afternoon and evacuate immediately. We marched through the night, this time to the city of Zhirardow. As the sky darkened, a heavy summer rain poured down on us. It was pitch dark. We couldn't see more than a couple of meters in front of us. As always, I was in the front row, and two Hungarian soldiers from the *keret* marched in front of us. At least they had good raincoats and shoes, but we poor slaves had nothing like that. And we had to *shlep* our bags, our backpacks with the heavy winter clothing and blankets soaked from the rain. As we were soaked through and through, our baggage became heavier and heavier. But the order was not to stop. The *keret* cursed even though they were well protected from the rain and didn't have anything else but their rifles to carry – *their* belongings were on the horse-driven wagons. On the one hand, we took great pleasure in the Russians chasing them as they fled, dragging us with them. But on the other hand, we were in a miserable situation. Normally, when we marched we talked quietly among us; this time the whole *szazod* kept silent. Everyone contemplated his own troubles. I tried to think positive thoughts to lift my spirits: "If G-d grants me life and I see the end of this war, I'll never forget this night, and I will tell my tale to my mother and brothers, and we will rejoice and be happy again."

Late in the night, it stopped raining; we kept marching. In the early morning we reached Zhirardow, a distance of more than 50 kilometers. As the sun rose, we could see steam rising from each of us as from a boiling kettle. We were put up in a large, empty factory building that had been a paper mill. There, we found bales of cigarette paper not yet cut, as well as cartons and other paper products. We spread them out on the floor and lay down upon them, exhausted.

To our good fortune, we didn't have to go out to work that first day. This was not because the Hungarian military took pity on us, but because they had pity on our guards, who also had had a bad night. Taking advantage of the situation, we got undressed completely, and tried to hang up our clothing to dry wherever possible. Zhirardow housed a Hungarian depot for materials and food supplies. So we did get provisions for a few days.

After two days, we were split into smaller groups and sent out to work. I was assigned to a group that worked at the train station. The Germans and the Hungarians used us to load all sorts of goods, even furniture, clothing and yarn, to ship back to Germany and Hungary.

Other groups worked in areas outside the city, building tank barricades, bunkers, trenches and so forth.

One day, as we were loading cargo, a carton broke open; inside was chocolate. Pleased beyond words, we all eagerly helped ourselves to the chocolate – eating enough to satisfy ourselves and never daring to stuff our pockets out of fear of being caught red-handed.

Those of us who spoke Czech or Ukrainian were able to converse in Polish with the local people who were also working at the train station. From them, we found out that the Russians had crossed the Wisla River around the area of Warsaw. When we were close to the battle lines like this, our *keret* and our commanding officers treated us very leniently. We figured they feared the Russians capturing us and setting us free, and that we'd take revenge against them.

In the beginning of August 1944, we again got our marching orders, still not knowing where we were going. But this time we heard from the locals that citizens of Warsaw had started to revolt against the Germans. We left Zhirardow in the morning and arrived in the afternoon at the village of Yezsorna, about 20 kilometers from Warsaw. There we settled in a barn. From there, every day, we marched about five or six kilometers to the nearby Wisla River, where again we dug trenches two meters deep and made bunkers on the river. The Russians had already taken up positions on the other side of the Wisla. Soil along the river was soft and we dug up enough dirt to form a heap two meters high, which obscured our view of the water and the Russians' view of us.

One day during our half-hour lunch break, I was sitting next to a friend, Willi Lorber, and somehow we decided to climb that heap of dirt to see what was happening on the other side of the river. Then we came back down and sat on the edge of the trench. Probably a Russian on the other side spotted us with binoculars, because after a few minutes a grenade flew over from their side and exploded just beyond us. Four of us were wounded, three slightly, and one very seriously. I was among the lightly wounded, hurt in my shoulder and elbow. Blood ran down my face, too, but I didn't notice that at first.

We immediately dove into the trench, and there was a second explosion. Doctor Ecker rushed over to check us and told the sergeant that we had to be sent back to the barn so he could treat us there. On our way to the barn via the *szazod's* wagon, Doctor Ecker examined and cleaned our wounds. One fellow by the name of Bloom said his leg injury was serious and deep, and Doctor Ecker asked that they transport him to the military field hospital, which they did. I got three days' rest since my wounds were only superficial. (Years later, in 1955, I suddenly developed a big boil on my face that wouldn't heal. I went to see my doctor who cut it open and was surprised to find a piece of shrapnel there. He asked me about it. I had totally forgotten about this wound for the eleven years that it lay dormant.)

The three days that I stayed in the Polish barn, I didn't work. One of my problems was that I had become temporarily deaf when the grenade exploded; my ears rang. A frightening feeling, but it cleared up in a day or so.

A group of us slept in an attic full of hay. It was such a treat to sleep in that hay – it almost felt like a real bed! During the day, I'd come down from the attic and go into the owner's "Garden of Eden" to pick ripe tomatoes, cucumbers, carrots, onions, gooseberries, plums and pears.

We remained in Yezsorna for about three weeks. For those first few days in August of 1944, the revolt in Warsaw was successful. But then the Germans brought in reinforcements, many in black uniforms, probably Ukrainian. From the air, they heavily bombed and completely overwhelmed the insurgents and the entire city. Having crossed the Wisla River, now the Russians pulled back, not because the Germans pushed them back, but for political reasons. The Russians didn't want the uprising to succeed because the underground movement leading it was an extension of the Polish government in exile in London, which the Soviets were planning to oppose. In fact, the Russians sat on the other side of the Wisla, watching the destruction of Warsaw and the uprising without lifting a finger to help. Without their assistance, the Polish people were unable to defend themselves from being crushed by the German boot.

Once the Germans completely choked off the uprising, the Soviets formed their own government in exile in the Polish city of Lublin. This was a Communist government that was to be a counterweight to the Polish government in London. When they finally crossed the river again and liberated Warsaw, the Soviets installed the Lublin Polish Communist government.

The flames from Warsaw rose in the night sky, a blaze so tremendous that from as far away as Yezsorna, we could see it illuminate the dark. Although I had little sympathy for the anti-Semitic Poles, and while I knew at this point that there were no more Jews left in Warsaw, I still found it hard to see such a great city go up in flames.

Again we were ordered to march. We slung our backpacks over our shoulders and this time headed closer to Warsaw. We couldn't understand why we were going to enter that burning city, and it was very frightening for us. We reached a place called Wlochy, at the outskirts of the town, and we put up there. Overnight we slept in the middle of a field. To this day I don't know what they expected us to do in Warsaw.

As we sat in the field, an old Polish man approached us with tears in his eyes, gesticulating with his hands to his head. He was practically wailing and said in Polish, "Warsaw has already been burning for 17 days."[4]

I asked him, "Did you also cry like this last year when the Germans burned down the Jewish ghetto?"

His face registered tremendous surprise. I could tell he didn't expect such a question. He probably hadn't realized we were Jews. All the time we'd been speaking among ourselves in Hungarian, and our yellow armbands had on them only the number 104/108 of the *szazod*, no Star of David. Abruptly, he turned away and left us.

---

[4] Polish: *"Yush Warsawa gorzhi shedemnasti dzhien."*

Chapter 26

Kol Nidre, 1944

THE ROAD FROM WARSAW WAS CLOGGED WITH CHILDREN without parents, holding white flags in their hands as they fled the burning city. German soldiers mixed with Ukrainian volunteer units, combing houses from block to block and emptying them of all valuables and expensive furniture. The Germans loaded these spoils of war onto anything with wheels: trucks, of course, but horse and buggy wagons, too. Later, they dynamited the houses or burned them down. This was typical of Nazi carnage and atrocities of war.

Our *szazod* commander suddenly wanted to go to Warsaw, supposedly to find a piano; he told a lower ranking member, a Hungarian of the *keret*, that he was going to find a piano in a house, and off he went. The rest of us remained camped on the field, waiting for him to return; he never did. Whether he really went to Warsaw in search of a piano and got killed or realized that the war was going badly for the Germans and Hungarians and deserted, I never learned.

Sporadic fighting broke out all the time. The Polish uprising lasted about two months. The officer left in charge decided to march us back to Zhirardow, where there was a Hungarian division command depot with military and food supplies. Fortunate we were that the officer was an elderly man and relatively tolerable.

Back in Zhirardow, we again settled in the former paper factory and rested. Our supervisor didn't know what to do with us. This was how pathetic we were, men stripped of all rights, whose destiny depended on the whim of some low-ranking officer. We sat around more than 10 days, waiting in vain for our piano-seeking commander.

At that point, the Hungarian division headquarters assigned a new commander to our *szazod*. A captain, he was a real bloodsucker, an extremely malicious man. Until then, our previous commanders were more humane. Because of his goatee, we secretly called him the *szokalos*, the bearded one; his cruelty still blocks my mind from recalling his name, and it's just as well. He lined us all up into a column four men abreast, cursing us, berating us, putting us down in the foulest language I ever heard from any of our commanders. We were stunned, and so were some of the *keret*.

He started off with the word *bipchik*. In Hungarian, *bipchik* is similar to the demeaning word "kike." "Listen, *bipchik*, you look too

human. At home in Hungary we're already making soap from scum
like you." The bearded one shook his head. "How they've let you do
such a pitiful job I'll never know. Dogs, I intend to change that; if
any of you don't carry your load, I'll bind you up for two hours."

He cursed and rattled on. "You dirty Jews. You are all
Communists. We will make soap out of you." To the *keret* he said,
"You're too lenient with those dirty *bipchiks*. If you don't act cruel to
them – as they deserve! – I'll bind you up too."

In Hungarian "binding up" is called *kikötes*. A person's hands are
bound behind his back, and the poor soul is hung from a post or tree
by his tied-up hands, his feet dangling off the ground, his agonized
face limply hanging down. Within 15 minutes he'd lose
consciousness. Then his tormentors would pour water over him,
cutting him down. When he regained his senses, he was hung up
again. Anyone who survived such a punishment was crippled for a
long time. Sadly, we were soon forced to witness such hangings of
men from our *szazod*. After the bearded bloodsucking beast dismissed
us, we returned to the factory, browbeaten and frightened. Now we
were in for it, in the deadly grip of a wild animal, completely
vulnerable to his cruel whims, and we were petrified.

At that time in 1944, the Hungarian government under Prime
Minister Kallay was replaced.[1] Later we learned that Kallay refused to
accede to the Germans. But there was a fascist movement, the Nylos,
in Hungary, and they were even worse than the German Nazis.
Szalasi was their leader. We knew nothing about the political climate
inside Hungary at the time, but Szalasi was reinforcing his grip with a
powerful military machine.[2] Those Hungarian military officers who
didn't align themsclves politically with the Szalasi movement or his
Nylos government tended to be slightly less antagonistic to us.

This, then, was our situation. Although we'd already heard the
rumors that in Hungary Jews were being shipped to Germany, we
hadn't yet learned of the existence of Auschwitz, Majdanek, Gross-
Rosen or other death camps. Dachau we had read about since it was

---

[1] In March 1944, Germans sent in troops to occupy Hungary; Kallay was ousted
and replaced by Döme Sztojay. This was an extremely anti-Semitic, pro-Nazi
government that lasted until August, when Sztojay was dismissed by Hungary's
Regent, Horthy, and replaced by General Géza Lakotos. The General was less
servile to the Germans, but his government lasted only until October, when the
Germans installed the Arrow Cross Party under the leadership of Ferenc Szalasi.
This sealed the fate of the majority of Hungarian Jews: out of approximately
850,000, only about 260,000 survived.
[2] After the war he was captured and hanged.

set up in the 1930s, but only when we were shipped to concentration camps did we learn all the sordid details.

What the eye doesn't see, the brain tends not to believe. We could never believe that human beings were capable of the atrocities we heard about, and hoped against hope that the rumors weren't true. But hearing our own commander's threats, we knew he meant them, and this terrified and depressed us that family members we had left behind by now were all murdered.

Soon we were on the march again. A week before Rosh Hashanah, we came to Gora Kalvaria (pronounced GOR-ah kahl-VAR-ah), a town along the banks of the Wisla River. It had to be the eighth or the ninth of September 1944. Shortly our *szazod* received mail. Whether the mail arrived that day or had been waiting for our arrival some time before, I never knew, but it wasn't distributed right away. This was the first time since we left Hungary that we received mail. I received a postcard from my brother Zvi. I forget the date of the card, but simply getting a sign of life from him exhilarated me. Unbeknownst to me then, he was in a place called Bor, somewhere in Yugoslavia.

From our secret code I learned he was in a precarious position. Still, because I held his postcard in my hand, I knew he was alive, and that was a great relief. Many more boys also received postcards, a few from parents who had been deported to Germany. The Nazis were very clever in the way they hid their crimes. They forced these parents to write their postcards with the return address of "*Wald am See,*" meaning "forest by the sea" – a euphemistic description of a concentration camp if ever there was one! I suspect our sadistic commander purposely let us receive mail so we'd know that our families had been deported.

Gora Kalvaria, 30 kilometers from Warsaw, was divided by the Wisla River. Its entire west side was devoid of people. All the houses closest to the Wisla were damaged, with their windows blown out. Some houses were destroyed by artillery fire. The Russians were quartered on the east side of the river, on a hill overlooking the west. Nothing about Gora Kalvaria suggested to us what this small town had been like before the war. We later learned it was a famous *shtetl* (Jewish village).

We settled in two relatively undamaged Jewish houses not far from the river. Always looking for *mezuzahs* on door posts – and recalling the one I'd discovered that night two years earlier near Horodenka – I gratefully sighted another *mezuzah* on a door. It pained me to see no one living there any longer. Close to the river banks, on the west side, were orchards of fruit trees – apples, pears and plums. Since the gardens around us were full of tomatoes, potatoes, cucumbers and corn, it was evident that the people had abandoned the city. There must have been a heavy shootout when the Russians succeeded in taking the east side of the Wisla River.

On the west side for a time we built bunkers and trenches. The Russians, located on the river's other bank, had the high ground. This was the first time during the war that we came so close to the battle line that we could see with our naked eyes the Russian soldiers on the other side. I'm sure they saw us even better. We were in a very dangerous place to build bunkers, especially during daylight hours.

When we arrived, a cease-fire seemed to be in effect. It was very quiet. This was probably because of Stalin's secret order not to cross the Wisla River as long as the Warsaw uprising was going on. Soon Rosh Hashanah came, September 18-19, 1944. I'm convinced that the Jewish enemies knew when the Jewish holidays were and deliberately chose that time to embitter Jewish life. Our captain suddenly appeared from nowhere to oversee us working. Normally, a commanding officer didn't physically monitor us at work; only the *keret* did. But this sadist was out for blood. He came screaming. He ordered us to line up, and picked two boys from among us. Who knew whether he spotted them resting for a minute, from a distance with his field glasses. He ordered the *keret* soldiers to hang the two up for half an hour. We had to watch this terrible punishment. When those two fainted, they were taken down; the soldiers poured water over them and as usual hung them up again.

As we watched the torture, next to me was a guy who was in his thirties, older than I, from the Maramaros region. His name was Binnem Holtz, and we called him Benni. So outraged was he that he was ready to throw a stone and try to kill this sadistic *szokalos*. I barely was able to quiet him down, knowing that if Benni took any action, he surely would be killed immediately, and also endanger all of us. All the while, the *keret,* with ready and loaded rifles and bayonets, surrounded us.

When the half hour was up and the two young men were released, they collapsed on the ground and lay like dead bodies. This half-hour scene still gives me nightmares to this day. Many nights I awake, weeping at that vision before my eyes. The *szokalos* quenched his thirst for violent sadism, and he kept on shouting abusively, "Dirty *bipchik*. I'll make soap out of you yet, if you waste time on the job." Finally, he left and we all felt the pain and frustration of our humiliation and helplessness. We could do nothing to defend ourselves against him.

That was our New Year's greeting on the Jewish New Year, 1944.

The *keret* took pity on the two fellows and allowed us to carry them back to the *szazod*; there was no way they could walk. After that horrendous event, we worked like machines, afraid to stop even for a moment, always keeping our eyes pealed on all sides. We still had our secret code to alert each other: "*geshem.*" When we heard it, we knew somebody was observing us. Under those conditions, we worked every day during the 10 days between Rosh Hashanah and Yom Kippur.

A day before the Yom Kippur observance, after a hard day's work, my buddy Willi Lorber and I made a stupid decision. To this day I can't explain it. We spotted pear and apple trees, full of fruit, close by. So we decided to pick some fruit before Yom Kippur. When we reached the trees, we shook them, and ripe pears fell like rain. As we started picking up the pears and putting them in a sack, the Russians lobbed grenades at us. Immediately, we dropped the sack and ran for our lives, lucky to escape without injury. Evidently the Russians had seen us and wanted to have target practice for the fun of it.

The next day, on the eve of Yom Kippur, we found out exactly what Gora Kalvaria was like before the war. A young man was milling around the two houses our *szazod* stayed in. As it turned out, he was the second Jewish person we encountered in all the time we wandered around Polish cities. This young Jew, maybe 17 or so, overheard some of our boys speaking Yiddish among themselves. He came over and asked, "Are you Jewish?"

We answered and then asked him if he knew Yom Kippur began tonight. Through tears, he said, "Do you know where you are? Thousands of Jews used to come here to be with their rabbi, the Gerrer Rebbe, for the holidays. Special trains used to come here from

Warsaw for this time of year. It's almost a year since the Germans, curse their names, murdered all the Jews of Ger."

We invited him to join us in chanting the inaugural evening service of Yom Kippur, the Kol Nidre, but he declined because he had been posing as a gentile and was afraid of being discovered. So we gave him some of our rations and he left. A member of our *szazod* was a cantor from a small Jewish community in Hungary and he led us in prayer. When it became dark we huddled in one of the rooms and sat on the floor without even being allowed to light a match; so close were we to the battle lines. We had no fear, but the *keret* feared that we would be spotted. As we sat in total darkness, the cantor recited the Kol Nidre prayer by heart. Everyone was immersed in his own memories of previous Yom Kippur nights. We could hear groans and moans, but soon everybody joined in and sang the historic melody. When one of the *keret* heard us quietly humming along, he ran into the room, screaming at us to shut up. The *keret* knew that this night was the holiest night of the year for Jews, but they stopped our prayers and reminded us where we were.

Tomorrow, once more, we'd have to dig trenches and work on bunkers; we hoped it would be a cool day so that it would be easier for us to fast. (Yom Kippur fell on September 27 that year, 1944.) In the morning, we received our regular assignments of so many meters to dig that day. Many of us tried to dig diligently in the morning when it was still cool, so that in the heat of the afternoon we'd have little to do to complete the quota. The majority of our young men fasted and prayed that the Yom Kippur decree for us and for our families should be for life and not for death.[3] This Yom Kippur passed and we managed to complete our quota for the day, even while observing the fast.

A few days after Yom Kippur, the *szokalos* discovered a good portion of our labor unit had *tefillin*, prayer books and, the married men, *tallesim*. Someone from our *keret* must have told him that some of us got up even earlier in the morning to lay *tefillin*. As we returned from work, tired, he ordered us to pack our belongings in 15 minutes and line up outside. Normally when we came from work, we had about 15 minutes time to leave our backpacks in the room, wash up, and then line up for the field kitchen. This time, we brought our backpacks outside and lined up. We assumed that we'd be ordered to leave the place immediately.

---

[3] In Jewish tradition, we stand before G-d on Rosh Hashanah to receive divine judgment; 10 days later, on Yom Kippur, our fate of life or death is sealed.

The *szokalos* ordered us to lay our backpacks down on the ground and sit next to them. Right away, we knew this sadist was up to something. He ordered everybody to open their backpacks, and had the *keret* empty them. Then he ordered the *keret* to remove all the Jewish books, *tefillin* and *tallesim*. Cursing, he yelled, "Dirty Jews, why do you drag this religious trash around?" For punishment, whoever had this "trash" in their backpacks would not get any supper that night. "Let your Jewish G-d give you supper," he laughed. One of the *keret* spread a *tallis* on the ground, and our items were dumped on it. Another soldier tied up the *tallis* and hauled it away. What he did with it, we never found out, but the whole *szazod* fasted until the next morning, shocked by this kind of violent rage, not to mention the desecration of our holy objects.

About two weeks later, sometime around the middle of October 1944, our situation improved. Unexpectedly, the sadistic s*zokalos* was recalled and replaced with a new commander, lower in rank, only a lieutenant. We were hopeful that the new commander would be more humane, because worse than the s*zokalos* we couldn't imagine. Sure enough, the new commander was a lot more reasonable. Only G-d knows what would have happened to us if the s*zokalos* had stayed any longer because, as I mentioned, the Hungarian government was by then taken over by the outspoken anti-Semite, the Hungarian Hitler named Szalasi. During his reign, the government surrendered all the Jews to the Germans with great zeal and joy. If, before that time, the Jewish *szazods* were considered only 50 percent outside the law, after Szalasi we became 100 percent without sanctuary.

Chapter 27

Germany

WE REMAINED IN THE VICINITY of Gora Kalvaria in Deblin until the end of October. Then we were ordered to move again. This time, we marched in the direction of Ostrovitz. Of course we continued to drag our winter-weight belongings with us – those of us who still had them. Many of our boys had been so sure that the war would end before winter set in that they got rid of their warm clothing. They would come to regret it.

From time to time, news filtered through to us that the Allies were exacting severe punishment on the Germans, especially from the air.

Our workload became harder and tougher. Our strength waned and we got less food to eat. Luckily, along the way, we still found crops, mainly potatoes and some fruit, in fields. That helped us supplement our diet and subdue our hunger. Inevitably, close to the front lines, the local population had abandoned their fields and gardens. The new commander didn't accompany us to our work, and we were able to tolerate the *keret*. Wherever the military passed through, the roads and streets were littered with empty can from conserves. We'd pick them up, wash them, throw in a few potatoes, and, adding a little water, cook our food. From all those potatoes, we managed to gain weight even if we had little strength. Still, comparing our situation then to being in a German concentration camp was like comparing day to night.

In the Ostrovitz area, the Wisla River runs the length of one or two kilometers, with an island in the middle. This battle line area was defended by the Hungarian military. So we were sent in to dig trenches on the little island. The Russians were close by, on the other bank of the river. We were quartered about six kilometers from the river, and the Russians observed all our movements, so we worked on the island only at night. To reach the island the Hungarian army built a small pontoon bridge, and every day the Russians would destroy the bridge with grenade launchers. The Hungarians tried to ferry us over with small boats, but that took too long, so they kept trying to build another little bridge, hoping it would survive the Russians' daily assault.

We would leave at 6 p.m.; it would take us more than an hour to reach our work assignment, so by the time we reached the river it was dark. We worked through the night, until the next dawn; this way the Russians never saw us. Sporadically, they fired across the river. The *keret* insisted we walk in single file, making it more difficult for random shots to hit our formation – and indicating that even members of the *keret* were very scared. It was hard on us to walk this way because it limited our ability to talk among ourselves. Talking not only helped us pass the time, but it allowed us to lend support to each other when someone was depressed. But the *keret*'s obvious fear gratified our need for revenge. We were very bitter by then. We'd hear the swish of bullets overhead and yet we were more numb than afraid at this point. The work itself, digging in the soft sand, wasn't very hard. What we really hated was that everything was wet. There was no place to sit down unless we found a plank or some chunk of wood we could put in the trench and sit on. Everybody suffered from the wet surroundings and we could never dry our clothing properly. At the end of October and beginning of November, we suffered terribly from staying in the damp trenches all night until dawn when we finished work. I was lucky that I still had fairly good shoes. But many of our boys went around in shoes so worn that their toes stuck out. Worst was when it rained: the trenches quickly filled with water, so we were ankle deep in it. A trench was two meters deep (roughly seven feet) and connected one bunker to another. To avoid the rain, we would dig a hole into the side of the trench wall parallel to the ground and big enough to lie down in. This way we could stay above the water that collected at the bottom. We risked doing this because we worked at night, and the Hungarian soldiers wouldn't check on us then for fear of the Russians' firing at them. The *keret* would hang out in the bunkers to keep dry. We, on the other hand, were totally at the mercy of the weather. Such nights one never forgets – they seem to last an eternity.

October through the middle of December 1944 in Ostrovitz was no doubt the hardest for us. Although some seven months earlier, we experienced difficult circumstances in the marshes of Malarita, we were still in fairly good physical shape at that time and had strength. What we went through since then drained our energy and pushed our health to the limit. We could not dry our clothing or shoes, and we didn't sleep well during the day. All of these factors, including the lack of proper nourishment, caused us to slip into a dangerous depression and fueled our apathy toward Russian bullets. We stopped fearing death; indeed, it seemed preferable to the situation we were in. Some of our *szazod* were very sick, in weak shape. Some of our boys were fatalistic, and perhaps rightfully so. Their illnesses got to them so badly that they cried, "Here comes our end." If they had 41 Celsius fever, they were allowed to remain in the barns and not go to work. But as soon as their fevers went down, out to work they had to go. It got so bad that our only hope, it seemed, was to be captured by the Russians.

But the Russians didn't move. Instead, they played cat and mouse, sporadically firing at us just to remind everyone that they were on the other side of the river. Some nights, when the weather was clear, they'd speak to the Hungarians with a loud speaker. (I don't know whether the Russians knew that there was Jewish *szazod* on the other side of the river.) In Hungarian, they'd ask us, "What did you get tonight to eat? We had ham and vodka." Then they'd pause as though waiting for an answer; naturally nobody from the Hungarian side responded. Then they started cursing with famous Russian four-letter words, and followed it with a barrage of fire from grenade-throwers and light machine guns.

They also told the Hungarians to surrender. "If you don't, you will suffer the same defeat you had in Woroniesh." Over the loudspeakers, they played popular Russian songs, easily heard, if not appreciated, despite the roar of the river.

Among ourselves, we discussed the chances of escaping across the river. Swimming would be impossible – the river was too wide and turbulent. Then, too, if a Russian spotted someone in the water, he'd probably fire at him. Only with a small boat, it seemed to us, could we safely get across. But where could we get a small boat? The *keret* and the other Hungarian units controlled the boats. We were also concerned for the safety of the boys who remained behind if some of us managed to escape. Our ears were filled with horror stories of the winter before when some fellows deserted to the Russians, and the Hungarians lined up the *szazod*, picked out every tenth man and shot him on the spot. No, we couldn't let such a thing happen. Either we don't go at all, or we all to together – a highly unlikely scenario – because most of us felt that we Jews are responsible for each other.[1]

One of our boys was an exception. He was originally from the Maramaros region (which belonged to the Romanians before World

---

[1] Hebrew: *Areivim zeh-la-zeh.*

War II), near Sighet, and he spoke Romanian. Along with a soldier in
the *keret* who was from the same area and also spoke Romanian, he
arranged to get a little boat. One night the two disappeared, but it
wasn't until we got through the usual morning line-up count that we
realized one of us and one of the *keret* were missing. A deadly scare
descended upon us. What kind of punishment would we suffer? Our
great *mazel* was that the *szokalos*, the bearded one, was gone. That one
of the *keret* was also missing undoubtedly helped our cause. Probably,
too, we got away without being punished because the Hungarians
knew the war was lost for them.

Of course we didn't know for certain what had happened to
those two until the next night when we went to work again. The
Russians blared on their loudspeaker, "Last night two of you came
over. Don't wait too long. There is still time for all of you to
surrender!" We knew then that the two of them made it successfully
to the other side. But did this boy survive the war? My friend Israel
Katz, who used to lived in Kingston, New York, knew the escaped
Jew; they both hailed from the same area. Often we discussed him,
and Israel told me that after the war he inquired about him to other
survivors who came from their hometown of Sighet. But nobody had
ever heard from him again.

After we finished digging the trenches on the island, we worked
on the west bank of the Wisla River. We dug holes in the ground, and
the Hungarian units poured cement into them. In the cement they
inserted steel bars that would stick out and were supposed to be tank
obstacles. We also laid barbed wire along the bank. Another
Hungarian team laid mines on the fields. For more than two months
we labored in this area.

Along the Wisla River, we neared Krakow. We found out from
locals that in Ostrovitz there were still some Jews left, working in a
factory that produced war materiel. This was in December 1944. We
never got a chance to contact them. More terrible news seeped
through to us that the Hungarians were constantly shipping our
people out to Germany. Every one of us was terribly depressed,
drained of strength. Our only hope was that the Russians would
liberate us.

When I realize now how close we were then to the hell-hole of
Auschwitz, I shudder. Local Poles kept it a secret and went about

their daily lives, partners in this great subterfuge, hiding and ignoring the great atrocities that were perpetrated day and night in that murder factory. In fact, it is unbelievable how not only they, but the whole world plugged their ears so as not to hear the cries from this inhuman place.

Around December 20, 1944, we were ordered suddenly to pack our belongings and, to our surprise, were marched to the train station and put on freight wagons. Since in Poland we had been walking, suddenly it seemed strange to ride on trains. Three more Jewish *szazods* arrived. Then roughly about 800 of us were loaded up together with our *kerets*. It was quite possible that the *keret* knew where we were going but didn't tell us. We thought they were shipping us away from the front lines because they were expecting an assault from the Russians. As it turned out, three weeks later, on January 12, 1945, the Russians did break through the German and Hungarian lines – and for the first time they took the war into Germany itself.

During wartime, trains moved very slowly. Many rail tracks had been destroyed from the Allies' bombs; as a precaution, we stopped in each train station for many hours. It wasn't until we arrived in Breslau, a large, German industrial city, that we finally knew they were taking us into Germany.

Breslau was pretty well bombed out. But many tall factory chimneys still billowed with smoke, indicating that they were in operation. After a few more days and nights of travel, around December 23, 1944, we reached Flossenburg, a city in Niederbayern, not far from the city of Nuremberg where, on September 15, 1935, Hitler proclaimed the infamous laws against the Jews, stripping them of their German citizenship. There, with our backpacks, we were taken off the train and lined up in columns, three in a row. My height put me at the head of the line, as usual. Our *keret* and an officer, all carrying rifles with fixed bayonets, escorted us. By then, Flossenburg was decorated for Christmas: we saw Christmas candles and evergreens in almost every window. People's faces looked cheerful, and they seemed to be going here and there in a festive mood, although we sensed that they had to feel the end of the war was near, which would mean their downfall. For better or worse, these Germans had a certain arrogance and conceit about their "Fatherland."

Flossenburg showed no damage from the war. Movement about town was hectic, people everywhere. Many soldiers on furlough strolled about with their girlfriends in the streets, smiling happily.

Some people showed us contempt and derision as we passed them by. A few onlookers even yelled at us, "*Verdammte Sau-hunde!*" ("You damned pig-dogs!"). I searched for signs of remorse or shame on people's faces, as I walked in the lead. I found none.

Suddenly German SS officers arrived. Our *keret's* Hungarian commander stopped our column and, with a viciousness he never expressed before, yelled, "*Bipchik!* Now you're going to what will be your Palestine." He was trying to impress the German SS that he also knew how to hate Jews.

The SS went to work. Surrounding us, they barked, "*Schneller, schneller!!*" to make us walk faster. They marched us up a hill on the outskirts of Flossenburg. "Faster, faster, you Israelites, go up the hill!" It felt bizarre to hear the Germans use the word *Israelittishevolk* because their habit was to call us *verfluchte Juden*, accursed Jews.[2] At a certain point, we saw a huge sign over a gate: *Kriegsgefangen Lager* (Prisoner of War Camp). That calmed me down somewhat and made me less afraid. I naïvely told myself, "If this is really a prisoner of war camp they're putting us in, they'll treat us according to international law."

At the camp gate, we were told to halt. Out came the camp commandant in SS uniform, a huge, plump SS redneck. His red face had a beastly expression on it. One of the German soldiers saluted him and reported that he was delivering 800 Hungarian Jews. Immediately, he gave the order to line up in fours. More SS came out and with sticks in their hands started to rearrange our lines, clubbing us over our heads as they did so. We were stunned and didn't know what to do; some boys, particularly ones at the end of the rows, were bloodied right away. Right off, we trembled at the sight of these SS. The gates opened and, as we passed through, the SS counted each of our rows. The Germans were very meticulous and had to see if their "new merchandise" checked out.

They herded us into a huge hall where a dreadful picture awaited us. There for the first time we saw so-called war prisoners: *häftlinge* (detainees or prisoners), as the Germans called them, half skeletons, dressed in striped black and white uniforms with a red and white

---

[2] If we could only have looked into the future and known that four years hence we would have our own State of Israel, how much better we would have felt.

"K/L" painted on their backs. On some of their lapels were triangles, some red, some green, and some yellow. Later we learned that "K/L" stood for *koncentration lager* (concentration camp) and the triangles were signs to classify the inmates: green triangles denoted criminals (mostly German), red triangles for political prisoners, and yellow for those of us who had transgressed German sensibilities by being Jews.

The hall was filled with people speaking different languages. Some had weird hairdos: a buzz-cut down the center of the scalp, with the sides left long. This made for easy identification. If someone tried to escape, his weird hairdo would easily give him away. To anybody seeing him, he was definitely an escaped prisoner. These men had sticks in their hands and shouted at us in many languages. At first we had no idea what their role was, but they certainly were acting like *kapos*.[3]

The hall could easily have been the setting for an insane asylum – or a different planet dominated by aliens. There was not one normal face in the bunch; all looked like zombies, barely alive. Their dead eyes protruded from two slits, expressing a fear of death and great hunger. It had to be that those men were driven mad by the horrible conditions in this hellish place.

Through the windows we spotted a group of young women marching by. All had their hair shaved off and were dressed in the men's striped pants and jackets. Their agonized Jewish faces made an awful impression on us. Now we knew for sure that this was not a prisoner of war camp. With such women here, this was a real concentration camp.

A few hours later they let in about 10 so-called barbers who were inmates also. They had orders to completely shave our heads. They all spoke different languages, and some broken German. We barraged them with questions, but nobody wanted to talk. They either responded, "You'll see," or asked us for something to eat and for cigarettes, both of which we still had in small quantities in our backpacks. So desperate were the barbers for cigarettes that they picked butts up from the floor. (Little did we know we would be doing the same a few months later.) Perhaps their only sign of hope showed through in their questions concerning the area we had last been, and in trying to discern the battle lines and where the war was headed.

---

[3] Concentration camp prisoners, often common criminals and frequently brutal to their fellow inmates, who were given privileges in return for supervising prisoner work gangs.

As night fell, the barbers, having shaved off everybody's hair, returned to their barracks. Outside it was very cold, and a howling, cutting wind made it feel even colder. On the hill all around us was a white sprinkle of snow. The watchtowers were lit up. A huge decorated Christmas tree was erected inside the compound, close to the entrance of the gate. The SS soldiers who stood guard on the watchtowers wore winter or fur coats and carried machine guns on their shoulders.

Then our group was rounded up and marched to another barrack, another block. More yelling. More clubbing. More screaming This was their method of dehumanizing people and robbing them of their human dignity immediately. They chased and clubbed us like cattle; but, then, not even cattle are clubbed. We entered another barrack, again in a huge hall. We had to undress completely. Every one of us wanted to lay out his clothing and shoes with his backpacks, as we were used to doing for the past few years. But then they clubbed our heads again, and screamed wildly, "*Schneller, Schneller.*" The hail of blows intensified because we couldn't move fast enough, not knowing what they wanted from us. To avoid getting clubbed, we quickly tore our clothing off and threw it down. Naked, we were driven in to another room. In this room, there was only a window; everybody had to leave the room via the window. Two SS men, one at each side of the window, screened everyone to make sure we had nothing hidden anywhere on or in our bodies.

They even checked our mouths for such things as gold rings or any other valuables that we might have had. One of the SS by the window spotted the silver chain around my neck given to me by my cousin, and ripped it off, clubbing me again for good measure. I had totally forgotten about it. Intentionally, though I deeply regretted it, I left my father's silver Swiss pocket watch, of priceless sentimental value, in my clothing. Those who had wristwatches and forgot to take them off received extra clubbing for that. We all had to run naked about 150 meters in the bitter cold Bavarian winter to a cellar shower room. A hanging sign identified it as "*Entlausungsanstalt*" (Delousing Facility). It was just as well that we didn't know yet that in these rooms the Germans also showered people with poison gas.

Since the Germans still wanted to use us for the hard work ahead, it made sense for them to save the gas for a later time. After the shower, they handed everyone a shirt, a pair of pants, a long jacket and shoes. Never mind the size or the fit. Everything was done to the tune of wild screams, "*Schnell, schnell!*" Again we were chased barefoot onto the frozen ground sprinkled with snow, again 150 meters to Block No. 20. There, we exchanged the uniforms and shoes among ourselves. At my size, I was very lucky to be able to switch with someone and find shoes I could wear.

Inside the block, we found a group of old inmates who were a bit more talkative. One Polish Jew had been in different camps for two years, and he responded to my questions. He replied in Yiddish. "You want to know what's going on here? Here death reigns supreme. Here is hell on earth. Hell. Have you ever heard of Dachau? Here it is a thousand times worse. Do you see?" He grabbed me by the hand and took me to the window. "Do you see the smoke coming out of that chimney? That is the crematorium. That's where you're going to end up. You and all the others. Here is only death. Even those who are still alive are already dead."[4]

From such a welcome, I became terribly depressed. I didn't expect a Jew to express such open hostility to another Jew. Yet, despite his frankness, I refused to believe him. Even when that goateed *szokalos* from our *szazod* threatened to make soap out of us, even in my wildest, darkest fantasies, I denied it. I wasn't the only one in our *szazod* who felt that way. We wanted desperately to believe that even the Hitler beast (I'm sorry to insult the animal world) could not do such a thing.

Such anger I felt in my heart toward that Polish Jew! Why did he have to speak to me like that? For a long time, I considered him a murderer – trying to destroy my hope. Even if he spoke the truth, he didn't have to be so outrageously cruel.

Bewildered and despairing, I turned away from this man; I didn't share his bitter remarks with my friends; I dared not. We tried to lift each other's morale, not bring each other down. "It won't be very long," we would say. "Hitler's demise is near and we will overcome it."

Block 20 had a large hall. Inside were rows and rows of wooden bunk beds stacked three to four high and only 20 to 25 inches wide – barely fit for animals. Close to the entrance on the right was a small

---

[4] "*Die vilst vissen vus du kumt for? Du ist der toid der herscher. Du ist dersh'ol ha-tachtit. Der g'henom. Host amul g'herdt vaig'n Dachau? Du ist toisand mul erger. Die zaist? Die zaist dem royich fun dem block dort dem koimen? Dus ist der crematorium. Du in dem crematorium vesti farending. Vie alle andere. Du is nor toid, afilu die vus leben noch zennen shoin ochtoid.*"

room. That room was for the block *ältester*.[5] He happened to be a
German, with a green triangle on his lapel. Close to this small room
stood a decorated Christmas tree. When we were all assembled in the
big hall, the block supervisor barked, "*Ruhe! Ruhe!*" ("Shut up"). We
became still, and then he began speaking. He gave a so-called
orientation lecture. But first he asked who among us spoke German
as well as other languages spoken by us newcomers to the block. A
Jewish doctor from one of the *szazods* volunteered to translate his
German speech into Hungarian for us, and the block supervisor
began reading his riot act.

"You are all very lucky people," he said. "Because tomorrow
night will be Christmas night and you will get a good meal to eat.
Potato soup and macaroni with marmalade." Then he enumerated
the laws of the concentration camp: "Here, for the slightest
transgression, the punishment is a death-sentence. And here in this
camp, we have our own crematorium that operates daily." He told us
what time in the morning we had to get up for the roll-call,[6] get
inspected for work assignments, and when we got our breakfast
coffee. He told us where the outhouse was located, along with some
other regulations. After this speech, the doctor added his own words
from the familiar psalm, "Even though I walk through the valley of
the shadow of death, I fear no evil because you, G-d, are with me."[7]

A strange feeling suddenly came over me after I heard the doctor
reciting this verse. Despite all the horrible experiences of this tragic
day, I somehow felt salvation was near and that Hitler would soon be
defeated.

A while later, they brought supper in for us: potato peel soup. It
was so bad we gave our soup to the older inmates. After this
miserable day, we suddenly lost our hunger. But the other guys
lapped it up like dogs. Slurping the soup down, they said, "In a day or
two, you too will eat that soup."

Later, the *kapo* screamed out, "*Schlafen gehen*" – Go to sleep – and
everybody squeezed into their chicken coop bunks. Probably none of

---

[5] Block supervisor (literally, the elder).
[6] *Appellplatz* (the word means both the "roll-call" itself and the courtyard where it
was taken).
[7] "*Gam ki elech b'gai zal mavet, loh irah rah, ki atah imadi.*"

us newcomers slept that night; and we could hear disheartening groans from time to time.

Next to my bunk was my friend, Willi Lorber. The whole night we whispered to each other. "We will live to see Hitler's defeat – it will come."

Chapter 28

Flossenburg – 40,688

ON DECEMBER 24, 1944, our *ältester*, a *kapo* and a few *stuben dienst* (assistants to the *ältester* and *kapo*) woke us early, screaming "*Aufstehen! Aufstehen!*" (Get up! Get up!) and banging their sticks on our bunks. Everybody jumped out of bed. As the *ältester* and his assistants passed by those still in bed, they struck them. Everybody dressed quickly. Soon two inmates brought in a huge kettle on wheels; in it was watery black coffee, with no sugar but very hot. When the *ältester* spelled out the orientation laws, we were all given an aluminum bowl with a handle for soup and coffee. With this ersatz coffee we also received a slice of bread. Everybody stood in line, and all the time the *kapos* and the *stuben dienst* kept shouting, "*Schneller, schneller.*" It was apparent that this yelling was ordered by the Germans in order to dehumanize and jangle the prisoners' nerves; it didn't take long for us to lose our sense of being created in G-d's image.[1] Slowly, more and more, I began to grasp the mindset of that old Polish Jew who spoke to me so bitterly; he'd been brutalized so much he couldn't think rationally any longer.

Now the *kapos* shouted at us to assemble for roll-call. The new inmates were ordered to remain in their so-called bunks. Things quieted down when the older inmates left, and we boys from the Hungarian *szazod* in Block 20 continued exchanging clothing with one another. Around 10 a.m., we had to report to a different hall and undress completely for a "health inspection." Fortunately, we didn't know then about the selection for life or death. The majority of our *szazod* were all young men, more or less still in good shape. Everybody was ordered to hold his clothing in his hands, keeping only his shoes on.

The selection started. The SS officer, a red-faced doctor, stood above us on a small elevated platform. His snake eyes pierced through everyone. I'm still haunted by his face. Next to him stood his assistant. When each of us passed by this so-called doctor, he ordered his helper to make a check-mark on the forehead of the fellow. Those who looked good to him were marked with a green check-mark; those who were very thin, with a hernia or any other imperfection that he noticed, he marked with a red check-mark and

---

[1] *Tzelem Elokim.*

separated them from us. We were marked like cattle, sheep or pigs, and assorted by different colors. Luckily, most of our *szazod* were marked for life, except for one poor soul who had a huge hernia and two others who were very thin and puny. This red-faced angel of death selected these three young men for the crematorium. After the selection process, we dressed again and went back to Block 20.

Since it was Christmas Eve, a time when Christians proclaim compassion and mercy and brotherly love, the Germans arranged a special Christmas spectacle. They brought in all the working groups around 3 p.m. and assembled them for roll-call. We who had remained in the block for selection joined them on the *appelplatz*. In our thin linen concentration camp uniforms, we shivered in the freezing temperature and cutting winds, as we joined a few thousand people already lined up. We wound up in the last rows, closest to the top of the hill, from where we could see the huge Christmas tree decorated and illuminated down by the concentration camp gate. Unaware of what kind of spectacle they had in store for us, we had to stand in place for two hours, until it got real dark. Terribly cold, we moved our hands and feet to avoid becoming frozen, and talked amongst ourselves. The *kapos* alongside the rows struck people, yelling at us to stand still and "*Ruhe! Ruhe!*" (Shut up!).

Finally, a car arrived. Two SS officers and four soldiers stepped out. With loudspeakers, they called out three prison numbers (we were just numbers at this point), and yanked these poor souls from the rest of us. They stood them up in front of the entire gathering so that we could all see them. Then I spotted a gallows nearby, and suddenly I grasped what was about to happen.

One of the SS officers announced through his loudspeaker what offenses these poor *häftlings* had committed. One of them had tried to escape. The other two were to be hanged for hitting back at *kapos*. This same SS officer announced their sentence in the name of the SS *Reichs Führer* Heinrich Himmler (head of the Gestapo). and he repeated this announcement for each of the victims. As the four German soldiers dragged them to their gallows, all three cried out in their last moments, "Comrades, comrades, don't despair! Hitler's Germany will pay for this! Germany will be defeated!" All of us were forced to witness this German atrocity. No one dared prevent it, surrounded as we were by an electric fence and armed SS guards in the watchtowers, poised and ready to fire their machine guns.

Although normally in wartime, windows in the cities and towns had to be covered with blackout curtains to shut out all light, our camp was ablaze with powerful searchlights mounted on the watchtowers. From the air, any pilot could tell this source of bright light was a concentration camp, but we now know that the so-called civilized world remained a mute witness to the murders that took place in the death camps.

The horrible spectacle numbed us; we no longer thought of the bitter cold. Still, once we were dismissed, we hastened to the barracks to try warming up. In Block 20, the Christmas tree was also illuminated. Waiting for us inside were the cooks with their portable kitchen, and we lined up for the holiday meal: macaroni with marmalade. To say the least, having just witnessed such a horror, we had no appetite. Most of us tasted a few noodles and left more than half. The older prisoners, who had been left inside, asked us for our leftovers. We nodded yes, and they licked our bowls clean. That second night, again I could not fall asleep. Through the night, we whispered quietly to each other, bolstering our hopes by reminding ourselves that we would overcome.

On Christmas Day 1944 we remained in our block. Across from our block was a *revier*,[2] Block No. 21. Around the *revier* was a wire fence. From our window, we could see everything in Block 21, and every morning I saw them open their doors and throw out the people who died the previous night. Called *musselmen* (a term coined after the Holocaust), these people had been reduced to skin and bones, just barely living skeletons, who finally died after a long, agonizing bout with hunger and disease. They were thrown onto a pile, like garbage to be cleaned up later. Several prisoners would show up eventually with a wagon, load the bodies onto it, and haul them away to the crematorium.

We remained in Flossenburg for a week. Forty-seven years have passed since I witnessed the Angel of Death at work day and night in that camp. Those horrifying memories haunt my dreams to this day and still wake me in a cold sweat.

After Christmas, all the old prisoners were marched out to their working places, while we, the new inmates, were told to remain in the barracks. Around 10 a.m., two SS men with a few German *kapos* arrived to take inventory of their living merchandise. They made a list

---

[2] A word that means "district" or "quarter," but in our particular case, referred to a hospital compound.

of our people and asked only two questions: everyone's age and trade, if any. I had no trade or vocation, but realized it would go better for me if I registered as having one. I listed myself as a carpenter since I knew something about lumber – boards, two-by-fours, how to saw wood, etc. – because of my father's and uncles' lumber mill. My buddy Israel-Katz, who was from a poor family and therefore had had to learn a trade, was adept at building furniture, so we got assigned to the same working group.

The day after Christmas 1944, I officially ceased to exist as Michael Jakubowics. By the end of that year, because of the huge number of inmates being brought in, camp authorities probably had no time anymore to tattoo all the people, so my forearm was not defiled with a number. Instead, they just assigned us numbers that we had to remember. The SS threatened severe punishment if we forgot our designation. I became number 40,688. Suddenly it wasn't important who my father or mother were, only that the number 40,688 was there. Those numbers were later stamped on the top of our prison uniforms.

I recall a line from a Yiddish song famous in Europe before the war: "Did a stone give birth to me? Did I not have a mother?"[3]

Such was our Jewish destiny. We were only numbers to the Germans who worked us as slaves until our dying breaths. After erasing our names so easily with numbers, it was easy for them to erase us completely, as if we hadn't existed at all. This was part of German *pinktlichkeit* (meticulousness). When they finished stamping numbers on everybody's jacket, they told us that all 800 new Hungarian Jewish arrivals would be sent to another workplace. Then they divided us into a number of groups. When the old *häftlings* returned to our block that evening after work, we told them we were being sent away – somewhere. They expressed envy, saying anywhere we went would be far better than remaining here. We remained in Flossenburg for abt eight days, possibly because the Nazi's didn't have any freight cars vailable for our transport right away. I hoped to leave this place as quickly as possible. Every day, through a window, I watched the *revier* in Block 21. I could not count how many victims were tossed on the heap and hauled away to the crematorium.

A large number of friends from our former *szazod* were assigned to the same group with me. Where we would be sent, we didn't know. Around January 3, 1945, they finally loaded us onto a freight

---

[3] "*Tzi bin ich fun a schtein geboiren? Tzi hot mich kein mamme gehat?*"

train. In our wagon, an old German soldier from the regular *Wehrmacht* guarded us with a loaded machine gun to prevent us from escaping. In his sixties, this old soldier only allowed himself to speak to us when we were in motion, for fear of being overheard by the SS officers in the adjacent passenger cars. We felt he had to know, deep down, that Germany had lost the war. That probably was why he was soft on us.

In our *szazod* was a young poet, Shonie Roth, who wrote in Hungarian. He also spoke perfect German, and asked the soldier where we were being taken. The soldier replied that he didn't know, but admitted it looked as though we were heading toward Nuremberg. He seemed to relax in speaking with Shonie, hinting that the war was coming to an end. Incidentally, Shonie Roth was then a group leader in our *szazod*. The Hungarian *keret* had some respect for him because he used the Hungarian language on a highly literary level. He somehow managed many times to stave off punishment for us. Often, he read his poetry to us; his work hinted at better days and gave us courage and hope.[4]

Although the distance from Flossenburg to Nuremberg isn't far, it took us a day and a night to get where we were going. We had to stop for hours at various stations. In many places the rail lines were destroyed by bombing. Finally, when we arrived at our destination, it was not Nuremberg at all where we had been headed, but the nearby concentration camp at Hersbruck. It was already dark, and a white blanket of snow covered the camp and its surroundings. After we disembarked from the train, the *stuben dienst* asked our group to pick a *kapo* from among us. Naturally, we opted for Shonie Roth, but he steadfastly declined. "Friends, this is no *munkoszazod*," he said. "This is a concentration camp." Knowing the situation we were in, he refused. So the block *ältester* pulled a fellow out of our ranks and ordered him to be a *kapo*. This inmate hailed from the city of Ungwar, and soon I heard very ugly stories about him. This was the German's method, the vicious plan during the entire war, to install *Judenrats* in the ghettos and Jewish *kapos* in the camps, to better control the situation.

---

[4] I later saw Shonie Roth in a *revier*, but I don't know whether he survived the war.

In Hersbruck, the Germans led us to the barrack. Bunks were set up here as in Flossenburg – three levels high. We were astonished how clean it was, and that it was also nearly empty, except for a few Czech gentiles and a few Hungarian Jewish prisoners from a former *munkoszazod* who had already been there for a couple of months. First off, they warned us not to drink the water; they advised us instead to wet our lips and quench our thirst with snow. We assaulted them with a barrage of questions. With brotherly feeling, they encouraged us by saying it wouldn't take too long before we saw Hitler's defeat. We also learned that our block *ältester* was a Polish *kapo* – a vicious sadist. Watch out for him, the old-timers warned, don't get in his way.

Over and over they warned us not to drink the water in the camp because something in it caused very bad dysentery and weakened people so much that they could barely move. Any sick men were put in the so-called hospital and never seen again. In fact, they were sent to Flossenburg and its crematorium.

Since I considered myself a Czech citizen and had attended Czech school, I tried to befriend the Czech nationals. As soon as I told them that I was from the Carpathian and a Jew, any friendliness and camaraderie toward me quickly disappeared. Among them was a former member of the Czech Supreme Court, and two more Czech big-wigs from high governmental positions.[5] The regular Czech inmates were very respectful of these three individuals, who enjoyed extra privileges in the block. For instance, they slept at the front of the barrack in wider beds, somewhat separated from the rest of our cages.

Our first night in Hersbruck was, thankfully, uneventful. For supper, we received a slice of bread with soup. The block *ältester* then ordered us to go to sleep "because tomorrow you're going to work hard." Still exhausted from the nightmare we'd gone through in the past few days, my pal Willi and I, despite our extreme emotional swings and sometimes fatalistic attitudes, soon fell fast asleep.

A couple days later, we were divided into work shifts. Day shifts and night shifts operated for 12 hours each without interruption.

---

[5] In Yiddish, we called them *karpin kep,* high-ranking officials.

Chapter 29

Zvi

I ALLOWED TWO WEEKS TO ELAPSE before continuing to relate my *Shoah* testimony because the next episode – the realization that perhaps I was the only one left alive from my whole family – was so difficult to write.

Although we hoped our salvation would come very soon, after several days upon arriving at the Hersbruck camp, I received the worst news possible about my brother Zvi. Three months earlier, I received a postcard from him and was relieved to learn he remained alive. It buoyed my spirits, and convinced me we'd outlast the Nazis.

At the time, my brother Zvi was nearly 37, and no matter what would happen to the rest of our family, I was certain he'd survive. Then I heard that another Hungarian Jewish *szazod*, in the next block, had the same number as my brother had. Overjoyed, I hoped to ascertain Zvi's whereabouts – and that maybe he was in that very compound. Though I knew it was forbidden to visit another barrack, I sneaked over to the block and asked inmates whether there was someone else with that particular *szazod* number. Someone pointed out a man, the *szazod's* doctor. Approaching him, I introduced myself and asked him about my brother. When I uttered "Jakubowics," the doctor looked straight in my eyes, then paused for a moment to gather his thoughts. "I have very bad news for you," the doctor finally said. "I can plainly see you're Zvi Jakubowics' brother. We had two Jakubowicses (in our *szazod*), your brother Zvi and your cousin Bainish. Both were shot dead near the city of Bor, in Yugoslavia. Killed on the last day of *Succoth*, on *Simchat Torah*, 1944. I'm very sorry to tell you that," he said. "The two Jakubowicses were very respected and beloved in our *szazod*."

The news numbed me. Tears ran down my face.

"I am sorry," the doctor repeated. "I am sorry."

I returned to my barracks safely without the block *ältester* noticing me. In a daze, I went over to the window and gazed outside, at the white snow covering everything. It must have been Sunday because we didn't work. For a long time, I stared out the window.

As I stood there, my eyes filled and overflowed with tears; the snow and everything around me turned red, as red as blood. My pal Willi came over to me. I had already informed him of my intention to go to the next block to find my brother Zvi. On seeing my condition, he immediately understood. With all his might, Willi tried to comfort me. But I was inconsolable. Life for me, I told him, wasn't worthwhile any longer. Hope had died in me, and my life no longer had a purpose or value. That's how I began my stay in the Hersbruck concentration camp in Bavaria – downhearted, without the will to go on. Yet my survival instincts remained with me. Maybe the force of hunger so overwhelmed me that it blocked any other thoughts or feelings of grief, sorrow and self-pity. Maybe that's why our sages warned us not to cave in to despair. "Never give up hope, even if a sharp sword is pointed at your neck."[1]

This may explain why so very few people committed suicide while living under such inhuman and humiliating conditions. Logic would dictate that being deprived of human dignity, being trampled on and treated as vermin to be exterminated would lead to suicide. Yet among Jews, there was no mass suicide; there was only mass murder – perpetrated by the greatest oppressor in human history, Adolph Hitler.

Hunger was a powerful force that kept us from going mad. Dutifully we rose at 5 a.m. for roll-call. January in Bavaria was always very cold, and we were dressed only in our light striped linen *häftling* uniforms. We literally froze during the morning roll-calls. Often we'd stand there for more than an hour, lined up in fours or fives, and the *kapos* would hit us with sticks if we moved while they counted us slaves and formed daily groups for various jobs. I was in a group that had to walk about one kilometer to a rail station and from there travel by freight train to a nearby village.

In this village, a huge German building company still in existence today, Hoch Tief, was digging a tunnel more than a kilometer deep into the side of a mountain. Inside the mountain they were erecting for the German airplane company Messerschmitt a factory that would be protected from Allied bombing. When I arrived there, the tunnel had already been excavated: two shifts of slave laborers worked day and night, 12 hours for each shift, so the factory was built very quickly. During the war, Hoch Tief employed thousands of us slave laborers loaned to them by the Germans, feeding us in return a little soup and a slice of bread.

In this village, the *kapos* further divided us into new groups. I fell into a group of predominantly non-Jewish Italians, army deserters who were sent to concentration camps by the Germans. I hardly understood them. I tried to speak to them in German, but most

[1] *"Al timnah mi-rachmin afilu cherev chadah munachat al tzavarecha!"*

spoke only Italian. Constantly they cursed, mostly when they got infuriated. To my untrained ear, the curse sounded like *"Porka Madonna!"* – curse words never far from their lips. I didn't understand what it meant, but I knew these were bad words.

My block was a mix of nationalities, including Jews, Frenchmen, Italians, Russians and Danes. Sometimes I spoke with the Danes who also worked on this one project. Many volunteer workers, Fascists from Yugoslavia, Poland and the Ukraine, wound up supervising us. Besides them, SS men milled about with rifles and bayonets. For a time, I worked using a circular electric saw, stripping boards and making two-by-twos. My civilian supervisor came from Yugoslavia. Aside from Serbian, he spoke German very well, and, at one time, he gave me a slice of bread and a cigarette butt. So, thinking he was a kind person, I took the ill-advised liberty of telling him that he should treat us fairly because the war would end soon and Germany would be defeated. He responded by saying, "You will not live to see that." I replied that the war would be over in six or seven weeks. He retorted coldly that "bigger heroes than you haven't lasted that long." My conversation with him left me terrified.

For a time, I labored at the foot of the mountain. They used a funicular railway to hoist supplies up and down the mountain, mostly building materials like cement and sand. But the long pieces of lumber didn't fit into the railway's cable cars, so we had to hoist them up on our shoulders. Usually two slaves, or sometimes when the *kapo* was in a good mood, three, carried this heavy lumber uphill. In this instance, it was my misfortune to be tall. Because I was either in the front or the back, I felt the whole weight on my shoulders. And with hundreds of people trooping up and down the mountainside to the tunnel's opening, the snow quickly turned into a brown slush. It was worse at the first of the morning; overnight, the mud and slush had frozen into a slippery sheet, making it extremely dangerous to carry heavy lumber. Apparently the *kapos* wanted to endear themselves to the SS, who were also overseeing our labor, so they'd hit us over our heads to speed up our pace. When we finally made it to the tunnel with our last ounce of strength, we had to unload the logs on bigger rail carts. Another group would then take over, transporting the lumber to various places inside, an area as long and wide as a football field.

One time, I worked inside the mountain. It wasn't as cold as working outside, so the work load felt easier. However, the air inside was heavy and had an unpleasant smell. Fortunately, I only worked inside two days and one night, and that was enough for a lifetime. I was part of a group that worked the day shift. Typically we left the tunnel area at four o'clock and rode the train back to Hersbruck, arriving around five o'clock. On one occasion, a big snowfall prevented the night shift from arriving to replace us, so we were ordered to continue working until the next morning. Of course they fed us well: some soup and a piece of bread. In that suffocating, stinking air, the night felt like it would never end.

With cold and hunger dominating our thinking, we mindlessly *shlepped* bags of cement from one place to another. Around us, empty paper bags abounded. A few of us got the bright idea to convert some empty cement bags into undergarments, by cutting out a hole on the top for our heads and two holes at the sides for our arms. We put these bags on under our shirts in order to preserve some body heat and protect ourselves a little bit from the wind. But I narrowly escaped a fatal beating in Hersbruck as a result of this tiny bit of inventive thinking.

Not knowing it was a corporal crime, I donned such a bag. These bags also had a thin wire for sealing the opening. Many of the *häftlings* whose shoelaces were torn used the wire to lace their shoes. One time as we came back to the barracks after work, Polish *kapo* noticed some of us had laced our shoes with the wires and had these empty cement bags under our shirts. With his ubiquitous stick, this sadistic *kapo* began to beat one of us, and didn't cease until foam came out of his mouth and he grew tired. Quietly I retreated to the outhouse, and quickly got rid of the cement bag under my shirt. As they say in Yiddish, to have escaped from a dangerous situation is as if your grandmother intervened from on high.[2]

That time I avoided a fierce beating. Other times I wasn't so lucky. As we marched from Hersbruk, we trooped in a column to the train station in the morning, approximately a mile away. Usually it was dark when we marched, hungry and cold, and the SS and *kapos* would order us to sing. Who in his right mind would want to sing under such conditions? But the *kapo* and the SS didn't care what we felt. It had to be for show – to impress the townspeople that in this so-called "Prisoner of War Camp" there were happy people. If we

---

[2] "*Velche babbe hot zich far mir gameet.*"

failed to sing on cue, the *kapos* would hit us over our heads. Since I was at the head of the line, I got clubbed many times.

The Russians prisoners were always the first among us to start singing, choosing a partisan tune. I still remember a couple lines of one song: "Three tank soldiers and one machine gun. Three machines of war."[3] I'm sure the German SS didn't understand these lyrics, and therefore didn't object to it. But we understood and joined in. The lyrics helped for two reasons: we avoided being clubbed, and we took heart because they predicted sure victory over the Nazis.

Along this marching route, we were struck by ordinary city sights: a bus station, illuminated buses in traffic, women dressed up in fancy clothing, a few men in warm overcoats and hats – all on their way somewhere, most likely to Nuremberg. When I saw these happy, well-dressed people, I wondered if I'd live to travel in a bus and be dressed like a normal human being. Even now, 50 years later, every time I travel on a bus, this image returns to me.

Around mid-February 1945, when we had already been in Hersbruck roughly 45 days, the cold and hunger began to take its toll. A number of us from our *szazod* couldn't bear it anymore, and some collapsed. We always warned one another not to register sick since previous Hersbruck prisoners alerted us to the consequences. We experienced for ourselves that those who did register were sent to Flossenburg and never seen again. Flossenburg meant the crematorium. But there's a limit to how much a human being can endure.

One day, as we did now all the time, we carried heavy lumber and cement bags from the foothills up to the middle of the mountain and into the tunnel. Among our group was my friend Israel Katz. Always frail and weak, he fainted while at work, close to four o'clock when our shift was nearly over. For some reason the train did not come that day, and everybody had to march back to Hersbruck – a distance of eight or 10 kilometers – definitely a two-hour walk.

The supervising officer of our group was an elderly German from the *Wehrmacht*. When Katz collapsed, the officer turned to us and asked for volunteers to carry him down the mountain to the main road, to a truck that would take us back to Hersbruck. Israel

---

[3] "*Tri tankista a yedna katiusha. Tri machini voyavoy.*"

was my buddy, so, despite having no idea what lay ahead, I volunteered for the job; so did another *szazod* mate – a married man, I'm afraid I don't remember his name, but he was older than us, probably in his late thirties. He also hailed from the Carpathian region. The German officer pulled both of us out from the group and ordered a young Ukrainian SS man to escort us. The Ukrainian SS were outfitted in dark, almost black uniforms, to distinguish them from the real German SS. Together, we lifted Israel up and carried him down to the main street and stood waiting for the truck, the Ukrainian SS man watching us so that we wouldn't run away. It soon got dark and a light snow started to fall. Still we waited. No truck, nothing. Sometime after nine o'clock, a Mercedes sped towards us, and when the passengers saw *häftlings* on the street corner, they stopped the car. A young German SS officer jumped out, screaming, "What are these *häftlings* doing here?" as though we were criminals.

Saluting the German officer, the Ukrainian explained that one of us couldn't walk and that he had been ordered to guard us and wait for a truck that would take us back to Hersbruck. The officer continued his tirade and ordered the four of us to walk back to the camp immediately. He also ordered the Ukrainian man to report to the camp commander upon our arrival and tell him to call a doctor to determine whether the three of us were fit for work or not. Although the two of us, neither sick, simply had been asked to help our friend, we dared not explain that to the German SS officer. *Häftling* "dirt" did not talk to the "master race."

We bore Israel Katz under our arms from both sides and started to march back to camp. The Ukrainian SS man followed behind with rifle and fixed bayonet. The snow started to come down heavier as we tramped on. We were really better off walking than standing around all those hours in the freezing cold. Fortunately, Israel revived a little and started to walk slowly on his own power, bracing himself by holding onto our arms. There was almost no traffic along the road. This SS man was patient with us and didn't try to make us walk faster.

It took us about three hours to reach camp. We arrived about twelve midnight – very hungry since we only had a little soup at noon. The camp was lit up, and the high-powered watchtower beams lit up the camp perimeter. When I think of this now, Allied planes could easily have spotted our well-lit camp. Meanwhile, the local population hid from Allied bombardment behind blackout curtains. Did the Germans purposely want to have the Allies see the camp and bomb us? Most likely, yes.

In camp, the Ukrainian SS man handed the three of us "criminals" over to the gate watch and also relayed the order to have us examined by a doctor. The gate opened and we were left standing inside. Soon a doctor, a Polish prisoner, arrived from the *revier*. He gave us a quick look-see and immediately pronounced his diagnosis to the German commandant who had by then appeared, too.

"This man," he said, pointing to Israel Katz, "is a sick man. The other two are healthy."

The commandant ordered Israel to be taken to the *revier* and, refusing to listen to our explanation of why we were there, ordered the two of us volunteers to be lashed 25 times. First, they marched the other fellow into an office by the gate. Waiting outside, I could hear him cry and yell as they beat him, and I knew what awaited me. A while later, my turn came. I was led inside; there were a number of *kapos* and two of them took me, one from each side, and bent me over a bench, pulled my pants down, and yelled out the punishment. I was ordered to count out loud or else get double the lashes. The two *kapos* held me down and the third started to hit me with a stick across my bare buttocks. I only had the strength to count to 12. I thought this would be my end, but my luck was that I was the second one, and it seems that they had already satisfied their appetite for savagery and sadism. They hit me four or five times more, then threw me to the ground and kicked me in the side several times for good measure, yelling, "March out fast."

But I wasn't able to get up fast enough to avoid more kicks. How I finally got out the door I'll never know.[4] Still this was not the end of my dreadful day. As I was being beaten, the German officer watched and enjoyed himself. The Germans first trained these *kapos* in savagery like police train their dogs to attack on command. In most cases, these *kapos* were first beaten up themselves by the Germans for not being brutal enough. That is how the Nazis built an army of sadists to help them in the vicious criminal acts they perpetrated all over Europe.

---

[4] In the early 1950s, I suddenly developed severe pain at the base of my spine and had to have an operation because of a boil growing there. The doctor who operated on me asked whether I had ever injured this area. Surely this condition must have been the result of my beating in Hersbruck.

I somehow managed to drag myself back to the barrack. There, the block supervisor told me there was no supper left for me. "But you must go to the *entlausungsanstalt* now, and that is an order," he shouted. I was completely bewildered. G-d in heaven, I thought to myself, do I deserve all this? All I want is to rest a bit on my cage-bed, and quiet my hunger pangs a little with a slice of bread and a little soup. Now I have to go to the showers.

I tried to explain to the block supervisor what happened to me and begged him to let me lie down and rest. But he began to yell, "Do you want to get more?" I realized that there was no justice, no pity in a concentration camp, not from the savage beast nor from the Angel of Death. So I went off to the showers, feeling pain with every step. At the showers, I had to undress and exchange my clothes. My old underwear was bloody. The *häftling* in charge of handing out clean clothing was a Jewish boy from Slovakia. He saw my bruised body, my swollen behind, and took pity on me; he searched for the largest garments he could find and handed them to me. This was a great kindness because usually they'd grab pants or a jacket, regardless of size, and that was that.

I tried to shower, but the hot water stung my wounds. Instead, I spritzed myself a few times and dried off. Finally around one o'clock in the morning, I got back to the barrack and lay down on my bunk bed, knowing that at 4:30 we would be awakened for the 5 a.m. roll-call.

G-d in heaven, I thought, How will I be able to do that? But in Yiddish there is a proverb: "A human being is weaker than a fly and stronger than steel."[5] Even thought I felt very weak, somehow I knew I could endure.

For the rest of that night I couldn't fall asleep. Willi was on a different shift for the past few days, and we didn't get to talk to each other. At 4:30 came the usual shouts to get up and the sticks banging on our bunks. With great effort I managed to get dressed and get down from my bunk. When you are 25 years old, as I was then, you possess hidden and unknown reserves of strength. I also believe that those of us who overcame our overwhelming situations then did so because we knew that the end was very near, and because of our driving need for revenge, to see justice done. Surely the Nazis would pay for their unspeakable crimes.

To my good fortune, that day I got assigned to work on the platform where freight was unloaded and hoisted up by cable cars.

---

[5] *"A mensch ist schvacher vun a flieg, en shtarker vun eizen."*

This was considered an easier job than dragging all the heavy lumber and building materials up the hill to the tunnel.

A day or two later, we arrived back in Hersbruck after work, in the dark evening. Our barrack was barely lit. As I got my supper ration of a slice of bread and a little soup, I held my bowl in one hand, and my slice of bread in the other. Suddenly, a *häftling* ripped the slice of bread out of my hand. In trying to hold onto it, I spilled all of my soup and was left with nothing to eat. In the great tumult that ensued, he disappeared. Bitterly disappointed, I went to my bunk and almost cried from hunger pains. What a great loss I suffered that day – a slice of bread and a little potato soup!

When I related the incident to an older Polish Jewish prisoner who had been in the concentration camp a few years at that point, he said, "You have to realize, we've all had these experiences from time to time. Also you should know not to save anything, be it a piece of bread or something, for later, because people steal here. This is a different planet we are on. Here the same supreme law rules as the one that rules wild hyenas."

I learned my lesson well. From then on, I guarded my soup and slice of bread as one watches over the most precious possessions, and never did I put anything away for later.

If a single hunk of bread was worth so much, you can imagine the value of an entire loaf! I witnessed the murder of a Czech boy in his 20s in front of all of us by a Polish beast because of one loaf of bread. One day, as was the practice, our block supervisor sent two prisoners to bring bread to our barrack from the main distribution block. The bread was allocated precisely: eight *häftlings* to one loaf. Slicing up the loaves with a machine, the cook then distributed a slice to each man. (You had great luck if you got a middle slice since it was usually bigger than an end piece.) This time, in counting up the loaves, the supervisor discovered one loaf was missing.

One of the two who went for the bread blamed the other, a Czech boy, and claimed that the Czech had eaten it. The block supervisor must have believed him because he started beating the Czech boy all over his head and body without stopping. When the stick broke, he ran into his room, grabbed another and continued beating the poor guy. The more the Czech fellow cried and pleaded, the more the supervisor beat him. The Czech's face was awash in blood. Never in my life had I witnessed such sadism. Everyone in the barrack held his breath and looked at the perpetration of this crime. No German was in sight in our barrack, and yet nobody dared stop this beast, not even the two inmates who were former high-ranking Czech government officials. Such was the terror that we lived under. That sadist beat him until white foam dribbled out of his mouth, as if he had an epileptic fit. Then the block supervisor went back to his private quarters, leaving the Czech boy there to bleed to death. He died the next day of his injuries.

After suffering my own beating, my strength declined rapidly. I think the culprit was two-fold: the cold weather and the hunger I suffered. My toes had become frost-bitten, and my ankles had started to swell. I could barely put my shoes on in the morning, but still had to go out to work. To make matters worse, in late February 1945, a heavy piece of equipment that another *häftling* and I were carrying fell across my left foot. I was in such excruciating pain that I couldn't put any weight on it as it now became even more swollen. Luckily that day the train came promptly and brought us back to Hersbruck. Limping, I barely made it to our barrack. I was fully aware that I couldn't go out to work anymore but had to register sick, despite my fears of being sent to the crematorium in Flossenburg. "The waters had reached the drowning point"[6] – meaning that I had no other choice. I couldn't go on any longer. I had no more strength. But G-d's ways are mysterious: I expected the worst, but registering at the *revier* turned out to be my salvation.

---

[6] *Ba-uh mayim ad nefesh.*

Chapter 30

Revier

RUSSIAN ARMY UNITS HAD ADVANCED CLOSE TO FLOSSENBURG by the end of February 1945. At roughly the same time, the Hersbruck camp had to be evacuated quickly because of the advancing allied armies. The German SS emptied Hersbruck of the *häftlings*, including those in the *revier* who were able to walk, and forced them to march deeper into Germany. Hundreds died on these death marches. Some succumbed to the cold or hunger, some were killed by the German SS. *Häftlings* who couldn't walk fast enough to keep up with the rest were shot on the streets like wild dogs. My condition had so deteriorated that I'm certain I'd have been a victim somewhere along that road.

Later I met some of the boys from our *szazod* who survived Hersbruck, and they told me horrifying stories of these death marches, as did prisoners from other evacuated camps. Even on the brink of defeat, the German beasts thought only of quenching their thirst for sadism. They saw the end coming, but persisted in killing off as many Jews as they could anyhow.

As I said, I had no other choice than to register sick. The *revier* doctors were also *häftlings* who operated under very severe conditions because they, too, were beaten up if a German doctor noticed them either being too lenient with the sick, or caring for them too well. One criterion for getting into the *revier* was swollen ankles. When a Czech doctor examined my legs, he immediately took me in. The *revier* block was very clean and much warmer than the barracks. For the first time in a little less than two months, I began to warm up. Inside the *revier* a Jewish doctor, who was once a surgeon in the Budapest Jewish Hospital, examined me. His name was Schwartz, and I can recall him very well. He wanted to inspect my injured foot, but now it was so badly swollen that he had to cut my shoe off with a knife. After a quick look, he told me he would have to operate on my foot the next morning.

When they assigned me a bed, it was in the same cages as in the regular barracks, three levels high. Since I had a foot injury, I got a bunk on the bottom so I didn't have to climb up. As I sat on my bunk bed, a fellow named Moshe from our *szazod* came over to me, very surprised, barely recognizing me because of how much my condition had deteriorated since he saw me last. "Michael, what's the matter with you?" he asked. I was very happy to see him, telling him I had fought like the dickens not to register sick for fear of being sent to Flossenburg.

"It's true," he said, "they were sending people to Flossenburg, but they haven't been doing that for the past three weeks." He also told me that our *szazod* doctor, Dr. Ecker, was in the *revier* along with two more boys from our *szazod* whom I knew. Compared to Moshe, who still looked like a human being, I was fast becoming a human skeleton. More than the constant hunger, the cold weather and not being dressed for the Bavarian winters, plus being beaten were all taking their toll.

In the *revier* the food was the same as elsewhere in the concentration camp – no less, and certainly no more. The only difference was that it was warm inside, and I didn't have to go out to do back-breaking slave labor. The next morning they took me into the so-called operating room. There was a long table on which the procedures were performed, with scissors and knives and no other medical equipment. They didn't even have gauze or bandages; naturally, no anesthesia. The doctor had two aides who placed me on top of the table. The two held me down tightly so I wouldn't move or jump. As he began, the doctor apologized to me by saying, "I must open this wound and clean out the infection or else it can spread all over your body. I'm sorry, I have no drugs to give you for the pain." But he assured me that after he cut it open, the pain would subside, and the operation wouldn't take long.

The operating room was like a butcher shop. One after the other, people were brought in with frozen toes or limbs and all sorts of other physical problems. Those waiting outside in the make-shift waiting room must have been frightened out of their minds, hearing the screams of the sick people who were having surgical operations without anesthetics. Dr. Schwartz didn't have so much as an aspirin to give his patients. He asked me whether I spoke Hungarian. When I said yes, he told me in Hungarian that the operation would not take long and I shouldn't be afraid. I mustered all my strength to keep from screaming when he cut the wound open and cleaned it out. Then he bandaged it up with crepe paper, the only substitute he had for bandages. (In fact, changing the crepe paper dressing every two or three days was more torture than the operation itself, because it adhered to the wound.) He wrapped the crepe paper tight enough to stop the bleeding, but the healing resulted in a permanent stiffening of my left big toe and the two next to it. They remain deformed to this day, and I must wear specially-made orthopedic shoes.

Dr. Schwartz was in his mid-50s when I met him. He appeared to be in good health. As the *revier*'s main surgeon, he operated and cleaned wounds all day long. The *kapos* respected him and he received better treatment from them and a bit more food – perhaps because they, too, might wind up under his knife one day. I heard in the *revier* that Dr. Schwartz studied medicine in Vienna and that the SS doctor in charge of the camp's so-called hospitals, and who occasionally inspected the camp, was a schoolmate of his. They knew each other from before the Hitler era in Austria. I believe that coincidence cost Dr. Schwartz his life, because the SS doctor had no intention of letting Dr. Schwartz survive and tell of the horrors that were perpetrated and the conditions that existed in the *reviers* of Flossenburg and Hersbruck. One day they announced in the *revier* that Dr. Schwartz was dead. I had just seen him about 12 hours earlier when he changed my dressing. All the *revier* patients were stunned by the news. Right away, the rumor spread that Dr. Schwartz was poisoned by that SS doctor who was the supervisor on a *revier* inspection just the day before.

We were evacuated from Hersbruck shortly after Dr. Schwartz disappeared. In all, I was in the Hersbruck *revier* for three weeks. Before we were shipped out, I got to know a remarkable Frenchman in a near-by "bed." He was a general who spoke very good German, so we could converse easily. One of his legs had been amputated and the other was very badly frost-bitten. Exactly how he sustained his injuries I didn't ask and he never said. All the French prisoners displayed great courtesy and respect to him and came over to his bunk regularly to talk with him. (Not knowing French, I didn't understand their conversations.)

By this time, March 1945, a few months before the end of the war, the Germans "generously" allowed Red Cross packages to be distributed – but only to the French, of course, not to the Jews. Two of the *revier*'s doctors were French, and from time to time I saw one of them bring the general some tablets, probably aspirin that had been included in the Red Cross parcels.

One evening, this French general was feeling very desperate and depressed, but he wanted to talk. Each day the Germans brought newcomers from other camps to our *revier*. They'd tell us news, including what camps they had previously been in and how close the battle lines were to us. The general knew the German map thoroughly, and he said to me, "I believe the war will end very soon." He explained where the Russians and Americans were inside Germany, and said, "You are young. You will live to see the end of this war. But as far as I am concerned, I don't believe I will." The only thing I knew was that we were close to Nuremberg. Where we were in relation to the front lines, I had no idea.

In the same conversation, he told me that they were going to amputate his other leg the next day because it was heavily gangrened. He was in a lot of pain and very worried when he confided these things to me. The next morning, they took him into the operating room, to that butcher shop, and amputated his leg below the knee. When they brought him back and put him in his bunk, he was in excruciating pain, groaning and screaming. I was all shaken up, listening to his loud moans. Despite the hellish situation I was in then, I realized there was always someone worse off than myself.

The two French doctors were able to give the general some medicine to ease his pain. The next day and night, I stayed by his side, empathizing with him. But there was nothing I could do to help him. On the third day after his operation, the camp commander, the highest ranking SS officer, came in to the *revier*. He walked straight over to the French general and said, "*Wie gehts, Herr Kollege?*" – "How's it going, my colleague?" The French general in his bitterness and pain answered in German, "*Ich bin nicht dein Kollege, du Schweinhund*" – "I am not your colleague, you pig-dog." When I heard that, I thought he would get a beating from this SS officer. How surprised I was to see the German commander just turn around and walk right out of the barrack without saying a word. That evening, I heard a murmur in the room. What happened, I wondered, sensing that an earth-shaking event occurred. That night, instead of the bitter black coffee we usually got for supper, we all got real milk. For those who had been in the *revier* for a longer time than I was, this was a first. Everyone wondered what had happened to warrant this great treat.

This occurred in the middle of March 1945. Remember, I had not seen a drop of milk since May 1944, when my buddy David Godinger bought me some in Mezeritch from a Polish woman. Almost a year's time. Yet I now offered my milk to the general. So did the French prisoners in the *revier*. In a few days, the general's pain subsided, and he stopped groaning and moaning. Unfortunately, sometime between March 15 and 20, only six weeks before the end of the war, he passed away in the bunk next to mine.

One week later, we began to hear explosions, bombardment and artillery fire. The battle lines were getting closer to us. I could hear cannon fire from miles away. One morning, the *kapos* got an order to evacuate us from Hersbruck to another place. Of course, no one knew where. All those capable of walking had to march with the rest of the camp, sick or not, no exceptions. For those of us who had injured legs or were legless, the Germans permitted us to travel in open freight trains. Mind you, it was still winter in Bavaria. I fell in among those lucky ones shipped by train. Every one of us was given one blanket to wrap himself with. *Kapos* stood outside the *revier* and distributed one loaf of bread to every *häftling* as he passed by. We invalids were transported on the backs of the *kapos* and other inmates. At the time, I probably didn't weigh more than fifty kilograms (110 pounds). As I passed the bread distributor, he handed me a loaf of bread. Right away I covered it up under my blanket. To my great *mazel*, the guy who carried me passed by another bread distributor. By mistake, I guess, he handed me a loaf of bread. So now I was the proud possessor of two loaves of bread – a G-d sent miracle. My greatest treasure was that bread hidden under my blanket.

I was carried all the way to the train. It was an open freight wagon, and I noticed lots of pebbles on the wagon floor, so most probably it had been used to haul stones. As I was hoisted into it, a *landsman* from a place called Yassena in the Carpathian helped me up and said, "Let's take this corner of the wagon and we'll cover ourselves with both blankets and keep warmer that way." He was less injured than I and in a little better shape. With our hands, we scraped the pebbles out of the corner so we might sit down; being just skin and bones, we could hardly have tolerated any stones underneath us. Sadly, I don't remember his name, and I don't know whether he survived the war.

Some 50 or 60 sick *häftlings* filled our open wagon. It was a cold Bavarian day in March. The first day and night of the train ride were very cold even under our two blankets. Near me was a Russian *häftling*, very sick with high fever. He kept groaning and crying, "Mamma moya, Mamma moya." His head was covered with a blanket, so we couldn't even see what he looked like. He begged for water, probably because of his high fever. Nobody could help him even with a little water. But as we left the station, it started to snow, and we suggested he take some snow off his blanket and eat it. That's when he told us that he was blind. Gathering some snow from the blankets, I put it in his hand. After eating it, he quieted down for a while.

We didn't travel too far before stopping for the rest of the night in a another village in Bavaria. By the morning, it had stopped snowing, and we shook the snow from our blankets as best as we could. My neighbor, the Russian, was again begging for water. As we waited at the station, we asked the civilian Germans milling around there to give us some. One humane German did bring us a bottle of water, which we promptly gave to the Russian prisoner. Again he quieted down. A few hours later, he was totally silent. Very early the next morning, we realized something happened to him. When I spoke to him, he didn't respond. Brighter daylight revealed that he was not the only one who breathed his last on the train that night.

Other dead bodies were strewn about the wagon (and, most surely, not on our wagon alone). The train began to roll again, but we traveled only a few miles before we stopped at another small village. In the bright sunlight, I spotted a large squadron of American planes flying overhead. Local air-raid sirens wailed, but all we could do was sit tight and gaze at the sky. Since we saw the planes headed somewhere, it was a good bet they had better targets than this little village. This relaxed us and made us unafraid of being bombed. We talked to each other and tried to revive each other with words of hope. "It won't be long now."

While our train waited in the village station, the German SS ordered the Ukrainian SS to empty the wagons of all the dead *häftlings* and load them in a covered freight wagon. But since the Germans didn't want the locals to see them carrying around dead bodies, they had their Ukrainian SS lackeys do the work for them under cover of night. The train was long – maybe 20 open and covered freight wagons – all filled with people from the Hersbruck *revier*, and maybe also from elsewhere. The German SS and Ukrainians rode in passenger cars that were attached to the train. They had no concerns that any of us might jump out of the wagons because we were in such poor condition: none of us could have or would have.

When it got dark, the Ukrainian SS took off the dead from the train. Before they did, however, we surviving *häftlings* removed their blankets. Before they carted away my dead Russian neighbor, I pulled his blanket over me; in it, I found a piece of bread that the poor fellow either hadn't seen or could not eat. I gave the bread to my

Yassina *landsman*. I didn't know how much longer we'd be traveling, but I considered myself the richest man in the group because I still had left a full loaf of bread.

A third night passed and still we sat in our open train wagon. We survived on a piece of bread and some snow. We passed urine, but I don't remember anybody having a bowel movement. Perhaps when a human being is so starved and dehydrated, over a period of four days and four nights, he has no such waste in him.

Overnight, the Ukrainian SS again pulled bodies off each wagon. To me, it looked as though they expected to find even more dead people than they did. Anyway, at least they didn't object to our taking the blankets from the dead. Most of us, just barely alive, now had an additional blanket. By this time my *landsman* and I had three blankets to cover ourselves with. As the train moved on, we weathered the third night a whole lot better.

At daybreak, the fourth day, we arrived at Dachau.

Chapter 31

Dachau

I REMEMBER IT WAS SUNNY WHEN WE ARRIVED It had to be about the 25th or 26th of March, 1945. For hours, we sat in the train wagon. Then in the afternoon, a group of *häftlings* from the camp unloaded Dachau's newest "merchandise." That's how we learned where we were, when we started to speak with them. By that time, of the 50 or 60 people loaded onto our wagon at Hersbruck, half were dead. Separating the living from the corpses, *häftlings* lifted us out of the wagon; we were so weak no one could make it on his own. Two other *häftlings* carted our dead away in a four-wheeled wagon. I overheard one say to the other in Polish, "He's still alive," referring to a body on the wagon. "Never mind," the other answered, "he'll die anyway." That's how cheap life was in Dachau.

Once inside the camp, the *häftlings* dumped us on the ground and told us to wait there until the camp command checked us out. Thankfully, it was not snowing or raining that day. The sun shone, although the ground was very cold. Half naked in our lightweight *häftling* garb, we waited, wrapped in blankets that did little to shield us from the cold. Finally, two *kapos* came. I think they were Germans, with red triangles on their uniforms. Standing over us with a clipboard, they started to register us. When they came to me, I gave my name as Mikhal Yanofsky, of Czech nationality. For the first time in my life, I actively tried to conceal that I am Jewish. It was naïve of me, of course, because I also gave them my concentration camp number: 40,688. They could have easily checked out my real identity against a list that undoubtedly was on the train from Hersbruck. Still I had to risk it: I was in such dreadful shape, and my instinct to survive was stronger than ever. I wanted to live to see the end of the war, so I was willing to try almost anything.

It was dark by the time my turn came. Two *häftlings* carried me into a barrack marked *"entlausungsanstalt."* They helped me take off my clothes and left me there. I didn't have the strength to stand on my one good foot, so I lay on the shower stall floor and, with great effort, managed to wash myself a bit. My left foot was still bandaged in crepe paper and I tried to keep it dry by keeping it out of the stall, but I didn't succeed too well. After doing what I could, I crawled out of the shower on my hands and knees. A *häftling* then handed me a pair of ill-fitting pants, shirt, undershirt and underpants. The two who brought me there earlier had appropriated my one shoe that I wore from Hersbruck on my good right foot. So I begged the distributor of the clothing for a pair of big socks. Pitying me, he handed me two pairs of socks and advised me to put both on my feet to keep warm. Then he assured me that someone would come to take me into the *revier*. I was almost the last one in the shower.

The pain in my left foot was excruciating and it had been occupying my thoughts. Now, suddenly, it hit me I was in the notorious Camp Dachau. I broke down and started to cry, lying on the floor unable to move or to walk. This was already my fourth night without sleep. I was totally helpless. All I could do was cry and hope for compassion. In despair, I fell asleep – or maybe I passed out. When next I opened my eyes, I found myself inside the Dachau *revier,* on the top bed of a three-tier bunk. There I remained until the Americans liberated the camp.

By late March 1945, the Russians, Americans and British were deep in the heartland of Germany. On the day of liberation in Dachau, there were 38,000 *häftlings* like me in the camp. Daily, hundreds of prisoners had been arriving at Dachau from various other concentration camps. Dachau was built to accommodate only a few thousand prisoners, but in the final few weeks of the war, the Germans crammed in 10 times its capacity. Already meager food rations were thus diminished to starvation rations. Here I suffered the most from hunger pangs. My body had no more reserves of fat; I was completely reduced to a *musselman*. And I wasn't alone. All of us were starving. For breakfast, we received only a cup of bitter, ersatz coffee. For supper, 12 prisoners had to share one loaf of bread; each got a tiny slice plus a few grams of margarine. Anyone unlucky enough to receive his slice from the end of the loaf got less – a real tragedy, because that was it for the day. Sometimes the bread was stale, covered with mold or mildew, and it simply fell apart. For the entire time I was in Dachau, I thought my stomach would fuse to my ribcage because my hunger pangs were so great. When I tried to complain to my neighbor across from me on the third bunk, a guy named Mertz, about how hungry I felt, he'd just tell me: "I'm already eight years in this camp. And you," he'd say in German, "you don't know how to shovel coal."[1] I asked him what he meant by that. He explained: "You don't know how to suffer yet." To him this was a skill that one could improve upon with time.

In the *revier*, French prisoners fared better. They received packages through the Red Cross, at least during the period that I was there. Perhaps, with the war nearing its end, the Germans feared the French the most. Their packages contained cigarettes, and the Frenchmen would sell them, one cigarette for one slice of bread.

Mertz often traded away his slice of bread for a cigarette. He'd smoke a bit, then put it out, to save it for later. Then he'd pull his blanket over his head and try to sleep or wait until the next morning for his bitter black coffee. Once I told him, "Mertz, you're doing a very foolish thing." But he just repeated: "I'm here eight years already, and you don't know how to go hungry."

After two weeks in the *revier*, I developed a boil on my rear end, which became very painful. I suspect it was the result of the Hersbruck beating. I couldn't lie on my back, only on my side. On the bottom level of my column of bunks, there was a Russian doctor whom everyone called *Wrach*. In the beginning I didn't know what the word meant, but I later learned that it was equivalent in English to calling a physician "Doc." He was a friendly person, and he examined my painful bottom. He told me that I'd have to have the boil cut open to obtain any relief, and offered to speak to the doctor in charge of the operating room. He did so, and the next morning I was taken there for the operation. How surprised I was to see the instruments and machines they had there, and how well lit it was. This was a real operating room, not the butcher's table they had in Hersbruck. I suppose because Dachau had gained notoriety the world over since early in the Hitler years, and the Germans were concerned about world opinion, that they tried to show how humane they were by providing a fully equipped hospital for their inmates. They put me to sleep. When I awoke, I was back on the top bunk and could also see that on my left foot the dressing was changed – this time not with crepe paper, but with real gauze. The pain was gone from my rear end, but I still couldn't lie on my back.

Mertz was one of the rare righteous men in Germany, and I still see his face in my mind. He confided to me that he had been sent to Dachau eight years earlier because he was a priest of the Subotnic church, and preached against Hitlerite crimes. We spoke a lot, and I discovered that he hated his own people even more than I did. He

---

[1] "*Du kannst nicht Kohlen schieben.*"

was a man with grace in his heart, and a man of conviction. He constantly encouraged and inspired me to have hope, saying, "We shall outlive them," *them* meaning the *kapos* and the SS. He was in his fifties, and I was only in my mid-twenties, but remarkably he was in better physical shape than I was. Possibly his family or friends sent him packages, though we never discussed it. But considering his fair condition after eight years in Dachau, it had to be that he had received some food from outside sources.

One day we were given a piece of liverwurst for supper instead of the one ounce of margarine on a piece of bread. Suddenly, Mertz tossed his piece of liverwurst onto my bunk, without saying a word to me. I tried to give it back to him. "Mertz, what are you doing?" He refused to take it back because "it has a lot of blood in it and I don't eat blood," he said.

This impressed me tremendously. Here was a man suffering from hunger and pain and he still possessed the moral strength to adhere to his faith and his beliefs. I took my slice of bread and tossed it on his bed.

During those last weeks in April, all kinds of rumors abounded. Nobody really knew how the war was going. The only news we received came from new arrivals who were evacuated from places all over Germany. Suddenly everyone became an expert in absolutely everything: not only were they military strategists, but they *knew* for certain when the war would end. Yet, at the same time, we feared that the Germans, in the final moments of their defeat, would extract vengeance on us by mining the barracks. We were so close to liberation and yet helpless to prevent our murder. We hardly slept or rested for worry of that possibility. Like strings pulled overly taught, my nerves felt like they'd break at any second.

After the war's end, Western psychologists came in contact with survivors in Germany in the Displaced Persons camps; they couldn't fathom, after hearing the horrors we suffered, how our faculties were still intact. In my view, hunger and starvation saved us.

Although I'd been deeply depressed and in psychological pain since the time I learned of the murder of my dear brother Zvi, in Dachau all I could think of was, "When will the hunger pangs stop?" This perhaps is not rational, but I firmly believe that had the Germans given us enough food to eat, many concentration camp inmates would have gone crazy or committed suicide, as the only means of escape from the wild brutality not only of the Germans but also of the *kapo* system, which pitted victim against victim. So focusing on our hunger had an ironic plus: it prevented us from going stark raving mad in our grief.

Roughly a week before the American army liberated us, an order came to remove all Jews from Dachau. I learned later the German intention was to march us to a forest in Bavaria. The Germans knew that many would perish along the way; those who didn't would be murdered. We in the *revier* were supposed to go, too. Because I had registered as a Czech national, I wasn't rounded up – initially. But my barrack supervisor, a Pole, suspected I was Jewish. One day, he came to my bed with two *kapos*, a pair of shoes and a complete *häftling* outfit. In Polish, he shouted, "You're a Jew!"[2] He ordered me to dress right away and go out to roll-call, where 5,000 Jews were already lined up in columns for the death march. As I lay there, the supervisor yelled again at me, "You are a Jew – get out!"

I'm unable to take even two steps, I told him, and added that I'm not going anywhere. They could shoot me, they could do whatever they wanted, but I was unable to move. He threatened to report me to the camp commandant for defying the order. In a concentration camp there was no such thing as a *häftling* defying an order – that was asking for death. But I wasn't trying to be a hero; I simply had no other choice. Dead in my bed or dead on the road, whatever would be would be. Angry, the block supervisor and *kapos* left the room, leaving the shoes and outfit on my bed. My left foot was still bandaged from surgery. Even if I had wanted to, I couldn't have put on a pair of shoes. Besides, I didn't have the strength. So, now, I waited for them to return, drag me down from my bed and finish me off. I was sure they would. But I think one of my grandmothers or grandfathers must have intervened on my behalf in heaven: the block supervisor and his two aides never came back. One week before liberation, I was saved.

That day the Germans marched all the Jews out of Dachau. Only later, in a hospital after the war, did I meet some Jews who had survived that forced march. They had marched all that day and half the night. Some of them were shot to death on the road along the way because they couldn't keep up; other escaped into the fields under cover of darkness. A large percentage of them survived because American troops intercepted the column on the road. A few

---

[2] "*Ty jestes zydem!*"

hours before that, the SS had disappeared. That's how that death
march ended. One thing I know for sure: had my block supervisor
dragged me from my bunk to join the march, I would not have been
at the head of the line and I wouldn't be here to write about it.

A day or two after defying the Polish *ältester*, I realized there
must have been great confusion among the camp authorities for an
action such as mine to go unpunished. I don't know whether denying
I was Jewish was a factor, but after that incident they didn't bother
me anymore.

Among the inmates left in the *revier*, the mood was a mixture of
hope and grave worry. We existed only to outlive the greatest
monster in human history, Hitler, and see his defeat. But we also
were filled with anxiety that as a last act of viciousness the Germans
would blow up the camp, denying us our freedom.

A day later, the most extraordinary thing happened: the
Germans started to distribute boxes of Ovaltine, one full box to
everyone in the *revier*. Never before had they done so, and we were
astonished. We took this to be a sign that we would soon be free. We
guessed that with the war ending, they didn't want all this food to be
found in warehouses within reach of thousands of people dying from
hunger.

Ovaltine is a very nourishing product. My brother Moshe used
to buy it for his children, Shloimi and Channi. It's made from dried
milk, egg yolks and sugar, so it's sweet and filling. When I got my box
of Ovaltine, I felt like the richest man in the universe. One spoonful
of Ovaltine had the power to save someone's life. My neighbor Mertz
told me that, in all his eight years in the camp, he never once saw a
German distribute a full box. And it was a sizable box at that –
maybe a full kilogram. Mertz wisely cautioned me not to take too
much of it: "Just a spoonful every hour or so, even less," he said.
"Just give it a lick, because our hungry stomachs cannot digest too
much at one time." I took his advice. As it turned out, many *häftlings*
in the *revier* consumed so much that they developed bad cases of
dysentery from it, and many died. Was that the German intention
when they gave us the Ovaltine? I think it was. I think they knew that
these hungry people would grab it and unknowingly gorge themselves
to death.

I guarded my priceless treasure under my blanket. I found it impossible to believe I could finally quiet my hunger pangs. From time to time I'd put a little Ovaltine on my spoon and lick it like a lollipop. That sufficed to quiet my hunger. Merely possessing it and knowing enough not to overdo it, was reassuring.

If I seem to dwell on the issue of hunger, it's because only someone who has felt it for weeks and months at a time, and has seen his body shrivel to skin and bone, can grasp the excruciating experience of near starvation. As the folk saying goes, "*Der satte kann nicht den hungrigen verstehen.*" A full and satisfied stomach can never really understand hunger.

Although in Hersbruck I had grown so downhearted that I considered death to be a salvation, now that I was at liberation's doorstep, my will to live was overwhelming. Each soul in the *revier* felt great exhilaration, envisioning the moment the concentration camp gates would break open and we would rejoice not only in our survival, but in living to see Germany demolished, and in having the world learn what had been done to us. At the same time, though, rumors still flew around the *revier* that the Germans would mine the barracks at night and we'd all perish in one great blast just before regaining our freedom.

Chapter 32

Liberation

I COULD NOT FALL ASLEEP those last nights at the end of April 1945. The four-year nightmare was about to end. Admittedly, my desire for revenge was very strong and drove me to hang on despite my weakened state. The concept of "mind over matter" was proven in the concentration camps. The mind empowered the body to endure and overcome the impossible.

At last, the long-awaited day arrived. On April 29, 1945, at a quarter to five in the afternoon, American tanks ringed the perimeter of Dachau. German guards were still stationed in the camp's watchtowers. I had no strength to get to a window, so I'm sad to say I did not see it with my own eyes, but Mertz described to me how American soldiers with machine guns cut down the SS guards in the towers. The German camp commander had disappeared a few hours before. The 20th Armored Tank Division liberated Dachau, and when American soldiers entered the camp, the *häftlings* cheered them wildly. From my bunk, I clearly heard the great roar of jubilation outside.

Mertz also detailed the revenge *häftlings* then took out on the *kapos*, *ältesters* and other German helpers still in camp. The crowd simply lynched them in the middle of the former *appelplatz*. I did not participate in any of these events because, although I was 25 and should have been in my prime, I lay half-dead in a bunk, barely capable of turning over. I don't remember having to go the bathroom even once during the weeks I was lying in bed in Dachau, although I'm still at a loss to explain this.

By dark, the Americans had secured the camp. They chased everybody back to their barracks because they had to battle nearby units of the German SS and the military who tried to retake the camp. Very heavy fighting ensued, judging by the explosions and barrages of gunfire. That night, cannon fire struck one of the barracks in the camp. Three *häftlings* were killed and many were badly wounded. Deathly afraid, we prayed the Germans wouldn't win this battle. And we mourned the tragic fate of the *häftlings* killed that night: people who survived until liberation yet still died at German hands.

Twenty-some years later, on my first-ever visit to Israel in 1966, I met a man by the name of Moshe Sheinfelt. He told me that my brother Moshe had been liberated in Allach, a sub-camp only a few kilometers from Dachau. Moshe died shortly after liberation, he said. There is no way for me to find out how accurate this information is or where Moshe was laid to rest. When they came into the camps, the Americans were forced to bury countless dead in huge mass graves in the camps and elsewhere.

The war ended on May 8, 1945. It wasn't until a couple weeks later that I found out President Roosevelt had died in April. News of his death pained me because I idolized him. I also learned of Hitler's death around the same time, but without any details. Although the world was now free of this monster, the news gave me little solace: he had already destroyed millions of lives.

Like others, I was the sole survivor of my dear family. By the end of the *Shoah*, I weighed 34 kilograms, something like 70 pounds – astounding at my height of six-foot-two-and-a-half inches. I still nursed a hope that maybe someone else in my family had survived, but it was not so. My brother Eliezer had two boys – the older one, Berzi, would have been 16 in 1945 and his brother Willi would have been 14 years old then. There were my brother Moshe's two children: Channi was 11 and Shloimi 8 in 1944. My brother Zvi had one boy, four years old, named Baruch, whom we called "Buchyk" as an endearment. All were dead.

Words cannot express the enormity of this tragedy. Of course, it was a war and people of all nationalities died. Men die in wars, but not necessarily their babies, mothers, wives, daughters, elders, or the sick. Only we Jews had to pay this enormous price.

Doctors and medicine didn't arrive in force until the middle of May, when the American army organized a makeshift hospital in Dachau to tend to the sick. There is one case I remember very well. In the same column of bunks that I was in, directly under me, a man lay in great pain because he couldn't pass urine. He was a Hungarian Jew, and he wept and begged for help. Pumping out his bladder wasn't a very complicated procedure, I think, but nobody was there to help him. The two or three *revier* doctors had disappeared. A few days after liberation, his groans and moans ceased. He had died. How ironic to live to be liberated and then to die a few days later. But so it was: hundreds died in the first few days after liberation; even a month later, there were 50 former *häftlings* dying every day in Dachau. For them help came too late.

Many *häftlings* brought on their own demise because they left their barracks, broke open the SS magazines and found lots of food. Ravenous, they wolfed down all kinds of supplies – conserved meats, canned ham, fish products and cheese. Then they brought some of these supplies into the *revier* and distributed them among those who, like me, couldn't walk. In a matter of days, people became even sicker with dysentery and began dying right and left. Scores of them succumbed because their weakened bodies couldn't absorb those rich fatty meats and other food. Thank G-d for Mertz, who strongly warned me not to eat any of it. I was fine.

After a while, the Americans, realizing why so many people were dying, clamped down on us and denied anyone permission to leave the barracks. For those of us in the *revier*, they ordered a very skimpy and lean ration. Of course, we weren't too happy with the amount, but I realized it was for our own good.

About a week after Liberation, Mertz and I bade each other goodbye. He headed home to his family somewhere in a German village. Remarkably, he was able to leave on his own two feet. I, on the other hand, was so sick and weak that I barely was able to roll over in my bed. For me and other Jews, Dachau had been the worst hell, especially during the last days.

On May 15, the Americans emptied out all the SS barracks in the camp, and installed regular beds from the city of Dachau. The beds were lined up in long rows, three or four across. Like a baby, I was carried over to one of those barracks, a huge room, by an American soldier. Gently he laid me down on a normal bed – the first one I had slept on in years. Then came Americans who spoke German, and they asked questions: Nationality? Citizenship? Name? Age? This time I gave my right name, but registered as a Czech citizen. I don't recall if they asked any other questions. But they hung a piece of cardboard with this information at the end of each bed. In two weeks' time, the American authorities completed the task of sorting out the sick.

Early one morning, two uniformed military nurses appeared to take our temperatures. For the first time in my life I saw an American thermometer being put into the mouth of a patient and measured in Fahrenheit. In Europe before the war, we always measured temperature under the arm and, of course, in Celsius. Later in the morning, the doctor and his assistant checked on my condition.

I had a high temperature, and my foot and back injuries weren't healing. When I lay on my back, I had no strength to turn onto my side without help. When I was given a bed pan by the nurses, I needed help to lift myself. Although our rations were lean, they were 100 times better than before. We were fed a spoonful of dried eggs, a thin slice of white bread and some juice in the morning. For lunch, it was a thin slice of bread and some more juice. For supper, a slice of bread with a piece of a chicken and more juice.

By the fourth day, we were more or less under the care of an American military doctor. He held the rank of major and he was attended by a male nurse, I guess, who spoke German. The doctor walked from bed to bed, asking questions and giving medical orders. His assistant translated for the patients while jotting down all the information. When the doctor reached my bed, I observed him intensively. He looked at me and studied the identification chart hung on my bed. "You're Czech?" he asked. "*Ja, ja,*" I answered in German. All this time I watched him closely, observing him and his expression. I detected some resignation in his eyes. He murmured something in English to the attendant that I couldn't understand, and started walking to the next bed.

Instantly, I realized he had given up on me. I called out to him in German, as loud as I could, "Doctor, doctor, don't go away! Come back!" He turned and returned to my bedside. I began to sob, still speaking in German, "Now that I've survived the war and lived to see the end of Hitler's Germany, now you are giving up on me? Help me, help me," I pleaded. "I want to live. I'm only 25 years of age." And as I cried out my plea, tears flowed down my face.

The doctor's aide translated all that I had said. The doctor then came closer to my bed and spoke gently in English. He stroked my sweaty forehead and my tear-streaked face. He said something to his aide. In turn, the aide told me in German that the doctor said someone would bring medicine for me at 3 p.m. that day. Then the two went on to the next bed.

Near me were three very sick people, in great pain. All three were from Yugoslavia, and spoke loudly among themselves. I picked up words here and there in Slavic that I understood, but couldn't make out the gist of their conversation. Later I learned that experiments had been done on them: the Germans kept them in ice-cold water to find out how long a human being can tolerate freezing temperatures. Their skin was horribly damaged, literally peeling off their bodies. Their pain was so excruciating that they couldn't lie down. With these patients the American doctor spent more time. I don't know whether he gave them something to lessen their pain, but they didn't stop crying and moaning the whole time.

At 3 p.m., two military nurses returned with my doctor's aide. They set up a blood transfusion contraption next to my bed, and connected it to me with great difficulty. Somehow they found a good vein in my skin-and-bone arm.

Then the group tended to the three Yugoslavs, and wrapped them with gauze bandages, top to bottom. I marveled at American medical efficiency and their abundance of medical supplies. Every day they removed the gauze and applied a fresh dressing. The three poor souls would cry and scream when the old gauze was removed. During this time, they were given no medication, only new gauze. Sadly, it did not save them. One night, after a week or so, two of them died; the third lingered for another day or two. Every day the Americans removed the dead from our block and the others.

I remained hooked up to the blood transfusion machine that first afternoon. To me, it looked as if it wasn't working. The bottle of blood plasma attached to the apparatus didn't appear to drain, and it didn't seem to me that I was absorbing any blood. Miraculously, though, the next morning I experienced relief and felt stronger. I don't know whether this was psychological or the real thing. But by morning, only a third of the plasma remained, so I must have absorbed it during the night. When the doctor made his rounds that morning, I noticed a look of relief in his eyes. Again he approached my bed and caressed my forehead. He said something I couldn't understand, but I sensed he was satisfied with my progress. When the doctor's assistant arrived around 3 p.m., he brought another transfusion bottle for me. He confided that the doctor had been in doubt that my body would be able to handle the first transfusion; pleased that it had, he ordered another one for me.

The second transfusion took only about 12 hours to empty. On the third day the doctor told me, through his aide, that he'd wait 24 hours to give me a third transfusion. Altogether, within 10 days, I received four blood transfusions. Feeling reborn, I began to regain some strength, able to turn from side to side and to lift myself onto the bed pan. Also, we got more to eat now in the *revier*, though I still remained a very hungry man. And I continued to suffer from a high fever.

No doubt this military doctor saved my life. No words can express my tremendous feeling of gratitude and thanks to this angel of G-d, and I hope he's still alive.[1]

I am deeply thankful, too, to the many Americans who donated blood to save our lives and to the American nation for helping me, literally and figuratively, to get back on my feet. After the war, I was nearly dead, and my savior was the United States of America. Later, the Jewish American Joint Distribution Committee did a wonderful job helping those of us who survived but who had nobody left in this world and who remained in hospitals for a long time recuperating, by giving us rations and small packages of food, clothing, coffee and cigarettes. As long as I live I will never forget these acts of kindness.

Slowly I started to regain my strength and my body mass. Nurses changed the dressings on my left foot and my back every day. In three weeks under American care in the *revier*, I gained three kilos. A week later, however, a new problem befell me: a rash, along with terrible itching. This rash covered my entire body. I think now that it might have been a reaction to the blood transfusions. But back then, the doctors thought it was leprosy, and prescribed some kind of cream that the nurses applied to my skin. Nothing seemed to help. I continued to suffer badly from it, and from high fever and shortness of breath.

In very early June 1945, the American military doctor in Dachau ordered a chest X-ray for me. Two assistants wheeled a portable X-ray machine to my bed and took a picture. The next morning, the doctor and his assistant came to my beside. Holding my chest X-ray, he informed me I was suffering from pleurisy and possibly TB, which explained why I had a temperature and was short of breath. He also told me that I would be sent the very next day to a special hospital where they cared for such illnesses. He left the X-ray next to my bed

---

[1] In 1977 or 1978, I chanced upon a letter to *The New York Times* by an American Army Colonel named Walter J. Fellans, who participated in the liberation of Dachau. I phoned him at his home in San Antonio, Texas, and related my story, in hope he could shed some light on the American doctor's identity. We had a long, emotional talk, but unfortunately Colonel Fellans was unable to recall the doctor's name with any certainty. He advised me to call the Pentagon and relate the few bits of data I did have: the American units involved; that for some reason I knew the doctor hailed from Boston; and that, as near as I could remember, his name-tag indicated the last name Killinger. Although my son and I tried to find him, unfortunately, our search bore no fruit. Some military records that might have shed light on the matter were destroyed in a fire at a military installation in St. Louis. Several times we thought we might be able to determine his identity definitively and whether he was still alive, but to no avail.

for me to take along with me. I had no idea what pleurisy was at that time, so the aide had to explain that I had fluid in the lining of my lungs.

Chapter 33

Gauting

TWO AMERICAN GIS IN THE MILITARY AMBULANCE CORPS put me on a stretcher and, on June 9, 1945, drove me and two other patients to a sanitarium on the outskirts of Gauting, in Bavaria. This place had been used by the German airforce and had the most modern equipment available at the time. I was carried in to Room 130 on the second floor of the B building, which was to be my address for the next 26 months. My room was very clean, painted white, with six normal hospital beds, night stands by each bed and a great window that let in lots of light.

In every way, Gauting Sanitarium was a real hospital; it didn't have a single dirty green military blanket or bare bunk without a mattress. A ray of hope returned to me, and I slowly lost my fear of being hopelessly sick. I steadily regained my strength. Although now I felt certain I'd recuperate, I surely never expected it would take more than two years to do so – that I would remain in Gauting until the summer of 1947.

This hospital was nestled in the middle of a pine forest. It was two stories high and built like a self-contained village. The building formed a perfect square with a huge center courtyard. Each patient wing, denoted A, B, C and D, was as long as a city block. Corridors connected all four wings, with the hospital staff being housed outside the square. It was constructed to accommodate 1,000 beds plus barracks for 500 more hospital staff; additional staff members commuted daily from the city. The American military occupation authority ordered the German military in charge of the hospital to immediately transfer their sick to other facilities; they then transformed Gauting hospital into a rehabilitation center for former concentration camp slaves from Dachau, Allach, and other parts of Germany. The Americans also ordered the German hospital personnel, doctors and nurses, to tend to the new patients. We three from Dachau may have been the first such patients brought to Gauting. In a very short time, however, all 1,000 beds were filled. Ninety percent of the sick and dying were Jews from concentration camps. Later, as the hospital needed more space, they moved the less-sick patients to another hospital in a city called St. Otillien, which had 500 beds. Other patients were sent to a hospital in nearby Munich.

Presiding over all of this was a French Jew put in charge by the American military government, through the United Nations Relief and Rehabilitation Administration (UNRRA), a Dr. Weiss. Two former *häftling* doctors, both Polish Jews, joined him a short while later to help supervise the German hospital staff. The staff included two German lung specialists who were assigned to B wing. One, Dr. Miller, was in his late 30s, and the other doctor, Hasler, was in his mid-50s. The nurses called Hasler *Herr Chefarzt* (literally, "Chief Doctor" – he must have been the former chief resident). Tall like me, Dr. Hasler held the rank of colonel and commanded a great deal of respect from the nurses and from Dr. Miller. Everyone listened attentively whenever he ordered anything for the patients. Every morning around 9 a.m., both doctors and a nurse entered our room and went from bed to bed. Nurses jotted down everything Dr. Hasler ordered. I well remember his first visit. Examining the X-ray I'd brought from Dachau, he showed something on it to Dr. Miller, and ordered new tests. Later, two nurses put me in a wheelchair and brought me to the first floor, where they fluoroscoped me. The physician administering the test peered into my lungs, and dictated his diagnosis before I was taken back to my ward. Later, they wheeled a portable X-ray machine right to my bed, sat me up and took X-rays right there.

Around 3 p.m., Drs. Hasler and Miller and a nurse visited me again and examined the new X-ray, after which Doctor Hasler ordered grape sugar injections for me: *traubenzucker*. It was a white powder that was to be injected into my bloodstream daily. This, they told me, would protect and strengthen my heart, which might otherwise be affected by the high fever that I continually suffered. I was still also very short of breath because the fluid collecting in my chest pressed on the lungs and the heart, making it difficult for me to breathe, so Doctor Hasler also ordered that the fluid be pumped out of my chest.

It was very strange at first, being tended to so well by German doctors and nurses, and I was very nervous about it for the first few days, worried that they might do something diabolical. I think I was not alone in this feeling. But I soon let go of these concerns, not only because I believed Doctor Weiss and the American military supervision would ensure the Germans didn't get away with anything, but also because in Gauting Hospital I experienced some genuine acts of good will.

Among the nursing staff were a number of German nuns who held supervisory positions. Sisters Luitgard and Luciola served as head nurses on my floor. I recall their names perfectly because they helped me so very much, more than their jobs required them to. Perhaps because of my young age and poor condition, or because their religious conscience bothered them, I found favor in their eyes. No matter how much I hated all Germans as murderers of my family, my conscience would trouble me if I did not acknowledge the help and care I received from these two nuns. At least they tried to atone for their brothers' sins. And due to their care in Gauting, I continued to recover. Yes, there were a few righteous people even among the German version of Sodom and Gomorrah.

Complying with Doctor Hasler's order to pump the fluid from my lungs, Dr. Miller attended me once he concluded afternoon rounds, usually around five o'clock. Two nurses helped me sit in a special chair and held me so I wouldn't fall off. Dr. Miller then stuck a long and fairly thick needle into my back, picking a space between my ribs. The needle was connected to a rubber hose; through it, the liquid building up in my body emptied into a big bottle on the floor. I was frightened by the size of the needle, but I never felt any pain, even when it was going in. From my body, the needle siphoned off a yellowish liquid; as much as a gallon drained into the bottle. Immediately my breathing eased, and I would have relief for about four or five days – until liquid again choked off my lungs and left me gasping for air. All this time my high fever never broke except for a short time in the morning. Then it would zoom up again in the afternoon and persist that way through the night. Sometimes I barely rested or slept. Since my fever abated in the morning, I was able to eat a good breakfast. There was plenty of food around: buttered rolls, juices and all kinds of cheese. My luck was such that, despite my lung condition and fever, I felt hungry all the time and ate my whole healthy ration in the morning and then some. Every week, I gained two or three pounds.

Sisters Luciola and Luitgard brought me something extra almost every day – an apple or orange or sometimes a bar of chocolate in the afternoon. But mainly, when I complained about my strong headaches and the high fever, they brought me a cup of real coffee to drink. That was quite a treat because real coffee, during the war and even for a while afterward, was a rare commodity.

For two months, the hospital staff pumped liquid out of me, like a farmer milks a cow. The more fluid they drained, the more collected in my chest. Finally the doctors decided to stop, but continued with daily *traubenzucker* injections. The wounds on my left foot and backside healed, but the rash all over my body – and the itching – still bothered me a lot. When I complained about it to Dr. Miller, he smiled. The cream I got from the Americans in Dachau was no good, he informed me; he would give me a different medicine, a *German* cream, which would better treat the leprosy. The nurses lubricated my skin with this German treatment and in about 10 days, the itching stopped and my skin cleared up.

At first, Room 130 housed six patients, myself included. To my right was a young man in his late 20s or early 30s, a Jew from Budapest. To my left was a middle-aged Jew, Natan, who spoke only Hungarian and a few words of German. Natan wasn't as sick as I was; he was able to walk around. In the bed across from Natan lay a middle-aged professor from Yugoslavia, who must have been in his 50s, by the name of Genesh. Although he wasn't Jewish, he had been married to a Jewish woman from Budapest, and they had one child. Professor Genesh taught at the college level in Budapest before and during the war. When the Hungarians rounded up the Jews, they arrested him, too. In reality, he confided to me, he could have stayed behind but he voluntarily went along with his wife. At first both of them wound up in Auschwitz; later they were put in different camps. He survived, but his wife and child were murdered. Professor Genesh was an expert linguist and a teacher of languages, mastering more than seven, including Russian, Serbian and Bulgarian. Having been born near the borders of Hungary and Yugoslavia, where mixed populations dwelled, he also spoke German, French, English, Hungarian and Turkish. His neighbor in the middle bed was a non-Jewish Turk who didn't speak a word of German, so the doctors had to rely on Professor Genesh to interpret the man's responses. On the other side of the Turk was a young Jewish fellow from the city of Bendzin, Poland, not even 20 years old; fortunately, he was ambulatory. Of the six of us in the room, I was the only one who couldn't even get out of bed without help.

The young Hungarian fellow, to my right, outwardly appeared to be in better shape than I was and could walk about on his own power. But he had two large cavities in his lungs and the doctors wanted to heal him with a procedure called "pneumothorax." As I understood it, this involved blowing air between the two sheaths of tissue that line the outside of the lungs and form a layer between them and the ribcage. This air was needed to compress the lungs and somehow help the cavities to heal. Every week or so, his lungs would be fluoroscoped to determine whether they were healing. In his case, the two tissue layers were fused together in places, leading the doctors to try separating them surgically. They rolled him to the operating room in building complex A, where all such operations took place. Sadly, he died during the procedure, and his death was a great blow to the morale of all of us in the room.

But the tragedy did not end there. This fellow's father also survived the war in Budapest, and learned through the Red Cross that his son was in Gauting Hospital. Right after the war, on all European radio stations, the Red Cross broadcast names of survivors who were still in Germany. Although travel right after the war wasn't easy, the father managed to make it to Gauting. When he arrived at Room 130, he learned that his son had died only a few days earlier on the operating table. I'll never forget the look of grief that transformed this man's face. Literally, he tore hair out of his head. "If only I could have come here one week earlier," he cried, and we all cried with him.

Fortunately, not every memory from Gauting was so sorrowful. The young man from Poland had an older brother who also survived the camps. Radio reports alerted the elder family member that his brother was alive in Gauting. He immediately set off in search of his sibling. The hospital enforced a strict nap time[1] rule from 1 to 3 p.m. All patients had to return to their beds for rest or sleep, and no talking was permitted during this period, to minimize disturbing other patients. I was dozing and didn't notice a man enter the room, but suddenly a great cry broke out. I awoke to see the two brothers embracing on the bed, kissing and crying out with unsurpassed joy. They asked each other an ongoing stream of questions about everything, starting from the time they got separated. "Where is Dad?" "Where is Mom?" "What do you know about our sister, Sonia?" "Perished, perished, perished," was the answer in each case. Of course, they woke everyone. Nurses, hearing the great commotion, rushed into our room to check. Grasping what was happening, they, too, wept openly.

---

[1] *Liegekur* (literally "bed cure").

Even now as I write these lines, my eyes become moist. For years afterward, whenever that scene would come to mind, I would fantasize a miracle: that I, too, would have a jubilant reunion with at least one member of my immediate family. I dreamt this often, even after I moved to the United States. In the end, though, I harbored no illusions about my family's fate. But even now, when I am in a public place like a theater or an airport, and notice a person similar in looks and height to one of my brothers, my heart beats faster, my pulse starts racing. It doesn't have to be an adult, either: children, the ages of my dear nieces and nephews as I remember them from over 50 years ago, provoke the same reaction. I know I must forget, but I've tried and I can't. Of course, I don't think about it *all* the time, only when I come across someone who reminds me of my family.

I always struggle with these questions: "Why was I spared? Was I more worthy than my brothers?" Definitely not. My brothers were more learned, more religious – especially my oldest brother, Eliezer, a talmudic scholar. He lived and died for the glory of G-d, as did the rest of those poor souls. I justify my survival because somebody must say *Kaddish* for my great but cut-down family, and I shall have to live with this until my last breath.

A few weeks after the Hungarian fellow died on the operating table, they wheeled a new patient into our room, a handsome young Jewish boy, 11 or 12 years old. They put him in the bed next to me. He was from the city of Nyearbator, and he only spoke Hungarian and a bit of German. As an endearment, we called him "Itskish." (In Hungarian, a younger brother is an "*itsem*," hence his nickname "Itskish.") He remained in our room for only about two months because the American Joint Distribution Committee (AJDC) began to collect sick Jewish children after the war and transfer them to a very famous lung hospital in Dawos, Switzerland, where they could get the best care. I was curious to find out how this young child escaped the gas chambers, and since my bed was next to his, I often had a chance to talk with him. Initially he was very uncommunicative. I had a hunch he survived because he had been used as a sex object, being that he was such a good-looking child. I gradually gained his confidence and he opened up to me. It turned out my hunch was correct: he told me that he had been kept by a *kapo*. Months later I received a photograph from him, from Dawos. I hope that he is alive and that his lungs were cured.

I feel tremendous gratitude for the great and noble humanitarian effort and help that the AJDC provided for all of us who were left sick or orphaned in Germany, and especially for the help they provided the young children who miraculously escaped the crematoriums. As for you, Itskish, I hope you've put aside your horrible experiences with the *kapo* and are living in Israel now as a free and proud Jew.

Sometime later, my roommate's brother from Bendzin took him out of Gauting Hospital; I believe they went to live in a Jewish Displaced Persons (DP) camp in Landsberg, Bavaria. The Turkish man also transferred from our room, either to another hospital or to be repatriated. Another Jewish patient, coincidentally also from Bendzin, was soon brought in: Stanislav Wygodzki, the Polish poet. Now only four of us remained in the room: the Yugoslav Professor Genesh, Wygodzki, Natan and I. After a few days of being together, we knew each other's histories very well, particularly the wartime miracles we all went through and how we survived. Wygodzki and I established a very friendly relationship. He spoke Yiddish very well (Natan and Genesh didn't know any Yiddish) and also Hebrew, so we were able to converse quite a bit.

Before the war, Wygodzki had already published two books of poems in Poland. A somewhat shy person, very genteel, sensitive and quite talented, he made a strong impression on me. I took great pleasure in speaking with him. I also learned much about his life, not from him, but from his friend who was also a patient in Gauting Hospital. Almost daily this friend, who had been a doctor before the war, visited him in our room, and they'd speak for long periods of time. After Wygodzki left Gauting, this friend (I'm afraid I don't remember his name) confided to me the double tragedy that Wygodzki went through.

When the Germans rounded up all the Polish Jews to transport them to Auschwitz or Treblinka, Wygodzki, his wife and their 5-year old son were put in one of those infamous railroad freight wagons with other people. Wygodzki and his wife decided to commit suicide. They fed their son poison, and then swallowed some themselves. A *landsman* in the wagon managed to revive Wygodzki; others' efforts to save his wife and son were futile. Though he never talked to me about this tragic and dark chapter in his life, I know from his friend that he suffered from it terribly.

With two books of poetry already to his credit, Wygodzki had a number of fans, among them a young Jewish girl from Sosnowiec, the sister-city of Bendzin. Although she had never met him, she fell in love with him after reading his poetry. Of course, this was a one-sided love affair. This young girl had survived the war with a sister and their mother. Thanks to their being able to procure Aryan papers, made easier by their blonde hair, they had come as voluntary Polish workers to Germany during the war. (Only women were able to hide their Jewishness so easily; it was impossible even for blonde Jewish men, who could be identified by the mark of circumcision.) When the war ended, this young lady, her sister and mother found themselves in the French zone of Germany. One day, thanks to the Red Cross, she heard the name of her beloved poet on the radio – that he was alive and now in the sanitarium in Gauting. She didn't wait too long before going to see him.

Nap-time in Gauting, it seems, was when the most interesting things happened! She, too, arrived when everyone was resting, and went straight to Room 130. This time I happened to be awake when the door opened, and I saw a beautiful, tall blonde enter. This must be a German nurse who works here, I remember thinking. She went straight over to Wygodzki's bed and introduced herself to him in Polish. Then she said to him, without fanfare, "I am very happy you survived the war. You don't know me, but I have been in love with you ever since I read your book of poems in Sosnowiec. And now I came here to help you get back on your feet and become your lawful wife."

I don't know if she thought that no one else in the room understood Polish, or perhaps she didn't mind if anybody did, because she had eyes only for the poet. Wygodzki was speechless. He began to stammer and was barely able to compose himself. Finally, he offered her a chair to sit down.

My roommate to my left, Natan, also noticed that something unusual was underway. Not understanding Polish, he asked me in Hungarian, "What happened? Our neighbor is so bewildered."

"Not now," I hushed him quickly in Hungarian, so I could continue listening. "I'll tell you later."

The young lady rented a room in the city of Gauting and commuted daily to see Wygodzki. I suspect he was very pleased with this unexpected adoration and devotion, particularly now that he was about 38. It inspired him to write a beautiful poem about her, which he recited to me later. He called it "The Young Lady with a Cigarette,"[2] because when she first appeared in Room 130, she had an unlit cigarette in her hand – even though she undoubtedly must have known that in a lung sanitarium even *carrying* cigarettes was strictly forbidden. But probably she needed the cigarette to camouflage her anxiety.

Wygodzki stayed in Gauting another month. Then he married the young lady, and they went off to live in the French zone, where her mother and her sister resided. It was a big problem for Wygodzki to get married, because he didn't have any clothing. But his friends, the Polish Jewish doctors, provided him with a decent suit to get married in.

Though we remained good friends, there was one issue about which the poet and I completely disagreed. He told me that after the wedding, he planned to return to Poland with his new wife. I was shocked by his decision, and tried to talk him out of it. "How could you go back as a Jew to the land of anti-Semitism – Poland?" I pleaded with him. "All that is left there for Jews in Poland are broken and desecrated gravestones and cemeteries." But his mind was made up.

"I'm a sick man," he said. "Where can I go? What can I do? I am tied to the Polish language and cannot write in any other."

That wasn't the whole truth, however. He knew how to write Yiddish and Hebrew very well. Before he returned to Poland from the French zone, he wrote to me in Yiddish for quite a while. He even sent me a couple of care packages at the hospital. It turns out that Wygodzki had told me only part of the story. I later found out that as soon as he returned to Poland, he became a member of the Polish government and was named Minister of Education. He must have had some idea he was going to get into the government and would hold a very high position. Initially, he genuinely believed in the Communist system, but later he saw the light. In 1967, after the Six-Day War between Israel and Egypt, the Polish government under Gomulka unleashed an avalanche of anti-Semitism against all Jews who lived there. Wygodzki managed to leave Poland with his new wife and their son. They fled to Israel, where he later became a contributing columnist to the daily paper *Ma'ariv*. In 1971, I had the pleasure of visiting him in Tel Aviv, and we had a very joyful reunion,

---

[2] *"Panna z Papierosem."*

reminiscing about our companions in Room 130 at Gauting. I refrained, however, from asking him any questions about Poland for fear of pouring salt on old wounds.

Chapter 34

Rosh Hashanah, 1945

ROSH HASHANAH ARRIVED FIVE MONTHS INTO MY STAY at Gauting. I was still struggling to get rid of my high fever, but at least I was getting strong enough to get out of bed. In the morning, I'd sit up in bed and read a little bit. There was no way for me to read in the afternoon or evening, once my fever rose.

By this time I weighed about 120 pounds – still much too light for my height and body frame, but moving in the right direction. X-rays showed I still had water between the lungs, but the doctors assured me the water level was on its way down. Every two weeks I was fluoroscoped; once a month I was X-rayed. Blood tests were also taken every two weeks. Of course, I had no idea then that all the fluoroscoping and X-raying were dangerous.

At one point a messenger came to Gauting Hospital from the Jewish brigade attached to the British army. He distributed small packages, gifts for the sick from individual soldiers in the Jewish brigade. Inside the packages were small personal items like toothpaste, brushes, combs, a few candies, chocolate and soap. In my package, I found a great treasure – a small book, 380 pages, entitled *Sepher l'ma'an ha-chayal*, a "Book for the Soldier." There, in capsule form, was a synopsis of Jewish history with major historical events and dates from very early on to the present time. It was divided into 12 sections, corresponding to the 12 months of the Jewish calendar. For instance, in the section called *Tishrei* (corresponding to September/October) it listed the slaying of Gedalia ben Achikam, which had taken place at that time of year. The book included many other important Jewish events that led up to the founding of the Jewish brigade. It even described the recent circumstances and struggles of *ha-appalah*, the daring immigration of Jews to Palestine right after the war.

I was so delighted with this small booklet that a million dollars would not have made me happier. It was the first Hebrew language publication I saw after the war. With bursting pride I read about my Jewish brothers and sisters in Palestine who were engaged in a difficult and bitter struggle for the survival of our Jewish people. One of the poems printed inside, "Our Fleet," is forever burned into my memory. Penned by Nathan Alterman, it referred to the small, dilapidated ships trying to bring Zionist pioneers to Palestine.

Alterman called them "ships of the sick, sailing in the shadows of death," because they were hunted by the mighty British fleet – like poor wounded rabbits being tracked by wild dogs. In this poem, he asked whether there was ever any other fleet in the world engaged in such a desperate battle.

Shortly before receiving this precious little book, something else happened in Gauting that left an indelible impression on me. It concerned the Yiddish poet Herschel Leivik, who was already living in the United States. Considered to be the greatest living poet in the Yiddish language, Leivik visited our hospital in 1945, a few months after the war. He gave a lecture for us in the A wing of the hospital, in a huge auditorium. I was heartbroken I couldn't go to hear him, because I was still too ill to get out of bed. How surprised and delighted I was when the next day Leivik visited all the bedridden patients. When he came to Room 130, he told me that he had also suffered from TB, but that he was over it by then. His words gave us encouragement that in time and with rest we would all be healthy again. When I told him I'd seen a play that he wrote, *The Golem*, before the war in Carpathia, and also that I had read his forceful poem *"Die keiten fun Moshiach"* ("The Messiah in Chains"), which he wrote just before the war, he was very pleased. After he toured a series of hospitals and DP camps where the remnants of Jewish communities from all over Europe were gathered in the American zone, he wrote another powerful Yiddish poem, "I Was Not in Treblinka." The first verse reads:

I was not in Treblinka	*In Treblinka bin ich nisht g'vaisin*
And not in Maydanek	*Oych nisht in Maydanek*
but I stood at the foyer of these camps.	*Ober ich bin g'shtanen oifn ganik.*

I felt privileged to meet and speak with this great man.[1] In later years, after I arrived in the United States, I read articles by Herschel Leivik regularly in the Yiddish daily, *Der Tag*, which published the

[1] In 1949, Leivik published a dramatic play called "The Wedding in Ferenwald" ("*Die Chasseneh in Ferenwald*"). Ferenwald was a Jewish DP camp about three kilometers from the town of Geretsried. It housed something like 4,000 Jewish survivors.

story of his imprisonment in Siberia and his escape. I was touched by his narrative. He was supremely talented at chronicling the best and worst in human beings.

More visitors from the US and Palestine began arriving. They toured DP camps and hospitals in the American zone, and that is how we bedridden people started to connect with the world again after having been totally isolated in Gauting for five months. Many of the Jewish survivors,[2] whose health was not badly damaged, recuperated quickly and were placed in DP camps. They traveled around Germany from zone to zone, and many also became involved in wheeling and dealing[3] on the black market. Most of those who were ambulatory right after the war also really enjoyed seeing big German cities in rubble. Meanwhile, I lay feverish in my hospital bed for 11 months, until March 1946.

To me it was unfathomable that former concentration camp inmates would play on the black market, acquiring beautiful clothes, high black boots, or gold wrist watches. It was, I suppose, a status symbol to have those things. But in my eyes such material things looked absurd. I felt contempt for the black market traders. What value was any of this when we were all orphaned survivors of entire families?

At that point in my life, I had not one article of clothing of my own. In bed, I pondered the line in Job I:21: "Naked I came out from my mother's belly and naked I will return." I had no desire whatsoever for personal things, even basics like clothing. I was clad in hospital shirts and underwear, and that was enough for me. I didn't need shoes because I was only now starting to walk a little, and simple hospital slippers sufficed. Besides, the operation on my foot left me unable to wear anything but specially made orthopedic shoes. I was now in the same position as a Buddhist monk: I desired neither clothing nor material possessions. But unlike the monk, I was in no position to achieve Nirvana, not with the heavy state of depression that gripped me. By then, I had given up all hope of finding someone from my immediate family. The longer my illness dragged on, the more depressed I got.

With or without clothes, and lying in bed most of the day, I had way too much time to think. Over and over, I pondered the unanswerable: "Why?" Why did it happen to us Jews? Why did European Jews wait so long until it was virtually impossible to

---

[2] *S'ridai ha-cherev* (literally, "leftovers from the sword").

[3] *Handl-wandl.*

escape? Why were we so blind? Why did we ignore dire warnings of leaders like Ze'ev Jabotinsky? I asked myself endlessly, "Why live on without family? Does life have a purpose for me any longer?" I never seemed capable of answering this last question. I just didn't know.

Hope is a powerful emotion – it's hard to live without it. But living with *false* hope, the kind we experienced in the years before and during the war, doomed us and brought the worst tragedies upon us. We always hoped that the monster named Hitler would suffer a crushing defeat. We latched onto any small fact that affirmed this possibility, and lulled ourselves into passivity. Had we really gotten hold of ourselves, we could have resisted as the Underground did, plotting secretly in the forests and the mountains to defend themselves. Instead, we left ourselves no escape.

I know I carry around a lot of "what-if" questions. What if, when we were in ghettos and labor camps, we resisted? In the beginning, more than half a million Jews were jammed into the Warsaw ghetto. By the time they did anything about their situation, 60,000 to 70,000 Jews were left. Only then did they revolt. But it was too late. What if they had resisted from the beginning? On and on, what if, what if, what if. Such thoughts tormented me while awake and invaded my fever-driven dreams.

Finally, in March 1946, the high temperature that plagued me for nearly 11 months dropped permanently. I began to feel a lot better. Many more visitors from the US and Palestine visited us in Gauting Hospital to lift our spirits and see what we needed in the way of material goods. From these visitors, we learned what was happening in the world, especially in the Jewish world. We heard all about the heroic struggle the *yishuv* (the Jewish population then in Palestine) was waging for a Jewish homeland in *Eretz Yisroel*.[4] Those events so consumed my consciousness that I began to emerge from my deep depression.

Finally strong enough to stand, I began to walk around the hospital corridors to meet with others who had also been bedridden. There's a Hebrew folk saying: "When you see others suffering, it reduces your own pain."[5] Everybody I met was a victim and, like me,

---

[4] Literally, the Land of Israel.
[5] "*Tsa'arat rabbim, chatzi n'chama.*"

the sole survivor of their families. I realized I wasn't the only one who had suffered, and each day this awareness helped lighten my heavy burden. A ray of sun started to pierce my dark sky, and slowly the black clouds dispersed. We had one great hope: in a State of Israel, a Jewish homeland, we Jews would cease being "an object of scorn and derision among the nations"[6] – this buoyed my spirits, speedily improved my physical and emotional conditions, healed my wounds fast, and strengthened my Jewish soul. Many times my heart raced when I thought of the Land of Israel, ours again one day and forever! With my heart and soul, I yearned for the day when I would leave the hospital and take part in this noble and just cause.

One year after my liberation from Dachau, I became a rich man. I received a pair of pants, a pair of very soft shoes and two dress shirts. Most likely, the Joint Distribution Committee donated the goods, and that was enough for me. I now could walk fully dressed in Gauting from B wing to A wing. I started to meet more fellow patients who also belonged to the Betar Zionist organization before the war.

Now in 1946, in my naiveté I felt that, after what we Jews had gone through in the *Shoah*, we shouldn't be divided into different parties or groups. Hitler didn't care to what political party a Jew belonged, or whether he was assimilated, Orthodox or a convert. He treated us all equally – like vermin. So I considered it ridiculous now for us to join different Zionist movements. At such a historic moment, we needed unity, not warring factions. When such axe-grinding politicos came to the hospital and preached their party lines, I couldn't stand it. Once, I interrupted a speaker who sounded very partisan in his speech, and I told him we should all be from one party, the party of Jews, the party for the struggle for a Jewish homeland. Ashamed, the speaker apologized and quickly said that it was not his intention to arouse sick people in the hospital.

By the spring of 1946, two weekly Yiddish newspapers were being published by *Shoah* survivors, whom I call "remnants of the refugees."[7] One was published at the Jewish DP camp at Landsberg; the other came from Munich, at the headquarters of the Central Committee of Liberated Jews. Both papers utilized the Latin alphabet because, after the war, there was no Hebrew print to be found,

---

[6] From a weekday morning prayer: "Look from heaven and perceive that we have become an object of scorn and derision among the nations; we are regarded as the sheep led to slaughter, to be killed, destroyed, beaten and humiliated. But despite all this, we have not forgotten Your name – we beg You not to forget us."

[7] *Sh'airit ha-plaitah.*

especially in Germany. After a time, from somewhere, Hebrew print arrived, and the Munich paper *Unserweg* (meaning "Our Way" or "Our Road") began to appear in Yiddish print. We received these newspapers in our sanitarium. In the isolated atmosphere of hospital confinement, these newspapers came as a big relief. We grew more informed about the condition of other "remnants," the state of Jewish affairs in the West, especially in the United States, and also of the *yishuv* in Palestine. The momentum toward Jewish statehood electrified me.

After the *Shoah*, there was no more important task for us than to strive with all our hearts and souls, with all our strength, to establish a Jewish homeland. Those who escaped the gas chambers couldn't remain on this bloody soil called Europe, the soil that bore the mark of Cain. This was how I felt right after the end of World War II.

Where Yiddish newspapers reconnected me with the Jews of the world, radio news fed my desire for revenge. I listened with anticipation for any reports from the Nuremberg Trials. The Allies put Nazi leaders like Göring, Hess and others in the dock. The trials had begun November 20, 1945, and dragged on for 10 months, until October 1946. Every day I eagerly waited to hear that they would all be hanged. This, too, kept me going and fueled my recovery.

Sometime later in June 1946, I received a letter from Stockholm, from my two cousins Etush and Piri Goldberg, formerly of Diosec, Romania. (This was the second sign of life from my extended family. The first was a letter from my older cousin, Eliezer Heimowitz, who lived in Palestine since before the war.) Etush and Piri came from a family of three sisters and two brothers. The two of them and a brother survived. The other sister, brother, their parents and Etush's husband all perished. They wrote to me that they were taken to Sweden from a camp in Germany after the war, possibly Bergen Belsen in the British zone. In a humanitarian gesture, the Swedish government retrieved some former camp inmates, mainly unmarried women, and transported them to a sanitarium in Stockholm to recuperate. Through the Red Cross broadcasts, my two cousins learned I was alive in Gauting Hospital. They wrote that they were okay now, had found work, were earning money and wanted to help me. I only had to let them know what I needed and they'd send it to me.

It was thrilling to receive their letter. In the same correspondence, they also related plans to return to Romania. I wrote back immediately, telling them how delighted I was to hear from them, but was very frank on the subject of their returning to eastern Europe. At the time, Romania was, or was on the verge of becoming, a Communist country. To me, surviving the *Shoah* meant joining the mass exodus to Palestine to reclaim the Land of Israel. Otherwise our survival had no meaning. My three cousins did go back to Romania, but quickly came to their senses and didn't stay very long. They managed to get to *Eretz Yisroel* through the efforts of *ha-appalah*, and now, thank G-d, reside in Jerusalem with their rebuilt families.

In a second letter from them, they again insisted that I tell them what I needed so they could try to supply it. I have everything I need in the hospital, I replied. If they insisted, the only thing I could use was some more shirts. Very soon, Etush and Piri sent me a letter indicating a package with six men's shirts and some socks, along with some chocolate, cocoa and coffee was on its way to me. I guess they knew that coffee and cocoa were like currency, both scarce commodities at that time. In the same letter, they enclosed the address in Sweden of a female cousin on their father's (Goldberg) side.[8] They would be leaving Stockholm soon, they said, but urged me to write to this woman if I needed anything, and she would try to procure it for me. Without ever having met me, she began writing to me on her own. In every letter she inserted an American dollar or two. I was very touched by this gesture, and 20 years later, on visiting my cousins Piri and Etush in Jerusalem, I met her and her husband at Piri's house. I thanked her for her nice gesture. Unfortunately, it was not destined for me to receive the package my cousins sent with the shirts and goodies. A month after they sent it, I received an official notification from the Swedish Post Office that a mail wagon carrying my package caught fire and was destroyed. In this memorandum they advised me to notify the senders so they could lodge a claim with the insurance company. But by then, my cousins had already left Stockholm.

Also in June 1946, with the help of the hospital nuns, I got a suit for myself. This seemingly trivial episode documents how slowly I returned to the human race. Although the AJDC distributed clothing as well as food ration packages among us, at my height, it was difficult to find clothes that fit, and I had precious little family to

---

[8] Etush, Piri, and I are related on their mother's side: their mother and my father were brother and sister. This other cousin was not related to me.

provide for me. Sisters Luitgard and Luciola saw all this, and procured five brand-new khaki-colored military blankets for me.

The nuns contacted a German tailor who then came to the hospital and took my measurements. In return, I gave him the five blankets, one package of food rations that I had saved from the AJDC, and about eight US dollars that I accumulated from my cousins in Stockholm. Out of these military blankets, he stitched a custom-made suit: a jacket and a single pair of matching pants. Somewhere I still have a photo of me in my khaki suit, which I wore with my soft-fitting shoes. True, it looked far more like a military uniform than a fashion statement. But as a patient in Gauting, in the twenty-sixth year of my life, I suddenly, finally, looked the part of a gentleman.

By chance, I learned that the Davidovich sisters from Torun – Montsi and Zipporah – survived and were in a DP camp not far from Munich. I yearned to see them, souls from my hometown. I told Dr. Miller that I wanted to make the trip, but he forbade me.

More good news came in a letter from Palestine from another cousin of mine on my mother's side, Zipporah Drimmer. In July of 1946, she wrote me that she had just arrived there with *ha-appalah*. I was overjoyed. It was like finding a sister, because she was also from Torun. We'd grown up together and our two families were very close. Sadly, she was the only survivor of the eight children of my Uncle Berel and Aunt Mindel Drimmer, all murdered in the fires of the *Shoah*. Her own miraculous survival story would require a book of its own. This new contact with my cousin Zipporah was rejuvenating to me, not only because I knew her so well, but also because she was as alone in the world as I was. We could empathize with one another in ways no two others could.

Zipporah and I began to correspond regularly. She knew how close I'd been to my boyhood friend Zvi Fixler, who left Torun in 1938 with the underground emigration movement to Palestine, called *Aliyah Bet*.[9] Eventually he joined the ranks of the underground organization *Aitzel* (an acronym in Hebrew for "*Irgun Tzva'i Leumi*,"

---

[9] Whereas legal immigration was called "*Aliyah*," the *Aliyah Bet*, or "Second Immigration," operated covertly to smuggle people without official visas into Palestine before World War II.

meaning National Military Organization), and took part in one of the group's attacks against the British, but was captured by them. Because he was under-age according to his papers, he was not hanged, but was sentenced to 15 years in the infamous Acre Prison. Later he was among those whom *Aitzel* liberated in their famous, daring attack on the prison. I knew nothing about this at the time, but Zipporah often visited him in prison and wrote to me about him. On one occasion, they were able to kiss, and he transferred a tiny piece of paper from his mouth to hers, which she was to send me. The paper contained these words in Hebrew, taken from the psalms of King David: "From the straits did I called upon G-d; He answered me with expansiveness."[10] It was signed *Ehud.* "Ehud" was Zvi's code-name in the underground. From his quotation of Psalm 118, which expresses faith and confidence, I knew that, despite his being in jail, his spirits were high and he felt he would soon be free.

I began to grasp a deeper understanding of the struggle in Palestine for self-determination and independence. The two Yiddish newspapers that were published in the American zone made it very clear that there was only one solution to our predicament: to return to our ancient homeland, *Eretz Yisroel,* from which we had been exiled by force. Nearly everyone in the DP camps and hospitals understood the impossibility of rebuilding a Jewish life on Europe's bloody soil. Those still in denial woke up in July 1946 when they came face to face with an act of pure brutality. In Kielce, Poland, local Poles savagely murdered 43 Jews, each a sole survivor of his or her family, who were trying to return to their birthplace. This incident made it clear that Europeans did not want to be confronted by victims of the *Shoah* – or, more specifically, to be forced to part with the Jewish property and goods that they had appropriated.

When the war broke out in September 1939, the Jewish population of Poland was 3 million. Approximately 180,000 of them saved themselves from the advancing German *blitzkrieg* by fleeing to the Soviet Union. When they tried to return after the war to their former homes in Poland, their neighbors greeted them with astonishment: "Are you still living? We thought you were all dead."

The pogrom in Kielce was an agonizingly obvious signal that Jews were not welcome in Poland any longer, and panic swept through the community. Now too terrified to live in their homeland, these Jews fled Poland into other European countries with the intent to go to Palestine. Most of them showed up in the American zone in

---

[10] "*Min ha-meitzar kara'ati yah, annani b'merchav yah.*"

Germany, thanks to the covert operations carried out by members of the Jewish Brigade of the British Army, working under the direction of the Jewish agency from Palestine, and with the help of various officers and soldiers of the American military stationed in the American zone. These clandestine operations were referred to as the *bricha* (from the Hebrew, meaning literally "to escape or run").

Once the Jews (not just from Poland, but also from other European countries, including liberated Jews from concentration camps) made it to the American or French zones in Germany and Austria, the next step was to get them to sea ports in France or Italy and smuggle them onto ships bound for Palestine. This so-called "illegal" emigration of Jews from Europe to *Eretz Yisroel* was called *ha-appalah*.[11]

The *bricha* and *ha-appalah* mark a beautiful and heroic chapter in the recent history of our people, in our fight for an independent *Eretz Yisroel* – a struggle made more difficult by Britain's betrayal of the Balfour Declaration. Issued in 1917, this declaration stated that the British government not only approved of a national homeland in Palestine for the Jewish people, but also promised to facilitate its establishment. During the 1920s and early '30s, Jewish emigration to Palestine (then a British colony) was fairly open, and the *yishuv* grew. But by the late 1930s, the British government tightened the gates: fewer and fewer of our brothers and sisters who were fleeing from Germany to escape Hitler were able to reach safety. Most remarkably, even after the atrocities of the Holocaust, they set even harsher quotas, limiting the amount of land that Jews could buy in Palestine and reducing the permissible number of immigrants even more. (I guess to the British, oil was more valuable than saving Jewish blood.)

October 1946 was a particularly terrible month. In Palestine, leaders of the National Council (*Va'ad Leumi*) were arrested by the British. Freedom fighters were deported or, as in the case of martyrs like Dov Gruner, Mordechai Alkahi, Eliezer Kashani and Yechiel Drezner, were hanged. I was completely obsessed by thoughts of the

---

[11] The Hebrew word *ha-appalah* stems from the word *va'yapilu* – "they went up" (Numbers XIV:44). The biblical reference is to the Children of Israel who left their encampment in the desert and went up to the top of the mountain to fight the Amalekites and Canaanites, despite the warning from Moses that their struggle would end in defeat.

heroic struggles of the *Aitzel, Haganah* and *Lechi*[12] – the underground organizations in the *yishuv* that were actively engaged in *ha-appalah* and defying the British government – including my friend Zvi Fixler who languished in Acre Prison. I focused on one thing: the condition of the Jewish people. The great pain over the loss of my whole family slipped to the back of my mind. I could no longer help them, but I could try to help my people, especially those in *Eretz Yisroel* in 1946.

One other episode from this time sticks out in my mind. As Jews flocked to reach the American zone in Germany, a husband, wife and daughter came to Gauting Hospital to pay a visit to a patient, a *landsman* of theirs. For the first time after the war, I met members of a Jewish family that had managed to remain intact. The parents looked to be in their 50s, their daughter in her 20s. The husband wore a beard typical of Jewish men in Europe before the war, just as my own father had. When I spoke to him at length about his harrowing wartime experiences, tears filled my eyes and ran down my face. To me he represented the hundreds of Jews from Torun and vicinity who were no more. All my life, I had been an anti-Communist, but this man told me he was able to save his wife, his daughter and himself because of the Communists. Stalin saved thousands of Jews by opening Russia's borders to the Jews from Poland – even if it wasn't for the love of Jews, but for his own self-interest – so I had to give Stalin some credit. When the Red Army retreated under the German invasion, he ordered his military to help anybody who wanted to flee. Of course, in 1946, none of us knew yet the full extent of the atrocities that Stalin committed under his own regime.

---

[12] All three of these groups were the forerunners of the present-day Israeli Defense Force.

Chapter 35

Anger, Shame and Grief

IN THE 1940S, DOCTORS BELIEVED SUNLIGHT WAS VERY
HARMFUL for people afflicted with tuberculosis. Medicine for
combating the TB bacteria was not available, so the only treatment
entailed *liegekur* – avoiding sunlight, resting a lot and breathing clean
air. Under these conditions, supposedly, the immune system itself
could combat the illness.[1] It was so universally accepted that the most
famous sanitariums in Europe, such as the one in Dawos,
Switzerland, relied extensively on this method. Use of penicillin was
in its infancy, especially in Europe. We'd heard about it in Gauting
and hoped we'd get some in time. Naturally, this didn't help our
mood. Without sunshine, what zest does life have? Before the war I
used to love to sun-bathe, and often we went to a place in Torun
called the Hady, by the Rika River, just to lie in the sun.[2]

It wasn't until sometime in September 1946 that Dr. Miller
finally allowed me to leave the hospital – for all of 48 hours. Montsi
and Zipporah Davidovich were in a DP camp near Stuttgart, and I
was determined to see them. After having been cooped up in the
hospital for almost 17 months, isolated from the outside world, I left
the hospital for the first time, feeling like a convict being freed from
jail.

Following this horrendous war, I was tremendously excited
about finally seeing people from my hometown. Would they, I
wondered anxiously, be worried at the prospect of my infecting them
with something? I resolved to make them understand the possibility
was remote. After many months in the hospital, only once did I test
positive for the TB bacteria, and that was at the beginning of June

---

[1] By coincidence, while I was writing about being in Gauting with TB, I received
the November 1992 *Smithsonian* magazine, which includes an article entitled "How
TB Survived Its Own Death," by Ken Chowder. He details the methods of treating
the disease in the 1940s, including a description of pneumothorax, which brought
on the death of our fellow patient, the Jewish boy from Budapest. The article gave
a history of the methods of healing TB over the past 100 hundred years and
confirmed my conviction that deprivation from the sun in fact brought on our
depression. Upon reflection, I'm grateful we didn't know then that the medical care
we were receiving was no more than a placebo.

[2] The Rika River flows from Torun in the Carpathian mountains to the river Tiso,
which later joins with the Danube.

1945. Once a month, doctors administered sputum tests to determine whether anyone was contagious. For the past 14 months, I consistently tested negative; otherwise, Dr. Miller would never have issued my hospital pass. Yet TB carried a strong stigma, as though people with the illness somehow brought it on themselves. No one felt this way about other diseases like kidney or heart ailments. But healthy folks steered clear of TB patients, afraid even casual contact would result in infection, and I felt ashamed.

My train trip to see the Davidovich sisters – the sounds and scenes – both frightened and exhilarated me. Riding in the coach, I kept holding my breath and trying to repress the feelings my ride evoked. Over and over I reminded myself, "No, I'm not being dragged somewhere unknown by our oppressor. I'm taking this train ride because I want to." Yet the clatter of wheels on the tracks and the engine's roar conjured up recent memories: boxcar rides, dead bodies, German machine guns pointed at my face, gloom and doom. Terrifying mental images kept popping into my head, and I tried very hard to free myself of them.

Another observation occupied my thoughts, as well. Only a year and a half after the war's end, I couldn't get over how well-fed and well-dressed the local population was. I, their victim, was still dressed in a suit made of a few military blankets. Also, the train stations and the connections worked in perfect order in all the villages that we passed. I witnessed no obvious signs of the war's destruction.

In a letter, I told the Davidovich sisters of my arrival date and time, so they were waiting for me at the station. As I stepped off the train, they ran toward me, recognizing me right away from my height. We embraced, and tears of joy ran down our cheeks. Our happiness to be together was tremendous, but it was matched by our sorrow.

"Mecheleh," they kept repeating through their tears, "Mecheleh, are you the only one left from your family?" – "Yes, yes," all of us agonized. Yes, we are the crumbs left from the 140 Jewish families from Torun and the neighboring Jewish communities of Lapishna, Schora and Prislip. We couldn't take our eyes off each other. It felt as though we had died and now had arisen from the dead.[3] The Torun we knew was no more. Close to 800 Jewish souls, large families of five or six children each, were totally wiped out. My uncle Zechariah's whole family was decimated. Not one soul left.

As I questioned them on name after name, the sisters grew sadder. Finally I blurted out, "Who survived?" The sisters mentioned

---

[3] *Techiyas ha-meisim.*

a handful of people. In a small Jewish community like Torun, we knew every family and we felt a kinship to one another, even if we weren't related by blood.

For me, our meeting was like a final liberation from the concentration camps. We exchanged the miracles of our survival, staying up almost all night, recounting our stories of how we were spared death at Hitler's hand. In the morning, as I prepared to return to the hospital, we spoke about the future. We agreed there was no way we would remain in Europe after the horrible way we'd been treated. I was very disappointed to hear that the sisters had an uncle, their father's brother, who lived in Cleveland, Ohio, and that they were making efforts to emigrate to America. "What kind of decision is that?" I asked, "to exchange one exile for another, even though a better one?" Little did I know then that I too would later seek this same exile in America. Having been in the hospital almost a year and a half at that point, I still hoped for a complete recovery so I could contribute something toward rebuilding our Jewish homeland in *Eretz Yisroel* and fulfill the biblical prophecy, the "return of the children to their borders."[4]

On the way back to Gauting, I peered out the train window and spotted a war slogan painted in huge bold letters on one of the station walls. It proclaimed that the wheels were rolling on for German victory.[5] Only a year and a half after the greatest destruction the world had ever known, there wasn't a trace of German remorse or shame for its crimes against humanity.

The dear and simple Jews from all the Toruns all over Europe are gone and will never return. May G-d avenge their blood. Before World War II, Carpathian Jews could own land. Many in my area earned their living by working the land. But when it came to *Shabbat*, each Sabbath was a majestic day of rest; inner and outer beauty and spiritual greatness. In my mind, I knew G-d would see that *Shabbat* was eternal, that it would never die no matter what had happened to our people.

Back in Gauting, I again descended into depression. I recognized a certain contentment in the Davidovich sisters: joy at having

---

[4] Jeremiah XXXI:16 – *"V'shavnu banim l'gvulam."*
[5] *"Die Reder Rollen für dem Sieg."*

survived together. Even though they lost the rest of their family, at least the sisters could share and ease each other's suffering. But I was alone with mine.

Shortly after my return from my first trip to the "free and normal world," I was asked to deliver a Rosh Hashanah greeting. The Hebrew year approaching wàs 5707, falling on the first and second days of October 1946. All rooms in Gauting Hospital were connected by intercom, making it possible to address the almost 1,000 Jewish patients. To use the intercom, I had to go to the administrative offices in A building. One of chief physician Dr. Weiss' secretaries was a Mrs. Kerbel, a *Shoah* survivor, as was her husband (who was also a patient in Gauting). It was Mrs. Kerbel who had asked me to deliver the New Year's address.

The task wasn't an easy one for me. Raging inside me were anger, shame and grief over the annihilation of our families. "Why did we go to the slaughterhouse without resistance?" I asked. Only two heroes, two Jews from among us, dared to avenge the atrocities that Hitler perpetrated against our people. Only two dared cry out to the world, to draw attention to what was happening to our people. They were David Frankfurter, who shot and killed the German ambassador Goodsloff in Switzerland in 1936, and Herschel Grynszpan, who took revenge on the German Embassy secretary in Paris, Ernst von Rath, in 1938. A mere two Jews out of nine million living in Europe dared to strike a blow against the bloody murderer.

But the heavy, narcotic sleep (*tardema*) that befell Europe's Jews never afflicted the *yishuv*. When they realized the extent of the tragedy that befell the European Jewish community, they raised the flag of revolt: on July 22 1946, *Aitzel* blew up the headquarters of the British government stationed in the King David Hotel in Jerusalem.

The *yishuv* believed in what our sages have always taught us: no longer can Jews wait for miracles. We have to create our own miracles, they cried, just as Mattityahu and his sons did in the Chanukah rebellion. That's a major reason, they proclaimed, why our sages urged Chanukah to be universally celebrated. On this holiday we recite, "You delivered the strong into the hands of the weak, the many into the hands of the few."[6] A new spirit ran through our people. No more Jewish blood would be spilled without cost to the aggressor.

In my speech I recalled these recent events, as well as the pain of our past. I also spoke with hope about the new heroes that had arisen

---

[6] *Masarta g'borim b'yad chalashim, v'rabim b'yad m'atim.*

from our midst to fulfill our destiny: that at long last our old/new homeland would arise again from the ashes and a Jewish state would be established. Our struggle now was our birth pains. "This new year of *taf shin zayin*," I said, "should bring to our sick in Gauting a full recovery, and to our brothers in the *yishuv* the strength to succeed so that the weak will defeat the strong."

My remarks found great approval among the patients in Gauting. Most of them felt the same way I did: ashamed and angry with ourselves, and sympathetic with the freedom fighters in the *yishuv*. Many came to my room afterward and admitted they were tormented by the same questions: *Why did it happen? Why didn't we resist?* Almost everyone offered the same answer: it was too painful to lose one's family. They wanted to be together, no matter what happened. To the bitter end, we thought there would be safety in greater numbers. What false hope!

At the hospital, we organized a group that met several times a week in the B wing. It consisted only of patients who tested negative for TB and were allowed to leave and return to the hospital. Our meetings helped lift our depression and lessen the monotony of hospital life. Clearly, this was the best therapy we could have had.

We also exchanged news about the outside world and what life looked like in the Jewish DP camps. After liberation, many in this group had gone initially to DP camps in Bavaria, such as Feldafing, Ferenwald and Landsberg, but when they contracted TB, they were sent to Gauting Hospital. They told us that these camps housed mostly sole-survivors. Either despite or maybe because of their condition as single-person remnants of families, their striving for freedom and independence was ignited. By 1946, these DP camps became hotbeds of Zionist activity. A Jewish homeland was on everybody's mind. All of us agreed we could not return to our former countries. We could not rebuild our lives on top of those cemeteries.

Only in the Land of our Forefathers[7] would we be able to rebuild our lives. Our pain was great, made greater because we now knew it was England that betrayed us, the England that we Jews all adored and praised before World War II. It was the current leaders of Great Britain – Prime Minister Clement Attlee and Foreign Secretary

---

[7] Hebrew: *Eretz Avotaynu.*

Ernest Bevin – who now closed Palestine's gates to Jews trying to reenter our homeland. And in hanging our Jewish sons who had the courage to fight against this betrayal and injustice, these English leaders became the new Hitlerite executioners.

We in Gauting, too, stood up. Our group organized a demonstration in the courtyard of the hospital, to protest the British court's sentencing of our freedom fighters in Palestine to death by hanging. I was the spokesman in this demonstration. Almost all the patients who were able to walk – a few hundred people – showed up in the courtyard. Taking my place once again at the head of the line (this time for a far better cause) I spoke of how the British government betrayed its own commitment both to help rebuild a Jewish homeland in Palestine and to cede control until the Jews were able to form a viable government of their own.

An American Jewish reporter photographed our hospital demonstration (a rare occurrence), and his newspaper published the photos with captions summarizing the essence of the demonstration: the outrage and anger of the Jews in the hospital against the British government. Sadly I no longer have any of the newspaper clippings, and I can't for the life of me recall the paper's name. All I have from the demonstration is a small picture somebody gave me as a memento.

All these events – the physical struggle going on in Palestine, the death sentences the British decreed against our freedom fighters, the operations of *ha-appalah* out of the DP camps, the illegal ships, the political efforts among the American Jewish community to help establish a Jewish homeland – absorbed 100 percent of my attention, to the point that I completely forgot about my illness. I believe that is what healed me. I started to feel better spiritually and physically. Before the war, we sang a Hebrew folksong exclaiming how good and pleasant it was for kinsmen to be together.[8] Now, after the war, this song took on new meaning.

Passover 1947 fell in mid-April. I was invited to the Jewish DP camp in Feldafing, to speak to a group who were students and disciples of Ze'ev Jabotinsky. Also an admirer of his, I readily accepted the invitation, and for the second time I left the confines of the Gauting sanitarium. In Feldafing, I spoke about the current Jewish situation and listened to other stories of survival. I picked up the *yishuv*'s new battle-cry: *Don't rely on miracles anymore.* I proposed

---

[8] The first line of the song reads: "*Hineh mah tov u mah nayyim sheved aḥim gam yaḥad.*"

that each of us must lend a hand to bring about our freedom. "These are our labor pains, and without pain there won't be delivery." I also spoke about anti-Semitism, saying that anti-Semitism would disappear if and when we had our own homeland. Now, more than 50 years later, I see how wrong I was. As our great commentator Rashi said, "It is well known that Esau hates Jacob."[9]

On April 27, two of our heroes, Meir Feinstein and Moshe Barzani, blew themselves up in Acre Prison, one day before they were to be hanged. They denied the British executioners the pleasure of putting a rope around their Jewish necks. For hundreds of generations to come, their names will be etched in our national memory.

After the worst war in human history, we survivors believed that evil was finally defeated forever, and that justice and righteousness would reign in the world. But when we saw the British hang our Jewish brethren, and the world community turn its back on these heinous crimes, we grew greatly disappointed in the so-called civilized world.

---

[9] *"Ki y'douah sheh Esav soneh et Ya'akov."*

Chapter 36

Geretsried

THE INTERNATIONAL REFUGEE ORGANIZATION (IRO)[1] opened a new Jewish DP camp near the village of Geretsried in the beginning of June 1947, situating it about three kilometers from Ferenwald. Camp Geretsried was tucked away inside a pine forest with enough housing units to accommodate roughly 2,000 people. It had a swimming pool, modern kitchen facilities, a theater, halls and offices, all completely hidden by the surrounding forest. It was built originally for a community of German laborers working in a nearby underground factory that the Nazis had erected to produce war materiel. The IRO decided this site, protected from the sun by the thick pine cover and bathed in pure mountain air, was suitable for housing former TB patients from Gauting.

I was transferred with a group of other patients to this camp, in mid-June or so. To say the least, I was somewhat scared to leave Gauting. After more than two years' stay under care in a hospital environment, to fend for myself was a daunting prospect. Notice of our transfer came abruptly, and we weren't prepared psychologically for the changes we were about to go through.

About a month before we were discharged from the sanitarium, a representative of the Jewish agency from Tel Aviv, Dr. Mayer, head of the *Kupat Cholim* (Health Insurance) in Palestine, paid us a visit. He was sent to evaluate patients' health and assess how many of us would be well enough to serve in Palestine's *Haganah* (military). After evaluating my condition, he advised me to stay put as long as possible, because the care I was receiving at Gauting was far superior to any I would receive then in Palestine. This upset me, because it reinforced the uncertainty of my condition. And given Dr. Mayer's medical advice, when notice arrived only four weeks later that I would be moved to Geretsried, it was a real shock.

When I arrived in Geretsried, my total net worth consisted of one pair of pants, three shirts, a single pair of shoes, and my one suit made from German military blankets. I could easily cope with this. Personal possessions and material things were still of no interest to me. What I found hard to handle was being so far from the great struggle for a Jewish homeland.

---

[1] This organization succeeded UNRRA, the United Nations Refugee Relief Agency.

Camp Geretsried began to fill up with about a thousand remnants of Jewish families from all over eastern Europe – Hungary, Czechoslovakia, Poland, Romania, Latvia and elsewhere. The IRO staff asked us to elect a committee to administer the camp locally. (In Munich, there was already a Central Committee of Liberated Jews in Bavaria, the organization which represented Jewish DP camps in the American zone of Germany; at the same time, there was also a central committee in the British occupied zone.) We held elections to appoint a camp committee and a camp leader for Geretsried. Each of the three branches of the Zionist movement, the *Mapai*, *Mizrachi* and *Hatzohar,* submitted a list of nominees. I was included among those nominated by the right-of-center *Hatzohar* branch. The outcome was such that the majority of the six or seven people elected to the committee were from the left wing of the Zionist movement, the *Mapai*. But I was elected to head the committee. This was a great honor for me: Geretsried was the only Jewish DP camp in all of Germany where a person from a minority slate was elected as camp leader.

Though fundamental ideological differences separated these Zionist groups from one another, our goal was the same: to end our homelessness, to cease being nationless wanderers. At the time, I wasn't politically savvy enough to discern any division or partisanship among the various means each party prescribed to reach its goals. Of all the committee members, I was the youngest – that, too, served as a great source of pride and satisfaction for me. Soon I came in contact with the staff of the refugee agency. While this may sound funny, I felt gratified that its staff respected me even though I only had three shirts to my name. (By that time, two years time after the war's end, most refugees had managed to attire themselves like normal human beings.)

Often, I addressed meetings in the great assembly hall in Geretsried. The gentile staff of the IRO would participate; it consisted mainly of Americans, but included Frenchmen and Englishmen, too. The French and Americans were sympathetic to our aspirations, but naturally the British weren't. Later we found out that the Brits placed spies in the DP camps to ascertain what we were up to. Regardless, at those meetings, I focused on only one theme: the establishment of our own homeland.

As Geretsried filled up with Jews from Eastern Europe, the *bricha* also managed to smuggle in a few hundred young Jewish boys from South Africa who volunteered to become soldiers for the *Haganah*. It bears mentioning that, in shaping the Jewish resistance against the British, Geretsried provided great assistance: because it was tucked away in a forest, away from the main road, it was the perfect choice for a secret military training ground.

Shortly after their arrival, these South Africans as well as many European Jewish refugees were trucked out. Later we learned that they became part of the 4,500 *ma'appilim*[2] who boarded the heroic ship *Exodus* to break the British blockade. Before they left, I became acquainted with many of them. A good number of them hailed from the same Carpathian region that I was from. Indeed, one young woman in that group, Tova Godinger, had attended school with me in Torun.

Enormous was our pain and sorrow when we learned that Great Britain captured the *Exodus* and forced it to return to Germany. But at the same time, I couldn't help thinking this malicious act ironically was our saving grace, as it was when "G-d hardened Pharaoh's heart ..." (Exodus II:34). Had the modern pharaohs of England, Attlee and Bevin, complied with the demand of President Truman to allow 100,000 Jewish DPs to enter Palestine, or had they not turned back the *ma'appilim* on the *Exodus*, G-d only knows whether a Jewish state would have been established. That Attlee's heart was hardened worked to our benefit. Rebuffing the *Exodus* was the straw that broke the camel's back. I am certain the saga of the *Exodus* was what finally aroused the attention of an indifferent world to the unjust ways in which Great Britain was treating the remnants of European Jewry. For one defining moment, the consciousness of the world was illuminated, and the two great powers, the United States and the Soviet Union, acted in unison on the side of justice (each of course, following its own agenda for acting this way).

Since Geretsried was a transit camp, people were coming through constantly. As I just mentioned, the British planted spies in the DP camps, and Geretsried was no exception. One such agent was a woman known by the name of Mary Weiss. She wore a necklace with a big Star of David on it, but I don't know if she was really Jewish or not. Her position as a social worker on the IRO staff provided her with good cover. In Geretsried there weren't too many families with children, but because she took great interest in and was

---

[2] Those who did daring things.

helpful with the children and the sick, people in the camp respected and loved her. After she left, I was told that she was a British mole sent there to report on the activities of the *bricha* and *ha-appalah*. During a time when hundreds of Jews passed through Geretsried in a few days' ume en route to Palestine, Miss Weiss probably had plenty to report.

As Geretsried's camp leader, I had the good fortune to meet some famous Jewish people, including David Dubinsky. He was the head of the American International Ladies Garment Workers Union (ILGWU) and was sent by President Harry S. Truman to tour the DP camps and report back to him. Leaders and representatives of Jewish organizations like the Joint helped DPs out a lot. Famous Jewish writers like Jacob Path and Isaac Rembah also visited our camp. Leaders of the World Zionist Organization such as Jacob Zerubavel and Yitzchak Tabenkin, who were two of the driving forces behind everything that was happening with the *bricha* and *ha-appalah*, also came.

All the Jewish DP camps in Germany joined forces to combat British barbarism by staging non-violent demonstrations: in Geretsried, we marched and gave speeches expressing our outrage, in hope of winning over public opinion in the world press. In this regard, I traveled to Munich quite often, to report on our activities to the Central Committee.

During the summer of 1947, I came to realize the scope of this gigantic struggle being waged to establish a Jewish state in Palestine. During the two years I spent in the hospital, I could only *listen* to stories about this work. Now I could actively participate in the effort to regain our ancient homeland.

These days were full of conflicting emotions. We felt tension, pain and humiliation because the British continued to imprison our leaders in Palestine, hang our freedom fighters or deport them to an internment camp Eritrea, and send to a detention center on Cyprus those *ma'appilim* who were caught trying to enter Palestine. But also we felt imbued by a Messianic vision and spiritual exaltation. I forgot the bad times, the hellish days and nights in the concentration camps; my heart filled with hope and conviction in our just cause. For that reason alone, it was worthwhile being alive – to bear witness not only to our greatest tragedy, but also to our greatest triumph: after nineteen hundred years, we were to be "the last generation of enslavement and the first generation of redemption."[3]

That summer, a young woman by the name of Nina Lubraniecka[4] arrived in our camp. Working in the administrative office, Nina altered the course of my life. Anyone who reads what I've written up to this point must surely wonder what kind of a hypocrite comments on these historic events with so much zeal and nationalistic conviction, and 'then, all of a sudden, as they say in Yiddish, *Bin ich oisgevaksen en America* – "All of a sudden I arrived in America." Why did I abandon all my aspirations and forego immigration to Israel? I must admit this is a very difficult question to answer. Perhaps my justification is feeble. But life has many contradictions and curiosities and compromises. What we call love is a lot stronger than all our dreams and aspirations. Our famous and wise King Solomon defined it this way in his Song of Songs (8:6): "Love is as strong as death" – and such a love changed the course of my life.

The period from mid-1947 until the middle of 1948 abounded with the happiest and most blissful days of my life. I found the will to live after the *Shoah*. I was proud to be a Jew. Gone were the shame and pain from which I'd been unable to free myself. In November 1947, the United Nations adopted the resolution to create a Jewish state in Palestine. Both the birth of Israel and the date of my wedding to Nina took place in 1948: *Medinat Yisroel* in May; our wedding, in July.

After meeting Nina, who helped restore my youthful zeal, I started to feel human again. I would have family again. There was no more feeling alone. At last I had my life's companion. My life suddenly took on a new flavor and purpose. I was certain Nina had these same feelings, because she also, like me, was the only survivor of her immediate family.

Although we came from different backgrounds, we formed a strong bond.[5] It may be hard for someone today to grasp the feeling we liberated war orphans felt about belonging to someone else, to form a family again. The greatest thing in family life is the feeling that you are a part of something, a larger whole. After the war, it was as if there were no borders, no differences for refugees. All the survivors felt like one body, one people. Wherever we came from, we all

---

[3] A Hebrew expression coined after the Holocaust: *"Dor achron l'sheibud v'dor rishon l'ge'ulah."*

[4] Loo-brah-NYET-ska.

[5] In Hebrew it's called the *ko'ach ha-moshaich,* the force that attracts.

suffered the same lot. Marriage to another sufferer ensured understanding. Of course we were different, but we had a good start in dealing with our differences, and we were more than willing to compromise with each other to maintain domestic peace.

So I came to live in the United States, as Nina wanted. This wasn't an easy compromise for me to make – but it was the second time in my life that I did so. As a teenager in 1936, I yearned to join a group that was training pioneers for Palestine. Back then, I considered the strong feelings of my parents, especially my mother's, and remained in Europe to please them. I was not alone. My brother Zvi also wanted to go; he, too, yielded to our parents' wishes. That's how strong our family ties were: we felt responsible for each other, holding these feelings sacred. In 1949, a similar struggle filled my head: the old desire to go to Israel versus the desire to nurture the new bonds with my wife, Nina.

Life in Israel was very hard then; housing and jobs were scarce. I questioned whether I had a right to ask Nina to join me in such a difficult place, especially since she had no Zionist upbringing. Life in America would be far easier than one in an Israel struggling against a thousand adversities. From correspondence with cousins who lived in Israel since 1928, I knew what it would be like. One relative, who lived in a kibbutz called K'far Masaryk, wrote that she could help us be accepted there. But she cautioned that my affiliation with the right-leaning *Hatzohar* group would be anathema in the leftist culture of the kibbutz – that my particular Zionist politics would be considered decidedly unwelcome.

Another argument swirled in my head: Aren't we war orphans deserving of an easier life, some respite? Haven't we struggled and lost enough? This thought and the letter from my cousin led me to my decision. It is why I write these words now from Allentown, Pennsylvania, and not Tel Aviv.

Chapter 37

America

WE SAILED FROM THE PORT CITY OF BREMEN, Germany on November 18, 1949. The vessel that brought us to the New World was the SS General S.D. Sturgis, a converted military troop transport whose namesake was a Union officer during the Civil War.

The eighteenth was a Saturday, but we boarded on Friday; according to Orthodox Jewish law you may not start your travels on *Shabbat*, but may board before sundown Friday night. Precisely 1,313 passengers of different nationalities boarded the ship (including, as we now know, many of Hitler's collaborators). Filled with mixed feelings of anguish, pain, delight and hope, Nina and I nevertheless were overjoyed to finally leave European soil that was saturated with the blood of our immediate and extended families. But we were apprehensive about arriving in a new land, not knowing the language (although Nina spoke a little bit of English already), having no trade and no relatives. The only family that we could expect was our co-religionists, the Jewish community. Young and full of hope, we were determined to overcome all the obstacles, the same as millions of other immigrants who came here before us and still do today.

The Atlantic was not very friendly; we encountered angry and stormy seas typical of November. Nina had a bad case of seasickness. I suffered less, but was not completely spared. Finally, 12 days and 12 nights later, we reached the American coast. On the morning of November 30, 1949, we arrived at a Boston pier. It took a whole day to go through the immigration procedures. Those immigrants who had relatives in the US had an easier time with the immigration officers. Since we had no one waiting for us, we and a few others wound up being the last ones to get through the formalities. By then it was dark outside.

A female representative of the HIAS (Hebrew Immigrants Association) worked with Nina and a few more people, as well as me. Although our papers listed our final destination as High Street, in Newark, New Jersey, the young woman recommended that we go to Allentown, Pennsylvania, instead – "truly a nice city," she said. This was the first time either of us had ever heard of it.

"Where is Allentown?" we asked her.

"It's between New York and Philadelphia."

"Fine," we responded, "we have no uncle in New York, and no aunt in Philadelphia – so let it be Allentown."

The HIAS woman (neither of us remember her name) then gave us directions. "First, from here you will travel to New York City, and from there another HIAS representative will direct you to Allentown."

Around 9 p.m., she took us with another group to the rail station in Boston, and put us on a train to New York. "In New York, when you get to Penn Station, the HIAS representative will be there to take care of you," she assured us.

We arrived in Penn Station in the early morning, but nobody was there to greet us. So we waited on the platform, not knowing where to go. Some of the immigrants were eventually met by their relatives and whisked off. But Nina and I stood there with our meager hand luggage and waited for a HIAS representative to come. Scared and bewildered, we waited probably no more than 50 minutes, but to us it felt like an eternity. Nina started to cry. Finally a man approached us, speaking in Yiddish and identifying himself as from HIAS. He apologized profusely for being late. Then he said it was very easy for him to recognize us. Why? we asked. Because, he smiled, only "greenhorns" would stand here on the platform instead of in the waiting room. Beyond that, our European clothing clearly gave us away.

The HIAS agent led us out to the street where he had a taxi waiting. When we got in, he told the driver to take us to the Hotel Marseilles on 103rd Street. (Nina and I learned that immigrants called this place "*Avraham Avinu's* Hotel," because our patriarch Abraham was known for his hospitality.)

My first impression of New York? Even though it was early in the morning and the streets were empty, I noticed how well lit everything was. And it was windy. I saw newspapers flying about the street. In Europe, even in 1949, paper was still very scarce, so I thought this had to be a very rich place for paper to be everywhere.

At the hotel, the man from HIAS registered us, and we got a room somewhere on one of the higher floors, 20 or 25 flights up. This was the first time in our lives that we were in so tall a building.

In New York, I had a friend named Max Steimetz, who had arrived a year earlier and lived in the Bronx. Between 1948 and 1949, we had corresponded. Max and I had been released from the sanatorium in Gauting together, and in Geretsried we were roommates. Now, so close to him again, I was very eager to let him know that we arrived in the Golden Land. Descending to the lobby, I asked at the front desk of our hotel how much it would cost to send a post card. Handing me one, the clerk said it costs one cent. I wrote to my friend Max that we arrived safely, and that I would try to come see him.

The next morning, December 1, Nina went to the Bronx to visit a very good friend of her mother's. Flora Adin came to America after the war, but earlier than we did. It was only after Nina left our hotel that I decided to go see Max. I was about to have my first experience on a New York subway. Along the way, I somehow managed to find people who could speak Yiddish and give me directions. In the middle of a workday, I arrived at his apartment; understandably, Max wasn't home. So I knocked at his neighbor's door. A woman opened it a crack, saw me – this tall man in European hat and long overcoat – and instantly slammed the door in my face. Calling through the door in Yiddish, I announced that I just arrived from Europe and that I'm looking for Max Steimetz. To my luck, she understood. She opened the door and now graciously let me in. Mr. Steimetz comes home between four and five o'clock, she said, so I asked her to please give Max the message that I was at the Hotel Marseilles on 103rd Street. Instead of simply taking the message, she became very concerned. She lived in New York all her life, she said, and never went on the subway alone! She was concerned about my traveling back to the hotel. I guess I was too naïve to be nervous about it. And I did manage to get back okay. Later that evening, Max came to see Nina and me. We were extremely comforted to see and talk with someone whom we knew from before – even though he cautioned us that life for new immigrants is not a bed of roses.

The next day, Nina and I left New York City by train and arrived in Allentown in the afternoon. At the station we were met by three ladies from an informal refugee aid committee responsible for housing new immigrants. These women were volunteer workers associated with the Allentown Jewish Community Center. Their deeds merit much gratitude: Mrs. Sadie Cohen, Mrs. Muriel Berman and a Mrs. Levitt or Levin (neither Nina nor I recall). I especially must single out Mrs. Cohen, who spoke fluent Yiddish and was a very warm, welcoming person with great empathy. These women brought us to the Jewish Community Center and introduced us to the Director, George Feldman, who told us that they have a room for us in the apartment of another immigrant family by the name of Gross. This family came to the United States before the war and knew German and Yiddish. Mr. Feldman felt this would help make our adjustment here easier. Also, their apartment was on 213 North 4th Street, close to the Jewish Community Center, on North 6th Street.

Mr. Feldman also advised us to change our last name from Jakubowics to Jackson. "It would be a good idea," he said, "because 'Jakubowics' is hard to spell, let alone pronounce." Here we were, two bewildered immigrants, and we thought that this man probably knew best: changing our name would be beneficial to our livelihood. "Jakubowics" literally means "son of Jacob," so "Jacobson" would have been a possible choice, but Mr. Feldman suggested Jackson, "because it's shorter." So we accepted his advice, and he had Mrs. Cohen escort us to the local refugee administration office. There, she spoke on our behalf to an official, a Mr. Boyle, that we wanted to change our name. All this took place within our first few hours in Allentown.

A year or two later I began to regret our decision, but by then it was too late. I thought about it a great deal. I was the only survivor of my martyred Jakubowics family and I had agreed to a name-change. At least I kept my Jewish name, Michael, given to me by my parents when they brought me into the covenant of Abraham. When one is called to the Torah, it's done by one's given Hebrew name and father's name. Hence I'm known in Jewish circles as Michael *ben* (son of) Avraham Zalman. Ultimately, I came to terms with this name issue. I realized that Slavic-sounding family names often were forced on our great-great-grandparents when they lived in Slavic-speaking European countries. Although I struggled with my name-change decision originally, I can say now that I am happy I discarded a name forced on my family, and adopted, of my own free will, an American name.

Our accommodations on 4th Street were extremely small and sparse – just a bedroom – but this was only temporary. A few weeks later, Mrs. Cohen found an apartment for us on 9th Street: a room in a small apartment building belonging to a lovely landlady by the name of Millie Schubert. Again it was a tiny room, but this apartment also had its own kitchen and bath, and we were very grateful for it, especially because apartments were hard to find after the war. Not only new immigrants were hunting for living space, but also returning soldiers and their brides needed housing, too, so there was quite a shortage.

The first 10 years in America were physically and emotionally very hard. We experienced the normal process that millions of immigrants went through in a new land, without a trade, without knowing the language and working at jobs that were not very fulfilling. In Yiddish there is a very appropriate saying for this process: *pok'n in muslan*, chicken pox and measles, meaning that everyone has to go through it. At the same time, despite the difficulties of those first years, they were also the most exalted and happy years in our lives here in America.

We stayed at Millie's for about two years, and then Mrs. Cohen, whose husband Isidore owned some apartment buildings in Allentown, rented us our very own, nice, big apartment on 1030 Hamilton Street, for even less money than the smaller apartment.

Here the sun rose for us again, and Nina and I were blessed with a son Jacob (Ya'akov, named for her father), who was born in 1954. One year later we were able to put a down-payment on a beautiful home at 1026 North 19th Street. Three and a half years later, in 1958, our daughter Renata (Rivkah, named for my mother) was born. There's no way to take out an insurance policy with G-d to have physically and mentally capable children. We were lucky and very grateful that both have grown healthy and strong. Having able-bodied children lightened the load of the already heavy concerns any couple has in building and supporting a family. Nina and I worked very hard at a number of jobs until we were able to start and build our own manufacturing company, Nina Sportswear.

Thank G-d we could afford to give our children a good education; most importantly, we were merited to create a new Jewish generation, to continue the chain that started with Abraham our Patriarch and has continued unbroken for nearly four millennia.

I know that Nina and I were probably overprotective with our children, and they may have resented this. When they were young, most likely they couldn't understand why we behaved the way we did. Unfortunately and indirectly, they too were victims of the *Shoah*. They never knew what it was like to have a grandmother or a grandfather, aunts and uncles and cousins.

Nina and I differed, in general, about mentioning the *Shoah* to our children when they were very young. Understandably, Nina to this day has difficulty talking about that dreadful time. I feel, on the other hand, that we dare not conceal from them what happened to our families. They needed to know why they didn't have any close relatives, where their Mom and Dad came from, and what transpired before they came into this world.

Jewish history is replete with tragic chapters. If my *Shoah* recollections contribute something worthwhile to our recorded history, part of the thanks must go to my children who over the years pushed and prodded me to jot down notes and write about our great martyred family, so gruesomely cut down.

But today, with Nina at my side, I am once again at the head of the line – our family line. We survived the Holocaust. We witnessed the birth of not one but *two* new generations of Jews, our children and then our grandchildren. Thank G-d, my family, nearly exterminated, thrives anew.

# # # #

Afterword

Purim

PURIM, THE HOLIDAY DURING WHICH WE CELEBRATE THE DEFEAT of our enemy Haman, seems an appropriate place to close my memoir. This festival commemorates the thwarting of his plot against the Jews by the timely intervention of Mordechai and Queen Esther.

During our long and troubled history, we Jews have escaped or survived many harsh and evil decrees, but the perpetrators were never punished for their wicked intentions. They were always left unharmed, only to scheme against us another day. Purim is therefore a joyous holiday not only because the Jewish people were saved from destruction in Haman's time, but also because we merited vengeance on our blood-thirsty enemies: Haman and his 10 sons were hanged.

I am constantly tormented by an unanswerable question: why didn't a miracle happen when Hitler, our latter-day Haman, declared his intentions to annihilate an entire people?

In the early 1930s, Ze'ev Jabotinsky wrote "In blood and by fire, Judea fell; in blood and by fire, Judea will arise."[1] I believe he foresaw what was to come in the later '30s and '40s. His slogan echoed the words in Ezekiel XVI:6, in which G-d said through the prophet Ezekiel, "I passed over you, and I saw you were downtrodden in your blood. In your blood you will live, in your blood you will live."

Was this a blessing or a curse? I don't know. But it seems it was our destiny to pay the terrible price of one-third of our people's blood in order to see the rise of Judea – the establishment of the State of Israel.

At the very least, the founding of the State of Israel made it possible for the Jews to capture and try the horrible executioner Adolph Eichmann, and to see him hanged like Haman. His own execution was certainly consolation for many of us survivors of the *Shoah,* for when Eichmann knew that the war was going badly for the Germans, he nevertheless with great zeal rounded up as many Jews in Hungary as possible and had them transported to the Auschwitz gas chambers. Eichmann's execution was a very personal revenge for me,

---

[1] "*B'dam v'ba'aish, Yehudah naphlah. B'dam v'ba'aish, Yehuda takum*"

since he was instrumental in destroying my immediate family in May and June of 1944.[2]

On Purim, it is not only customary but considered a *mitzvah* to go to the synagogue and listen to the reading of the Scroll of Esther (*Megillat Esther*), in which is told the story of Haman. Interestingly, the Talmud tells us that "whoever reads the *Megillah* backwards does not fulfill his obligation." Our sages explain that "backwards" does not only mean in reverse order; it also means that whoever reads the *Megillah* merely as ancient history has missed the point. The Purim story, like the *Shoah*, is directly relevant to our contemporary world. As the *Megillah* itself tells us, when we celebrate Purim, the miraculous events of that era are "remembered and reenacted in our lives."

During a Purim festival a few years ago, I went to hear the *Megillat Esther*. When I arrived at my synagogue, it was already filled with lots of children, beautiful Jewish children from toddlers to eighth graders and beyond. I was delighted to see them all. But suddenly, images from my past flashed before me.

I saw old Reb Yaikel starting to read the *Megillah:* "And it was in the days of King Achashveirosh ..."[3]

And there, listening to his every word, were the beloved children of Torun. All the children of my brothers Eliezer, Moshe and Zvi were also holding *groggers* (noise-makers) in their little hands, ready to make noise, shout and stamp their feet at the sound of the accursed name of Haman. Everybody in the synagogue was fully connected to a 2,500 year-old piece of Jewish history.

Other images of previous Purims flooded my mind's eye. I was 15 and traveling with a group of boys and girls from Torun to the village of Volova, which had a larger Jewish community than Torun and was only 20 kilometers away. There, the Zionist organization put on a drama called *Uriel Acosta*. It was based on the real-life story of Uriel Acosta and his family, a story that had its roots in the expulsion of the Jews from Spain and Portugal around 1492, although the Acosta tragedy took place between 1590 and 1640. (I was the

---

[2] That Hitler committed suicide is no consolation, because he knew he nearly accomplished his goal before taking his own life.

[3] "*Va-y'hi b'yemai Achashveirosh...*"

youngest in that group of boys and girls, and I know that at age 15 I couldn't have comprehended the contemporary significance of the drama.) We returned to Torun very late that night, but my house was still lit up, full of jolly people continuing to celebrate Purim.

Then another Purim. In Torun, my Zionist youth organization used to organize its own plays also. I took part in three such plays. One was called *The Two Kunyeh Lemmels*, a silly comedy about two dimwitted young men. Another was called *Moishe Chayet* ("Moshe the Tailor"). The third, *Green Fields*, was a love story with many lyrical songs in it. All these plays took place on alternate Purims and at *chol ha'moed Pesach*. Many Jews from neighboring villages would flock to Torun to see the performances, and the income generated from them would go to the purchase of books for our Hebrew school library.

Then another Purim, and then another … .

Back in the synagogue, coming out of my reverie, understandable tears of sadness and nostalgia welled up in my eyes.

On the *Shabbos* morning prior to Purim, it is also customary to read from the Torah portion in which we are warned to "Remember what Amalek did to you."[4] (We survivors of the Holocaust, however, hardly need to be reminded of this: our painfully indelible memories, emotional and physical scars, do the job for us.) Back in 1993, Purim happened to fall on a Saturday evening, so I went that *Shabbos* morning to the synagogue, not only to abide by this custom but also to commemorate my father's *yahrzeit* with an *aliyah*.[5] My father went to his eternal rest in 1943. I am grateful that he accumulated merits enough to be buried in a Jewish cemetery in the Hungarian city of Debrecen, and died knowing that all his children were still alive in spite of the Tisha b'Av pogrom that the Hungarians perpetrated against the Carpathian Jews in the year 1941.

I think very often about living and dying, and about destiny. I recall reading somewhere in an old Jewish book that every human being must think that each day of his life may be his last, and that thinking so may make him a better human being. It was said that this attitude also makes your days more meaningful and your life more satisfying and gratifying, because then each day of your life is as if you have picked the winning lottery number.

Sometimes I think that since the Holocaust I've lived my life too focused on death and dying. Yet, to me, life and death are

---

[4] *Z'chor et asher assah lechah Amalek.*

[5] Purim falls on the 14th of Adar, whereas the anniversary of my father's death, his *yahrzeit*, is on the 18th. But it is customary to be called up to the Torah, to have an *aliyah*, for a *yahrzeit* on the *Shabbos* prior to the actual date.

inseparable. And what kind of a *chutzpah* would I have to complain about death, since I have already reached the age of 81. It's an age no one in my immediate family had the good fortune to reach. My father was 67 when he died. My mother was 67 or 68. My eldest brother, Eliezer, died when he was 47 years of age; my second oldest brother, Moshe, at 44; and my brother Zvi, at 36. They all died martyrs, *al kiddush Hashem*. Hardly a day passes since those horrible days of 1944 that I don't think of them or of their wives and children in one way or another.

Is it a wonder then, that the Angel of Death rents space in my thoughts and in my mind? But I fear him not. For with G-d's help I defeated him, when I was victorious in 1945.

Souls Not Forgotten

Victims and Survivors

On the paternal branch of my family, my grandfather Chaim Jakubowics wed Miriam Debora Kirsner and bore 10 children (8 daughters, 2 sons). From eldest to youngest they were:

	Perished	Survived
Sara, wed Moshe Leib Heimowitz		
16 souls in their immediate family	10	6
Avraham Zalman (my father), wed Rivkah Drimmer		
14 souls in our immediate family	13	1
Bayla, wed Yitzchak Zoldan		
12 souls in their immediate family	10	2
Rifka, wed Leib Fixler		
17 souls in their immediate family	12	5
Channah, wed Alter Goldberg		
8 souls in their immediate family	5	3
Faiga, wed Isaac Popper		
14 souls in their immediate family	11	3
Zecharia, wed Sarah (maiden name unknown)		
6 souls in their immediate family	6	0
Rachel, wed Alter Fried		
9 souls in their immediate family	8	1
Etya, wed Yitzchak Zoltan		
7 souls in their immediate family	3	4
Jutta, wed Zisya Nojovich		
9 souls in their immediate family	9	0
Totals for 112 members of my father's extended family:	87	25

Victims and survivors from the family's Drimmer (maternal) branch. Grandfather Efrayim Drimmer wed Hudyeh (Judith) Jakubowics (no relation to the paternal Jakubowics branch) and together had 10 children - 7 daughters and 3 sons. One son, Moshe, and one daughter (whose name I do not know) died before World War I and are not listed below. From eldest to youngest they were:

	Perished	Survived
Malka, wed Berel Jakubowics (no relation to paternal Jakubowics)		
11 souls in their immediate family	5	6
Rifka, my mother, wed Avraham Zalman		
(listed and counted on my father's side)		
Yenta, wed Samuel I. Davidovich		
7 souls in their immediate family	6	1
Zvi (Armin Darvos), wed Molvin (maiden name Reich)		
8 souls in their immediate family	6	2
Kyla, wed Lazar Jakubowics (no relation to paternal Jakubowics)		
10 souls in their immediate family	9	1
Berel, wed Mindel Markowitz		
10 souls in their immediate family	9	1
Leah, wed Moshe Joseph Weiser		
13 souls in their immediate family	12	1
Sara, unmarried		
1 soul	1	0
Totals for 60 members of my mother's extended family:	48	12

Glossary

A

adar (Hebrew) Twelfth month in the Jewish (lunar) calendar. In a leap year, an extra month is intercalated after Shevat (the 11th month) and is called Adar Rishon (the 1st Adar), immediately followed by Adar Sheni (the 2nd Adar).

ad hashmadah (Hebrew) Until total destruction.

aitzel (Hebrew) Acronym for *Irgun Tzva'i Leumi*, meaning National Military Organization.

aktion (German) Action; roundup.

aliyah (Hebrew; *literally* "ascent") Being called to partake in the communal reading of the Torah; immigration to *Eretz Yisroel*.

al kiddush Hashem (Hebrew) To the glory of G-d.

ältester (German; *literally* "the elder") A supervisor of a concentration camp barrack.

amalek (Hebrew) Wicked and cruel Biblical enemy of Israel.

ani Ma'amin (Hebrew) "I Believe," which is the title and first words of a song of faith that the Messiah will come.

appellplatz (German) Location in the camps where roll-call was taken.

ashmedai (Hebrew) Devil; demon.

asseret y'mai teshuva (Hebrew) Ten days of repentance (between the Jewish New Year and the Day of Atonement).

B

ba'al tefillah (Hebrew) One who leads the congregation in prayer.

badchen (Yiddish) A wedding entertainer specializing in humorous and sentimental improvised rhymes.

balegula (Hebrew/Yiddish; *literally* "owner of wheels") A person who has a one-horse carriage and works as a cabby, or one who has a two-horse wagon and is a freight carrier.

b'merchav (Hebrew; *literally* "with expansiveness") A metaphor for one's feeling free from strife, even when in dire straits.

bar/bat Mitzvah (Hebrew) A Jewish boy of age 13, or a girl of age 12; the ceremony initiating him or her into religious duty and responsibility.

bau (German) Building.

BCE Before the Common Era.

bench (Yiddish) To say Grace after meals.

bipchik (Hungarian) Disparaging epithet similar to "kike."

bitachon (Hebrew) Very strong faith.

bricha (Hebrew; *literally* "run" or "escape") The underground operations that helped get Jewish Holocaust survivors to the American or French zones of Germany or Austria, as the first step in getting them to Palestine.

buchar (Hebrew) An unmarried yeshiva student.

b'zaiyut apechah tochal lechem (Hebrew) "By the sweat of your brow shall you eat bread."

C

CE Common Era.

chaim (Hebrew) Life.

chalif (Hebrew/Yiddish) Knife used to slaughter animals according to Jewish ritual dietary laws.

challah (Hebrew) A loaf of bread baked in honor of the Sabbath and festivals.

Chanukah (Hebrew) An eight-day festival that begins on the 25th of Kislev, commemorating the Maccabees' rededication of the Holy Temple in the second century BCE. And marked by the kindling of lights.

chaver (Hebrew) Friend; buddy; learning partner.

cheder (Hebrew/Yiddish) Jewish primary school.

chol ha-mo'ed (Hebrew) Intermediate days in the middle of Passover.

chometz (Hebrew) Leavened bread or other substances prohibited to be enjoyed or even possessed during Passover.

chorban (Hebrew) Destruction; catastrophe.

chorban shlishi (Hebrew) The third destruction.

chovavai Zion (Hebrew) Lovers of Zion, which was one of the earliest Zionist organizations.

Chumash (Hebrew) Pentateuch; the Five Books of Moses; Torah.

D

dayin (Hebrew/Yiddish) A judge.

E

Emek ha-Bachah (Hebrew) The Valley of Tears.

entlausungsanstalt (German) Showers; de-lousing establishment; gas-chamber.

Eretz Avotaynu (Hebrew) Land of our Fathers.

Eretz Yisroel (Hebrew) The Land of Israel.

erev (Hebrew) Eve; the evening prior to a holiday.

erev Shabbos (Hebrew) Sabbath eve (Friday night after sundown).

esrog (Hebrew) Citron; one of the four species used during the Feast of the Tabernacles.

ezredesh (Hungarian) Commander; the rank of colonel.

F

farchnyoket (Yiddish) Fanatically religious.

fartumult (Yiddish) Very confused.

filvaruk (Polish) Wealthy farmer's estate.

finantzen (Yiddish) Border police.

G

Gan Eden (Hebrew) Garden of Eden.

g'derrim farknipung (German) Intestinal knot.

gehinnom (Hebrew) Purgatory; hell.

Gemara (Aramaic; *literally* "completion") Rabbinic commentary on the Mishnah, forming part of the Talmud.

geshem (Hebrew) Rain.

ge'ulah (Hebrew) Redemption.

goyim (Hebrew/Yiddish; *singular* "goy") Gentile nations; non-Jewish people.

guten morgen (German) Good morning.

gymnasium (Yiddish/Latin) Public European secondary school, resulting in a diploma beyond that of American high schools, and which was mandatory for entrance to college.

H

ha-appalah (Hebrew) Daring emigration under difficult conditions; refers to the underground operations that helped Jews get from Europe to Palestine after World War II.

hachsharah (Hebrew; *plural* "hachsharot") The training for young pioneers preparing to emigrate to Palestine.

häftling (German) Concentration camp prisoner.

haganah (Hebrew) Military defense organization.

Ha-Makom (Hebrew; *literally* "The Place") One of G-d's many names.

handl-wandl (Yiddish) Wheeling and dealing.

Har ha-Zetim (Hebrew) Mount of Olives.

Hashem (Hebrew; *literally* "The Name") One of G-d's many names.

hatzlachah ba-derech (Hebrew) A successful journey.

Hatzohar (Hebrew) Acronym for *Ha-Zionim Revizionim*, the Revisionist wing of the Zionist movement.

hefker (Hebrew/Yiddish) Unclaimed, ownerless property; not protected under the law.

HYD (Hebrew) Acronym for *Hashem Yimkom Dammo*, meaning "May G-d avenge his blood."

I

ir v'aim b'Yisroel (Hebrew) A Jewish metropolis in the Diaspora (even though the literal definition is "a mother-city in Israel"; often used to refer to Warsaw, which was once the largest Jewish cultural center in Europe.

J

Judenrat (German) A Jewish council created under German orders which was responsible for internal matters in a ghetto or town.

K

kabbalah (Hebrew; *literally* "received tradition") Jewish mystical teachings.

Kaddish (Aramaic) From the word meaning "holy," it is a prayer in praise of G-d. Mourner's *Kaddish* is recited by the immediate family of the deceased.

kapo (German) A blended word-form from "concentration camp police"; a concentration camp inmate chosen by the Nazis to police his fellow inmates.

kappoorahindl (Yiddish) Whipping boy.

karpin kep (Yiddish) High-ranking officials.

keret (Hungarian; *literally* "fence" or "frame") Hungarian military guard.

kichel (Yiddish) Small cookies.

kikötes (Hungarian) Binding up.

Ki thissa (Hebrew; *literally* "When thou takest") One of the chapters in the Book of Exodus, referring to Moses taking the census of the Children of Israel.

kittel (Yiddish) Outer white garment worn by religious Jews in the synagogue on the Day of Atonement.

klal Yisroel (Hebrew) The entire Jewish people.

ko'ach ha-moshaich (Hebrew) The force that pulls.

kokoshok (Hungarian; *literally* "roosters") Hungarian policeman whose headgear was adorned with rooster feathers.

Kol Nidre (Aramaic; *literally* "all vows") Opening words of the evening service for the Day of Atonement.

kremslach (Yiddish) Potato pancakes.

kristalnacht (German; *literally* "crystal night") The night of broken glass, that is, the night in 1938 when the Nazis burned the synagogues all over Germany.

L

lager (German) Camp; labor or concentration camp.

lais din v'lais dayin (Hebrew/Yiddish) Without justice or judge.

landsman (Yiddish; *plural* "landslite") Fellow countryman or compatriot.

langer moit (Yiddish) A very tall maiden.

Lechi (Hebrew) Acronym for *Lochamai Chairut Yisroel*, meaning Freedom Fighters for Israel.

liegekur (German; *literally* "bed cure") Naptime.

M

ma'appilim (Hebrew) Daredevils.

ma'ariv (Hebrew) Evening prayer service; also the name of a daily evening newspaper in Israel.

meitzar (Hebrew) Oppressor.

mala<u>ch</u> (Hebrew) Angel.

mammalandische Yidden (Yiddish) Jews from the Hungarian motherland.

matan Torah (Hebrew) Giving of the Torah at Mount Sinai.

mazel (Hebrew/Yiddish) Luck.

mazeldik (Yiddish) Lucky.

me<u>ch</u>areif u'megadeif (Hebrew) Blasphemer and insulter of G-d.

Medinat Yisroel (Hebrew) State of Israel.

mensch (Yiddish/German; *plural* "menschen") A gentleman; a decent, understanding human being.

meshorer ha-za'am (Hebrew) An angry poet.

meshumid (Hebrew) A Jewish convert to Christianity.

mezinkeh (Yiddish) Youngest child.

mezumin (Hebrew) Three adult Jewish males saying the grace after meals.

mezuzah (Hebrew) The tiny parchment scroll affixed to a door post that identifies a Jewish home.

midrash (Hebrew; *plural* "midrashim") Commentary forming part of the Talmud; homiletical interpretation of the Bible.

mikvah (Hebrew) Ritual bath.

minyan (Hebrew) Quorum of ten Jewish men required for regular prayer services.

Mishnah (Hebrew) The code of Oral Laws, which form part of the Talmud.

mitzvah (Hebrew; *plural* "mitzvot") A good deed.

m'konen (Hebrew; *plural* "m'konanim") Mourner; witness and recorder of tragic history.

mo'ar (Yiddish) Stone house.

mogen David (Hebrew/Yiddish) Star of David.

moshavah (Hebrew) Collective farming settlement, where (in contrast to a kibbutz), a person can have some private ownership.

moshiach (Hebrew) Messiah.

munkoszazod (Hungarian) Military unit consisting of no less than 100 men, but usually double in wartime; by the early 1940s, Jewish "inductees" were used as slave-laborers. This term is used interchangeably with the word "*szazod*."

munkotabor (Hungarian) Military labor camp.

munkotabornikas (Hungarian) Slave-laborers.

musselmen (Yiddish/German) People reduced to skin and bones.

myra (Hebrew) Flattened dough for matzo.

N

nachalah (Hebrew) Inherited land.

nais (Hebrew; *plural* "nissim") Miracle.

neshama y'seira (Hebrew) Additional soul.

netzach Yisroel (Hebrew) The eternity of the Jewish people.

niddah (Hebrew) Menstrual cycle.

n'kumah (Hebrew/Yiddish) Revenge.

nusach (Hebrew) The prayer rites traditionally followed by a particular group.

O

oberleutnant (German) First lieutenant.

oborokee (Ukrainian) Storage place.

olam ha-emmet (Hebrew) World of Truth.

örmester (Hungarian) An officer under the rank of lieutenant.

P

pais (Hebrew) Sidelocks.

pecklech (Yiddish) Small bag or bundle of belongings.

Pengas (Hungarian) Hungarian currency.

Pesach (Hebrew) The holiday of Passover, commemorating the Jews' exodus from Egypt.

Pirkei Avot (Hebrew; *literally* "Ethics of the Fathers") Part of the Talmud concerned with ethical teachings.

prohalina (Ukrainian) A grassy patch of land or a field in the middle of a forest.

R

rachamim (Hebrew) Compassion.

rasha m'rushah (Hebrew) An extremely cruel person.

Rashi (Hebrew) Acronym for *Rabbainu Shlomo Yitzchaki*, author of the 11th century commentary on the Bible and Talmud.

Rav (Hebrew) Rabbi.

Reb (Hebrew) Title of respect, akin to "mister" or "sir," used by a younger person addressing an elder or person of higher education.

refuah (Hebrew) Medicine; cure.

revier (German) Makeshift hospital.

rodaif (Hebrew) Pursuer.

Rosh Hashanah (Hebrew) The Jewish New Year.

rozias (Hungarian) Roundup; random search.

S

schvartz-tummah (Yiddish) Black and impure.

sefer (Hebrew; *plural* "seforim") Book.

seforim chitzonim (Hebrew) Secular books.

Selichot (Hebrew; *literally* "requests for forgiveness") Special prayers recited before dawn during the week preceding Rosh Hashanah.

Shabbos, Shabbat (Shabbos, Yiddish; Shabbat, Hebrew) Sabbath; day of rest.

shadchen (Hebrew) Matchmaker.

sh'airit ha-plaitah (Hebrew) *Shoah* survivors.

shalom (Hebrew) Peace.

shalom aleichem (Hebrew/Yiddish) Peace be with you.

shalom bayit (Hebrew) Marital peace and harmony.

Shavuot (Hebrew; *literally* "weeks") Festival commemorating the giving of the Torah at Mount Sinai.

sheitel (Yiddish) A woman's wig.

Shema Yisroel (Hebrew) "Hear, O Israel"; the opening words of the prayer confessing Jewish faith.

shiva (Hebrew) The seven-day period of intense mourning for the dead, beginning immediately after the funeral.

shlep (Yiddish) To drag, proceed or move slowly, tediously, or awkwardly; someone who moves slowly.

shloshim (Hebrew) Thirty-day mourning period after a person's death.

shmurah matzo (Hebrew) Special matzo that is used solely during Passover.

Shoah (Hebrew) Catastrophe; holocaust; the destruction of the Jews in Europe during WWII.

sho<u>ch</u>et (Hebrew) Butcher who performs ritual slaughter, that is, one who follows the prescribe procedures for slaughtering kosher animals.

shtetl (Yiddish) Village.

shul (Yiddish) Small synagogue.

siddurim (Hebrew) Prayer books.

Sim<u>ch</u>at Torah (Hebrew; *literally* "rejoicing in the Torah") A celebration that in the Diaspora falls on the 9th day of *Succoth*, while in Israel it is commemorated on the 8th day.

sinat a<u>ch</u>im (Hebrew) Hatred among brothers.

sitches (Ukrainian) Local militiamen or civil guard.

s'ridai ha-<u>ch</u>erev (Hebrew; *literally* "leftovers from the sword") Survivors.

strohmann (German; *literally* "straw man") A gentile front-man for a Jewish business.

stuben dienst (German) Assistant to the barracks *ältester* and *kapo*.

Succoth (Hebrew; *literally* "booths") Feast of the Tabernacles.

szazod (Hungarian) Military unit consisting of no less than 100 men, but usually double in wartime; by the early 1940s, Jewish "inductees" were used as slave-laborers. This term is used interchangeably with the word "*munkoszazod.*"

szokalos (Hungarian) Bearded one.

T

ta'am (Hebrew) Taste.

ta'amim (Hebrew) The musical accents written in the Hebrew Bible as a guide to correct cantillation.

tallis (Hebrew; *plural* "tallesim") Prayer shawl with four fringes.

Talmud (Hebrew; *literally* "instruction" or "study") The collection of many books of Jewish beliefs and customs, civil and criminal laws and regulations, Rabbinic opinion, commentary and debate.

Tammuz (Hebrew) The fourth month of the Jewish calendar, corresponding roughly to June or July.

Tanach (Hebrew) Acronym for the Torah (the Five Books of Moses), *Nevi'im* (the Prophets) and *Kesuvim* (the Writings, i.e., the Hagiographa).

t'chum Shabbos (Hebrew/Yiddish) Sabbath boundary.

techiyas ha-meisim (Hebrew/Yiddish) Resurrection of the dead.

tefillah (Hebrew; *plural* "tefillot") Prayer.

tefillin (Hebrew) Small black leather cubes containing parchment scrolls inscribed with *Shema Yisroel* and other biblical passages, bound to the arm and forehead by leather straps and worn by men at weekday morning prayers.

tehillim (Hebrew) Psalms.

tirzach (Hebrew) Murder.

Tisha b'Av (Hebrew) The ninth day of the month of Av; fast day commemorating the destruction of both the First and Second Temples in Jerusalem; Tisha b'Av nidcheh is the postponement of the fast to the 10th day of Av.

Tishrei (Hebrew) Seventh month of the Jewish calendar, corresponding roughly to September or October.

tizedes (Hungarian; *literally* "ten") A low commander in charge of only ten soldiers.

tochacha (Hebrew) Curses; the passages of chastisement and rebuke in Leviticus XXVI:14-43, as well as in Deuteronomy XXVIII: 15-68.

Torah (Hebrew; *literally* "teaching") Specifically, the Five Books of Moses (Pentateuch or *Chumash*); in general, connotation, the entire body of Jewish law and teachings.

tsuris (Yiddish) Troubles.

tzaddik (Hebrew; *plural* "tzaddikim") A pious, righteous person.

tzarah (Hebrew) Tragedy.

tzelem Elokim (Hebrew) The human being created in G-d's image.

U

überziedlung (German) Transfer.

V

va'yehi (Hebrew) "And it was in those days …."

verfluchte Juden (German) Accursed Jews.

W

Wehrmacht (German) Defense force.

Y

yahrzeit (German/Yiddish) The anniversary of a parent's death.

yeshiva (Hebrew/Yiddish) Talmudic academy.

yishuv (Hebrew) Jewish community in Palestine.

Yom Kippur (Hebrew) Day of Atonement, which is a fast day falling on the 10th of Tishrei and climaxing the Days of Awe.

yontif (Yiddish) Jewish holiday.

YS (Hebrew) Acronym for *Yemach Shemo*, meaning "May his name be erased."

y'shias Hashem (Hebrew) G-d's help.

Z

Zidos (Hungarian) Jews.

ZL (Hebrew; *plural* "Zichronam L'vracha") Acronym for *Zichrono L'vracha*, "Of blessed memory."

Zohar (Hebrew; *literally* "radiance") Classical work embodying the mystical teachings of the Kabbalah.